A Pirate's Life No More

EARLY
AMERICAN
PLACES

ADVISORY BOARD

Vincent Brown, *Duke University*
Cornelia Hughes Dayton, *University of Connecticut*
Nicole Eustace, *New York University*
Amy S. Greenberg, *Pennsylvania State University*
Ramón A. Gutiérrez, *University of Chicago*
Peter Charles Hoffer, *University of Georgia*
Karen Ordahl Kupperman, *New York University*
Mark M. Smith, *University of South Carolina*
Rosemarie Zagarri, *George Mason University*

A Pirate's Life No More

The Pardoned Pirates of the Bahamas

STEVEN C. HAHN

The University of Georgia Press
ATHENS

© 2025 by the University of Georgia Press
Athens, Georgia 30602
www.ugapress.org
All rights reserved
Set in 10.5/13.5 Adobe Caslon Pro Regular
by Rebecca A. Norton

Most University of Georgia Press titles are
available from popular e-book vendors.

Printed digitally

Library of Congress Cataloging-in-Publication Data

Names: Hahn, Steven C., 1968– author.
Title: A pirate's life no more : the pardoned pirates
of the Bahamas / Steven C. Hahn.
Other titles: Pardoned pirates of the Bahamas
Description: Athens, Georgia : The University of Georgia Press, 2025. |
Series: Early American places | Includes bibliographical references and index.
Identifiers: LCCN 2024046656 | ISBN 9780820373430 (hardback) |
ISBN 9780820373447 (paperback) | ISBN 9780820373454 (epub) |
ISBN 9780820373461 (pdf)
Subjects: LCSH: Pirates—Bahamas—History—18th century. |
Piracy—Government policy—Great Britain—History—18th century. |
Pardon—Bahamas—History—18th century. | Pirates—Bahamas—Biography. |
Pirates—Great Britain—Colonies—Biography. | Piracy—Atlantic Coast (U.S.)—
History—18th century. | Piracy—Caribbean Area—History—18th century.
Classification: LCC F2161 .H165 2025 | DDC 910.4/5—dc23/eng/20250203
LC record available at https://lccn.loc.gov/2024046656

Dedicated to the memory of John D. and Barbara L. Hahn
You did good!

CONTENTS

LIST OF ILLUSTRATIONS XI

ACKNOWLEDGMENTS XIII

INTRODUCTION. Young, Resolute, and Wicked Fellows? 1

CHAPTER 1. The Call of the Sea 17

CHAPTER 2. A New Madagascar 49

CHAPTER 3. "All Mad to Go a Wrecking" 68

CHAPTER 4. The Pardon and Its Discontents 94

CHAPTER 5. "Pirates Expelled—Commerce Restored" 128

CHAPTER 6. A Pirate's Life No More 168

CHAPTER 7. The Respectable Pirates of New York 204

CONCLUSION. Noncanonical Pirates 238

APPENDIX. Pearse's List of Pardoned Pirates 249

NOTES 269

BIBLIOGRAPHY 313

INDEX 335

ILLUSTRATIONS

ORIGINAL MANUSCRIPT PAGES OF
PEARSES'S LIST OF PARDONED PIRATES   3

DOCUMENTED MERCHANT VOYAGES
OF PARDONED PIRATES   31

LOCATION OF PROVIDENCE IN THE
EIGHTEENTH-CENTURY CARIBBEAN   51

SOUTHERN CAROLINA GOVERNOR JOHNSON'S
PARDON OF PIRATES   96

ACKNOWLEDGMENTS

No man is an island, and therefore I could not have willed this book into existence without the support and encouragement of numerous institutions and people. Conducting research in far-flung archives is costly, and it could not have happened without significant financial support. First, I would like to thank my employer, St. Olaf College, for providing professional development grants that facilitated summer research in London, Jamaica, and New York City. St. Olaf's Interlibrary Loan staff likewise deserves much credit for tracking down many resources that went into the making of this book. I am lucky to have a home institution that is so supportive of my academic endeavors. Likewise, an American Philosophical Society Franklin Grant funded yet another of my sojourns to London. I am grateful for the support APS has given me through the years, for this and my two previous books. The American Council of Learned Societies awarded me with a project development grant that enabled me to devote time to writing the manuscript. I am honored by the trust ACLS placed in me to finish it!

A number of individuals contributed in ways big and small toward the completion of this book. From afar, I have long admired the work of the late Trevor Burnard, and I wish to thank him posthumously for providing thoughtful responses to my questions (posed out of the blue via email!) concerning travel and work in the Kingston area. Meanwhile, Joshua Piker and Denver Brunsman devoted considerable time writing letters on my behalf that helped secure funding from grant-lending agencies. I am humbled by your support, and grateful for the inspiration each of you have given me to contribute in my small way to both Muskogee (Creek) and maritime history. I am also thankful to Arne Bialuschewski for providing research suggestions, feedback on drafts of several of this book's chapters, and for sharing his knowledge of and enthusiasm for all things pirate. In addition to these professional scholars, St. Olaf students should know that they too contributed mightily to my development as a historian. The hundred-odd students who have taken my course on pirates have encouraged me to think deeply about piracy while contributing to a stimulating and joyous learning environment. Among my former students, two deserve special notice. Alexi Garrett and Claire (Bents) Steele, now budding scholars in their own right, each served as my summer research assistants in a program funded by St. Olaf. Alexi helped me launch the project by investigating Bahamian records. She is the one who first identified the Bahamas Council's factionalism recounted in chapter 5. A few years later, Claire assisted me in wading through the Massachusetts and New York shipping returns. In addition to identifying likely pirates in these records, Claire deserves credit for correcting errors I first made transcribing the names of pirates on Pearse's list, and especially for discovering the pirate ring in New York City featured in chapter 7. Her great insights encouraged me to dig deeper into the New York records, and I hope I have done justice to her painstaking work. Nathaniel Holly of the University of Georgia Press has given me great encouragement over the past year as I worked toward the completion of the manuscript. Finally, I wish to thank the anonymous reviewers chosen by UGA Press, and my copyeditor, Lori Rider, for their attentive reading of my manuscript and for offering many valuable suggestions that helped sharpen its focus. Any remaining errors and omissions are my own.

Importantly, I wish to thank my family for their love and support, and for making my life a fulfilling one. On numerous occasions, my wife Mary attended to matters at home while I worked overseas in the archives. This book could not have happened without you. My children Erin and Luke, now adults with careers of their own, make their father proud every day. I love you all more than words can say. Finally, my parents, John and Barbara Hahn, were alive at the time I finished my previous book. Since that time, they have passed on, so I dedicate this one to their memory. I miss you both!

A Pirate's Life No More

INTRODUCTION

Young, Resolute, and Wicked Fellows?

After three months at sea guiding the HMS *Phoenix*, on August 15, 1717, Captain Vincent Pearse dashed off a letter confirming his safe arrival at New York. Pearse, one of several British naval captains sent to American waters to suppress piracy, optimistically reported, "There has been lately no pirates on this coast," noting only the rumor of a suspicious ship bound for Newfoundland.[1] For the next few months, Pearse cruised along the North American coast protecting merchant convoys, stopping in Annapolis and Williamsburg to confer with colonial governors before returning to New York.[2] In late January, he received a letter from Admiralty Secretary Josiah Burchett that included a copy of the royal pardon for pirates issued four months earlier. Pearse conferred with New York's governing council, and together they determined that he should deliver the offer in person at their lair in the Bahamas.[3] On February 6, 1718, Pearse sailed, and two weeks later he approached the harbor at Nassau, Providence Island. Predictably, the naval captain had nothing good to say about the pirate lair now in his view, whose inhabitants he described as "young, resolute, [and] wicked fellows." Only time would tell if these pirates, who had used the island as their home base for nearly three years, would accept the offer of clemency.

Pearse arrived in the harbor at ten o'clock on the morning of February 23 and sent First Lieutenant Richard Symonds ashore with a white flag of truce and a copy of the royal pardon. Symonds returned that afternoon to report that the pirates had given him a cordial reception. Over the next few weeks, pirates clamored before Pearse seeking the benefits of the Act of Grace. Among the first to surrender was the notorious Benjamin Hornigold, who had been terrorizing Caribbean waters and local Bahamians for more than three years. Fellow pirate commanders Josiah Burgess, Francis Lesley, and Thomas Nichols, along with their crews totaling 114 men, also surrendered. Staying at Providence through the month of March, contrite pirates continued to trickle in seeking pardons, including some of Britain's most wanted criminals. Once pardoned, many of the pirates fled, catching rides on sloops bound for other colonies. To document his success, Pearse compiled a list of 209 men, noting that twenty of them had resumed engaging in piracy. Pearse's list of pardoned pirates, now tucked away among the admiralty records at the National Archives of Great Britain at Kew, constitutes the most extensive census of pirates dating to that period.[4]

I first learned of this census while perusing the footnotes of a book written by a prominent British maritime historian, who recounted Pearse's voyage but never identified the men whose names appeared on it.[5] Curious to know, I ventured to Kew in May 2012 to view the document myself. Located southwest of London, near the famous Royal Botanical Gardens, the National Archives is a behemoth edifice that holds records documenting more than a thousand years of Britain's past. The collection is so vast, in fact, that it requires an assembly-line system just to deliver documents from the massive vaults to patrons waiting in the expansive reading rooms. The very first hour of my first day there, I requested a bound volume catalogued "ADM 1/2282," a collection of letters written by British naval captains whose surnames begin with the letter P. When the tome arrived a half hour later, I grabbed it and rushed to a nearby seat, where I impatiently flipped through its tattered, yellowing pages. In almost no time, I located Pearse's list, which filled three pages arranged in three columns featuring the names of 209 men, with a crucifix etched next to those who, according to Pearse, had returned to piracy.

My eyes initially gravitated to the names of those I recognized and were likely to ring a bell with many a pirate enthusiast, such as Benjamin Hornigold and Charles Vane. However, as I made my way through the list more systematically, I was surprised to find that most of their names were unknown to me. Who had ever heard of the pirate John Mitchell? The dread pirates James Fasset and George Raddon? Scourges of the high seas John Mutlow, John Sipkins, and William Pinfold? How could anyone make sense of the tangle of nondescript names like John Smith or John Richards? Were Joseph and Thomas Pearse somehow related to the naval captain by that name who pardoned them? So it was that in a matter of minutes I realized Pearse had bequeathed to historians a list of mostly nobodies. But then it occurred to me that these nobodies constituted a majority of pirates and that their stories might be worth telling.

Original manuscript pages of "A List of the Names of Such Pirates as Surrendered Themselves at Providence to Capt. Vincent Pearse." Enclosed in Vincent Pearse to Secretary Josiah Burchett, June 3, 1718, ADM 1/2282, National Archives, Kew. Several well-known pirates such as Benjamin Hornigold, Richard Taylor, and Palsgrave Williams appear on page 1. Note the presence of crucifixes next to the names of individuals who, according to Pearse, had "gone out a pirating again."
Photos by the author.

Nº	Persons Name	Nº	Persons names	Nº	Persons names
73	Henry Barnes	105	William Rouse	137	William Chew
	Jaq.ᵉ Champion		Joseph Papp		Abra. Adams
	John Rowals		† Peter Guidet		Joseph Thompson
5	William Willis		Mark Holmes	140	James Peterson
	Tristram Wilson		Danl. Stillwell		Peter Mallet
	Daniel Jones	110	Inº Edwards		William Tito
	Philip Calverley		Chas. Garrison		John Arterile
			Joseph Pearse		† John Mounsey
80	James Brown		Wm Grahame	5	John Johnson
	John Sutton		Alexr. Campbell		John Isley
	Geo. Radden		James Nevile		John Turren
	Adam Forbes	5	James Fasset		Samuel Ady
	Cornelius Mathow		Edw. Berry		John Magnes
5	Tho. Pearse		Inº Andrews	150	Thomas Treuter
	David Ross				Echo. Miller
	† Jacob Johnson		† David Nearne		Davd. Snow
	Wm. Bridges	120	Garrt. Peterson		Rects. Earle
	Robt. Brown		Richd. Twelty		Anthony Hen
90	Rt. Moggridge		† Charles Veine	5	John Carge
	Henry Shipton		Rogr. Houghton		Robt. Shew
	John Cullemore		R. Valentine		† Inº. Michill
	Peter Johnson	5	Samuel Boyce		† Edw. Rogers
	Charles Morgan		Richd. Legatt		Mich. Roger
5	John Auger		Rd. Rawlings		
	William South		Darby Connelly	160	John Kemp
	Mazmadke Gee		Arthr. van pelt		John Sipkins
	James Morat	130	Inº Richards		Clencias Lan
	Benjn. Turnor		Saml. Beach		Wm. Penfold
100	John Mutlow		Wm. Peters		Pearse Boyse
	John Stout		Jona Smith	5	Jacob Robert
	Tho. Reynolds		Geo. Sinclair		Wm. Miller
	James Wheeler	5	Wm Hasselton		Edw. Potts
	Alexr. Little		Wm Darris		Inº. Cochran

Persons Names	No	Persons Names	
Joseph Fryers	202	Thomas Emly	
Geo. Rouncivall		Nich.ᵗ Woodall	
John Creysh		Edward Days	
Wm Roberts	5	Chris.ⁿ Peters	
Math.ᵘ Revcere		John Jackson	
Joseph Mickelbro		Cha.ˢ Whitehead	
Robert Ross		Edw. Arrowsmith	
Isaac Kerr	209	John Perrin	
Edward Kerr			
† Tho. Williamson			
† Tho.ˢ Chandler			
Samuel Moodey			
Wm Spencer			
William Hunt			
Nath.ˡ Hudson			
William Smith			
Acontjah Stanbury			
Edward Bead			
Edw. Parmyter			
† Tho. Stoneham			
† John Crow			
Wm Edmundson			
Rich.ᵈ Hawks			
Andrew Davis			
Thomas Pearse			
Rich.ᵈ Ward			
Henry Glinn			
Legh Ashworth			
Denis.ⁿ Dwooly			
Geo. Crisom			
David Turner			
Cors Perickson			
Tho. Bradley			

Who were these men, and what brought them together at Providence at a critical moment in history? Moreover, what does a pirate do after he is pardoned, and how does a pirate lair transform itself into a functioning civil society? These questions first sparked my research on seafaring men who, with the exception of a handful of notorious criminals, remain largely unknown to historians. Bringing them before the light of history was itself a quest, requiring a decade's worth of extensive and intensive archival work in Great Britain, as well as several mainland and island colonies. My first impulse was to see if any of the pirates remained in the Bahamas, thinking that temporal and geographic proximity to the site of the pardon was the most effective way of tracking them down. To my satisfaction, many of the names on Pearse's list—upward of fifty—surfaced in Bahamian documents. Here I found them engaging in a range of everyday affairs: acquiring land, registering ships, marrying and baptizing their children, paying taxes, appearing in court, and giving depositions. My hunch being confirmed, and knowing that many of the pirates derived from Jamaica, I conducted a similar survey in those archives, including official government correspondence as well as local administrative records. Once again, the Jamaican paper trail turned up a number of pardoned pirates, many of whom appeared in the Governor and Council's 1716 piracy investigation (the subject of chapter 3), while others surfaced fleetingly in church, court, and property records.

From there, I turned my attention to shipping returns, which the Naval Office kept, albeit irregularly, for each colony under royal authority beginning in the 1680s. Because of the incompleteness of these records, I supplemented them by scouring the shipping notices that routinely appeared in colonial newspapers. Together, these invaluable records enabled me to identify the names of captains and their vessels, as well as track their customary sailing routes. The "sailor geographies" I reconstructed helped me identify a conspicuous subset of mariners from Pearse's list engaged in intercolonial trade who frequented the Bahamas during the key years of 1714–1720. In turn, the fact that these captains derived from virtually all the British American colonies compelled me to expand my research into local administrative records from Rhode Island to Barbados. While I was fortunate to visit in person archives in South Carolina, Jamaica, the Bahamas, and New York, this work would have been impossible without access to digitized records made available through several well-known genealogy websites, university and public libraries, and regional and local historical societies. By combing through these sources, I found brief references to pardoned pirates in many colonies, with a number of individuals concentrated in the greater New England area and New York, the subject of this book's final two chapters.

Throughout the research process, I continually asked myself: How do I know? That is, how do I know that the names on Pearse's list correspond to those of individuals I uncovered in the archives? The task was easy for high-profile pirates like Charles Vane and Benjamin Hornigold. Having an uncommon name, like Adonijah Stanberry, also made it easier to ensure that the individual in question was in fact a pardoned pirate. The more difficult objective was to identify persons with ubiquitous names, à la William Smith. To guide me, I adhered to the Occam's razor principle, whereby the simplest answer is usually the right one. First, I assumed that individuals who resurfaced nearby as pirates shortly after the pardon were the same men who accepted the Act of Grace from Captain Pearse. Second, I presumed all the men on Pearse's list were maritime workers from port towns, eliminating all but those who self-identified as such in the historical record. At the same time, I had to keep open the possibility that persons engaged in related crafts, like shipbuilding, sailmaking, carpentry, and even medicine, might also have plied their trades among pirate crews. Third, I focused on mariners who were temporally and geographically in close proximity to the Bahamas at the time Pearse arrived in 1718. I call this the "proximity principle," and it enabled me to identify mariners who regularly frequented Bahamian and/or Caribbean waters. At the same time, I eliminated mariners who engaged mostly in transatlantic trade or never sailed in the Caribbean. The proximity principle also holds that individuals possessing the same surname were likely to be relatives. Through these efforts, I have been able to identify and track about 150 of the pardoned individuals, before and after their encounter with Captain Pearse. The pages that follow recount their stories as a collective biography connecting land and sea and illuminating the entangled histories of far-flung places of the wide Atlantic.[6]

Thanks to a profusion of both scholarly and popular books, much is known about the rise and fall of the so-called golden age of piracy (ca. 1714–26), a phase of sea robbery centered in the Caribbean that commenced after Queen Anne's War (1702–13). While the Bahamas had long served as an occasional pirate refuge, Spanish and French attacks during the war rendered the colony ungovernable, thereby making the islands an even more inviting rendezvous for lawbreakers. In particular, the July 1715 hurricane off Florida that destroyed most of the Spanish silver fleet attracted a substantial number of British treasure seekers to the Bahamas, which were used as a staging point for "wrecking" or salvage activities off the Florida coast that evolved into piracy. At first, some pirates vowed not to attack British vessels, but many abandoned this pretense and thus began the golden age of piracy. Because of their lawlessness and proximity to the Spanish wrecks, the Bahamas became a lair where pirates referring to themselves as "the flying gang" shared prizes, outfitted their ships, and traded with anyone willing to do business with them. Driven from the Bahamas after the institution of a royal government in 1718, many of these same men were eventually hunted down and executed, but they became the stuff of legend thanks to contemporary publications featuring the exploits of Stede Bonnet, John Rackham, and Edward Thache, better known as Blackbeard.

Why would anyone become a pirate? Most historians agree that economic considerations are fundamental to the equation. Britain's demobilization of the navy after Queen Anne's War left thousands of mariners working in American waters—already schooled in the art of wartime privateering—unemployed. Piracy furnished out-of-work sailors not only the opportunity to continue practicing a familiar trade but also the profits generated by sea robbery far exceeded the paltry salaries earned by British mariners in the Royal Navy and in the merchant marine. For a time, port towns did business with pirates because of certain economic advantages they brought. Piracy enabled some port towns to acquire goods that were otherwise scarce or unavailable, and trading with pirates increased the flow of much-needed gold and silver specie.

If scholars agree that piracy's origins are at the most basic level economic, they tend to disagree when assessing pirate motives. On the one hand, some scholars depict piracy as "a business" akin to modern organized crime, as Cyrus Karraker did six decades ago. More recently, economist Peter Leeson has advanced the Karraker thesis by imaginatively illustrating how piracy conformed to the rationalist economic laws—the "invisible hand"—articulated by Adam Smith.[7] Conversely, a number of historians emphasize the pirates' radical origins and depict piracy as a class-conscious form of protest against merchant capitalism, as Marcus Rediker has posited in several influential works. Rediker notes the lower-class origins of most pirates and demonstrates how pirates developed an alternative social order where ship governance was more democratic, and in which pirates received more equitable shares of the wealth their activities generated. More than that, pirates were outsiders who developed a subculture of defiance that mocked authority and embraced symbols of death, like the skull and crossbones. Rediker implicitly celebrates these and other manifestations of pirate culture, typified by the most notorious outlaws who were "at war with all the world."[8]

Alternatively, a number of historians have investigated Britain's administrative and naval response to sea robbery—the "war on piracy"—in an attempt to explain its demise in the mid-1720s. Metropolitan officials, we learn, passed anti-piracy laws and extended the jurisdiction of vice-admiralty courts in an attempt to win convictions. Where they were able to do so, British officials instituted royal governments and put new men in office who shared in the metropolitan desire to root out piracy. Along with these and other administrative changes, Britain increased the Royal Navy's presence in Atlantic waters and empowered naval captains, like Vincent Pearse, to hunt down pirates. Although scholars differ as to which, if any, of the above strategies were most effective in eradicating piracy, most nevertheless attribute its demise to metropolitan changes in attitudes and to the agency of British officials.[9]

Recently, a new wave of historians has sought to dismantle some of the shibboleths established by their predecessors.[10] These works provide more nuanced explanations for the origins and demise of piracy, and call into question the monolithic category of "pirate." Historian Guy Chet, for instance, finds that most scholars have overestimated the capacity of the early modern state to suppress piracy, noting, "Britain's anti-piracy policy more commonly involved accommodation and negotiation rather than confrontation."[11] Following similar logic, Douglas Burgess and Mark Hanna attribute the relatively rapid end of piracy after Queen Anne's War to a change of attitude in the colonies rather than policies conceived in London. Burgess's study zeroes in on port towns like Newport, Rhode Island, where local officials gradually—and grudgingly—relinquished some (though not all) of their admiralty jurisdiction and began convicting rather than acquitting pirates.[12] Hanna's comprehensive study, encompassing several centuries, depicts the post–Spanish Succession era as the desperate last gasp of British piracy rather than its golden age. Its demise, Hanna argues, derives from the maturation of colonial economies, whereby piracy—once permitted, and even encouraged, as a source of economic stimulus—had become a dangerous liability for staple-producing colonies reliant on trade with the mother country. Hanna avows that piracy's relatively rapid demise also stems from a concerted effort by writers such as Cotton Mather and Daniel Defoe to reframe the preexisting historical narrative. Their efforts, he illustrates, brought about "a shift from the heroic pirate" depicted in seventeenth-century literature to that of the "horrific pirate" more common in early eighteenth-century publications.[13]

Meanwhile, historians David Wilson, Arne Bialuschewski, and Matthew Bahar eschew simplistic explanations for the rise and fall of piracy, as well as the identities and motives of pirates themselves. Bialuschewski and Bahar, for instance, explore the intersections between maritime and indigenous history, illustrating how Native peoples allied with English buccaneers operating on the Spanish Main, and, in Bahar's case, how New England Indians adapted European maritime technologies to conduct piratical raids against English settlements.[14] Wilson, in turn, avows that in the early eighteenth century "an outright war against piracy was beyond the capacity of the British imperial administration." In his view, piracy arose due to local circumstances, and its repression was orchestrated by local interest groups that often "competed as much as they collaborated" for resources.[15] In all, these historians view pirate motives as multifaceted, localized, and mostly opportunistic. As Bialuschewski observes, "the pirate trade was mostly a haphazard and opportunistic affair." If at times piracy resembled organized crime, it nevertheless was a "product of particular and mostly short term" economic conditions.[16]

The literature on English piracy in Atlantic waters is therefore abundant. What is still lacking are thorough investigations of individual pirates who left their mark on the administrative records of the colonies. By asking new questions and probing different kinds of sources, the lives of these 209 men offer the opportunity to integrate the study of piracy on the high seas with the land-based communities that once nurtured it.[17] Moreover, a study such as this enables one to explore some of the implications of recent scholarly work. If piracy was opportunistic and short-term, as Bialuschewski and Wilson suggest, then it stands to reason that we need to explore what these mariners were doing when they were not engaged in piracy. Meanwhile, Burgess and Hanna imply that the demise of piracy involved a process of "othering," both in law (Burgess) and in literature (Hanna). First, metropolitan and colonial officials criminalized a form of robbery that they had formerly tolerated or actively promoted. Second, they identified a new kind of deviant human being—*hostes humanis generae* or "enemy of all mankind"—whose robberies at sea were deemed significantly worse than those committed on land.

A Pirate's Life No More seeks to reclaim the humanity of the 209 pardoned men and situate them more firmly within the normal currents of colonial life. The use of local administrative records—court files, deeds, shipping returns, and land and church records—is fundamental to this work. These sources capture quotidian moments where ordinary men conducted ordinary business, enabling the historian to reconstruct more holistically their careers as mariners, but also their lives as husbands, fathers, parishioners, and property owners. Such records allow us to paint a picture different from that derived from the official correspondence of naval captains and colonial governors, and especially celebrated published works, such as the pseudonymous ["Captain Charles Johnson"] *A General History of the Robberies and Murders of the Most Notorious Pyrates* (1724). Official correspondence of this kind, typically routed through a chain of command leading back to London, was explicitly agenda driven and therefore subject to various kinds of conscious and subconscious bias. Colonial governors, for instance, sometimes inflated the pirate threat in order to justify requests to have Royal Navy ships stationed in their harbors. Conversely, they could conveniently obscure the role a colony's own officers sometimes played in encouraging pirates by looking the other way when ships appeared with hauls of suspicious cargo. Royal Navy captains, meanwhile, often wrote defensively with their own career advancement in mind when reporting on pirates that slipped away or when explaining circumstances leading to the arrest of men who later proved innocent. Importantly, official and published records reflect the perspectives of metropolitan officials and the merchant class, who, in the interests of curtailing piracy, were quick to demonize pirates as "enemies of all mankind" to generate popular support for Crown policy.[18]

The critical distinction is that local administrative records were never meant to be read more than once. Therefore, they are less subject to the agendas of writers seeking to impose their views on a wider audience. So, for example, an individual might have a property deed recorded by the colonial secretary in order to establish good title, with the hope that no disputes would arise requiring it to be dusted off for inspection, at least until said property had to be sold or bequeathed. Merchants, meanwhile, recorded their clients' debts in account books intended for their own eyes; these typically only saw the light of day when debt lawsuits required their inspection by a court. In a similar vein, a church's registry of baptisms, marriages, and deaths was typically for internal use and constitutes a historical record more likely to be combed through centuries later by genealogists than to have been read by contemporaries.

By focusing on such documents, a picture of everyday life emerges.[19] Take, for example, the rather unexceptional affairs of a man who wound up in Pearse's dragnet, Boston mariner Abraham Adams. Born in 1693, Adams's father, also named Abraham, was a respectable innkeeper who owned a couple properties in Boston. The elder Adams died in April 1700, as can be inferred from a will he wrote that year. At that time, the future pirate was one of seven children, all minors, whose father bequeathed half of his estate and movable property to their mother, Abigail, so that she could support the family after his death. Meanwhile, the younger Abraham embarked on a maritime career, probably in his early teens. In 1715, now an adult, Adams borrowed ninety pounds from a local gentleman, using as collateral his share of his father's property. His mother died about a year later. Adams's seafaring adventures continued, and one can surmise that a voyage to South Carolina commencing in November 1716 would have enabled him to learn of shipwrecks off the coast of Florida and opportunities for trading with the pirates in the Bahamas. Evidently, Adams tried his luck trading there at least once and was on hand around March 1718 when Captain Pearse arrived offering pardons. Adams limped home and never again raised the suspicion of naval authorities. Adams last appears in Massachusetts records in June 1723, when he sold his late father's Boston property for seventy-five pounds. Such was the humdrum life of Abraham Adams, one of Captain Pearse's "young, resolute, [and] wicked fellows."[20]

Investigating obscure pirates like Adams, in turn, calls for a more nuanced assessment of golden-age piracy. Although pirates hailed from virtually every colony and some were British born, the 209 persons who are the subject of this book inhabited several key population centers, namely, the Bahamas, New England, New York, and, most importantly, Jamaica. Slightly different local circumstances drew each of these groups into piracy. It is noteworthy, for example, that local Bahamians first engaged in piracy as a means of revenging themselves against the Spanish, whereas the Jamaicans at first descended on the Bahamas to find sunken gold off the nearby coast of Florida.[21] Many North Americans, in turn, came to the Bahamas primarily to trade with the pirates and got caught in Pearse's dragnet for being accessories to crime.

One common misperception I seek to address is the notion that this polyglot, transient community of sailors formed a short-lived "pirate republic" and envisioned creating a social, economic, and political order that was more democratic than that of Britain. This idea is problematic for several reasons. First, many of the men who gravitated to the Bahamas had property and families in other more prosperous and well-established colonies, and thus they had no incentive to contribute to a social experiment in a faraway place. Along those same lines, transient individuals capitalized on the Bahamas' lawlessness merely to hide from the authorities, repair and resupply their ships, and sell illegally acquired goods. They had little interest in the colony's long- or short-term development and no patience for the difficult work of building a colony, republican or otherwise. In fact, the men who accepted the pardon referred to themselves as "marooners," a self-perception reflecting the impermanence of the Bahamian pirate community. Ironically, the minority of pardoned pirates who resided permanently in the Bahamas contributed in ways large and small to the functioning of the royal government instituted by Woodes Rogers in 1718; they paid taxes, held minor offices, and defended the colony from external threats. Pardoned pirates remained deeply committed to British institutions, and, for them, the pirate lair at the Bahamas was little more than a glorified (and temporary) fencing operation.

What is more, the modest level of success experienced by some former pirates is indicative of preexisting class divisions within their ranks. The royal proclamation issued in September 1717 (and renewed several times thereafter) had the effect, intentionally or not, of dividing the pirate community along class lines. Those who owned property and had access to credit, or had influential friends, were more likely to escape the noose and resume legal maritime activity than their less fortunate peers, which largely explains why they are more visible in the paper trail.[22] Importantly, the royal proclamation drove a wedge between hard-core criminals engaged in capturing ships and those who merely acted as their accomplices by trading with or protecting them. The relative ease with which some erstwhile pirates slipped back into legitimate trades, and into the local social fabric, indicates that, for many men, piracy and the trade in stolen goods was but an opportunistic phase in a longer maritime career, and existed on a continuum with other kinds of seafaring work.

It mattered that some rose to the officer ranks (like captain, master, or mate) and others languished as common sailors. New Yorker William Smith, to name one of the most noteworthy individuals, enjoyed a decades-long career in maritime trade and climbed his way into the merchant class. He appears in New York records conveying property, serving as godfather for children of relatives, and suing others in court.[23] Smith even has the rare distinction of having two grandchildren who married into the family of a U.S. president.[24] Thanks to recent historical work, we know that piracy was not an aberration but rather played an integral role in the formation of the economy and society of colonial America. *A Pirate's Life No*

More takes the argument a step further by focusing on individual mariners like William Smith whose lives are illustrative of that process. Nonetheless, most of the pirates who appear in these pages disappear from the historical record by 1730, and some barely lived beyond their pardons. Presuming that the average pirate was in his late twenties in 1718 means that the typical seafarer expected to die before reaching the age of forty, a reflection of the dangers of seafaring.[25] All told, the reality that sailors' lives could be nasty, brutish, and short lends credence to the idea that pirates risked their lives knowing that death was looming anyway. "A merry life, but a short one" indeed.[26]

Vincent Pearse, of course, could not have known the long-term effects of delivering the Crown's offer of grace to the Bahamas pirates. He had reasons to be skeptical; after all, about half the men who frequented the Bahamas fled at his approach, and for the next decade, the Crown and colonial governments spent much blood and treasure trying to eradicate piracy. The ongoing exploits of legendary pirates such as Blackbeard, John Rackham, and Bartholomew Roberts attest to the limitations of the pardon. Yet the pardon catalyzed a wave of surrenders that proved to be the first steps toward rehabilitating a generation of temporarily wayward seamen, many of whom jumped at the chance of a fresh start. Vincent Pearse's deft handling of a tense situation, combining a show of force with clemency, had the effect of projecting the king's magnanimity into one of the British Empire's most neglected, lawless places.

Or so Pearse would like us to believe. Ordinary pirates held their own views on the drama unfolding in the Bahamas, and their perspectives sometimes challenge the stories told by Crown officials, Captain Vincent Pearse included. Although Pearse's writings depict a virtuous naval captain doing his duty to pacify "young, resolute, [and] wicked fellows" gathered at Providence, pirates knew an altogether different man. A month after his departure from the Bahamas, Captain Pearse returned to New York City to have a prize sloop condemned in the local vice-admiralty court. The alleged pirates who manned the sloop turned the table on Pearse by testifying under oath that he acted belligerently, traded with pirates, and committed other violations of the law. Pearse, who eventually married the daughter of New York attorney general (and future governor of New Jersey) Lewis Morris, never faced justice to answer these accusations. But that doesn't necessarily mean the allegations were untrue. Men of power and influence may have been in a better position to tell their side of the story, but the words and actions of ordinary pirates enable us to flip the script to uncover new dimensions of the golden age of piracy. Rather than the hackneyed tale of extermination of the "common enemies of mankind," I submit a new script, one of otherwise decent men who risked reputation and livelihoods to make lives at sea pay for their ambitions on land.

Overview

This study will unfold in largely chronological fashion, while also focusing on regionally specific storylines. Chapter 1 establishes context; it explores how the men on Pearse's list, originating in Britain and its American colonies, became mariners in the first place, and explains how almost ceaseless war and privateering provided them with opportunities to hone the skills they later deployed as pirates. Where possible, I explore the careers of captains engaged in the merchant trading system preceding their brush with piracy. It culminates with an in-depth investigation of William Rouse of Charlestown, Massachusetts, illuminating how his experiences at sea intersected with his landed interests. In chapter 2, I turn to the Bahamas, recounting how the archipelago's geography, its past history as a pirate lair, and its sufferings during Queen Anne's War contributed to piracy conducted there. I emphasize how Bahamian piracy resulted from local concerns and preceded the larger wave of piracy dubbed the golden age. From there, chapter 3 explores the singularly important contribution of Jamaicans to piracy. While I revisit the well-known story of Governor Archibald Hamilton's encouragement of treasure seekers off the coast of Florida, I focus on the Governor and Council's 1716 piracy investigation. This, I argue, backfired by alienating the mariners from the merchant community and government that encouraged their activities in the first place. Partly to escape justice and partly out of spite, many of Jamaica's mariners fled temporarily to the Bahamas and escalated attacks on foreign as well as British shipping. Subsequently, chapter 4 recounts in detail Captain Pearse's efforts to suppress and pardon the pirates in the Bahamas. I reveal a mad scramble to trade with the pirates there emanating from major port towns in the British American colonies, identifying individuals who accepted the pardon as accessories to piracy. Thanks to a detailed investigation of a prize sloop brought into New York, I argue that Captain Pearse himself probably also traded with pirates during his sojourn in the Bahamas, and that his writings on the affair tell only the heroic side of his story.

Chapter 5 constitutes a shift in focus to my original question of what happened to the pirates after the pardon. Focusing on the Bahamas, I consider fifty-odd individuals who remained there, many of whom resumed maritime careers, accepted privateering commissions, and, perhaps surprisingly, contributed to civic life in the colony. Peter Goudet of London, who became the Bahamas' customs collector and assemblyman, best illustrates the process of pirate rehabilitation. Following those same themes, chapter 6 explores the pardoned pirate diaspora that formed in the wake of the pardon, encompassing many colonies and Britain itself but focusing more in depth on New England mariners. While a few noteworthy individuals returned to piracy, and others served as privateers, I illustrate that many quietly resumed their careers as sailors in the merchant marine. Most typically forged ahead by marrying, forming families, accumulating property, and ensuring that their legacies would be passed on to the next generation. Chapter 7 carries this story to New York, where a circle of former pirates became pillars of the local maritime community. I feature the life of William Smith, the former pirate who rose to the rank of the merchant class and whose descendants married into the family of a future U.S. president. The conclusion attempts to synthesize the various observations I have drawn from this study of "noncanonical" pirates, as I have dubbed them, emphasizing the ephemeral nature of opportunistic piracy and the ordinariness of pirates.

Finally, a brief word on nomenclature. For the sake of brevity, I am electing to use the term "Providence" rather than "New Providence" for the Bahamian Island that forms the setting for much of the action that unfolds, although the island was often known by the latter name to distinguish it from a short-lived English Caribbean settlement founded in the 1630s.

CHAPTER I

The Call of the Sea

O'er the glad waters of the dark blue sea,
Our thoughts as boundless, and our souls as free,
Far as the breeze can bear, the billows foam,
Survey our empire and behold our home!
These are our realms, no limits to their sway—
Our flag the sceptre all who meet obey.
Ours the wild life in tumult still to range
From toil to rest, and joy in every change.

—George Gordon, Lord Byron, *The Corsair*

In the month of May 1677, yeoman John Richards and his wife Mary baptized their infant son John at the Congregational church in Lynn, Massachusetts.[1] On September 7, 1684, Marmaduke Gee, son of Marmaduke and Elizabeth Gee of Fivefoot Lane, was baptized at the Church of St. Mary Magdalen Bermondsey in London's Southwark borough.[2] On June 10, 1688, at the Dutch Reformed Church in New York City, Jan Sipken and his wife Else baptized a son, who, as was increasingly common among the descendants of New York's Dutch settlers, went by his Anglicized name, John Sipkins.[3] In January 1690, Edward and Elizabeth Berry of the parish of St. Andrews in Jamaica baptized their eldest son, named Edward after his father.[4] On January 10, 1692, a male child born to John and Eleanor Pearse was christened as Joseph at the St. Catherine's parish church in Spanish Town, Jamaica.[5] On March 21, 1693, at St. Paul's Church in Wyke Regis, county Dorset, England, one George Rouncifull was baptized before his parents Joshua and Mary.[6] In April 1693, a baby boy was baptized at the Church of Our Lady and St. Nicholas in Liverpool, England. Son of John

Ashworth, the boy was christened as Leigh.⁷ South of Edinburgh, Scotland, in the small hamlet of Temple, on January 26, 1696, Archibald Murray received baptism before his mother, Anne, and his father, James Murray, Laird Deuchar. As fate would have it, all these infant boys would grow up to be pirates. Somehow, each of them gravitated to Nassau, Bahamas, where in 1718 they stood penitently before Captain Vincent Pearse to accept the Act of Grace of King George I.

How does anyone become a pirate? That is, by what tangle of circumstances does a person of ordinary birth and parentage, often with no criminal past, wind up a sea robber? Moreover, how was it that individuals birthed in England, Scotland, and a multitude of British colonies appear in the same time and place engaged in the same nefarious activities? The answer to these questions is never straightforward, and each of the 209 men pardoned by Pearse probably could have told a different story about their motivations and the paths they took into piracy. However, by situating them in time and place, certain patterns emerge that are broadly illustrative of the entire cohort. Most grew up in or near port cities, often following a father or other relative into the maritime trades. Timing also mattered, and the maturation of interimperial shipping networks at the dawn of the eighteenth century promoted geographic mobility, particularly in waterways encompassing the greater Caribbean. Timing also explains how imperial warfare may have impacted these individuals, who, coming of age during a conflict known as Queen Anne's War, had ample opportunity to hone piracy skills while serving on armed merchant vessels, as privateers, or as enlisted men in the Royal Navy. Although they spent much of their time at sea, most retained key commitments on land, as exemplified by one William Rouse of Charlestown, Massachusetts. His story, which concludes this chapter, illustrates how one man under financial duress stumbled into pirate trading to provide for his large family.

"Bred for the Sea"

Only the faintest details can be known about the childhoods of most pirates. Even for renowned sea criminals details are lacking, and for that reason, most pirate biographies begin *in medias res* with the first reports of their criminal activity. The pseudonymous author of the *General History* (1724) candidly admitted the difficulties he faced tracking down their origins, largely because of their obscure parentage.⁸ Still, he must have sensed that his readers hungered to know more about the origins of pirates, so he sometimes used his imagination to fill in the gaps in his knowledge. As was common in English crime literature, he posited that the criminal disposition was forged in youth, as if certain young children were destined from an early age to become pirates because of their lack of education, previous criminal activity, and, in the case of two infamous female pirates, deviant gender identities.[9]

While it is possible that childhood poverty and innate dispositions could have led the 209 men on Pearse's list to turn pirate, a more reasonable strategy is to situate them more broadly in the maritime world of the early English (after 1707, British) Empire. First, we know that the vast majority of the men who accepted the pardon in 1718 had been born in the last quarter of the seventeenth century. As the historian Marcus Rediker has noted, the average pirate was about twenty-eight years of age, not a youth by contemporary standards, but rather a seasoned sailor with at least a decade of maritime experience.[10] By that calculation, we can infer that many of our subjects were born around the year 1690. Baptismal records enable one to positively identify relatively few of the pirates, but most who can be traced were born within a decade of that year, as indicated by Ashworth (b. 1693), Berry (b. 1689), Murray (b. 1696), Pearse (b. 1689), Rouncifull (b. 1693), and Sipkins (b. 1688). A few of the men were a bit older, like John Mitchell (b. 1677), and some were probably older still.

Most of the pirates hailed from Anglophone seafaring communities scattered widely across the Atlantic littoral, from Liverpool to Port Royal, Jamaica. Although the occasional landlubber appears in their ranks, most pirates were sea people who grew up near the docks and in places where making a living depended on maritime trade. As it was common for boys to assume trades practiced by their fathers, it can be surmised that many of the pardoned pirates were the sons of mariners. In a few rare instances, we know this for certain. John Mitchell, who grew up in Charlestown, Massachusetts, was the son of mariner Thomas Mitchell, a reasonably prosperous man who owned shares of at least three sloops.[11] John Sipkins and John Stout of New York both had mariners as fathers.[12] William Williams of Kingston, Jamaica, was the son of a sailor who also shared his name.[13]

If not mariners by trade, many of our subjects' fathers indirectly made their livings by sea. Francis Lesley's family, for instance, lived in St. John's Parish, Barbados. His father, Colonel John Lesley, owned at least one trading sloop and probably supported the family, in part, through the carrying trade.[14] John Williams, father of the pirate Palsgrave Williams, had been

Rhode Island's attorney general and owned properties in at least two seafaring communities, Boston, Massachusetts, and Block Island, Rhode Island. Never far from the ocean, John Williams engaged in the carrying trade as a one-third owner of the brig *Anna & Mary*. Williams probably traded to destinations in the Caribbean; after his death in 1687, his inventoried property included a parrot cage, indicating he kept tropical birds as pets.[15] Situated in London, Peter Goudet's father, a Huguenot immigrant, was a merchant who imported silk and wine from his French-speaking contacts on the continent.[16] Leigh Ashworth's father, John, was a customs officer in charge of inspecting ship cargoes at the port of Liverpool.[17] At least one of the pirates under consideration, Abraham Adams of Boston, was the son of an innkeeper, whose clientele included visiting seamen.[18]

In port towns, proximity meant that the call of the sea was a strong one. Benjamin Franklin, the great printer, scientist, and statesman of the early U.S. republic who witnessed the golden age of piracy as a boy in Boston, was not immune to its call. In addition to growing up in a vibrant port town, Franklin had many relatives who made their livings directly or indirectly by sea. Reflecting on his childhood in his celebrated *Autobiography*, Franklin recalled how, after trying his hand as a tallow chandler (his father's line of work), "I disliked the trade, and had a strong inclination for the sea, but my father declared against it." Although discouraged by his father, the young Benjamin could not escape the call, stating, "Living near the water, I was much in and about it, learnt early to swim well, and to manage boats." As his dissatisfaction working with tallow continued, Franklin related that his father "was under apprehensions that if he did not find [a trade] for me more agreeable, I should break away and get to sea" as his older brother Josiah had done. Benjamin was eventually bound to his brother James as a printer's apprentice, which ultimately led to a celebrated career in Philadelphia. Even though the printing trade was ideally suited for the bookish Franklin, he confessed that he "still had a hankering for the sea," a hankering that never fully escaped him.[19]

Like Franklin, most mariners probably experienced the call of the sea in their early teens, as typified by mariner (and pardoned pirate) James Moodie, who in a deposition given at age forty indicated that he had been "bred to the sea" for twenty-six years.[20] On one level, gravitating to maritime work could be a practical decision.[21] After all, such employment could provide steady wages, and ambitious individuals could aspire to become masters of vessels. Those who earned enough money, in turn, sometimes were able to buy their own ships, and the most business-savvy and fortunate individuals might retire from active seafaring after a couple of decades and enter into the ranks of the merchant class.[22]

An individual could enter into the seafaring ranks in a number of ways. The sons of mariners presumably learned at their fathers' sides, joining them on voyages when they reached their preteen years. In some instances, youths entered into formal indenture contracts with master mariners, agreeing to work for them upward of seven years in exchange for their training. Others still may have gotten their start in the Royal Navy, which instituted a formal process by which adolescents or young men entered as unskilled landsmen, and gradually advanced to the ranks of "ordinary" and "able" seamen as their skills progressed. Individuals demonstrating particular abilities might advance further still into the officer ranks, although most pirates never did so within the navy.[23] A majority, perhaps, received training that was more informal by joining a ship's crew as an adolescent and sticking with maritime work because it was the only thing they knew. Their training would have progressed in stages. Ships boys, like the "landsmen" of the Royal Navy, would have started out running errands for the crew, like fetching water and cleaning the deck. From there, they would have learned how to work the sails and anchors, and those who showed the most aptitude gradually learned the art of navigation.[24] Becoming a master of a vessel, however, required at least basic literacy, for it was necessary to be able to read a merchant's written instructions, ship manifests, and other forms of commercial paper. For the aspiring master or captain, mathematic skills likewise were essential, both for conducting trade and for navigation, which relied heavily on geometry.

At the same time, seafaring might have had a romantic appeal, as the epigraph from Lord Byron attests. The ocean itself kindled feelings of the sublime due to its vastness, depth, and unpredictability. As a conduit for escaping the constraints of ordinary life on land and exploring faraway places and peoples, the oceans beckoned. At the time, pirate stories encountered by word of mouth or in print also had a romantic appeal. English boys inherited a proud seafaring tradition, typified by their pirate national hero, the renowned Sir Francis Drake.[25] These boys could have learned about Jamaica's buccaneers, notably Captain Henry Morgan, who, like Drake, received a knighthood for his exploits, as well as a position as deputy governor of Jamaica.[26]

The well-known exploits of Captain Henry Every only solidified the romantic appeal of piracy. In 1693, Every, then a midshipman on the *Charles II*, spearheaded a mutiny of disgruntled sailors near Spain, seized control of the ship, and renamed it the *Fancy*. His crew turned its sights to the Indian Ocean, where they remained for about two years, capturing a massive ship called the *Ganj-i-sawai*, which means "exceeding riches." Known by its Anglicized name, the *Gunsway* had been commissioned by the Mughal emperor Aurangzeb himself, carrying treasure valued somewhere between 200,000 and 500,000 pounds sterling, and a "female relative" of the emperor, sometimes thought to be his daughter or granddaughter. It was the richest ship ever taken by pirates. Soon afterward, Every and his crew made haste to the Bahamas, where they secured safe passage by bribing Governor Nicholas Trott. Although a worldwide manhunt ensued, Every was never found, and most of his crew slipped away unpunished to seaports in North America and beyond. Published accounts of Every's exploits burnished the legend further by crediting him with founding a pirate utopia at Madagascar.[27]

Every may have inspired young seamen to emulate him and perhaps dream of founding their own pirate utopias. Walter Kennedy, an English pirate who was executed in London in 1721, was known to have memorized stories about him. While awaiting his execution in prison, Kennedy enjoyed recounting Every's exploits to fellow inmates. Likewise, the pirate Edward England, who raided the Indian Ocean a generation later, captured a Dutch East India Company ship in 1720 and renamed it the *Fancy*, clearly invoking the memory of Every and his ship. When his crew later mutinied and ousted him as captain, England drifted to Madagascar, where he appears to have lived for several years. Even though he died an impoverished alcoholic and founded no pirate utopia, Edward England, historian Colin Woodard speculates, nevertheless may have come "closest to living out the Every legend."[28]

In addition to inspiring the next generation of sailors, there is tantalizing evidence to suggest a possible direct link between Every and the pardoned pirates of 1718. That linkage comes in the form of one James Brown of Rhode Island. Possessing a surname that is common there, James lived in Newport and was probably a first cousin of the Browns of Providence, where James's contemporaries—the sea captain also named James and his brother, the merchant Obadiah—established a mercantile dynasty. The Browns of Newport, descended from patriarch Chad Brown's younger sons, James and Jeremiah, were of more modest means. Nevertheless, they were a respectable family, with their father James serving in various minor offices for the Newport town government.[29] James's brother, Robert, also appears on Pearse's list, and their brothers John, William, and Jeremiah all worked as sea captains in the first quarter of the eighteenth century.[30]

In 1695 Brown joined the crew of a privateer vessel, the *Susannah* of Boston, under the command of Thomas Wake, who held a commission from the governor of Rhode Island to attack pirates in the Indian Ocean. The following year, Wake encountered Every at sea. Some said Wake and his crew, rather than hunting down the pirates, joined in Every's attacks on foreign shipping. Others claimed that the *Susannah* had been plundered by Every and had not engaged in sea robbery. For his part, Brown claimed that he had grown "weary of being abroad in those parts" and joined Every after learning of his intention to sail for the Bahamas. From there, Brown ventured to Pennsylvania to assume a new identity. In addition to trying his hand as a planter, Brown married Anne Markham, none other than the daughter of Pennsylvania lieutenant governor William Markham, who was notorious for encouraging illegal trade and sheltering pirates in the Quaker colony.

When proprietor William Penn returned there in 1700, he seized Brown and had him, along with several other piracy suspects, sent to Boston for questioning before the Earl of Bellomont. Brown, naturally, gave a self-serving deposition in which he insisted he had only been a passenger on the *Fancy* on its return voyage to the Bahamas. Although Penn rightly suspected his guilt, Markham and two self-confessed members of Every's crew confirmed Brown's story and Brown was released.[31] Presumably, he returned to his wife in Pennsylvania. James and Anne (Markham) Brown had three children together, and by 1708 James resumed sailing to the West Indies.[32] In 1718 Brown commanded and owned a Rhode Island sloop, the *Dolphin*, which traded between Rhode Island and New York, where the Browns and surviving members of the Markham family now resided. Additionally, Brown owned two other sloops, the *Endeavor* and *Tweezers*, which he registered in Rhode Island and used to trade locally between New York and Connecticut. Brown remained active until dying on a voyage to Martinique in 1723, leaving Anne and a surviving daughter.[33] If in fact the "James Brown" denoted on Pearse's list is the same Rhode Island mariner by that name, it constitutes a singular direct link between the Indian Ocean pirates of the 1690s and those of the later golden age.

Young boys who came of age in the final decades of the seventeenth century thus inherited popular historical traditions that tended to celebrate, rather than denigrate, piracy. As such, impressionable young minds would have been predisposed to look on them not simply as criminals but as daring adventurers, bold men of action who gained wealth and fame, serving their own interests as they simultaneously expanded England's global influence. In addition to admiring pirates, mariners of this generation perhaps conceived of the colonial enterprise itself as inherently piratical in nature. The historian Mark Hanna describes England's earliest overseas ventures as "piratical colonization" whereby plunder of Spanish riches worked hand in hand with the establishment of settler colonies in the Americas. Colonies ranging from Massachusetts to Pennsylvania to Jamaica actively supported maritime predation. Piracy therefore was commonplace, and most colonial subjects would not have regarded the plunder of enemy shipping as a "crime" in the strict sense of the word.

"This Part of the World Is Full of Privateers"

While their proximity to the sea and legends of famous pirates may have inspired the 209 men on Pearse's list, warfare constituted a more direct influence. During their formative years, England fought two major wars between 1689 and 1713, the former known as King William's War (1689–97) and the latter known as Queen Anne's War or the War of the Spanish Succession (1702–13), pitting the English against the Catholic powers and their respective allies. Consequently, men of their age would have found it difficult to conceive of a world without war. In particular, naval warfare had the most direct effect on England's colonies, as their archenemies, France and Spain, routinely targeted the maritime communities in the Caribbean and North American mainland. As one observer writing from Barbados in 1695 bluntly put it, "This part of the world is full of privateers."[34]

Virtually all the men who accepted the 1718 pardon would have been far too young to actively participate in, much less remember, King William's War. Therefore, the latter Queen Anne's War provides the best context for understanding how young sailors came about their professions, honed their skills, forged their worldviews, and, eventually, gravitated into piracy. More so than previous conflicts, naval operations factored significantly into strategy during Queen Anne's War, which, like its predecessor, was nearly global in scope.[35] For a decade, England's colonies again lived under the near constant threat of French and Spanish privateers. Otherwise known as *guardacostas*, Spanish America's formally commissioned private naval defense force, with origins dating to the 1670s, operated from bases such as Santiago and Barracoa in Cuba.[36] Seemingly no colony avoided Franco-Spanish attacks, and English ships faced threats everywhere on the high seas. To combat their enemies, early in the war Queen Anne incentivized privateering by waiving Crown fees for prizes.

Whether inspired by patriotism or financial incentives, sailors working in American waters at first appear to have responded enthusiastically to the call of war. Boston provides a case in point. In the summer and fall of 1702, nine ships commanded by veteran Boston skippers engaged in privateering expeditions. Typically, the crews manning these ships consisted of forty or more men, meaning that even a conservative estimate indicates that perhaps up to four hundred of New England's mariners experienced privateering in that short time span. And they were successful; extant maritime records from Massachusetts indicate that, in the fall of 1702 alone, local authorities condemned ten French and Spanish vessels captured by privateers.[37]

Maritime records from Massachusetts fortunately preserve the names of each man who served aboard the privateering vessels outfitted from Boston. Only one of them would later appear on Pearse's list as a pardoned pirate: John Richards of Lynn, Massachusetts. Richards would have been about thirty-five years of age when he signed up to join the crew of the brig *Adventure*, commanded by John Halsey.[38] Rather than guard the nearby coast, Halsey and company ventured into Caribbean waters, capturing two French ships and a third one of disputed origins they hauled before the vice-admiralty court at Barbados in December 1702.[39] By now a seasoned mariner who had settled in Boston, the following spring Richards appeared before local officials as master of the brig *Sarah*, built in his hometown of Lynn, to register it on behalf of three owners from Boston. In recognition of his status and experience, Richards soon assumed distinction as "Captain" John Richards of Boston, and in October 1705 he wed Mary Allen of Salem, daughter of ship captain Benjamin Allen.[40]

As the enthusiasm among American sailors for the war effort waxed and waned, reliance on privateering presented numerous problems for British officials. First, privateers competed with the Royal Navy for manpower, causing naval officials to organize press gangs to force sailors to serve on board men-of-war. Impressment was legal, but also the source of fear and resentment among common sailors, who sometimes responded by escaping, rioting, and fighting off press gangs. Merchants involved in the American trade lobbied against impressment, as the practice threatened commerce by diminishing the number of able seamen available to conduct trading voyages. Second, privateering inadvertently stifled the clandestine trade with the Spanish Americas, which continued even as the two countries waged war. By 1708, Jamaican officials, whose island was heavily dependent on clandestine commerce, complained of a "dull" trade that threatened to impoverish it, indicating that privateers regularly exceeded their orders by attacking Spanish subjects on shore, and by plundering nonthreatening Spanish ships.

In order to encourage privateers and keep them within "just bounds," in 1708 the British Parliament passed a vital piece of legislation, officially titled "An Act for Encouragement of the Trade to America" (6 Anne, cf. 65). Commonly known as the "American Act" or the "Sixth of Anne," the statute first abolished the impressment of sailors working in American waters. As the historian Shinsuke Satsuma illustrates, the American Act also indicated a "revival of interest in active colonial maritime war" by promoting privateering. It did so by allowing privateers to keep more of their spoils. The Crown, for instance, relinquished its right to the "Royal tenth" from the proceeds. Moreover, the act established a new system for adjudicating prize cases, employing civil law procedure (rather than maritime law) to interrupt the meddling of colonial officials, who often pocketed shares that rightly belonged to crew members.[41] The act succeeded in greatly reducing impressment for a short time. Instances of privateering appear to have increased, with Jamaica emerging as the epicenter of activity. For example, naval records from Jamaica indicate that from 1709 to 1712 (the last year of substantial fighting), at least twenty-seven ships designated as a "foreign prize, made free" registered with customs officials in Port Royal harbor.

Of the twenty-seven captains who commanded these ships, approximately nine of them made their homes in Jamaica, including two who later appeared on Pearse's pardon list. John Lewis of Port Royal served on the *Anne* privateer in 1709 and a year later commanded a prize ship named the *Port Royal Merchant*.[42] In 1711 Lewis appeared once again, this time in Rhode Island aboard a prize ship captured by his friend, fellow Jamaican William Tempest.[43] The second pardoned man, Port Royal mariner Robert Brown, took a turn in 1710 on a privateer vessel, the *Dragon*.[44]

If privateering allowed one opportunity to develop skills in seamanship and artillery, Royal Navy service offered another. In some instances, mariners enlisted in England but exited their service at various ports in the Americas, where they remained after the peace of 1713. More commonly, American-based sailors enlisted in one of the colonies, often for short stints lasting but a few weeks or months. The most famous example of this kind of itinerant service is Edward Thache, or Blackbeard, who enlisted on at least two navy vessels.[45] Like Thache, the future pirate Edward England saw navy service during the war. In 1712 he enlisted on the HMS *Sorlings*, receiving a discharge at New York in July 1713.[46]

No fewer than fifteen men on Pearse's list served on Royal Navy vessels that circulated in Caribbean and North American waters during Queen Anne's War. Michael Rogers, for instance, enlisted on the HMS *Ruby* as a pilot from July to October 1702, and served again in that capacity on the HMS *Anglesey* during a layover in Jamaica spanning February to May 1704.[47] Most others served only during the war's latter stages, often circulating between a select number of vessels, which offered the opportunity to forge networks that later could be called on for the formation of pirate crews. From 1709 to 1711, Henry Berry, Packer Adams, Dennis McCarty, and George Sinclair completed stints on the HMS *Sweepstakes*. Each of them ended their enlistments in Barbados only to turn up later in the Bahamas.[48] Henry Hawkins, Robert Brown (of Jamaica), and the aforementioned Michael Rogers joined Edward Thache on the HMS *Windsor*.[49] Jamaican Anthony Jacobs saw two years of service (1711–13) aboard the HMS *Seaford*, and Griffith Williams, arguably the most seasoned of all the navy men, spent three years aboard the HMS *Foweys* (1711–14) before being transferred to the HMS *Shoreham* in 1715, on which another future pirate, James Neville, also served.[50] New Englanders John Mitchell and James Brown each enlisted for service on the HMS *Sapphire*, most notably Mitchell, who piloted the vessel in 1711 for an unsuccessful attack on Canada.[51] Others still joined the navy in the immediate postwar period, receiving discharges in American ports that placed them near emerging hubs of piracy. David Champion served six months on the HMS *Roebuck* before being discharged at Martinique in March 1716.[52] Meanwhile, in South Carolina, Henry Chick joined the crew of the HMS *Shoreham* in August 1715 and received a discharge there the following March.[53] Tristram Wilson, who enlisted at the English port of Poole in January 1713, served more than two years on the *Speedwell* and *Scarborough* before disembarking at Jamaica in September 1715.[54]

Based on circumstantial evidence, then, a few hypotheses may be generated to assess the assumption, held by historians and contemporary naval and colonial officials alike, that many of the golden-age pirates were former privateers. First, almost all the men on Pearse's list were too young to have actively participated in King William's War or the early stages of its successor named for Queen Anne. While it is possible that a few had begun their training as mariners at this time, serving as novice "landsmen" or shipboys, by 1708 many would have been approaching or past the age of majority and would have acquired enough nautical experience to make them valuable crew members. Most future pirates seem to have cut their teeth as mariners around the years 1708–12, perhaps encouraged by the provisions of the American Act. With the exception of John Lewis, John Mitchell, and Robert Brown, however, there is no direct evidence that others on Pearse's list captained or served on privateer vessels operating at that time. However, given the prevalence of privateering at Jamaica, the sense among naval officers that the pirates had been privateers is plausible. Importantly, a select number of the men on Pearse's list acquired valuable navy experience that, in the future, could be put to use for nefarious purposes.

The Carrying Trade

Privateering was not a full-time job but rather an interruption of the more common activity of sailing trading vessels. By the turn of the eighteenth century, many of the elements of a more systemized intra- and interimperial trade were falling into place, encouraged by a consumer revolution in Britain and the demographic expansion of the colonies. Historian David Hancock describes this system as "self-organized complexity," indicating that trading connections emerged not because of centralized planning but through the initiative of merchants and ship captains in Europe and the many nodes of trade located throughout the global empires.[55] Within the empire, a degree of specialization occurred. In the Caribbean, an economy of plantation slavery emerged, producing the sugar and molasses that was in demand in England and North America. The Caribbean colonies supplemented their trade by providing tropical goods such as the turtle shells used for making combs, along with logwood (primarily harvested on the Spanish Main) used for dying wool. As the Caribbean colonies devoted most of their arable land to sugar cultivation, they became dependent on other colonies (as well as England) to meet many of their daily needs. For instance, North American farmers supplied the Caribbean colonies with foodstuffs, including fish caught in New England, wheat grown in New York, and South Carolina rice.[56] In addition to food, the North American colonies were an important source of lumber, which was scarce in the Caribbean due to deforestation.

To ensure that the fruits of colonial enterprise would benefit the mother country (retroactively described as "mercantilism"), in the latter half of the seventeenth century Parliament passed a series of laws, referred to collectively as the Navigation Acts. These required the conduct of colonial commerce in English ships, staffed primarily with English sailors; applied duties to a range of enumerated goods; and established vice-admiralty courts to adjudicate maritime disputes, including those related to piracy.[57] Prior to 1690, Britain did little to protect its trade in the Americas. However, during the wars of the late seventeenth and early eighteenth centuries, it developed a "convoy and embargo regime" to address that deficiency.[58]

The decentralized nature of the British Empire promoted a culture of smuggling and also enabled individual colonies to carve out independent niches within the Atlantic commercial system. For instance, the historian Mark Peterson depicts Boston as a "city-state," a largely self-governing polity that flaunted mercantilist laws, which led to a brief revocation of the Massachusetts charter in the 1680s. Like other colonial projects, its founders were initially obsessed with finding gold but soon discovered that codfish was its most viable commodity. Left to its own devices, Boston carved out a trading niche in the West Indies, supplying the region with salted fish that helped sustain its settler population and rapidly growing number of slaves. In the seventeenth century, Boston issued its own coinage and printed paper money that funded the local war effort against France.[59] The colony of Bermuda provides a similar example. Historian Michael Jarvis details how Bermuda first concentrated on tobacco production, but after 1685 reoriented its economy toward the sea "largely without imperial direction, promotion, or supervision." By the 1690s, he argues, Bermuda had become "perhaps the most intensively maritime colony within the British empire" through its shipbuilding industry and role as carriers of commercial products to and from Britain's colonies. This positioned Bermuda, as Jarvis phrased it, "in the eye of all trade."[60]

Many of the 209 seamen who accepted the pardon had been actively involved in the carrying trade for a decade or more prior to encountering Captain Pearse in the Bahamas in 1718 (see table 1). This was their principal occupation. Many appear to have begun their sailing careers by specializing in a select few local routes, gradually expanding the scope of their operations as they gained experience. Boston's John Mitchell, for instance, initially confined his activity to New England but later specialized in trade to North Carolina.[61] His first recorded voyage to North Carolina took place in 1708, when his sloop (of which he was one-third owner) was cleared outward from Boston. From 1708 to 1712 Mitchell made at least three more runs to North Carolina and one voyage to St. Thomas, indicating a capability of conducting lengthier Caribbean voyages. In 1714 alone, Mitchell made three voyages to North Carolina, returning once more in the spring of 1715 and at least twice more the following year.[62] Fellow Bostonian Samuel Boyce (Boyes) began his career as a master of vessels by specializing in the trade to Virginia. His first recorded voyage dates to 1700, the year he appeared in Virginia from Boston as master of the sloop *Dolphin*, in which he made a repeat voyage, arriving in Virginia again on May 4, 1701. From that point on, Boyce began extending the scope of his trading voyages, leaving Virginia on June 21, 1701, and continuing on to Barbados. By 1706 he was making regular trips to South Carolina in the brig *Susannah*. Eventually, Boyce would sail directly to the Caribbean, conducting an eight-month round trip between Boston and the island of St. Christopher's in 1716–17.[63]

Where a ship captain made his home naturally would have had an impact on the destinations to which he traded and the corresponding navigational expertise he acquired. In Jamaica, for instance, the island's geographical position, which facilitated a long-standing clandestine trade with the Spanish colonies, influenced the maritime career of John Lewis. Beginning at least as early as the 1680s, Jamaicans were actively engaged in cutting logwood on the Spanish Main, particularly at the Bay of Honduras and Campeche in the Yucatán Peninsula. Lewis gravitated to this trade. As captain of the brig *Martha*, between June 1709 and May 1710, Lewis made two voyages to Campeche and one to the Bay of Honduras, each time bringing home logwood. As with his Boston counterparts, Lewis expanded the scope of his navigation, clearing for London in October 1710. Around that same time, Lewis made connections in New York and got married there, conducting two trading voyages back and forth to Jamaica between 1712 and 1713.[64]

As a former Dutch province, New York maintained commercial links to Dutch colonies in the Caribbean, which shaped the nautical expertise of its mariners. John Sipkins, for instance, specialized in the trade between New York and Curaçao. In March 1711 he cleared outward for that island, returning in January 1712. The following July he returned to Curaçao, and by 1713 he was making stops in Jamaica. Sipkins also made "deep water" voyages across the Atlantic Ocean, which required considerable skill and entailed greater risk. Sipkins ventured to the Netherlands in 1715, which included a stop at the English port of Cowes on the return voyage. In the future, Sipkins confined his navigation to Caribbean routes, making voyages to St. Christopher's and Jamaica in 1716 and another to St. Thomas in June 1717.[65]

In addition to acquiring a growing familiarity with maritime geography, these sailors came to understand the economic role of their local community within the Atlantic trading system, as well as the nuances of local consumer demands, and the varying productive capacities of numerous colonies. Predictably, the inventories of cargoes reflect the regional special-

TABLE 1
Documented Merchant Voyages of Pardoned Pirates before 1718

[BLANK spaces denote lack of information]

Name	Vessel	Origin	Destination	Date	Cargo	Source
Adams, Abraham		Boston	Antigua	Nov. 1708		*BNL*, Nov. 15, 1708
	Kitty and Mary	Boston	Antigua	Apr. 1711	gunpowder, guns	CO 152/10
		Antigua	Boston	May 1711		*BNL*, May 21, 1711
		Boston	South Carolina	Nov. 1716		*BNL*, Nov. 26, 1716
Barker, John	*Diamond*	New York	St. Thomas	Sept. 1715	provisions, lumber	CO 5/1222
	Diamond	St. Thomas	New York	Nov. 1715	coconuts, sugar, molasses, cotton	CO 5/1222
	Diamond	New York	Antigua	Dec. 1715	flour, bread, peas, onions, lumber	CO 5/1222
Boyce, Samuel	*Diamond*	Virginia	Boston	Oct. 1700	tobacco	CO 5/1441
	Diamond	Boston	Virginia	May 1701		CO 5/1441
	Diamond	Virginia	Barbados	June 1701	tobacco	CO 5/1441
	Diamond	Virginia	Boston	Oct. 1701	tobacco	CO 5/1441
	Diamond	Boston	Virginia	June 1702	Corn, pork, staves	CO 5/1441
	Diamond	Virginia	Boston	June 1702	tobacco	CO 5/1441
	Susannah	Boston	South Carolina	Jan. 1706	'	*BNL*, Jan. 14, 1706
	Seaflower	Boston	registration	Dec. 1711		MAC, vol. 7
	Friendship	Boston	St. Christophers	Dec. 1716		*BNL*, Jan. 14, 1706
	Friendship	St. Christophers	Boston	Aug. 1717		*BNL*, Aug. 12, 1717
	Friendship	Boston	St. Christophers	Oct. 1717		*BNL*, Aug. 12, 1717
Brown, James	*George*	Pennsylvania	Antigua	Apr. 26, 1708	Lumber, provisions, pitch, tar	CO 157/1
	George	Barbados	Pennsylvania	July 1709	rum	CO 33/14
Chandler, Thomas	*Content*	Leeward Islands	Barbados	Sept. 1701	No goods subject to duties	CO 33/13
	Content	Barbados	Leeward Islands	ca. Feb. 1702	No goods subject to duties	CO 33/13
Creagh, John	*New Sea Flower*	South Carolina	Antigua	July 1705	lumber, pitch, tar	CO 157/1

Name	Vessel	Origin	Destination	Date	Cargo	Source
	Sea Flower	South Carolina	Antigua	March 1705/6	Two Indian slaves	Salley, *SCCHJ*
Glinn, Henry	*Mermaid Galley*	Guinea Coast	Jamaica	Jan. 1711	Two hundred "negroes" imported; sugar, fustic, indigo, and pimiento for export	CO 142/14
	Mermaid	Jamaica	unknown	ca. Sept. 1713	Sugar, logwood	CO 142/14
Harris, William		Boston	unknown	ca. Aug. 1699	Attacked by pirates "east of Boston"	CO 5/860
	Good Intent (crew)	Barbados	Boston (cast away at New York)	ca. Dec. 1703		MAC, vol. 62
	Hopewell (crew)	Boston	shipwrecked	Mar. 1703/4		MAC, vol. 62
		Piscataway	Jamaica	Aug. 1704		CO 142/13
	St. Christophers	Boston	St. Christophers	Mar. 1, 1716	onions, shingles, fish	*BNL*, Feb. 6, 1716; CO 5/848
		Rhode Island (via Boston)	Connecticut	Aug. 1717		*BNL*, Aug. 27, 1717
Hudson, Nathaniel		New York	St. Thomas			*BNL*, April 30, 1711
Jackson, John	*Speedwell*			Registered in Boston, Apr. 1698		MAC, vol. 7
	Speedwell	Virginia	Boston	Nov. 1706		*BNL*, Nov. 18, 1706
		Boston	Virginia	June 1708		*BNL*, June 28, 1708
		Virginia	Boston	Nov. 1708		*BNL*, Nov. 15, 1708
		Virginia	Boston	Dec. 1708		*BNL*, Dec. 20, 1708
Lewis, John						
	Brig *Martha*	Jamaica	Campeche	ca. June 1709	ballast only	CO 142/13
	Brig *Martha*	Jamaica	Bay of Honduras	Feb. 4, 1709/10	ballast	CO 142/14
	Brig *Martha*	Honduras	Jamaica	May 1710	logwood	CO 142/14
	Brig *Martha*	Jamaica	Honduras	June 1710	ballast	CO 142/14
	Port Royal Merchant	Jamaica	London	Oct. 1710	logwood, sugar, sasparilla, ginger, pimiento, fustick, cinnamon, "bark of citranian"	CO 142/14

Name	Vessel	Origin	Destination	Date	Cargo	Source
	Charles (crew)	Jamaica	Rhode Island	June 1711	prize ship	*BNL*, June 4, 1711
		New York	Jamaica	July 1712		*BNL*, July 7, 1712
	"Privateer snow"	Havana	New York	Oct. 1712	prize ship; gold, silver, elephant tusk	*BNL*, Oct. 6, 1712
	Brig *Lark*	New York	Jamaica	Sept. 1713	flour	CO 142/14
Mallet, Peter	*Success*	Nevis	South Carolina	July 1706		CO 157/1
	Success	Nevis	South Carolina	Oct. 1708	sugar, rum	CO 157/1
	Defiance	Monserrat	Barbados	Feb. 1713	no goods liable to pay duties	CO 33/13
	"barque"	St. Thomas	St. Christophers	Nov. 1713	cotton, sugar	Book of Duties, St. Thomas
	Martha and Mary	Nevis	St. Christophers	July 1715		CO 157/1
	Neptune	Nevis	Boston	Aug. 1716		*BNL*, Aug. 27, 1716
	Neptune	Boston	New York	Sept. 1716	mackerel, cod, European goods	*BNL*, Sept. 10, 1716
Martin, John		Boston	Campeche	Jan. 1714		*BNL*, Jan. 17, 1714
		Turks Island	Boston	Oct. 1714		*BNL*, Oct. 25, 1714
		Boston	Campeche	Dec. 1714		*BNL*, Dec. 27, 1714
Mitchell, John	"His father's sloop"	Boston	Pirate attack 100 leagues east of Boston	Sept. 1699	Fishing voyage	CO 5/860
	Centurion	Boston	Nova Scotia	May–October 1704	Transport sloop	MAC, vol. 122
	Hannah and Mary	North Carolina	Boston	Oct. 1708		*BNL*, Oct. 25, 1708
	Hannah and Mary	Boston	North Carolina	Nov. 1711		*BNL*, Nov. 26, 1711
	Hannah and Mary	North Carolina	Boston	Mar. 1712		*BNL*, Mar. 31, 1712
	Hannah and Mary	Boston	North Carolina	Apr. 1712		*BNL*, Apr. 14, 1712
	Hannah and Mary	Boston	North Carolina	July 1714	rum, European goods	CO 5/848
	Hannah and Mary	Boston	North Carolina	Dec. 1714	rum, molasses	CO 5/848
	Hannah and Mary	Boston	North Carolina	May 1715	rum, molasses, European goods	CO 5/848
	Hannah and Mary	Boston	North Carolina	Oct. 1715	rum, molasses	CO 5/848
Mutlow, John	*William and Thomas*	New York	Jamaica	Dec. 1716	provisions	CO 5/1222

Name	Vessel	Origin	Destination	Date	Cargo	Source
	William and Thomas	Bahamas	New York	May 1717	Appurtenances from a Wrecked vessel	CO 5/1222
	William and Thomas	New York	St. Christophers	June 1717	provisions	CO 5/1222
Perrin, John	Betty	Virginia	South Carolina	Mar. 1716	wine	CO 5/1442
	Lucy	Virginia	South Carolina	July 1717	wine	CO 5/1442
Rawlings, Richard	William and Sarah	Boston	Barbados	Sept. 1710		T 64/47
Richards, John	Endeavor	Boston	Newfoundland	Sept. 1706		BNL, Sept. 9, 1706
	Endeavor	Boston	Barbados	Apr. 1708		BNL, Apr. 26, 1708
	Endeavor	Boston	Barbados	Oct. 1708		BNL, Oct. 11, 1708
		Fayal	Boston	Apr. 1713		BNL, Apr. 6, 1713
		Boston	Antigua	May 1713		BNL, May 4, 1713
	Joseph and Mary	Boston	Portugal	June 1714	fish, boards, staves, corn, oil	CO 5/848
	Joseph and Mary	Boston	Barbados	Dec. 1714	fish, oil, lumber	CO 5/848
	Joseph and Mary	Boston	Barbados	Apr. 1715	fish, oil, lumber, horses	CO 5/848
	Samuel	Boston	Barbados	Apr. 1716	fish, lumber	CO 5/848
	Samuel	Boston	Barbados	Dec. 1716	oil	CO 5/848
Richards, Richard	Rebecca and Catherine	Anguilla	Barbados	Jan. 1716	no goods	CO 33/13
Rouse, William	Andrew and Samuel	Boston	Madeira	ca. Mar. 1697		MAC, vol. 7
	Hopewell	Boston	Ship registration, voyage unknown	Mar. 1698		MAC, vol. 7
	Andrew and Samuel	Boston	Suriname	Sept. 1701		MAC, vol. 7
	Andrew and Samuel	Suriname	Barbados	Jan. 1702		CO 33/13
	Andrew and Samuel	Barbados	Suriname	Feb. 1702	"no goods lyable for duties"	CO 33/13
	Brig William	Boston	Registered in Boston as co-owner	Sept. 1702		MAC, vol. 7
	King of Spain	Boston	Jamaica	Sept. 1710	fish, boards, staves, mackerel, flour, pork, soap	CO 142/14
	King of Spain	Boston	Jamaica	Feb. 1711		BNL, Feb. 11, 1711

Name	Vessel	Origin	Destination	Date	Cargo	Source
	King of Spain	London	Boston	Nov. 1711		*BNL*, Nov. 19, 1711
	King of Spain	Boston	London	Feb. 1712		*BNL*, Feb. 16, 1712
	King of Spain	Boston	Jamaica	May 1712		*BNL*, May 19, 1712
	King of Spain	Rhode Island	London	Apr. 1713		*BNL*, Apr. 6, 1713
	King of Spain	Boston	Jamaica to Campeche	Sept. 1713	Madeira wine, sugar	CO 142/14
Sipkins, John		New York	Curaçao	Mar. 1711		*BNL*, Mar. 17, 1711
		Curaçao	New York	Jan. 1712		*BNL*, Jan. 26, 1712
		Curaçao	New York	May 1712		*BNL*, June 9, 1712
		New York	Curaçao	July 1712		*BNL*, July 7, 1712
	Rachel and Anne	New York	Jamaica	Dec. 1712	oil, lumber, flour, bread	CO 142/14
	Rachel and Anne	Jamaica	New York	ca. Jan. 1713	sugar, rum	CO 142/14
		Campeche	New York	Apr. 1714		*BNL*, Apr. 26, 1714
		New York	Campeche	May 1714		*BNL*, May 31, 1714
	John and Elizabeth	Holland/ Cowes	Marblehead	ca. Jan. 1716		*BNL*, Jan. 30, 1716
	John and Elizabeth	Marblehead	New York	Mar. 1716		*BNL*, Mar. 26, 1716
	John and Elizabeth	New York	St. Christophers	June 1716	provisions, European goods	CO 5/1222
	John and Elizabeth	Jamaica	New York	Sept. 1716	European goods	CO 5/1222
	John and Elizabeth	New York	Madeira	Oct. 1716	provisions, grain, wax, lumber	CO 5/1222
	John and Elizabeth	St. Thomas	New York	July 1717	lignum vitae, sugar, cotton, wood, ginger	CO 5/1222
	John and Elizabeth	New York	Jamaica	Aug. 1717	provisions, oil, lumber, pump boxes	CO 142/14
Smith, John	Loyal Tibble	Barbados	New York	July 1712	rum	CO 33/14
	Abigail	New York	Jamaica	Feb. 1713	butter	CO 142/14
	Abigail	Jamaica	New York	Mar. 1713		CO 142/14
Smith, William	John and Elizabeth of Connecticut	New York	Barbados	Dec. 1715	provisions, lumber, one horse	CO 5/1222

Name	Vessel	Origin	Destination	Date	Cargo	Source
	Love	Bermuda	Barbados	July 1717	brasiletto wood, seal oil, turtle shell, 40£ cash, gold	Bermuda deeds, vol. 7
Spencer, William	*Pineapple*	Boston	Montserrat	July 1716	mackerel, lumber, horses	CO 5/848
Sutton, John	Unnamed sloop	Barbados	Jamaica	October 1702		*CSP*, vol. 20
	Unnamed vessel	Exuma	New York but "belongs to Barbados"	June 1708		*BNL*, June 7, 1708
	Sloop *Anne*	Barbados	South Carolina	ca. October 1708	Rum	CO 33/13
Taylor, Richard	*William's Endeavor* of Philadelphia	Maryland	Barbados	June 11, 1716	Not yet laden	CO 33/15
	William's Endeavor	Barbados	Philadelphia	July 11 to Aug. 30, 1716	sugar, cotton, rum	CO 33/15; *BNL*, Sept. 10, 1716
		Antigua	Philadelphia	Dec. 12, 1716		*BNL*, Dec. 31, 1716
		Philadelphia	Antigua	Feb. 6, 1717		*BNL*, Mar. 11, 1717
		Barbados	Philadelphia	May 2, 1717		*BNL*, May 13, 1717
		Antigua	Philadelphia	June 27, 1717	"Brings no news"	*BNL*, July 8, 1717
		Antigua and Providence	Philadelphia	Feb. 21, 1718	"brought seven of the pirates who surrendered"	*BNL*, Mar. 17, 1718
Wishart, Robert	*Providence*	Bahamas	South Carolina	ca. Nov. 1716	Only ballast	CO 5/508
	Providence	Bahamas	South Carolina	ca. Feb. 1717	Only ballast	CO 5/508

BNL = *Boston News Letter*

CO = Records of the Colonial Office, National Archives, Kew, United Kingdom

CSP = Sainsbury et al., *Great Britain Public Record Office, Calendar of State Papers, Colonial Series: America and the West Indies*

MAC = Massachusetts Archives Collection

SCCHJ = A. S. Salley, *Journal of the Commons House of Assembly of South Carolina*, March 6–April 9, 1706

T = Great Britain, Treasury, Miscellaneous Records, Colonial, Barbados: Ships Entered and Cleared with Cargoes

ization of trade contributing to this knowledge. In each of John Mitchell's voyages from Boston to North Carolina, for instance, he carried rum distilled in New England from the molasses carried there from the Caribbean. In two of the four voyages for which Mitchell's cargoes are known, rum was the exclusive product he carried, supplementing one 1714 voyage with cider, wood, salt, and "European goods," and another in 1715 with molasses and more European manufactures. Another Bostonian, John Richards, made numerous trips to Barbados carrying fish, whale oil, lumber, and corn harvested in New England, occasionally supplementing these goods with other local products like wheat, horses, and, on one occasion, a lamb.[66] Likewise, Boyce, sailing between Boston, Virginia, and Barbados, loaded his vessel with corn, pork, wood staves, and tobacco produced in Virginia, knowing that such commodities were in demand in sugar-dependent Barbados.[67] Knowledgeable in the macroeconomic workings of the empire, a substantial number of these ship captains would have understood the market incentives of trading with or joining pirates in the Bahamas.

Captain William Rouse on Land and at Sea

One of the most commonly held misperceptions about pirates—and perhaps all sailors—is that their occupation, which entailed spending months away from home on the high seas, diminished their connections on shore. According to this view, they were stateless men who lived beyond the boundaries of law and displayed little loyalty to any community on land. Inhabitants of a "wooden world" of sailing vessels, it is sometimes assumed that mariners forged their deepest human connections with other mariners, and were frequently deprived of familial bonds established through birth, marriage, and parenthood, as well as those forged with onshore neighbors. Pirates, in particular, formed a "subculture of defiance" that was at odds with the societal norms on land.

Although some maritime drifters lacked long-term commitments to people on land, many of the 209 men on Pearse's lists maintained considerable ties to persons and institutions in their home ports, as well as those to which they frequently sailed. Many enjoyed multigenerational connections with their families of origin, and they frequently married, establishing nuclear families of their own. They went to church; some appear to have gone regularly and baptized their children. Although most were never wealthy, these mariners owned property and maintained business connections with persons at home and in multiple locations where they conducted trade. In a word, they were solid subjects who appear as beneficiaries of wills, buyers and sellers of land, and sometimes even minor officeholders.

Far from being rootless, a more realistic assessment indicates that these so-called enemies of all mankind had put down deep roots in their home communities, and that those roots spread outward to ports in other colonies. Given the frequency with which they traveled, mariners were perhaps the most cosmopolitan people in the Atlantic world, possessing knowledge of people, places, and events transpiring far from their homes.[68] Perhaps no one fits this profile better than the erstwhile pirate William Rouse of Charlestown, Massachusetts, for whom the paper trail enables the most complete reconstruction of his life before the pardon. Rouse's presence in maritime Boston is ubiquitous, indicating the intimate connection between land and sea and the financial concerns that may have caused him to stumble into piracy.

William Rouse (Rous, Rowse) was of solid English Puritan stock, the likely descendant of Faithful and Suretrust (Starr) Rouse, who settled in Massachusetts during the "great migration" of the 1630s.[69] Existing baptismal records do not indicate when or to whom William was born, but it can be inferred that he was born in the late 1660s, making him one of the oldest of the pardoned pirates. Contemporary documents always refer to him as being "of Charlestown, mariner" or as "Captain Rouse" to distinguish him from several persons by that same name in nearby towns. Captain Rouse presumably was reared in Charlestown, and since he knew how to read and write, he likely attended the Charlestown grammar school.

The earliest documented evidence of Rouse's presence in the Boston area comes in February 1689, when he signed on as a crew member of the HMS *Rose*, which had arrived several years before to enforce the revocation of the Massachusetts Bay Company's charter and support a newly installed government under Sir Edmund Andros. Rouse appears in the ship's pay ledger as an "able" seaman, indicating that he probably had at least two years of sailing experience at that time. Although the date of his discharge is not recorded, his compensation totaled above ten pounds, meaning that Rouse probably spent upward of one year on board.[70] Rouse's stint in the Royal Navy was not without incident. As the Glorious Revolution unfolded in the winter of 1688–89, it exposed the divided loyalties of the *Rose*'s captain and crew. Captain John George and some of his followers proposed sailing the *Rose* to France in order to support King James. The majority, however, supported William and Mary, and rose up to arrest Captain George.[71] William Rouse was among those who supported William and Mary, and he provided a deposition before Boston officials in which he chronicled the seizure of the captain and the ship.[72] Rouse surfaced again in the fall of 1691 when, as captain of the sloop *George*, Rouse brought to Barbados a cargo of flour, shingles, and barrel staves.[73] Shortly after his return from Barbados, Rouse wed Mary Peachee (Peachie, Peachey), a twenty-year-old, relatively poor woman from Charlestown.[74]

Together, William and Mary Rouse created a large family. Their first child, William Jr., was baptized in December 1692. Mary would produce at least eleven children, giving birth well into her mid-forties: William Jr. (b. 1692, d. 1715), Mary (b. 1695, d. 1703), Thomas (b. 1697), Katherine (b. 1700), John (b. 1702), Joseph (b. 1708), Mary (b. 1710), Peachie (b. 1712), Elizabeth (b. 1714), William (the second b. 1716), and Ruth (d. 1722).[75] Like most families in the early modern world, William and Mary Rouse experienced the loss of children. Their first daughter named Mary died at age eight. William Jr., a mariner like his father, died in a tragic drowning accident at age twenty-six in British Guyana. Ruth died in early adulthood.[76]

True to his upbringing, the Congregational church played a significant role in Rouse's life, and that of other family members. Their primary place of worship was the First Church of Charlestown. While Mary was not baptized as an infant, at the age of twenty she took advantage of the "Half Way" covenant, a procedure adopted in 1662 enabling persons to become partial communicants of the church. Importantly, these "partial" members of the church were allowed to baptize their children (a function many churches denied to nonmembers), which may explain Mary's rationale in becoming one, just nine months before marrying William.[77]

For his part, William became active in church affairs later in his life, shifting his loyalties to King's Chapel in Boston, the area's first Anglican establishment. A local historian relates a story about Rouse that, if true, may indicate why he decided to make the switch. As the story goes, it was customary among Charlestown's "influential citizens" to purchase a family pew in the local church there. Around the year 1709, Rouse purchased an "interest" in a pew owned by the late captain Thomas Russell. Russell's surviving relatives, however, continued to assert their rights to the pew, and crowded into it on Sundays alongside the Rouse family. This caused Rouse to complain to the selectmen (the church's governing body) that he was "something disturbed by others taking up part of the same pew." The selectmen confirmed Rouse's ownership of the pew, but only on the condition that he allowed Russell's children to continue occupying it alongside his family.[78] Rouse perhaps did not like the way the dispute was resolved, so he baptized his three youngest children at King's Chapel beginning in 1714 and served as a vestryman from 1715 to 1720. He also bought his own pew there, which remained in the family until 1733.[79] The Rouse family's shift to the Anglican Church may explain why Mary Rouse was summoned to court in 1730 for failing to attend Sunday services in Charlestown.[80]

Still, temporal concerns occupied Rouse, especially his work as a mariner. He surfaced again in 1694, when Massachusetts officials deposed him in proceedings that led to the recall of Governor William Phips.[81] While Rouse would have been a witness to the many naval operations of King William's War, there is no direct evidence to indicate that he was ever involved in privateering. Instead, Rouse spent his time conducting trade. By March 1697, Rouse was at the island of Madeira trading for wine as the master of the ship *Andrew and Samuel* of Boston.[82] One year later, he captained the trading sloop *Hopewell*, owned by the prominent Boston merchant Samuel Lillie.[83] Rouse did, however, experience a short, peacetime stint aboard Massachusetts's officially sanctioned privateering ship, the *Province Galley*, funded and commissioned by the colony in 1694 to defend New England waters. Between November 1698 and February 1699, Rouse served as lieutenant under the galley's longtime commander, Captain Cyprian Southack. Along with two members of the Massachusetts council, Southack negotiated a treaty with French-allied Indians in Canada and retrieved several English prisoners.[84] Although Rouse would have had little say in those proceedings, he learned that diplomatic missions provided an opportunity for clandestine trade, a temptation to which he eventually succumbed.

During the interwar years, Rouse enhanced his profile as a captain of trading vessels and started investing in them himself, suggesting a rise in his personal wealth. In January 1701 Rouse was in London on a trading voyage. Ironically, for the return trip to Boston, Rouse received a black box intended for the governor of Massachusetts Bay, Lord Bellomont. Although he was forbidden to open it, Rouse was aware of its contents: a commission for Governor Bellemont to try the pirates, primarily those associated with William Kidd.[85] Three months later, in Boston, Rouse received a let pass as captain of the *Andrew & Samuel*, which granted him permission to conduct trade in Suriname. Rouse had clearly developed familiarity not only with sailing routes to Britain and West Africa but also South American waters. A year later, in September 1702, Rouse registered the brig *Samuel*, but this time as a quarter owner, not as its captain. His partners at that time were two prominent merchants from Boston, including future Massachusetts councilman Andrew Belcher.[86]

That he was able to associate with prominent men illustrates that Rouse was, in fact, a man of property by that time. In January 1700 Rouse made his first real estate purchase, paying two Charlestown mariners and their wives £150 for a house and tract of land off Wapping Street, near wharves that today constitute the Boston Naval Yard. Four years later, in June 1704, Rouse paid forty-five pounds for a three-and-a-half-acre plot near Breed's Hill (site of the famous Revolutionary War battle erroneously named Bunker Hill) that included "fruit trees" and pasturage.

These purchases invite several observations.[87] First, like most ship captains, Rouse conveniently lived near the wharves; the ships he sailed and owned were only a short walk away and would never be far from his sight. Furthermore, that Rouse purchased land from fellow sailors may indicate that he felt most comfortable doing business with them, a sign of nascent trade consciousness. Additionally, his purchase of an orchard and pasturage that would have sustained farm animals indicates that Rouse, like many ship captains who aspired to greater status, tried to diversify his economic activities and preferred to own productive capital rather than simply work for wages—this, at a time when his growing family would have required Rouse to maximize his earnings. Finally, the individuals involved in these transactions reveal the kinds of personal connections Rouse relied on to conduct business. To perform the legally mandated duty of witnessing the conveyances, Rouse called on his brother-in-law John Peachee for the home purchase. Nathaniel Dowse, a prominent relative of one of his sellers, witnessed both transactions.

Rouse seemed to be living a charmed life, but during Queen Anne's War, he fell into an illicit trading scheme that landed him in jail and nearly ruined his career. While not a privateer, Rouse contributed to the war effort by conducting prisoner exchanges with the French. In December 1705 he sailed to Port Royal (in modern Nova Scotia) to conduct one such exchange, returning to Boston in February 1706 with seventeen former English captives. Evidently earning the trust of the French governor, la Bonaventure, Rouse convinced him to dismantle an English brig, the *Mayflower*, which the French had captured and retrofitted as a privateer ship. At the same time, he proposed having the English redeem it and several other captured vessels that the French impounded at Port Royal.[88]

Rouse's success caught the eye of Governor Paul Dudley, who ordered him to sail in the sloop *Anne* to Port Royal that April to conduct yet another exchange for twelve English captives languishing in prison. Meanwhile, in Boston, at least eleven French prisoners taken by English privateers remained in confinement. Rouse's orders were explicit. He was to carry letters Dudley had written to Port Royal's governor, la Bonaventure, accompanied by a French diplomat who was in Boston negotiating the exchange. Three high-ranking French prisoners "on parole" also accompanied Rouse. Dudley reminded Rouse that these three men were expected to "return hither" with him to Boston, requiring him to "demand this of la Bonaventure" should he balk. Ordered "not to tarry" more than six days, Rouse was to return promptly to Boston with the redeemed English prisoners.[89]

It was common knowledge that prisoner exchanges, a regular occurrence in the war zone between New England and New France, presented inviting opportunities for ship captains to conduct clandestine trade. Commerce of this kind, routinely tolerated in peacetime, threatened the colony's security, as Franco-Indian attacks were often facilitated by the gunpowder, shot, and steel weapons sometimes traded to French subjects and their Indian allies. To put a stop to the practice, in 1703 Governor Dudley issued a proclamation outlawing trade with the enemy, and the policy received legislative support two years later when Parliament passed an act forbidding it. Governor Dudley, who was suspected of having a financial stake in this illegal trade, was rather lax in enforcing his own proclamation.

In March 1706 (a month before Rouse sailed) Dudley allowed an enterprising Scotsman (and future governor of Nova Scotia) named Samuel Vetch and his trading partner, John Borland, to conduct trade in New France as a means of collecting debts predating the war.[90] Rouse arrived in Port Royal that May and exchanged the prisoners as planned. He also redeemed the brig *Mayflower* by paying off Governor la Bonaventure. Perhaps sensing that he would receive lenient treatment like Vetch, he allegedly traded with the French governor and his subjects. On top of that, Rouse convinced Governor la Bonaventure to issue a let pass for the *Mayflower*, now commanded by John Phillips of Charlestown, enabling him to fish in Acadian waters. Under the cover of that let pass, Rouse and Phillips proceeded to trade with the Indians and more French subjects on the Acadian shoreline. Rumors of this illicit trade quickly filtered back to Boston, and the authorities rounded up Vetch, Borland, Rouse, and Phillips, along with two other accomplices, Roger Lawson and Ebenezer Coffin of Nantucket.[91]

An investigation ensued that summer, and things did not go well for Rouse and the others. Dudley, an unpopular governor, sought to score political points by bypassing the normal common-law process and holding the trial in the Massachusetts Assembly—an impeachment. Many of its popularly elected members came from frontier districts that were currently suffering from Indian attacks and wanted to clamp down on clandestine trade.[92] During those proceedings, Rouse's boat pilot, Andrew Miller, turned on him, testifying that Rouse did in fact trade salt, molasses, sugar, fish, pickles, tobacco, and brass kettles with the French at Port Royal, receiving beaver fur in return. Miller alleged that Phillips, acting under Rouse's orders, had traded with the Pemasquid Indians, as evidenced by the quantities of beaver fur that had been loaded on his ship.[93]

The English prisoners redeemed by Rouse turned on him as well. One of them, Henry Darling, complained that Rouse had put the prisoners to work restoring a brig to seaworthiness and having them haul cargoes of beaver fur on board Phillips's sloop. Darling reported that many French subjects came and went from Rouse's sloop to purchase goods, and that Rouse sometimes went on shore to trade sugar and iron implements. When Rouse and Phillips rendezvoused at the mouth of the Pemasquid River, they invited forty Indians, including women and children, to come on board with them to trade, exchanging tobacco and iron plowshares for beaver products. Darling, under the impression that Rouse and Phillips had traded there before, also reported the existence of a storehouse filled with English woolens and other goods provided by Rouse. Darling estimated that Rouse had amassed £2,000 worth of beaver furs.[94] Former prisoner John Collins confirmed many of these details, additionally accusing Rouse of loading Phillips's sloop with yet more trade goods off the coast of Maine with the intent of trading illicitly again.[95]

In the end, the Assembly found Rouse guilty of "high misdemeanors" and on September 3 passed a private act (a law applied to one citizen) punishing him with a fine of £1,200, plus court costs. Rouse was to remain in jail, where he had been since June, until he could pay the money he owed. Governor Dudley later confided that the fines imposed on Rouse were "especially" beyond his ability to pay, effectively making the financial penalty a perpetual jail sentence. Additionally, Rouse was forbidden to hold any public office in the colony of Massachusetts.[96]

From jail, Rouse, along with Coffin and Phillips, proclaimed their innocence by drafting a petition to Queen Anne asking that she rescind the private acts issued against them by the Massachusetts Assembly and revoke their fines. In Rouse's version of the story, he intended to use the trade goods as barter in exchange for the English brig and several other vessels in Port Royal harbor. Rouse claimed that Dudley had inspected the goods to ensure he carried no contraband, that is, gunpowder and weaponry. Rouse claimed that, after paying for the brig, he and Governor la Bonaventure could not agree on a price to redeem the other vessels. With extra trade goods at his disposal, Rouse exchanged them for coal, which was "much needed" in Boston, and traded the remainder for beaver fur with Indians who were known to be friendly to the English, not French allies. Rouse claimed that, at the time he stood trial, the province was in an uproar due to Indian attacks on the frontier, and the Assembly felt pressure to make an example of him and the others. The Massachusetts acts, he argued, were "an extraordinary proceeding, and unprecedented" and thus should be disallowed.[97]

Unable to ply his trade, Rouse could not pay the fines he owed to the government. Consequently, he spent a total of eighteen months in jail. One must presume that his large family endured significant material want during that time, and we are left to ponder the degree of psychological stress Mary endured back home trying to raise her family with no husband nor income. Just as important, the jail term posed a significant threat to William and his family's sense of honor. Now a convicted criminal, William must have wondered if he would ever again be able to captain a ship. As it was a relatively small village, virtually everyone who lived in Charlestown would have known Rouse and his family, who must have endured occasional whispers about his criminality, and perhaps at times withered under the glares of hostile neighbors who spoke ill of him. Indeed, virtually all of Massachusetts knew what Rouse had done, as indicated by a 1707 pamphlet written by Cotton Mather under the pseudonym "Philopolites." The focus of Mather's ire was Governor Paul Dudley, whom he accused of permitting clandestine trade with the enemy. He cited Rouse's case as a prime example of the government's "tenderness" toward criminals, insinuating that Rouse and the others deserved to hang rather than pay a fine.[98]

As he was languishing in prison, the petition Rouse had sent to the queen wound its way through various branches of the British government. Finally, on September 24, 1707, the queen's Privy Council repealed the acts, ordering Massachusetts officials to conduct a "fresh trial in the ordinary course of law." At the same time, the Privy Council recommended restoring the fines and setting the men free if they posted bond for good behavior.[99] Rouse must have received word of the Privy Council's order in November 1707, when he petitioned the council for his release. Jail time had been hard on him, physically. Rouse complained of "indisposition of body," stating that another winter in confinement constituted a threat to his very life. Rouse asked for permission "to return to [my] own house," agreeing to post bond for good behavior, and return to prison, if required, when warmer weather came. The council, which included Rouse's business partner, Andrew Belcher, consented to his request. It helped to have friends in high places.[100]

Although he returned home, Rouse's legal battle continued for more than a year. In May 1708 the formerly imprisoned men, eager to clear their names, pressed to have their case heard in the Massachusetts Superior Court of Judicature, the colony's highest appellate court. After several delays caused by attorneys sparring over technicalities, Rouse's case was finally heard on January 25, 1709, in Charlestown, Middlesex County. Although no records of the deliberations survive, the court evidently decided that Rouse had suffered enough for his indiscretions, and a day later, it discharged him after he paid court fees.[101]

Finally a free man, Rouse attempted to resume a normal life. He started sailing again; in April 1710 he became master of the ship *King of Spain*, a square-stern ship of two hundred tons. Evidently, Rouse's brush with the law had not alienated him from local owners of the vessel, who trusted Rouse with their ship for the better part of three years. From 1710 to 1713, he made at least two voyages to London, and two more to Jamaica, which included one stop at the Bay of Campeche.[102] The captaincy of the *King of Spain* must have promised to be lucrative, for Rouse resumed purchasing real estate in Charlestown, perhaps with an eye toward providing more living space for his growing family, and to have sufficient property to bequeath his children. The year of his discharge, Rouse purchased additional pastureland bounded by the Mystic River. In 1710 alone, Rouse made three more purchases: two town lots adjacent to his home and some "wharf land" near the Charlestown battery.[103] Just as he had done before his arrest, Rouse invested in sailing vessels. In 1713 he registered the sloop *Neptune* on behalf of himself and a Boston merchant. A year later, Rouse collaborated with three Charlestown men in ownership of yet another vessel, the sloop *Friends Adventure*.[104]

In certain respects, then, it would appear that Rouse had recovered his status within the community. At the same time, there were signs that he faced an uphill battle trying to recover from the financial duress caused by his prolonged detention and court battle. In November 1711 Rouse arrived from London on the *King of Spain* and had to quarantine in the harbor after one of his crew contracted smallpox. Rouse succeeded in having the quarantine lifted two weeks later, but in early January 1712 Royal Navy captain James Campbell impressed four of his sailors, causing him to delay another voyage and miss an opportunity to earn money ferrying fish from Newfoundland. Rouse sued Campbell for eighty pounds in damages plus his legal costs. In the meantime, the four impressed sailors sued Rouse for unpaid back wages totaling fourteen pounds. Rouse went to court one more time that May, asking for restitution and declaring the impressment illegal by virtue of the 1708 America Act. The court ultimately sided with Rouse and ordered Campbell to pay, but it is clear that the legal squabbles caused him to lose valuable time and money.[105]

Rouse, who had largely avoided legal entanglements before 1706, soon began appearing in court more frequently for the adjudication of debt cases, as both plaintiff and defendant. Rouse's woes principally derived from a dispute he had with one of the owners of the *King of Spain*, London merchant Herman Lewis. When Rouse departed from London on that ship around August 1712, he signed a bond promising to pay Lewis the sum of £2,000. Following a voyage to Jamaica that ended in Boston, Rouse failed to honor that agreement, made worse by his inability to sell six hundred pounds of lead gunshot that remained in his possession. In January 1714 the case went to arbitration, resulting in an order that Rouse pay Lewis's attorneys £800 and return the unsold gunshot. The case eventually went to the Court of Common Pleas, which decided in favor of Lewis. Rouse paid £640 and in January 1715 appealed to the Superior Court to absolve him of the remainder. The Superior Court, again, decided in favor of Lewis, ordering Rouse to pay another £160 to cover the remainder of the debt, plus some court costs.[106] Rouse's financial entanglements with Lewis were so aggravating, in fact, that Rouse's own son, William Jr., initiated a suit against him for an undisclosed amount in his capacity as Lewis's attorney.[107]

Strapped for cash, Rouse sued those who owed him money. In December 1713, as the Lewis case was unfolding, Rouse initiated a lawsuit against a Roxbury card maker named John Paige for the sum of six pounds. One month before, Rouse had paid in excess of five pounds on Paige's behalf for provisions that were loaded onto the HMS *Phoenix*, ironically the same ship Vincent Pearse commanded five years later. In January 1715 Rouse sued a Boston shopkeeper for a twenty-three-pound debt contracted less than two months earlier. The fact that Rouse tried to collect such small debts, so quickly, suggests that he needed all the money he could get his hands on.[108] Ironically, in June 1715, just as he paid off his debt to Lewis, Boston merchant John Oliver sued Rouse for forty pounds.[109] Rouse luckily dodged at least one more lawsuit due to the plaintiff's inability to appear in court.[110]

As a sign that these debt cases had squeezed him financially, Rouse began mortgaging his Charlestown properties to obtain liquid capital. Rather than borrowing from a private individual, William and Mary Rouse took advantage of a 1714 act that established a land bank enabling individuals to take out loans by using their real estate as collateral. In January 1715 he and his wife Mary took out a loan of £200 worth of bills of credit. They put up all their properties as collateral, ranging from the town lots they owned to the wharfage and orchard, promising to repay within a year at 5 percent interest. Again, in September 1717, the Rouses mortgaged all their property to obtain another loan of £200. In effect, the latter government loan required Rouse to pay back the capital and interest (at 5 percent) within nine years. The final payment on the loan was scheduled for February 13, 1726.[111]

A decade of legal and financial struggles may have forced Rouse to start taking desperate measures. Curiously, Massachusetts treasury records indicate that Rouse conducted two missions on behalf of the government to search for sunken merchant ships, an activity that was entirely new to him. In 1716, just as a mad scramble off the coast of Florida for the sunken Spanish treasure fleet commenced, Rouse received a small sum as master of the sloop *Endeavor*, which he sailed to the coast of Maine in search of a merchant ship that reportedly sank there. In May 1717 Rouse commanded the sloop *Elizabeth and Mary* on a mission to Sable Island, some 175 kilometers off the coast of Nova Scotia, in search of two more sunken merchant ships.[112] Although we may never know what compelled Rouse to begin doing business with pirates in the Bahamas, it is plausible to suggest that he encountered mariners with wrecking experience and became enticed with the prospect of finding gold and silver off the coast of Florida. Massachusetts shipping returns from that period are devoid of any mention of Rouse, indicating that he was sailing off the radar of government officials by the summer of 1717. He would not appear in the historical record again until encountered by Vincent Pearse in 1718, which raises the questions: How did he get to the Bahamas, what was he doing there, and why would he accept a pardon for piracy?

William Rouse was older and wealthier, and he had a higher profile than most of the pirates who surrendered to Vincent Pearse in 1718. Nevertheless, his experiences as a mariner in Charlestown, Massachusetts, are broadly representative of those of other seamen throughout the Anglophone Atlantic world. Rouse grew up near the water and, perhaps like Benjamin Franklin, felt the call of the sea in a visceral way. Through the printed word, or by word of mouth, Rouse likely knew the many laudatory stories about Francis Drake and Henry Morgan. Chances are good that he even met a few of the men who sailed with Henry Every, perhaps even admiring their ability to steal the Mughal emperor's money and get away with it. As England had been at war with France and Spain for his entire adult life, Rouse might have considered a world full of privateers to be the norm, reflecting the idea that there could be "no peace beyond the line" separating the Americas from Europe. Like most successful mariners, Rouse established a firm footing in his hometown, by marrying, producing a large family, buying property, and forming partnerships with many local mariners and merchants. Although not criminally inclined, Rouse nevertheless had opportunities to operate in the grey area between legal and clandestine commerce, which nearly cost him his livelihood and his life. In straitened financial circumstances, Rouse began borrowing money, and he rolled the dice by assuming the risks of doing business with pirates in the Bahamas in a desperate attempt to pay it back.

CHAPTER 2

A New Madagascar

John Graves tried to warn everyone. Having resided in the Bahamas since the mid-1680s, he had seen a lot. After a brief stint as the colony's secretary, from 1696 Graves had struggled to exercise his duties as the Bahamas' commissioner of customs. Although presiding over the customs office could be a thankless job in any colony, the Bahamas posed special challenges. The inhabitants, long accustomed to living outside the purview of royal authorities, chafed at the prospect of having their trade regulated under the auspices of the Navigation Acts, which they routinely flaunted. Pirates sometimes frequented the islands, where Bahamian governors, often enticed by bribes, treated them with kid gloves. Governorship of the islands, such as it was, changed hands frequently and was hotly contested, as rival claimants routinely acted in an arbitrary manner and arrested each other on charges of piracy. Sparsely populated and poorly defended, the Bahamas also made inviting targets for French and Spanish privateers, who harassed and invaded the islands frequently during Queen Anne's War. In a 1706 letter to the Board of Trade, Graves provided a grim description of the islands after suffering from a series of Spanish assaults two years before. Due to killing, kidnapping, and emigration, the Bahamian population had been reduced to less than five hundred persons, Graves estimated, noting that because they were "scattered [over] some 200 miles distance" and were without a government, the islands were indefensible. Lacking food and other basic provisions, Graves compared the inhabitants to "Wild Indians," stating, "At the best they are very ready to succour and trade with Pirates." Unless the Crown could provide protection, Graves predicted that the Bahamas were likely to become "a second Madagascar."[1]

Within a few short years, Graves was proven correct. By 1718, Britain's colonial governors were bemoaning the fact that pirates were in the process of turning the Bahamas into a "new Madagascar," a licentious pirate nest that posed a challenge to royal authority.[2] As is well known, from 1714 to 1718 the Bahamas, particularly the de facto capital of Nassau on (New) Providence Island, served as a refuge for hundreds if not thousands of golden-age pirates. Lacking any form of constituted authority, lawlessness prevailed, and conditions on the islands came to resemble, for a time, those found on Madagascar two decades earlier, the memory of which lived on as the utopian kingdom of "Libertalia" conjured by the author of the *General History*.

The rise and fall of the pirate lair at the Bahamas is well known and has been the subject of innumerable historical works dating to the *General History* itself. What is often overlooked, however, is that piracy resumed first in Harbor Island and Eleuthera before the pirates were able to establish a foothold at Providence. Furthermore, Bahamians carried out piratical attacks more than a year before the 1715 wreck of the Spanish *flota*, and almost two years before crews from Jamaica began salvaging treasure there. We must therefore attribute the Bahamas' turn toward piracy to local causes, and avoid the temptation to depict it a mass movement that happened instantaneously everywhere in the British Atlantic. Whereas the Bahamian pirates—like all pirates—longed to procure valuable treasure and vendible commodities, revenge against Spain and France was their principal motive at this particular point in time. Only later did the actions of the Bahamians become swept up in a broader regional phenomenon that transcended these local concerns.

The Bahamas became a pirate lair largely because of its geographical situation, forming an archipelago consisting of 29 islands, 661 smaller cays, and over 6,000 exposed rocks. Altogether, the land mass comprises less than six thousand square miles, which combine to form 2,201 miles of coastline.[3] The Florida Strait, through which flows the Gulf Stream, separates the North American continent from the archipelago and was the principal route by which oceangoing vessels returned from the Caribbean to Europe. In addition to their proximity to major shipping lanes, as the author of the *General History* noted, the Bahamas attracted pirates because "there are so many uninhabited little islands and keys, with harbours convenient and secure for cleaning their vessels."[4] Large vessels, such as the men-of-war commanded by Royal Navy captains, had a difficult time navigating through the Bahamas, making it easier for smaller pirate sloops to escape.

Although the Spanish repeatedly conducted expeditions to enslave the

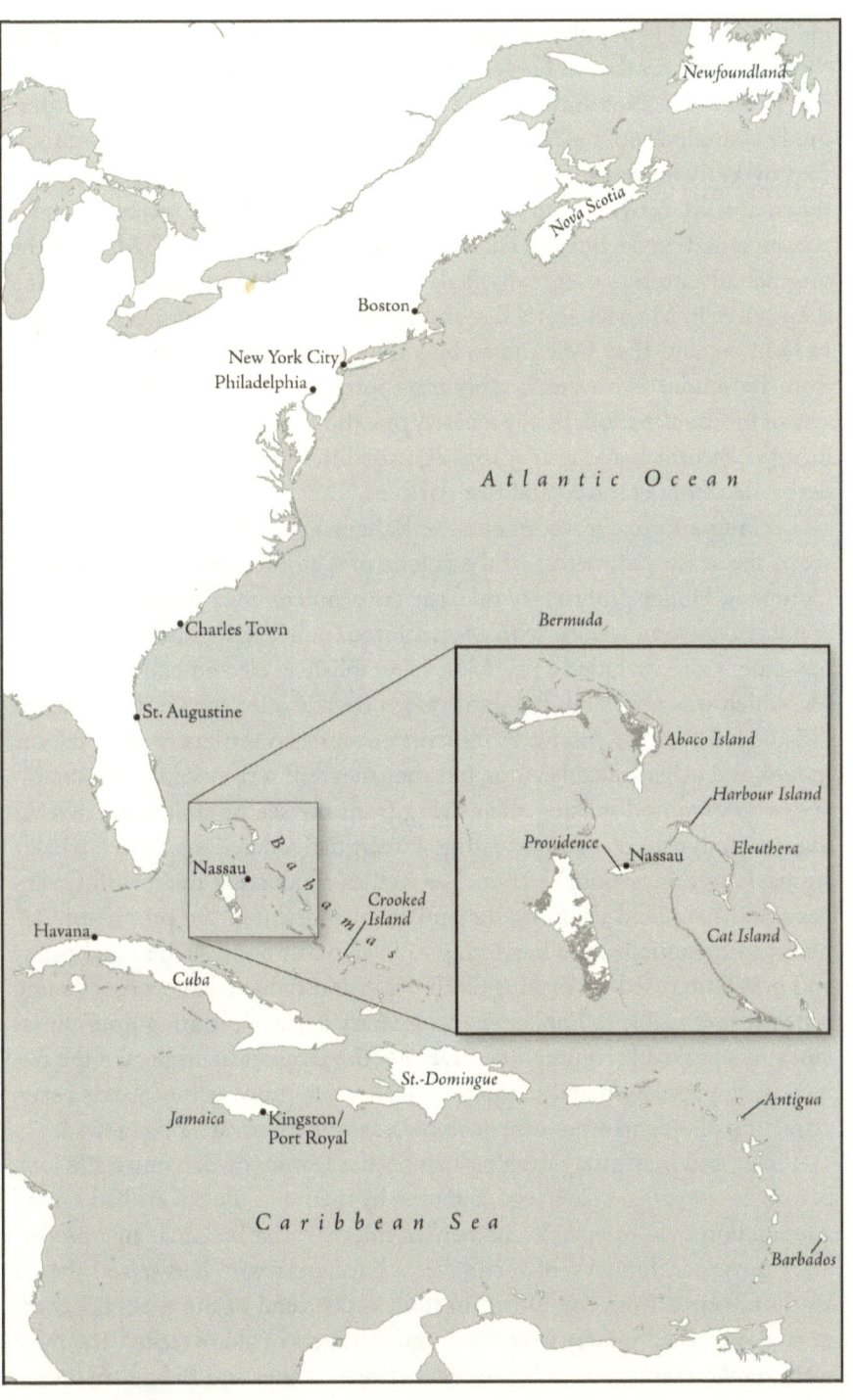

indigenous Taino population, the earliest attempt at European settlement in the Bahamas was that of French Huguenots, who created a short-lived colony in the 1560s. Not until 1647 did a group of religious dissidents from Bermuda (founded 1608) establish the Company of Eleutherian Adventurers. Led by William Sayle, the company settled at an island they called Eleuthera, a word derived from Greek, meaning "free." About seventy persons accompanied Sayle, but the colony struggled to sustain itself. Most of the original adventurers eventually fled, returning to Bermuda or establishing themselves in Massachusetts Bay and Jamaica. Still, a few families managed to hold on, and they were joined by a number of enslaved and free Blacks from Bermuda, who were forcibly transported to the Bahamas for various acts of insubordination. By 1670, nearly one thousand persons may have been living at Eleuthera and nearby islands, two-thirds of them white and the rest descended from enslaved and free Africans.[5]

Lacking a formal government, the Bahamas received one in 1670, when six of the seven proprietors of the colony of Carolina formed the Bahamas Company. Under proprietary rule, the government consisted of a formally appointed governor, along with an appointed council and judiciary. The original patent also included a provision to establish an elected house of assembly, which was not instituted until 1729, a decade after the Crown assumed jurisdiction over the colony. Proprietors encouraged settlers to plant cotton, indigo, and other valuable crops, but they met stiff resistance from Bahamians, who preferred making their living from the sea by smuggling, wrecking, turtling, fishing, and harvesting ambergris (concretions from a whale's stomach used in making perfume) as well as conducting trade with Caribbean and mainland colonies. Bahamians also resented the proprietors' attempt to monopolize the harvesting of local hardwoods, such as mahogany and brasiletto (used for making cloth dyes), and Bahamian governors found it nearly impossible to implement proprietary goals of profiting from the islands' most valuable commodities. Despite the proprietors' neglect of the Bahamas, its population and economy continued to grow, as the islands began attracting dissidents from other colonies, as well as privateering crews.[6]

Piracy and maritime salvaging had been a feature of Bahamian life long before the so-called golden age, and even by the 1680s the colony had earned a reputation as a "receptacle and pen" of thieves.[7] The Bahamas' first proprietary governor, John Wentworth, was a buccaneer who had seized the island of Tortola from the Dutch in 1665, and several of the ensuing governors also courted pirates, privateers, and salvagers of shipwrecks.[8] The most well-known example of collaboration between pirates and Bahamian governors was that between Governor Nicholas Trott and Henry Every's crew. In March or April 1696, a ship called the *Fancy* arrived at Eleuthera, where its captain, who called himself "Henry Bridgman," asked for permission to enter the harbor at New Providence. Trott, who undoubtedly knew that Bridgman was actually Every, allowed his crew to land there, upon which Every paid off his crew and dispersed his loot. Trott allegedly received a large bribe for looking the other way.

Trott's apparent complicity with Every coincided with a series of imperial reforms instituted in 1696 and the Treaty of Ryswick (1697), which potentially might have curtailed privateering. All colonies came under closer scrutiny, and the Bahamas proprietors sought to restore law and order, creating a vice-admiralty court and expanding the number of government offices. In 1699 Governor Nicholas Webb put into effect an act against piracy and issued letters of marque to a former Bostonian named Read Elding, who embarked on a mission to capture a pirate named Kelly who terrorized local waters. Instead of capturing Kelly, Elding apprehended a vessel named the *Bahamas Merchant* and submitted a prize claim in Nassau, insisting that he had found it wrecked and abandoned. When the case was tried in the vice-admiralty court, the former captain of the *Bahamas Merchant* insisted that Elding had seized it from him "in a piratical manner." The court nevertheless found in Elding's favor. Disillusioned, Webb left the colony, and Elding's pirates plundered Webb's abandoned estate. Improbably, before his departure Webb named Read Elding as his deputy governor. Elding was popular and ruled the island for nearly two years, albeit without a proprietary commission. He has the distinction of presiding over the first execution of a pirate on the island, a Dutch freebooter named Hendrjik van Hoven (alias "Captain Hind"), who was hanged in 1699.[9]

The Bahamas proprietors eventually replaced Elding with Elias Haskett, another New Englander with preexisting economic ties to the Bahamas, who arrived early in 1701. Historians Michael Craton and Gail Saunders describe Haskett as a "tyrant and rascal" who enforced laws arbitrarily to punish his political opponents and tried to line his pockets through nefarious means. In October 1701 Haskett arrested former deputy governor Elding on charges of piracy and corresponding with pirates. He was in the process of negotiating with Elding for his release in exchange for a bribe when a local posse stormed the jail and released Elding. In the meantime, a group of rebels headed by John Graves and Ellis Lightwood (a prominent planter) apprehended Haskett and forcibly sent him to New York to face charges of piracy.[10] The result was the "Revolution of 1701," whereby Bahamians drew up twenty-four separate charges against Haskett, who was relieved of his duties. Ellis Lightwood served as governor until 1704, when the proprietors named Englishman Edward Birch to replace him. Birch happened to arrive shortly after a Spanish attack on the islands, and he was so troubled by the colony's backwardness and poverty that he promptly returned to England, choosing to leave the inhabitants "as he found them." Three years later, the proprietors tried to entice one Robert Holden to be governor, but he refused. For the span of fourteen years (1704–18) the Bahamas effectively had no government.[11]

Politically dysfunctional, the Bahamas was unable to defend itself during Queen Anne's War. Assaults against the colony began around September 1703, when a combined squadron of Spanish and French ships struck Providence, where the attackers supposedly "[put] the men to the sword" and threatened to burn the women. A passing Dutch privateer vessel managed to turn away the enemy and carried away about eighty persons to safety in Philadelphia.[12] The enemy struck again around January 1704, when Spanish and French ships landed upward of five hundred men at Providence. They met no resistance from the local inhabitants, except for one unfortunate man who fought back and had his hand cut off. The soldiers carried off the inhabitants' personal goods, burned the church to ashes, spiked and destroyed the fort's cannons, and carried off gold, silver, and slaves. Enemy ships appear to have lingered in the area for several months.[13] In April a French ship attacked a wrecking expedition led by James Roisie of Boston, who, along with a majority of his crew, was killed while attempting to haul up the remains of a Spanish ship near San Salvador Island.[14] On August 3 the Spaniards returned to Providence. A galley with sixty-five men captured an English sloop then proceeded to land on the island, which, with only twenty men capable of bearing arms, could not stop the Spaniards from terrorizing the population. Spanish forces plundered the town again one month later, taking forty slaves and committing further damage to the now dilapidated fort.[15]

Although reeling from enemy attacks, Bahamians did fight back. In the fall of 1704, one Thomas Williams received a privateering commission from Nathaniel Johnson, the governor of South Carolina. Bahamians constituted the vast majority of his crew, which was successful in capturing several Spanish prizes that they brought back to Providence that November. Lacking a government, the crew petitioned John Graves to constitute one so that the prizes could be adjudicated properly in an admiralty court. As they explained, "Our wives and children are in a manner starved for want of clothing and provisions," adding that some even lacked "a shift to cover their nakedness."¹⁶ A few weeks later, Graves departed for England, commencing his lengthy quest to have the Bahamas placed under royal authority. Then, in 1706, Governor Johnson commissioned a second privateering vessel, this time under the command of Thomas Walker. Featuring a crew of at least twenty-two men, Walker's company targeted the coast of Cuba, destroying nine vessels and taking twenty-four Spanish prisoners. Walker's crew reported the good news in a letter they wrote to Governor Johnson in January 1707, stating that they had treated the prisoners "civily" by lending them a vessel to return home. They likewise affirmed the "prudent, just & honest" conduct of Walker, who later emerged as the Bahamas' leading anti-piracy crusader.¹⁷ Despite their ability occasionally to mount a defense, many Bahamians fled the colony, such as those who boarded a vessel in the summer of 1707 and arrived at South Carolina. There, they reported how the Spanish had stripped them of everything they owned and warned that they would "not suffer [allow] the English to settle Providence any more," claiming that the Spanish intended to found their own colony there.¹⁸

The attacks that weakened the Bahamas in 1704 resumed and intensified two years later. Around October 1706, undisclosed "enemies" targeted Providence Island, where they stole and spiked the fort's guns, burned many outbuildings, and stole movable property.¹⁹ Then, in July 1708, a French privateer named Martel, with a company fitted out from Santiago de Cuba, landed at Exuma and later proceeded to Eleuthera. Martel's intention seems to have been to terrorize the islands' female inhabitants. As one escapee, Elizabeth Stroude, testified before authorities in Bermuda, Martel's men had some of the Exuma women "hoisted up by the hands tyed behind them," sparing not even those who were "bigg with child." Dangling in midair, the French beat them violently with their cutlasses to extort confessions of their "supposed hidden wealth." Stroude herself suffered a beating so severe that she "was hardly able to stir for some time." Not content with simply meting out violence, the French burned the houses and stole food. "They left us neither food, lodging nor anything that might be of use," Stroude added, "except some small trifle provisions." Stroude also had heard that the women of Eleuthera received the same treatment, relating one story she heard of a pregnant woman who was beaten and lost her child to miscarriage, another who died, and a third who was tortured "by burning with matches put bewixt her fingers and toes." Another woman was tied up in her house, tortured, and killed when Martel's men set the house on fire. As the justice of the peace who took the deposition added in a postscript, Mrs. Stroude cut short the interview, "for that she was ashamed to declare what she saw and heard of their brutalities," inferring that Martel's men had also raped them.[20] Reports indicated that one of the victims was the wife of Perient Trott, one of the colony's leading men.

French attacks continued for several more weeks. Around the same time Martel was ransacking Exuma, a French captain named Bartholomew Martin, with a crew of twenty-three men outfitted at Santo Domingo, detained Bermuda mariner Samuel Harvey as he was collecting salt at Turk's Island. Martin's crew later captured another Bermuda sloop and set its captain, along with Harvey, adrift in a small boat with four days' provision.[21] In August, Martel struck again, this time at Harbor Island. Sea captain Edward Holmes testified that, on his return home from a mission on behalf of the government, he found a sloop anchored in the harbor flying a British flag. As Holmes approached, the sloop's crew lowered the flag and replaced it with a French standard. Accompanied by two canoes filled with armed men, Martel promptly attacked and boarded Holmes's ship. Holmes's family had also joined him, and the French men took hold of his wife and stripped her naked, then the quartermaster "presented a pistol at her breast" in an attempt to discover hidden valuables. After searching "the very hair of her head to find what was hid there," Martel's men threatened to fling her overboard. They later carried Holmes and his wife on shore, tying both of them to a tree. Captain Holmes was hit five hundred times with a cutlass and burned with matches between his fingers and toes, enduring verbal threats that they would also burn his "privy members." After this beating, the French carried them eight leagues from their habitation and let them go, forcing them to trek home injured.[22] Small-scale hit-and-run attacks on land likely continued throughout the islands, such as the one reported many years later by Mary Fox, a free person of African descent, whose two sisters and three children had been captured by the Spanish around 1710 and sold into slavery.[23]

In addition to making landfall, French and Spanish privateers targeted Bahamian shipping, as well as other unfortunate trading vessels trying to make their way through the Florida Strait. In the summer of 1708 alone, a French privateer named Pajoean intercepted seventeen British vessels. Bahamian Benjamin Sims suffered one attack and had to seek shelter in South Carolina. Meanwhile, one Captain Williams, who carried a number of passengers on board, suffered two attacks at the hands of the French. Following the second attack, Pajoean's company marooned Williams and his passengers on a deserted island, where for several weeks they subsisted on conch and whelk. As victims trickled into Charles Town, South Carolina's William Rhett, the future pirate hunter, warily observed that the Spanish and French had essentially occupied the Bahamas Islands, which they used as bases to cruise nearby waters. "Noe vessel will be able to escape them that are bound for that place [Bahamas] or Jamaica," Rhett mused, adding that more attacks were planned for the following summer.[24]

Ship captains who passed by the Bahamas testified to the devastating effects of these raids. Capt. Samuel Chadwell, who guided a sloop to Providence in 1706, described how fearful inhabitants "live scatteringly, in little huts, ready upon any assault to secure themselves in the woods." Chadwell observed that the Bahamians, although seemingly well stocked with "small arms" and ammunition, "chuse theyr Commanders as they please," noting that there was "no administration of Justice: the strongest man carrys the day."[25] In 1710 navy captain Nicholas Smith confirmed many of Chadwell's observations. At Eleuthera, Smith came ashore to listen to stories of French predation, reporting that the thirty-two families who lived there would "abandon their houses and retire to the woods for shelter, where they lay every night" to avoid being captured and tortured. At Harbor Island, he found longtime resident Thomas Walker, who had assumed the ad hoc role of "Commander in Chief," and had managed to build a small battery mounted with four guns. Harbor Island seemed to be "pretty well provided" with gunpowder, shot, and small arms, which discouraged the French from attacking there again. Smith failed to make it to Providence, but he heard rumors that it was in as poor condition as Eleuthera, with thirty-odd families clinging to existence in the woods, and defended by a "demolish'd" fort that was "of no use to them."[26]

Thanks to a truce Britain enacted with France in 1711 and a suspension of arms negotiated with Spain a year later, fighting between the belligerent nations—on paper, at least—more or less ceased by the beginning of 1713. The Treaty of Utrecht officially terminated the war that summer. Yet, as was common in the colonies, an undeclared war continued. Spanish *guardacostas*, which had served as private navy during wartime, shifted their focus to combat smuggling, preying on English ships engaged in clandestine trade. In May 1713 a South Carolina vessel captained by Joseph Ellicot was taken by a *guardacosta*, which in turn captured two vessels from New England and another from Bermuda. Their crime: loading salt in the Bahamas, which many Spaniards still refused to recognize as a lawful British colony.[27] Meanwhile, the privateer Louis Martel, who had ravaged the Bahamas during the war, continued terrorizing Bahamian waters, this time armed with a commission from the governor of Santiago de Cuba to "take all vessels that had [brasiletto], logwood, and salt," which the Spanish perceived as contraband harvested illegally within the Spanish dominions.[28]

Given the wartime traumas they experienced, it stands to reason that many Bahamians would have been eager to revenge themselves. Although few definitive eyewitness accounts from the Bahamas exist from 1713 to 1715, there are a number of clues suggesting that local Bahamians, in conjunction with newly arrived mariners from elsewhere, began attacking Spanish shipping around August 1713. Bermudians, who by their central position within the interimperial trade system also served as the empire's most reliable conveyors of news, were the first to hear about what was happening in the Bahamas. In April 1714 Bermuda governor Henry Pullein reported that "three sets of pirates" had been operating in the Bahamas for "eight months past," meaning that the attacks started around August the previous year. With crews of about twenty-five men each, Pullein reported that they have taken at least £3,000 worth of goods from the Spanish. Pullein also identified two of their captains, both of whom had only recently "resign'd [resided] amongst them." One was Benjamin Hornigold, who was about to become the most notorious British pirate of his day. The other was John Cockram, a smuggler who traded brasiletto and logwood to Curaçao and had recently married Catherine Thompson, the daughter of Harbor Island merchant Richard Thompson, perhaps the wealthiest man in the Bahamas at that time. Pullein specified that their targets were exclusively Spanish, lamenting that Spanish customers were now refusing to trade. At the same time, however, Pullein seemed to justify the Bahamians' actions. "In reality," he wrote, the Spanish were "served in their kind, as they have committed piracies on us under sham commissions," referring to recent attacks by the *guardacostas*.[29]

As people engaged in illicit activity were not inclined to record their activities in writing, details of these early piracies are hard to come by. Nevertheless, the existing evidence suggests that the first pirate voyages originated on the island of Eleuthera, where a group of "strangers" had arrived and worked in conjunction with a local population that welcomed them. The strangers included Hornigold and Cockram, along with one Benjamin Linn, Thomas Terrill, and Ralph Blankenshire. Daniel Stillwell, John Kemp, Matthew Lowe, John Carey, and James Bourne were all identified as married men, indicating that they were locals or persons from elsewhere who had recently married into local families. Hornigold, Cockram, Stillwell, and Carey later accepted a pardon from Vincent Pearse. Another local accomplice was Zaccheus Darville, the seventeen-year-old son of John Darville, who was

Stillwell's father-in-law and evidently consented to having his teenage son join the pirate crew.

These pirates conducted at least three major voyages in 1713–14. For the first voyage, Stillwell and Hornigold fitted out Stillwell's sloop, the *Happy Return*, capturing dry goods, tallow, and a "negro" slave valued at 8,000 pieces of eight. Using the same sloop, Stillwell commanded a second voyage that netted 1,100 pieces of eight, some "dressed skins," and other cattle products valued at 300 pieces of eight. More details are known about the third voyage. Hornigold, Stillwell, and an unnamed "stranger" bought an "open boat" from the inhabitants of Eleuthera and sailed to Cuba in December 1714. There, they apprehended a *lammet* and *caow* (two types of small vessels) owned by one Petir Barrihone of Port-au-Prince, French St. Domingue. The company made off with goods and money valued at a whopping 46,000 pieces of eight, making it by far the most lucrative of the three voyages. The pirates also apprehended several Spanish subjects and took them to the Bahamas, perhaps in order to ransom them. Barrihone later testified before Cuban authorities, who in turn made their displeasure known to Jamaican officials.[30]

While the inhabitants of Eleuthera welcomed the pirates, it was not yet apparent that they would find a similar reception at Providence. Thomas Walker, who had briefly served as a customs officer under Governor Haskett, assumed duties as the colony's ad hoc leader and identified himself as a "pursuer, prosecuter and disturber of all pirates, robbers & villains." As such, piracy conducted from Eleuthera deeply disturbed him, fearing reprisals by Spain and the erosion of trade in the Bahamas. To combat the breakdown of law and order, Walker recommended resettling Eleuthera's inhabitants at Providence, where they could be watched more closely. Alerted by Jamaican officials of the attacks at Cuba, around the end of December, Walker went to Harbor Island and staged some kind of "surprise" to apprehend Stillwell, perhaps in conjunction with two pirates, who later submitted depositions revealing Stillwell's crimes. Walker also claimed to have apprehended another of Stillwell's accomplices. In an attempt to round up more pirates, Walker employed an unnamed individual "to take the others at Ileatheria which are fled into the woods & defend themselves by fforce of arms." Walker appointed Captain John Chase of the sloop *Portsmouth* to convey Stillwell to Jamaica, where he could stand trial. In the meantime, Walker conducted a diplomatic mission to Cuba, presenting a letter to Governor Marques de Casatorres indicating the steps he had taken to bring Stillwell and the others to justice. Embellishing his success, Walker claimed to have apprehended eight of the pirates, now on route to Jamaica for their trials. Perhaps angling for a gubernatorial appointment, Walker also claimed to have averted an attack on the islands that the Spanish had planned. Unfortunately, for Walker, Stillwell never stood trial in Jamaica, as he managed to bribe the first mate of the *Portsmouth* and escape.[31]

Following the Stillwell incident, a power struggle ensued in the Bahamas between Walker and Hornigold and his pirate allies. In March 1715 Walker began corresponding with and forwarding depositions to British officials, alerting them to the piracy threat. Walker depicted the islands as "a recepticall and shelter of pirates and loose fellowes," adding that the local population was "inriching themselves by sideing and dealing with, entertaining and relieving such villains."[32] Walker warned that the pirates were mounting guns at the fort to repel anyone who attacked them. In the meantime, Hornigold expanded his base of operations beyond Cuba. In August 1715, near the Yucatán Peninsula, an anonymous passenger on an English logwood vessel encountered a "pirate snow" commanded by Hornigold. He and his men hailed the ship and boarded it, then made all the passengers give up their hats. Hornigold explained that his men had been drunk the night before and, in a stupor, threw their own hats overboard.[33] Although Hornigold did not confiscate any of the valuable logwood, the fact that his men would steal the hats from fellow countrymen indicated that his acts of piracy were taking a dangerous turn. Instead of targeting foreign ships, he was now inching toward a policy of attacking all ships indiscriminately. Later that fall, Hornigold captured a Jamaican ship off the Spanish Main, the sloop *Mary*, which he brought back to Providence in November, and by that point he was clearly willing to use violence against his local nemesis, Thomas Walker.[34] When Hornigold appeared in Nassau in November, he encountered Walker's son, Thomas Junior. He asked Walker Jr. "where ye old rogue his father was," prompting the younger man to say that he was at his home three miles away. Hornigold continued to harass Walker Jr. by calling his father "an old rogue," declaring that if he laid eyes on him "he would shoot and kill him."[35]

Although Hornigold never acted on his threat to kill Walker, by January 1716 he had gained the upper hand and was now using Providence, rather than Eleuthera and Harbor Island, as his home base. That January, he sailed again from Providence with 140 men in the *Mary*, which was described as having six guns and eight *pattararoes* (smaller-caliber swivel guns). Hornigold returned to Providence soon thereafter with another Spanish prize sloop, and perhaps feeling guilty about apprehending an English ship, he returned the *Mary* to its Jamaican owner. Now commanding the Spanish sloop, Hornigold went cruising again in March, evidently near Cuba. By then, Providence's evolution into a pirate lair was more or less complete, as crews from several Jamaican ships began landing there to share gold, silver, and goods taken from Spanish ships wrecked off the coast of Florida, along with booty derived from the capture of several French and Spanish ships off Cuba.[36]

Also by that time, British officials had launched a manhunt for the Jamaican mariner John Lewis. Lewis had been contracted to ferry the Spanish governor of Papian (in modern Columbia), the Marquis de Navarres, from Jamaica to Cartagena carrying goods and valuables estimated to be worth £16,000. Around the first of May 1715, Lewis and Navarres departed Jamaica in his brig, the *Lark*. Instead of bringing the marquis to Cartagena, however, Lewis put him ashore at Tholu on the coast of modern-day Mexico and absconded with his goods. In June, Lewis appeared in South Carolina, where Governor Charles Craven apprehended him and impounded the stolen goods. Lewis escaped from jail shortly thereafter, and Craven was later charged with keeping the marquis's goods for himself. Craven nevertheless proclaimed his innocence, citing the distractions involved in conducting a war against Indians who had staged a massive uprising that spring, known as the Yamasee War.[37]

Lewis's whereabouts were unknown at that time, but the mate of his ship, Jamaican Thomas Barrow, had taken up residence at Providence, indicating perhaps that Lewis or more of the crew were hiding out there. For a brief time, Barrow proclaimed himself the "governor of Providence," threatened to make it "a second Madagascar," and estimated that more than five hundred Jamaican mariners would join him there to engage in piracy. Barrow also resolved to continue the war against French and Spanish shipping, but as for English ships he insisted they "don't intend to meddle with them, unless they are first attack'd by them." Despite these reassurances, Barrow fielded a pirate crew that took one New England ship and another from Bermuda near Providence. On shore, the newcomers, estimated to be about fifty men "who have deserted the sloops that were upon the wrecks," committed "great disorders in that island, plundering the inhabitants, burning their houses, and ravishing their wives."[38]

The extent to which the pirates terrorized the local population is questionable, for such statements often come without corroboration, and may intentionally conceal the fact that many Bahamians were happy to do business with them. Nevertheless, Thomas Walker and his family were concerned enough for their safety to flee Providence, and in late June 1716 he took refuge in Charles Town, South Carolina. Walker alerted government officials there about the activities of Hornigold and other pirates. With firsthand information provided by Walker, around the first of June Deputy Governor Robert Daniel arranged for a preemptive strike.[39] He commissioned one Matthew Musson, master of the sloop *Edward & Sarah* and its seventy men, to search for pirates in the Bahamas and seize their persons and goods. Musson, himself a Jamaican privateer, knew many of the individuals now sheltering at Providence and would later play a small role in implementing the 1717 pardon. In the Bahamas, Musson encountered Benjamin Hornigold and talked his way onto his ship. On board, he found Virginia mariner John Perrin (who would also accept a pardon from Pearse) and "sundry goods which Perrin pretended to have bought of Hornigold." Musson seized Perrin and the contraband goods, forced Perrin to load them on a sloop "he properly owns," the *Betty*, and accompanied him back to Charles Town. Musson and Perrin arrived there sometime in early July, and Perrin's sloop filled with contraband anchored in the harbor.

The fate of Perrin's illegally obtained goods soon catalyzed a fight over them between Deputy Governor Daniel, on the one hand, and Customs Surveyor William Rhett and Thomas Howard, captain of the HMS *Shoreham* (stationed at Charles Town at that time), on the other. Determining who was in the right depends on whose side of the story one was inclined to believe. Lieutenant Governor Daniel, who submitted his own self-serving deposition with others corroborating it, spun a story implicating Rhett and Howard in interference with gubernatorial attempts to prevent "imbezelment." On the morning of July 4, Rhett's deputy, Richard Wigg, went on board Perrin's sloop, ordering the hatches opened so that he could seize the Crown's share of the goods. The sailors on board refused, saying it was contrary to their orders and proclaiming they would "knock out the braines" of anyone who tried to seize the goods aside from Deputy Governor Daniel, who had commissioned them. Rhett went to complain to Daniel, who affirmed that he alone was in charge of securing the goods to "prevent imbezelment."

Later, Daniel sent Nathaniel Partridge, his admiralty marshal, to inspect the sloop, but he was shocked to find that Rhett and Captain Howard's men had already broken open the hatches and were in the process of seizing the goods. Howard's men were all armed and violently threatened Partridge, causing Daniel to call out the local militia. With 140 men backing him, Daniel went to the harbor, where he found Rhett and Howard just offshore in three vessels onto which the goods had been loaded. Daniel shouted at Captain Howard and Rhett, demanding they return to shore. While Howard ignored him, Rhett stood up in his boat brandishing a sword and leading his men in a "chorus of huzzahs." Rumor even had it that Rhett flashed his backside at the deputy governor. Daniel then had his men lob cannon and small arms fire over the boats, in an attempt to bring them back to shore as they rowed away toward a wharf owned by Rhett. Deputy Governor Daniel, in the company of a local lawyer named George Rodd, boarded a boat and chased the three vessels. He soon came upon one of the boats carrying Rhett, Howard, and his lieutenant, James Fellowes. Brandishing a gun at Daniel, Lieutenant Fellowes started swearing at him and threatened to kill him as Captain Howard looked on with a drawn sword and a "surly" look on his face. Daniel backed off, and as he was leaving, Rhett flew into a rage, threatening to climb overboard with his sword to attack the deputy governor. At that point, Captain Howard had to step in and physically prevent Rhett from rashly inflicting bodily harm on Daniel.[40]

Conversely, the barrage of paperwork Captain Howard and his allies submitted to the British Treasury accused Daniel of seeking to deprive the Crown of its rightful prize. While the depositions Howard compiled adhered much to the same story line, they spin the events in a manner clearly emphasizing Daniel's obstructionism, the naval officers' devotion to duty, and the reasonableness of Rhett's actions. One witness, British mariner Michael Cole, revealed that Rhett never lapsed into a fit of frenzy during the ordeal, only giving verbal orders to his crew for the conduct of the vessel.[41] Another thing the deponents insisted on was the militarism of Deputy Governor Daniel and the militia. Deponents commented on how the militia beat drums and raised banners as if in preparation for war. Rather than harmlessly firing shots over Rhett and Howard, they did so with the intent of harming them. At least three shots struck Howard's boat, and cannon shot was directed at them from Granville's Bastion. Importantly, one slug penetrated the left breast of William Rhett, seriously wounding him and causing many observers to fear that he would die. Howard's deponents also emphasized the pugilism of Musson's crew, who attempted to stymie the customs office's attempts to impound the goods on board the *Betty*. In addition to insulting officers Richard Wigg and John Hogg by calling them names—"dog" was a favorite epithet—crewmembers beat them with frying pans, and the quartermaster pistol-whipped Hogg. They also tried to force Wigg, who could not swim, to jump to his death in the Ashley River. That the colony's lieutenant governor seemed to be orchestrating this belligerence confirmed the opinion held by navy officials that Daniel "was an old rogue who countenanced pirates."[42]

One individual who shared that opinion was Howard's lieutenant, James Fellowes, who reputedly went around town calling "all the inhabitants" of the colony pirates and threatened to turn the *Shoreham*'s guns on them to "make the government shake." He later engaged in fisticuffs with one of Daniel's crewmen, Joseph Swaddell, and was arrested after hitting him in the face. In addition to charging him with assault, Deputy Governor Daniel charged Fellowes with high treason for calling him "an old rogue." Fellowes was soon released from jail, however, after obtaining a writ of habeas corpus. In the meantime, Joseph Swaddell ended up in jail for trying to kill William Rhett, misfiring a musket three times as he pointed it in his face. Deputy Governor Daniel then had the South Carolina Commons House of Assembly draw up charges of high crimes and treason against Rhett, Captain Howard, and James Fellowes. On August 2 the Assembly rejected the charges, discerning they were "false and spurious." As Lieutenant Fellowes remarked, "I think it is very hard that we should lay under the character of being rebels and being guilty of high treason for assisting the officers of H.M. Customs in the execution of their office according to our instructions."[43]

The incident in South Carolina illustrates the difficulty colonial governments and naval officers had suppressing the pirate lair at Providence in its infancy. John Perrin's presence there, and his willingness to trade with Benjamin Hornigold, foreshadowed the mad scramble to the Bahamas that ensued for the next two years (a subject taken up in more detail in chapter 4). Although not inclined to commit acts of violence themselves, many ship captains and merchants were happy to trade for piratically obtained goods, presumably offered at reduced prices, as well as to procure scarce gold and silver specie.

Also complicating matters is that colonial governors frequently had to rely on captains like Matthew Musson to carry out their orders. Although he gave the appearance of acting against the pirates by capturing Perrin's contraband goods, Musson was no innocent. Rather, the previous December Governor Archibald Hamilton of Jamaica had issued privateering commissions to him, along with nine others, ostensibly to search for pirates. The reality, as everyone knew, was that Hamilton had tacitly given permission to the privateers to search for the Spanish treasure fleet that sank off the coast of Florida a few months before. Most of the ten captains commissioned by Hamilton would later commit acts of piracy against French and Spanish merchant ships, as well as the Spanish salvaging crews camped out on the coast of Florida.[44] Musson, who did not return to Jamaica until October, had in fact fished the wrecks, attacked Spanish shipping, and shared the spoils with his crew at Providence.⁴⁵ William Rhett alleged that Musson first captured a Spanish sloop called the *St. Michael*, apprehending over £1,500 worth of silver and logwood. Soon after, Musson captured two Spanish long boats and yet more goods, and he unloaded them at Port Royal, South Carolina, outside the purview of customs officers. Despite his alleged criminality, Musson obtained a commission to hunt pirates from Deputy Governor Daniel, but rather than track them down, Musson ventured to Providence to report to his friends that they might find "favorable usage" in South Carolina. The seizure of Perrin's sloop had been staged, the intent being to allow Perrin to offload his prize goods at Sullivan's Island and slip away unscathed back to Virginia.

If William Rhett's testimony is credible, Deputy Governor Daniel was not the solution to piracy but part of the problem. Rhett alleged that the antipiracy commissions Daniel issued to Musson and others were a "great absurdity" because, initially, the intent had been to empower ship captains to attack Indians on the coast of Florida in the ongoing Yamasee War. Deputy Governor Daniel also looked the other way when Musson and his companions unloaded goods at Port Royal and, in his capacity as judge on the vice-admiralty court, ensured that pirates received the full share of their prizes.⁴⁶ Regardless of who was in the right, jurisdictional disputes between colonial governors and royal officials such as naval captains and customs officers, particularly in proprietary colonies like South Carolina, complicated their ability to coordinate and root out the pirate's nest. As historians such as Mark Hanna and Douglas Burgess have ably demonstrated, proprietary governors operated without direct oversight from the Crown. South Carolina, in particular, had a long track record of governors who looked the other way from piracy, partly to accommodate locals who traded with pirates, but also because these same governors had a financial stake in their activities. Some accepted bribes or reserved a share of their prizes for themselves. Given the rank animosity between Deputy Governor Daniel, William Rhett, and Thomas Howard, it is highly likely that financial considerations, rather than a philosophical jurisdictional dispute, caused the rupture between them.⁴⁷

The question of who had the authority to seize and try pirates, however, did add another layer of complexity that initially made it difficult for colonial governments to enforce laws against them. Since the reign of Henry VIII, English law held that pirates who committed crimes on the high seas had to be tried in the High Court of Admiralty. Enforcing that law was impractical, as it was logistically difficult (and expensive) to apprehend someone in the Americas and conduct them to London for trial. The first colony to pass an anti-piracy law of its own was Jamaica in 1681.[48] In the 1680s, Crown officials attempted to convince other colonies to adopt their own version of the "Jamaica Act," and several followed suit. However, as historian Mark Hanna demonstrates, the 1684 South Carolina anti-piracy act contained so many loopholes that it was nearly impossible to procure convictions and executions. The establishment of vice-admiralty courts in 1696, along with the Piracy Act of 1698 (passed in response to the piracies of Every and Kidd), formalized the procedures by which piracy cases were to be adjudicated, at least on paper. In practice, however, implementation of the 1698 act was slow, as several colonies—particularly Rhode Island and Jamaica—claimed expansive admiralty jurisdiction for themselves. As such, they conducted their affairs according to local custom, including common-law jury trials in which many pirates were acquitted. Some colonial governors were unsure whether their gubernatorial commissions empowered them to try piracy cases, and colonial charters sometimes could be unclear as to the nature of provincial admiralty jurisdiction. Simply put, the wheel of justice moved slowly, and in the early months of 1716, many colonies were not yet institutionally prepared—nor ideologically committed—to hunt pirates.[49]

Still, anti-piracy colonial governors took notice of what was happening and began alerting Crown officials of the problem brewing in the Bahamas.[50] In May 1716 the Lords of the Admiralty began instructing ship captains assigned to American waters to be on the lookout for pirates. These instructions lacked specificity, offering only the rote order to "take, sink, burn, or otherwise destroy" any pirate ships they encountered. Still, the Admiralty's words represent a marked shift indicating a growing awareness of the emerging pirate threat.[51] Thomas Walker's testimony reached anti-piracy governors like Francis Nicholson at Nova Scotia and Alexander Spotswood of Virginia. Around late June 1716, Spotswood sent mariner Henry Vickers on a reconnaissance mission to the Bahamas, and he returned in July to confirm much of what Walker said was transpiring there. By September, Spotswood, naval captain Thomas Howard, and others, had expressed their concerns about the Bahamas to leading government officials in Britain, including naval secretary Josiah Burchett, members of the Privy Council, and King George I himself. On November 30, the Privy Council, with the support of the naval secretary and king, wrote to the Board of Trade asking them "to consider means for dislodging these profligate fellows or pirates from the Island of Providence."[52] Developing a comprehensive anti-piracy policy, however, would take months.[53] Consequently, the pirate lair at Providence grew.

The story of how the Bahamas became a pirate's nest has been recounted many times. Nearly all works on the subject confirm that the islands' geographical features, history as a pirate refuge, and lack of a government made it a welcoming place for sea robbers after Queen Anne's War. While the suffering of the Bahamians during that war contributed to its lawlessness, the immediate cause of the so-called golden age of piracy was a desire on the part of hardscrabble settlers at Eleuthera and Harbor Island to attack Spanish and French shipping. The war did not "end" in 1713 for them, as *guardacostas* continued to harass their shipping, and they had not yet recovered from the impoverished state in which the war had left them. Abetted by the arrival of mysterious "strangers," the Bahamians conducted at least three piracy voyages that enabled them to exact revenge and, just as importantly, to begin restoring the local economy. Eventually, pirates such as Hornigold strong-armed their way onto Providence, and the port town of Nassau became their base of operation. For upward of two years, piracy had been a local solution to a local problem, but events transpiring in Jamaica and off the coast of Florida produced a convergence of interests that would make Bahamian piracy truly Atlantic in scope.

CHAPTER 3

"All Mad to Go a Wrecking"

On May 13, 1716, after spending more than a year in the Caribbean, Captain John Balchen of the HMS *Diamond* anchored at the Nore, a sandbar at the mouth of the Thames River. There, he composed a letter directed to Naval Secretary Josiah Burchett, who had asked Balchen to report what he knew "relating to sloops at Jamaica going upon the wrecks in the gulph of Florida," alluding to the remains of the 1715 Spanish treasure fleet submerged near modern-day Vero Beach. The previous November, Balchen told him, Jamaica governor Archibald Hamilton had issued privateering commissions to two sloops, identifying their captains as Edward James and Henry Jennings. Officially, Hamilton's motive was "for suppressing piracys" committed by Spanish *guardacostas* on Jamaican vessels, "but their design, as they said themselves was to go upon the wrecks."

After heading out to sea, the sloops returned "in a shorter time than could be expected" with a massive haul of money. "The common report," Balchen revealed, was that the sloops had landed on the Florida coast and "forc'd from the Spaniards . . . the money which they had saved out of the wrecks" totaling 100,000 dollars, or pieces of eight. Balchen considered this "the greatest piracy," noting that Jamaicans believed their actions to be "just." In all, Balchen estimated, twenty Jamaican sloops headed for the wrecks to seek their fortune, depleting the supply of available sailors. "If I had stay'd a week longer," Balchen surmised, "I do believe I should not have had men enough to bring me home." Ten of Balchen's own men had deserted him two days before his departure in favor of joining crews headed to Florida. As Balchen put it, the sailors "were all mad to go a wrecking," for the majority of Jamaicans believed "they have right to fish upon the wrecks, although the Spaniards have not quitted [left] them."[1]

Captain Balchen has the rare distinction of being a firsthand observer of the dawn of golden-age piracy in Jamaica. There, mariners responded to some of the same grievances and incentives that catalyzed piracy in the Bahamas two years earlier. Following the peace of Utrecht, Spanish *guardacostas* continued to harass British shipping, which Jamaicans likened to piracy and wanted to combat by making reprisals against them. Likewise, the constriction of Jamaica's clandestine trade with Spain's colonies had impoverished the island during wartime, and new imperial trade monopolies instituted after the war threatened to prolong Jamaica's economic slump. Yet there are critical distinctions between circumstances in the two colonies, which meant that piracy would unfold somewhat differently in Jamaica. First, the July 30, 1715, wreck of the Spanish *flota* offered astronomical financial rewards. Captain Balchen lamented the "madness" for wrecking, but Jamaican mariners had good reason to think salvaging gold and silver off the coast of Florida was worth the risk. Although the Bahamas were closer in proximity to the wrecks, Jamaicans were in a better position to salvage them because they had the manpower, technical expertise, and capital to fund expeditions. Second, unlike the lawless Bahamas, Jamaican piracy unfolded with the approval of its governor, Archibald Hamilton. In addition to issuing commissions to ten sloops, Hamilton had a financial stake in their activities. Once alerted to their criminal behavior, Hamilton dragged his feet trying to put a stop to them and subsequently lost his position as governor.

Contemporary observers like Balchen were keenly aware of the push and pull factors motivating Jamaican sailors to go wrecking, which catalyzed piracy on the island and amplified ongoing piracies in the Bahamas. Modern historians have likewise recounted Governor Hamilton's role in facilitating the piracies of 1716, as well as the role Henry Jennings and others played in that drama. However, most have overlooked crucial evidence indicating how Jamaica's governing and mercantile elites contributed to the spread of piracy by funding wrecking expeditions, and then by criminalizing the behavior of the island's mariners. When Governor Hamilton was deposed as governor in May 1716, he was replaced by Peter Heywood, from a leading Jamaican mercantile family. Beginning in August of that year, Heywood presided over a detailed and lengthy investigation conducted by the Jamaican Council. In addition to uncovering the former governor's and the mariners' roles in the illegal wrecking and piracy, the council revealed the extensive financial entanglements of the merchant community, which had financed the expeditions to the wrecks and received large shares of the proceeds. Several prominent merchants did jail time during the investigation, and some ultimately had to restore goods and money to their rightful Spanish and French owners. But the merchants largely avoided criminal prosecution, and many were able to abscond with shares of plunder that could not easily be tracked down. Merchants dissembled when questioned about their own complicity, and they had the financial means and political capital to contest their prosecutions in a court of law.

The seamen, in contrast, provided an easy target. By virtue of gubernatorial proclamations issued in August 1716, Jamaica's mariners faced criminal prosecution for piracy. Sensing that governing authorities and the merchants had betrayed them, vast numbers of mariners fled to Providence to evade capture, but also out of spite. As several leading Jamaicans predicted at the time, throwing the book at ordinary seamen backfired, as the pirates of Providence began attacking British ships with as much frequency as they did those of the Catholic powers. Jamaicans turned to piracy because their government, as well as the merchant community that incentivized their activities, had thrown them under the proverbial bus.

The Groans of Jamaica

The economic underpinnings of Jamaican piracy derive from Queen Anne's War, which took a massive toll on the economy, particularly affecting the maritime trades. Jamaican merchants previously enjoyed a flourishing clandestine trade with Spanish colonies, but when war came in 1702, the British government banned all such commerce. Two years later, Britain rescinded the ban, but by that time French ships had begun to fill the void. Throughout the war, French and Dutch traders supplanted those of Jamaica. The war also interrupted Jamaica's profitable role in the slave trade. For many years, Portugal had held the *asiento* (contract) to provide slaves for the Spanish colonies. As Portuguese ships alone could not meet the demand, they subcontracted out the work to English slaving vessels. Navigating from West Africa to the West Indies, English slave traders frequently landed their enslaved human cargoes at Jamaica. From there, Jamaican vessels fanned out to distribute the enslaved to destinations throughout Spanish America, and especially its close neighbor, Cuba. In 1701 King Phillip of Spain revoked the Portuguese *asiento* and awarded it to the French, who served as the principal suppliers of slaves for the remainder of the war. In addition to French competition, profits from trade diminished due to the cost of the island's convoy system, which in Jamaica alone totaled £100,000 annually. Much of this cost had to be borne by merchants, who were charged prohibitive fees by naval captains who organized the convoys. Sailors suffered indirectly as merchants curtailed their trading activities.[2]

Privateering also contributed to the decline of Jamaica's economy, ironically because Jamaica's privateers proved to be more successful captors of enemy ships than their counterparts in the Royal Navy. For example, in 1703 forty-three foreign ships were condemned in Jamaica's prize courts, thirty of them having been captured by privateers. The problem, however, was that, although instructed not to "meddle" with nonthreatening commercial vessels, Jamaica's privateers attacked shipping indiscriminately, targeting Spanish trading vessels venturing to Jamaica, as well as British vessels trading to Spanish colonies. Because of the high risks, many Jamaican and Spanish merchants simply stopped trading with one another, thereby diminishing employment opportunities for Jamaica's maritime workers.

The 1708 America Act, which was intended to incentivize privateering, also backfired due to the way it was implemented in Jamaica. By virtue of the act, the Crown gave up its traditional claim of one-fifth of the value of each prize, as did the Lord High Admiral, who relinquished his right to one-tenth. However, the America Act still required the captors to pay Crown duties on enumerated goods, including cocoa, brandy, tobacco, and wine. In addition to Crown duties, prizes could also be subject to those owed to colonial governments. To increase its wartime revenue, the Jamaican assembly passed an act in 1709 that placed high duties on many goods, thereby compounding the financial stress imposed by the Crown.[3] In fact, in some cases the duties were so prohibitively high that privateers (and the merchants who provided financial backing) actually suffered losses on their captured prizes. In 1710, for instance, the captured French ship the *St. Joseph* netted 336,000 pounds of cocoa, which sold at auction for approximately 4,846 pounds sterling. However, Crown and Jamaican duties assessed on the cargo totaled in excess of £6,759, resulting in a net financial loss of approximately £1,912. Likewise, the 512 gallons of brandy confiscated from another French ship had a market value of about £472, but its captors owed duties exceeding £321, thereby reducing the profit margin by a factor of 75 percent.

Jamaicans with a financial interest in privateering naturally protested these excessive fees and launched a short-lived print war advocating for relief. Merchants who fitted out privateering sloops complained that the bonds they paid for the "good behavior" of the crews far exceeded the value of the prizes. In 1711 the Jamaica Assembly published a petition to Queen Anne, asking that she reduce Crown duties so that much-needed local duties could remain in place.[4] Representing the Crown, Jamaica's customs collector fought back with a missive justifying the duties on the grounds that many of Jamaica's privateers neglected to pay them. Some, he argued, shared their prizes on the "Spanish coast" where duties were difficult to collect, while other privateer crews simply distributed prizes on the high seas. The author also chastised privateer captains who took their prizes to be condemned in other colonies that were lax in enforcing customs procedures, singling out William Tempest for bringing a Spanish vessel all the way to Rhode Island for condemnation.[5]

Although the duties expired in 1711, they remained a hot-button political topic. In 1714 an anonymous author published a pamphlet chronicling the island's economic woes titled *The Groans of Jamaica, Expressed in a Letter by a Gentleman Residing There to a Friend in London*. In the process of indicting a "triumvirate" of corrupt politicians, the author singles out the duties as one of many sources of Jamaica's "groans," accusing the government and merchant bondholders of depriving the mariners of their money. "Many of the captors [referring to commissioned privateers and their crews]," he wrote, "being in the meantime, dead, or removed to other parts," never were paid. "Such as those [privateers] who remained in Jamaica," he added, "were brought into despair," because their work had yielded "little or nothing."[6]

Because of Jamaica's wartime customs policies, the island hemorrhaged mariners. In 1709 at least one hundred Jamaicans went rogue by joining a Canary Island captain named Mitchell who established a privateering base on the San Blas Islands off the coast of Panama.[7] A year later, a similar number of Jamaican sailors joined privateer crews from South Carolina, which one observer believed "tends to the ruin of all our trade."[8] By 1710 it had become obvious that the dearth of sailors not only affected trade but also weakened the Royal Navy's ability to man its ships. As one member of the Jamaica Council put it, "The British men of warr now attending there [Jamaica] are in some measure disabled for want of seamen." Staffing the island's twenty-five to thirty privateer ships, he estimated, resulted in the loss of two to three thousand seamen. Most of them, he added, "are driven from the said island by the vigorous and too severe execution of the customs officer's power ... for collecting duty's arising upon prize goods."[9]

The restoration of peace did little to improve Jamaica's economy, due to the institution of royal monopolies that cut into its trade. Cuba, Jamaica's principal partner in the clandestine trade, had once provided a lucrative market for those who carried the island's main cash crop of tobacco. In an attempt to keep tobacco profits within the empire, Cuban officials ceased doing business with the Jamaicans, and in 1717 Spain established the Real

Factorías de Tobacos, a company that enjoyed a monopoly of all tobacco products shipped to Spain, thus bypassing Jamaican interlopers. Most importantly, in 1711 the British government established the South Sea Company. Although the company is best known for the speculative stock "bubble" that burst in 1720, it originated with a grand vision for tapping into the wealth of Spanish America through legally sanctioned trade, and the company's founders even aspired to secure trading rights with Spain's colonies in the Pacific. By virtue of the Treaty of Utrecht, however, the company had to settle for the lesser prize of Spain's *asiento* contract. The contract, which was to endure for thirty years, required the South Sea Company to provide Spain annually with 4,800 *piezas de Indias* or slaves, all subject to duties. In addition to providing slaves, each year the company was allowed to send one ship of no more than 500 tons burden to trade in Spanish ports. To facilitate trade, the company established factors, or agents, in several Spanish ports, including Havana, Cartagena, and Veracruz.[10]

Most Jamaicans hated the South Sea Company. As articulated in a well-known 1714 pamphlet, Jamaicans feared that its monopoly powers would subvert Jamaica's "private" trade with the Spanish colonies. Among many grievances, they complained that the duties required for each slave were excessive and would render the South Sea Company incapable of making a profit. At the same time, Jamaicans feared that the company's monopoly would raise the general price for slaves, as rates for those sold by the company exceeded their market value. French and Dutch traders, the writers observed, would fill the void left by the British because they would not scruple to abide by trade restrictions. Although the pamphlet speaks mostly to the concerns of Jamaica's planters and merchants, mariners also disliked the company, as evidenced by their recent decline in numbers. One contributor to the pamphlet reminded his readers that, three years earlier, several thousand sailors had vacated Jamaica due to declining trade opportunities. Because the plantation trades provided for the "breeding of seamen," it was also thought that the depletion of commerce would lead to "the decay, loss, or destruction of the trade and maritime strength," of not only of Jamaica but all of Great Britain.[11]

Attacks of Spanish *guardacostas* compounded Jamaica's economic vulnerability. Importantly, the continuation of these attacks after the peace of 1713 may have enabled Jamaicans, including their governor, to justify reprisals against Spanish and French shipping. In March 1713 Governor Hamilton complained, "The coast of this island has been very much infested with privateers with Spanish commissions," adding that "pirates and freebooters" were also on the loose. The privateers sometimes targeted the island's more vulnerable north side, and Hamilton cited the example of one planter who was "interely ruin'd by the loss of all his slaves and movables."[12] Hamilton's observations are confirmed by Hovenden Walker, who, as admiral of the West Indies fleet, sent one of his subordinates to Havana around that time to complain of Spanish attacks on the island.[13] The *guardacostas*, of course, also attacked British ships. In November 1713 Spanish *guardacostas* captured the ship *Kensington* carrying £11,000 worth of goods.[14] Spanish attacks like these, and Jamaican protests, only intensified during the ensuing two years.[15] In all, Jamaican officials tallied thirty-seven British ships that the Spaniards had seized since the Peace of Utrecht.[16]

Although the British usually depicted themselves as innocent victims of Spanish "pyracies," in truth they were anything but. Benjamin Hornigold and several other crews operating in the Bahamas had been attacking Spanish ships since the summer of 1713. John Lewis's heist of the Marquis de Navarres's goods had already prompted talks between high-ranking diplomats from both nations. Given the frequency of complaints against pirates on both sides, Spain and Britain's subjects in the Americas arguably remained in a low-scale state of war in the summer and fall of 1715. *Guardacostas*, seeking to enforce Spanish trade laws, stepped up tit-for-tat seizures of British ships. Things might have gone on like this for a while, at least until the next war between the two countries was declared. As it turned out, a summer hurricane proved to be the perfect storm that accelerated piracy in the region.

The Wrecks

In order to transport the valuable silver and gold derived from mining operations, the Spanish Empire devised a fleet system to ensure its safe arrival in Spain. Each year, as was the goal, two squadrons, all carrying European goods needed in the colonies, sailed from their home port of Cadiz to the West Indies. One, the *Tierra Firme* squadron, headed to the port of Cartagena to load silver mined in South America. Meanwhile, the other fleet, known as the *flota* of New Spain, anchored at Veracruz to acquire Mexican silver. Typically, the ships comprising the two fleets spent months—and sometimes years—in port while they waited for shipments of silver to arrive, and in the meantime they would sell off the goods in their holds. Once the ships had been sufficiently laden with bullion, the two fleets disembarked and rendezvoused at Havana, Cuba. There, the captains repaired and resupplied their vessels to make the Atlantic crossing. From Havana, the entire fleet navigated through the Florida Strait, following the Gulf Stream northward to their port of origin at Cadiz.

The Spanish treasure fleet had long been the envy (and target) of other European nations, so the objective was to provide safety in numbers. The recent war, however, had disrupted Spain's fleet system. In 1702 English and Dutch naval vessels caught up with the entire silver fleet at Vigo, a port in Spain, sinking many of the ships and apprehending some of the bullion. In 1708 English naval vessels intercepted the *Tierra Firme* fleet near Cartagena, destroying one of the treasure ships and capturing another. Spain lost another of its ships to a hurricane in 1711. Because of the dangers involved, Spain dispatched its fleets with less regularity in wartime, and another would not sail homeward until 1715. That year, the New Spain fleet, consisting of five vessels, was under the command of General Don Juan Esteban de Ubilla. The *Tierra Firme* fleet, captained by Don Antonio Echeverz y Zubiza, consisted of six ships. A French vessel that had joined the convoy, the *Griffon*, which was on a special mission for the governor of Veracruz, sailed with the fleet, totaling twelve ships.[17]

By the time Ubilla and Echeverz arrived at Havana, it had been more than four years since the last treasure fleet had made a return voyage to Spain. Consequently, the 1715 fleet accumulated an unusually large amount of treasure. Ubilla himself sailed on a ship carrying 1,300 chests stuffed with three million silver coins. Additionally, the ship held gold coins, gold bars, silver bars, and jewelry, as well as emeralds, pearls, and Chinese porcelain. One of the military ships that protected the convoy, known as a *refuerzo*, was stocked with eighty-one chests of silver coins and more than fifty chests of silver objects. Echeverz's ship, meanwhile, carried vast quantities of gold and silver coins, gold and silver bars, gold dust, and tropical commodities. Altogether, the fleet's estimated value was 15 million silver pieces of eight, or, according to one calculation, in excess of $887 million in today's U.S. dollars.

Departing on July 24, 1715, the voyage was uneventful for the first five days. However, on the morning of July 30, as the fleet made its way through the Florida Strait, it encountered a somewhat rare July hurricane. Ubilla's ship was destroyed, killing Ubilla and all 225 persons on board. Eleven of the ships sank offshore between 28 and 27 degrees latitude, roughly encompassing the shoreline between Cape Canaveral and Port St. Lucie in modern Florida. Of the estimated 2,500 crew and passengers, at least 1,000 persons died, with the survivors erecting makeshift camps onshore as they waited for relief. The only vessel to survive the hurricane was the *Griffon*, which managed to make it to Cadiz relatively unscathed.[18]

Word of the wrecks reached Spanish authorities in Cuba two weeks later. Havana's governor quickly organized salvage operations. They set up a base camp near Palmar de Ays and recruited diving crews that consisted of many enslaved persons and nearby Ais Indians.[19] Although the Spanish tried to keep information about the wrecks to themselves, it was impossible to do so. Nearly every ship passing through the Florida Strait would have had the opportunity to view the wrecks, which lay in shallow water, as well as the ongoing salvage efforts. News conveyed by mariners traveled fast. South Carolina received word no later than September 30 when Samuel Meade, captain of the HMS *Success*, reported that Spanish officials detained South Carolina diplomatic envoys so "that they might not bring the news that eleven sail of Spanish and French ships with immense riches on board . . . were lost upon the shoals of the gulph of Florida."[20] In turn, a New England vessel that had been in communication with Meade notified Captain Josiah Soanes, stationed at St. Christopher's, of what had happened in Florida.[21] Word reached Virginia in late October, when Governor Spotswood transmitted news of the wrecks, even musing that local mariners ought to be "encouraged" to try their luck searching for silver there.[22] In mid-November a detailed report of the wrecked fleet reached London via Madrid, which appeared in the city's newspapers and remained a top story for several weeks.[23] By December, New Englanders learned of Spain's misfortune from a report published in the *Boston News Letter*.[24]

News of the wrecks must have reached Jamaica quickly, although nobody seems to have reported it until Governor Hamilton mentioned it in a letter that November.[25] Jamaicans had good reasons to remain silent, for in the meantime, several sloop captains were busy outfitting their vessels for wrecking expeditions. As revealed months later, the "common report" was that the sloop captains made it no secret that their destination was the wrecks. Jonathan Barnet later admitted that he had readied his ship before seeking a commission. One Jamaican captain, a mixed-race individual named Francis Fernando, allegedly circulated a printed advertisement to recruit his crew.[26] After readying their vessels, these sloop captains went to Governor Hamilton asking for commissions to go to the wrecks, but Hamilton denied them, saying he would only issue commissions for tracking down Spanish pirates. Between November 21 and December 12, Hamilton issued ten such commissions. In all, 650 sailors joined these crews, although British officials later revised this number upward to 800, indicating that eager mariners continued to sign on.[27]

While on paper the commissions empowered these vessels only to hunt for pirates, Hamilton gave verbal encouragement to the captains to fish the wrecks, even tacitly approving the use of violence. "The wrecks [are] free for everybody," Hamilton opined before Jamaica merchant Lewis Galdy. When Galdy asked the governor what to do in the event ships from Spain and other countries beat them to the location, Hamilton is reported to have said, "The strongest ought to keep the money out of the wrecks." Captain Barnet, meanwhile, said that he and the governor had an understanding that it would be permissible to employ violence to drive off the Spanish. Barnet recalled the encouragement Hamilton gave him, stating, "If the Spanish were stronger he would get no money . . . if he were stronger than the Spanish he might get all the money."[28]

Importantly, fishing the wrecks not only concerned the mariners; it also involved Jamaica's merchants, who posted bonds for the "good behavior" of the crews and owned the vessels on which the crews sailed. By the customs that governed privateering and wrecking voyages, each of these individuals would have been entitled to a share of the plunder proportional to their financial investment. For instance, twelve Jamaican merchants, along with the ten ship captains, paid for the security bonds. One of them, merchant William Hayman, provided financial backing for four of the ships, the *Eagle*, *Bersheba*, *Bennet*, and *Edward and Sarah*. Meanwhile, Kingston merchant Christopher Feake backed two of the vessels (*Diligence Galley* and sloop *Henry*), and eminent merchants such as John Beswick, William Wyllis, John Lewis (not the pirate), and Charles Chaplin each had invested in at least one.[29] In addition to those posting bonds, at least twelve more persons, all of whom owned shares of the ten vessels, also expected a cut of the profits. Merchant John Warner, for instance, owned a one-eighth share of the *Bersheba*, as well as a smaller share of the *Bennet*. Archibald Hamilton himself was a silent partner for another two sloops, the *Eagle* and *Bennet*, claiming a one-eighth share of each. One Jamaican woman was even involved, Sarah Lopes Tores, the widow of a prominent Jewish merchant, who had a one-twenty-fourth stake in the *Bennet*.[30]

Because of the financial backing they provided, Jamaica's merchants exerted added pressure on the ship captains to return home with enough loot to make the voyages profitable. For instance, in March 1716 Captain Samuel Liddale of the sloop *Coconut* had readied his vessel for a trading voyage to South Carolina. Although Liddale did not enjoy the cover provided by an anti-piracy commission, the sloop's owners, merchants James Knight and John Lewis, nevertheless ordered Liddale to "go look for a wreck."[31] Merchant Thomas Bendysh likewise exerted tremendous pressure on Captain Francis Fernando to engage in illicit activity. In one instance, he chastised Fernando for neglecting to seize a Spanish packet boat, and in exasperation Fernando asked Bendysh, "What do I have to rob everybody for you?"[32]

As further evidence of their fervor to reap the spoils of wrecking and piracy, a small number of Jamaican merchants appear to have hopped on board vessels bound for the Bahamas to partake of the activity themselves, or at least to oversee the distribution of prizes. One of them, William Willis (Wyllis), accepted a pardon from Captain Pearse in 1718, presumably to absolve himself of providing material support to the pirates. Willis owned a share of the *Bersheba* and was later subjected to questioning for his role in abetting piracy.[33]

Having fanned out toward the wrecks in December, the first Jamaican sloops to reach the Florida coast were the *Eagle* and *Bersheba*, captained by Wells and Jennings, respectively. On Christmas morning, Jennings apprehended a Spanish mail boat and forced the pilot to reveal the location of the wrecks. Heading north through the Florida Strait, Jennings was able to observe that salvage crews had already recovered the cargo from two of the wrecked ships. Sensing that vast amounts of recovered money would be onshore at the camp erected at Palmar de Ays, Jennings and Wells handpicked 150 of their toughest men, divided them into three companies, and landed on shore at 2:00 a.m. on December 27. At daybreak, with Jennings taking the lead, the Jamaicans descended on the Spanish, who, with only sixty-five men, were badly outnumbered. The Spanish commander overseeing salvage operations raised a white flag and tried to negotiate with Jennings, offering him 25,000 pieces of eight to go away. Jennings refused, absconding with an estimated 350,000 pieces of eight, worth roughly 87,500 pounds sterling. Like many of the crews that followed, Jennings's company headed for Providence to divide the spoils.[34]

Meanwhile, on route to the wrecks on December 31, Francis Fernando and the sloop *Bennet*'s crew of eighty men caught up with a Spanish vessel anchored near Bahia Honda, a bay on Cuba's northern coast the English referred to as "Bay of Hounds." Fernando hailed the vessel, perceiving that it was in fact a prize vessel formerly owned by Jamaicans, the *Kensington*, which Spanish *guardacostas* had seized two years earlier. Seeking a pretense to reclaim the *Kensington*, Fernando conducted a search, finding a cargo of silk stockings he believed "were enough to condemn her." After rifling through the captain's papers, Fernando and company seized the valuables on board, which included between 150,000 and 250,000 pieces of eight, or 3,100 pounds of silver. The cargo also included casks of indigo, cochineal (used for dyes), and other commodities. Fernando loaded all the goods onto the *Bennet*, and the crew divided the prize on January 5. Fernando then put twenty-five of his crew on the *Kensington*, ordering them to take it to Port Royal for condemnation. With 125 men still on board the *Bennet*, Fernando headed toward Florida and seized the captain of a small Spanish launch, confiscating some salt and forcing the captain to pilot him toward the wrecks. How much his crew salvaged there was never reported, but Fernando did spend time at Providence dividing the spoils.[35]

Fernando's capture of the *Nuestra Señora de Belen* alerted Cuban officials to the Jamaicans' hostile actions. On January 8, 1716, the governor of Havana penned a letter to Archibald Hamilton describing what happened, and he sent a Havana lawyer, Don Juan del Valle, to Jamaica to demand the restoration of the ship and its contents to its rightful owners. Valle arrived in Jamaica on January 20, delivered the letter to Hamilton, and met with the Jamaican council on January 26. By that time, Valle had witnessed the return of Jennings and Wells and had learned about their robberies on the Florida coast. Valle pressed for more information and demanded that Hamilton produce a list of the commissioned vessels and return any money from the wrecks. Valle continued pressing his case, appearing before the council again on February 9 to submit a petition he had drafted, again seeking restitution for stolen Spanish property.[36]

Had Governor Hamilton taken meaningful action at that time, he might have averted further piracies and perhaps retained his position as governor. Although he acknowledged that Jennings might have gone too far by stealing salvaged bullion from the encampment in Florida, Hamilton downplayed Valle's grievances at every turn. Hamilton justified the right of British subjects to work the wrecks, musing that they might be "derelict" and thus free for anyone to salvage. He also seemed to think the seizure of the *Nuestra Señora de Belen* was legal, and Hamilton reassured Valle that he would have a chance to make his case in the vice-admiralty court. Hamilton conveniently reminded Valle that Spanish *guardacostas* had seized a great number of Jamaican vessels since the peace of 1713 and that Spain owed a great deal of money to British subjects. In Hamilton's mind, the Cubans had no more right to complain about stolen property than did the Jamaicans.[37]

Nor did Hamilton summon the commissioned vessels home, as Valle was pleading with him to do. In fact, Hamilton did the exact opposite, issuing a new let pass to Henry Jennings and the *Bersheba*, empowering him to return to the wrecks. As was later divulged, Jennings arranged a secret meeting with Hamilton on February 28, long after the governor had learned of what transpired on the Florida coast. They met at night on the "back piazza" of Hamilton's residence at Spanish Town, with only Jennings, Hamilton, and the governor's secretary, Samuel Page, in attendance. Hamilton signed the let pass Jennings had requested, seeming not to question his behavior in Florida. Page, however, challenged Jennings, asking him, "Why will you go out again on such dangerous undertakings when you know that complaints have been made about your last voyage?" Page also warned Jennings that his continued predation on the Spanish wrecks would "tarnish your honorable reputation." In reply, Jennings allegedly said that he "had not yet sowed all his wild oats," adding that "if he returns home safe he would give up sea employ." In other words, Jennings was planning to use the spoils to retire.[38]

In turn, Hamilton's inaction, which mariners interpreted as gubernatorial consent, only intensified the activities of Jamaica's ship captains. Around mid-March, Jennings on the *Bersheba*, Leigh Ashworth now in command of the *Mary*, and James Carnegie, commanding a noncommissioned sloop called the *Discovery*, rendezvoused at Bluefield Bay on Jamaica's southwestern coast, intending to return to the wrecks. On the passage to Cuba, these three ships met the *Coconut*, commanded by Samuel Liddale, another captain operating without a commission. As they rounded Cuba's northern side, the convoy approached Bahia Honda. There, they were joined by a sloop captained by Benjamin Young, who was towing two pirogues he had found abandoned by logwood cutters in the Bay of Honduras. Jennings and Ashworth, meanwhile, had spotted a French ship, the *Lovely Mary of Rochelle*, thought at first to be a pirate. Jennings and his crew, however, observed two canoes from the *Lovely Mary* paddling toward the coast, and Jennings learned that the canoes were ferrying money on shore. On the night of April 3, Jennings manned the two pirogues with volunteers from all four ships and captured the *Lovely Mary*.

Four days later, another French ship appeared, the *Marianne*. Jennings sent Captain Carnegie to apprehend it, but seemingly out of nowhere, Benjamin Hornigold appeared and intercepted the *Marianne* before Carnegie could close in. Hornigold took the *Marianne* back to Providence, where Jennings, Ashworth, Carnegie, Liddale, and Young followed him to divide their prizes.[39] Less lucrative robberies also seem to have occurred around that time. Henry Isaacs, who commanded a pirogue named the *Samuel and Anne* and also lacked a commission, captured a small Spanish sloop filled with 207 bags of snuff, which had previously been taken by a Dutch crew out of New York that had turned pirate after coming to the Florida Strait to work the wrecks.[40] As the presence of the New York sloop indicates, vessels from virtually everywhere in British America eagerly got in on the wrecking action.

Jamaica's policy of granting supposed anti-piracy commissions clearly spiraled out of control. Not only did many noncommissioned ships join those operating with gubernatorial permission, but the pirates at Providence under Hornigold stepped up their attacks, sometimes justifying their actions by claiming falsely that they too had commissions from Jamaica.[41] Finally, Governor Hamilton took action, issuing proclamations on April 24–25 ordering the commissioned vessels to return home, and forbidding all Jamaican vessels from going to the wrecks. Hamilton even launched an investigation, focusing on the actions of Francis Fernando.[42] On May 11, Fernando brought in a sloop, the *Dolphin*, on which were said to be piratically obtained goods. Customs officers at Port Royal immediately impounded the vessel. One night later, twenty armed men overpowered the two customs officers guarding the sloop and confiscated the goods. Hamilton learned that the *Dolphin*, captained by James Spatchers of Providence, was owned by Jamaican merchants Daniel Axtell, John Warner, and Thomas Bendysh. The goods on board were supposedly the owners' share of those from the *Lovely Mary* taken by Ashworth, Jennings, and Carnegie. Fernando, however, had a grievance with Axtell, who was rumored to be paying the Spanish ambassador Valle's legal fees, and to have called Fernando a "pirate and a rogue" behind his back. Bendysh and Axtell had orchestrated the robbery to make sure they got their shares of the prize instead of Fernando.

On May 15, Hamilton called Axtell and several other witnesses before the council. Axtell refused to speak and was taken to jail. The perfunctory investigation confirmed Fernando's capture of the *Nuestra Señora de Belen* and little more.[43] A few weeks later, Hamilton wrote to the Board of Trade, blaming the Spaniards for being the "first aggressors" and professing his innocence by blaming the ship captains for violating their commissions. In fact, Hamilton stressed his reluctance to issue the commissions, saying he did so only after being "prevailed upon by the clamours of our trading people." Hamilton added that "all necessary precautions were taken to prevent any inconveniencys by such commissions" but that the wreck of the Spanish *flota* had diverted "two or three" of the sloops, clearly lowballing the actual number involved. Hamilton acknowledged that "some ill uses had been made of these commissions" on the coast of Florida, and he affirmed his actions of April 24–25, in which he called in all the sloops. On July 9, Hamilton created a commission of five men to investigate the piracies, still trying to cover his tracks. By then it was too late, as Hamilton received news a few days later that he had been replaced as governor and would himself be the object of an investigation.[44]

Inquest

On July 25, Peter Heywood, born in Jamaica to a prominent family and the island's former attorney general, received official word that he had been named acting governor. Hamilton, meanwhile, was ordered home to appear before the "royal presence" and answer the charges leveled against him. Heywood's instructions provided by the Board of Trade ordered him "to make strict inquiry" into the commissions Hamilton had issued "and into all abuses, piracies and robberies committed of late upon the Spaniards in the Gulph of Florida or elsewhere." Ominously, these instructions required him "to seize all persons they shall find guilty, and send them over hither with their effects and such evidence as may be proper to convict them according to law."[45]

Heywood and the council got to work on July 31, issuing a summons to Captain Charles Chapman, asking him to deliver the commission that Hamilton had issued to him the previous December. The following day, two French ambassadors from Saint-Domingue arrived, consisting of one Mr. Moret, an infantry captain, and Captain Escoubret, commander of the *Lovely Mary of Rochelle* apprehended by Jennings, Ashworth, and Carnegie previously in April. The two men delivered letters from French governing officials and presented the council with a memorial from the governor of Saint-Domingue, the Count de Blenac. In it, Blenac recounted piracies committed against four French ships. The council responded expeditiously, issuing that same day instructions to apprehend John Wells, Francis Fernando, Leigh Ashworth, James Carnegie, and their entire crews, totaling upward of three hundred men. On August 3, the council had the order publicized and "dispatched to the various precincts of the island."[46] Given the large numbers of mariners who had been to wrecks or preyed on foreign shipping, seemingly all Jamaican mariners stood in the council's crosshairs.

Perhaps more than any single action, the Jamaica Council's launch of the investigation and attempt to round up hundreds of sailors contributed most to the golden age of piracy. Fearful of being caught in the council's dragnet, Jamaica's mariners fled the island in droves, accelerating a process that began during Queen Anne's War. While Francis Fernando managed to hide in Port Royal, the rest of the ship captains fled, many to Providence.[47] Knowing that the Bahamas lacked a proper government and that Benjamin Hornigold had taken charge in Nassau, mariners understood that they might evade the council's reach by hiding. Many who had gone to the wrecks had spent time there, so Providence was familiar turf. Again, word in this maritime network seems to have spread fast, and the news of the council's investigation caused panic among the sailors.[48]

At the time, Jamaican officials perceived that the council's investigation might backfire, causing more sailors to turn pirate rather than resume honest seafaring. Even Archibald Hamilton predicted as much, stating that "rigorous prosecutions" might cause all the sailors to flee the island. Instead of bringing the full force of the law against them, Hamilton recommended making examples only of the most "notorious offenders."[49] Despite presiding over the council's work, Peter Heywood also came to that same point of view. Writing to the Board of Trade ten days into the investigation, Heywood stated, "I have great reason to fear they [pirates] will increase [because of] the search we make for the person [Jennings] that committed the depredations on the Spaniards ashore on the coast of Florida." By issuing arrest warrants as well for Fernando, Ashworth, Carnegie, and others, Heywood believed the council "has drove from the island great numbers of both the sea-faring men and others that were therein concern'd for fear of being took and brought to punishment."[50]

Jamaican merchant John Bowes, who was deposed during the investigation and thus well informed about the council's work, assessed the situation in the same way. "The inquiry," he observed, "will be so far from rendering the evil, that it will rather increase it. The attempt of taking up of some of the piratical sailors," Bowes continued, "has so alarmed the rest that it seems they are gone off by swarms."[51] South Carolina customs collector William Rhett, writing on August 3, confirmed the widespread panic in the maritime community. "The men dare not go to Jamaica," Rhett wrote, "for they fear being tried as pirates." This was for good reason. Rhett noted that acting governor Robert Daniel had issued commissions to fish the wrecks, which Rhett described as a "pretence" for ship captains to capture Spanish vessels in Florida. South Carolina mariners also had been trading with Henry Jennings, and Rhett observed that "most of the French goods taken by Jennings have been here."[52]

Aware that the investigation might backfire, the council pressed on, issuing orders on August 21 to apprehend Jennings, Wells, Fernando, Carnegie,

Ashworth, and a merchant, Peter de Reimer, who was involved financially in the robberies. When this second order failed to turn up the wanted men, on August 30 the council issued a proclamation against all the men suspected of piracy who were in hiding or had fled Jamaica. The proclamation did not outright charge them with the crime of piracy; rather, it gave the men until December 1 to turn themselves in, after which they were to be declared pirates.[53] Most sailors suspected of "unwarrantable activity" would not have bothered to read the fine print, so most of the leading suspects, and many of the unnamed crewmen, remained in hiding or at Providence.

From August 1 until mid-October, the council devoted itself almost exclusively to the investigation. In that span of time, they deposed upward of fifty individuals, including sailors, merchants, and naval officers, as well as Hamilton and a few members of his inner circle. The council also deposed French and Spanish ambassadors, as well as ship captains and owners, and read from several petitions they submitted asking for the restoration of their property. The sailor depositions in particular are valuable for what they revealed about hostile actions taken at sea. Samuel Liddale, deposed on August 7, provided a blow-by-blow description of how Jennings, Ashworth, and Carnegie captured the French ship, the *Lovely Mary of Rochelle*, near Bahia Honda. Liddale likewise alluded to dissensions among the crews, indicating that Hornigold had preempted Carnegie in taking the second French ship. Perhaps seeking to exonerate himself, Liddale said that he had twice refused to attack the French ship because it was used for trading, rather than a pirate vessel.[54] Liddale even tried to exonerate Alan Bernard, the *Bersheba*'s quartermaster, confirming that he was sick at that time and played no role in the capture of the French vessel.

Bernard himself appeared before the council three days later. In addition to explaining how his infirmity incapacitated him, Bernard provided more details, such as that the men in the pirogues were a "parcel of villains" from the Bay of Honduras, presumably logwood cutters who had been driven away by the Spanish. Bernard also recounted how some of the sailors mocked him for not taking an active role, chastising him for "sitt[ing] with your fingers in your mouth." As with Liddale, Bernard alluded to tensions arising within the fleet, as the sailors threatened mutiny and pressured the captains to sail on to Providence to share the spoils for themselves. The ship captains Jennings, Ashworth, and Carnegie preferred to send their prize back to Port Royal to have the *Lovely Mary* condemned in a proper court of law, but they ended up deferring to the wishes of their crews.[55]

The sailors' testimony also revealed Archibald Hamilton's role and their understanding of the unspoken agreement about the real purpose of the commissions. Jonathan Barnet, captain of the *Tyger*, provided some of the most damaging testimony in his important August 10 deposition. Barnet revealed, for instance, that he initially haggled with Hamilton, complaining that the anti-piracy commission "would do him no service upon the wrecks." At that point, Hamilton seemingly gave him verbal approval to use force against the Spanish, inferring that "the stronger" would get the money. Barnet likewise admitted that he had readied his ship before seeking the commission, inferring that other captains had done the same.[56] In every single deposition, sailors casually admitted that their intention was to go to the wrecks, and almost no one conceived of their mission principally as one to suppress piracy, undermining Hamilton's assertion that the ship captains had violated their orders.[57]

In addition to apprehending the ship captains and their crews, another of the council's main goals was to untangle the complicated financial agreements behind the piracy and unsanctioned wrecking. Where it was possible to do so, the council hoped to retrieve the stolen goods and money and restore them to their Spanish and French owners in an effort to maintain the fragile peace of 1713. While the council targeted substantial members of the merchant community, the big prize was Archibald Hamilton, who was suspected of having a financial stake in at least one of the sloops and stood to gain personally from their lawbreaking. British officials were made aware of Hamilton's potential financial entanglements the previous May, when two Jamaicans, Samuel Page and Walter Adlington, voyaged to London and submitted depositions indicating that Hamilton claimed a share of the *Bennet* (Fernando's ship). These men also alleged that Hamilton had exerted undue influence on the vice-admiralty court in the March 16 condemnation of the *Nuestra Señora de Belen*, from which Hamilton was due a share of the prize money.[58]

As a group, the merchants were better educated and thus had a firmer grasp of the legal process. Because of their wealth and standing in the community, they could mount a better defense than could the mostly unlettered sailors. In order to get the merchants to talk, the council, whose members derived from the same socioeconomic class, offered amnesty to many of the merchants in exchange for their testimony. In English common law, this arrangement is known as *nolle prosequi*, derived from a Latin term meaning "to be unwilling to pursue."[59] In effect, these agreements shielded the merchants from criminal prosecution, enabling them to divulge self-incriminating information without the threat of criminal charges hanging over their heads. The council may have resolved to make such offers after their unsuccessful attempt to depose merchant Daniel Axtell, who refused to speak and went free after posting bail.[60]

Evidently fed up with Axtell's stonewalling, the council began offering *nolle prosequi* protection to witnesses on August 14, when merchant George Daws was called to testify. Two days later, William Wyllis, Edward James, and John Cavalier agreed to be interviewed after being offered protection. William Hayman, who had a share in at least four of the suspected sloops, finally agreed to testify on August 17 under the same arrangement. William Leaver, Edward Sandys, John Beswick, and John Reeves testified under *nolle prosequi* agreements on August 19. Jasper Ashworth, brother of the suspected pirate Leigh, agreed to testify on August 21, and the council offered protection to one woman they deemed an important witness, Sarah Fernando, Francis's wife. Thomas Bendysh, who had been deposed weeks earlier, agreed to testify once more under *nolle prosequi* on September 10. Although merchants benefited most, the council did offer the same protection to three mariners: James Roche and Joseph Gosling, the mate and quartermaster of the *Bennet* under Francis Fernando, and Joseph Eels, who was quartermaster of the *Mary* under Leigh Ashworth.[61]

If the mariners were mad to go wrecking, the depositions reveal that the island's merchants were equally mad to claim a share of the spoils. One noteworthy revelation was the clandestine methods by which ship captains transferred money and goods to the merchants. Captain Fernando, for instance, deposited plunder from the *Bennet* at the home of Thomas Bendysh, who lived at Anotto Bay on the northern side of the island, rather than Port Royal, where naval officers might observe his activities. Bendysh in turn conveyed a share of the prize to Hamilton, who furtively lodged it in the home of John Rigsby to avoid suspicion. For weeks, the owners of the *Bennet* warned Fernando not to return to his home at Port Royal, perhaps fearing that he might talk about their activities and entrap them in the investigation.[62] Likewise, their testimony revealed the rank bribery involved in the condemnation of the *Nuestra Señora de Belen*. Thomas Bendysh, for one, paid Attorney General James Broderick in excess of fifty-six pounds to "stand neuter" during the admiralty proceedings. Several lawyers and other officers received in excess of fifty pounds to put their thumbs on the scales of justice in order to have the ship condemned without hearing the testimony of its Spanish owners.[63]

The merchants, then, clearly knew that they were breaking the law by trafficking in stolen goods. In fact, once word of Jennings's theft and the piracies against the Spanish and French vessels reached the island, many of the ship owners started selling off their shares to cover their tracks. For instance, Dr. Nicholas Harris, a shareholder of the *Bersheba*, claimed that he sold his share because "he did not like Capt. Jennings first action," referring to his attack on the Florida coast. Harris was evasive, however, when asked to identify the precise day he sold it.[64] Similarly, merchant William Wyllis admitted to conveying his share of the *Bersheba* to John Warner but somehow failed to recall how much money he received for it. John Cavalier and John Reeves also relinquished their shares of the *Bersheba* after learning of Jennings's attack.[65] While the *Bersheba*'s owners, in particular, had reason to be nervous due to the nature of Jennings's crimes, the owners of other ships also nervously divested their shares. John Wright sold his share of the *Bennet* after Francis Fernando became a piracy suspect. Finally, Archibald Hamilton tried to unload his share of the *Bennet* but could find no buyer.[66]

Archibald Hamilton appeared before the council for two long days on September 7–8. Fielding a barrage of questions, the former governor maintained his innocence, insisting that issuing commissions was justified legally, and on the grounds that naval ships were inadequate for the task of capturing pirates. Hamilton insisted he "was not apprised" of their plans to go to the wrecks, about which he knew only vaguely "by common fame." When asked about his financial interest in the voyages, Hamilton conceded that he had been involved in trading ventures since beginning his term as governor, and that he had "reluctantly" agreed to a one-third stake in the *Bennet* after being pressured to do so. Pleading his naivete, Hamilton claimed that "he did not pretend to understand trade, only concerned himself with those who did, and did not do anything irregular." The owners of the sloop *Eagle* had also made a habit of including the former governor in their ventures, and Hamilton conceded that "he did expect they would concern him as they did formerly." Because Henry Jennings of the *Bersheba* had stolen money from the Spanish salvage camp on the coast of Florida in conjunction with the *Eagle*—an action everyone regarded as illegal—Hamilton was wise enough to refuse his share of the silver Jennings had looted.[67] However, Hamilton conceded that he accepted his 458 troy weight of silver share from the *Bennet*, but he justified his actions by saying he wanted to "keep it safe" while the *Nuestra Señora de Belen* case went to admiralty court. After the ship was condemned, Hamilton kept the money, but he denied that it was for "private use," insisting he retained it merely to defray the costs of the army regiment that Hamilton paid out of his own pocket.

While uncovering Hamilton's financial entanglements, the council also tried to understand Hamilton's apparent inaction toward the ship captains suspected of piracy. The former governor claimed that he had no "good proofs" against Henry Jennings and denied ever giving him a let pass for his second voyage. Hamilton likewise delayed apprehending Francis Fernando because he was unconvinced his actions were "piracy as is" and did not want to betray the captain of a vessel in which he was financially concerned. Hamilton also stated that his primary objective was to secure the money and goods libeled by Don Juan del Valle in admiralty court. Issuing arrest warrants for Fernando and the others would have simply caused them to flee and distribute the proceeds among the mariners. Hamilton likewise depicted Valle as reluctant to stage a vigorous prosecution, even blaming the outcome of the admiralty court proceedings against the *Nuestra Señora de Belen* on Valle's absence; he took a monthlong visit to one of Jamaica's hot springs. When Hamilton finally issued proclamations calling for the arrest of Fernando and other suspects, he blamed naval officer William Norris for failing to apprehend them.[68]

In the end, a divided council voted five to four to arrest Hamilton and send him home to face trial.[69] But they were never able to recover all the money nor reveal the full scope of the robberies committed in Florida or on the high seas. Mariners had shared much of the prize money offshore or at Providence (where most remained in hiding), and they were able to sell many of the goods to sympathetic people on land. In one instance, the quartermaster of the *Bersheba* even gifted "hams and olives" to people he encountered onshore at Bluefield Bay.[70] It is just as doubtful that the merchants under investigation revealed the full value of the money and goods received. For more than a year, the owners of the *Lovely Mary of Rochelle* and *Marianne* continued pressing Jamaican officials to restore money and goods still owed to them, totaling upward of £30,000 in value.[71]

The council did manage, however, to track down some of the money and effects stolen by the *Bersheba* and *Bennet*, which was now in the possession of several merchants, as well as the former governor. In addition to Archibald Hamilton's 458 pounds troy weight of silver, John Beswick and Edward James confessed to receiving shares of about £1,500. William Wyllis, one-eighth owner of the *Bersheba*, received £400, while John Reeves, who owned a one-twelfth share, received 1,000 pieces of eight. George Daws, Nicholas Harris, and John Cavalier each received 1,500 pieces of eight for their one-ninth share of the same vessel. The *Bennet*'s owners also had money in their possession. Edwyn Sands and William Leaver each confessed to receiving 108 pounds of silver for their one-twelfth shares of the *Bennet*. Sara Lopes

Torres, meanwhile, received twenty-six pounds from Henry Jennings in lieu of an outstanding debt he owed to her. Additionally, some cochineal and indigo had been impounded by naval officers and remained in their possession.

Few merchants, however, faced criminal charges for their involvement in piracy thanks to *nolle prosequi* protection. Instead, the council forced them to turn over the goods to the rightful French and Spanish owners, which was done accordingly. The guilty parties also lost the security money they posted for the commissioned vessels. John Beswick and William Hayman had to forfeit the £1,500 bond they had posted for the *Eagle*, as did Cavalier and Hayman for the *Bersheba*. Hayman and John Wright forfeited another £1,500 bond for the *Bennet*.[72] Thanks to his connections and an aggressive public relations campaign, Archibald Hamilton was eventually acquitted and elected to the House of Commons in 1718.[73]

As directed by the council's August 30 proclamation, a few mariners suspected of piracy trickled in before the December 1 deadline, offering information in exchange for clemency. William Bryan, who sailed on the *Bersheba*, provided convincing evidence of Henry Jennings's complicity in the capture of the *Lovely Mary of Rochelle*, adding further details of the contents of its cargo and the manner by which the crew shared the proceeds at Providence.[74] William Quarrel returned to Jamaica in mid-October describing the activities of the *Francis and Sarah*, and he provided the names of the two dozen men who left him and were hiding at Providence.[75] On October 19 Matthew Musson suddenly appeared, admitting that he had fished the wrecks and had taken another commission from Robert Daniel, the deputy governor of South Carolina. He also confirmed Jonathan Barnet's assertion that Governor Hamilton knew that he intended to go to the wrecks before offering him a commission.[76] Joseph Gosling of the *Bennet* arrived on October 26. In addition to giving a blow-by-blow description of the capture of the *Nuestra Señora de Belen*, Gosling provided the names of 136 men who received shares of the prizes.[77]

Investigating pirates thus became a routine part of the council's business, and it began inquiring into other acts of piracy that had come to its attention. On December 19 Henry Timberlake, master of the brig *Lamb* of Boston, appeared before the council to inform its members of his encounter off Hispaniola with Benjamin Hornigold in the sloop *Delight*. Hornigold approached Timberlake's vessel and, after firing several shots at it, commanded Timberlake to come on board. He depicted a man brimming with self-confidence, as Hornigold bragged that he had recently taken two ships, and urged Timberlake to "give my [invitation] to the captain of the man of war and tell him I assign to have his ship from him when I meet him," before ransacking the *Lamb* for provisions. An hour after being restored to his ship, Timberlake encountered Edward Thache, who sent his crew on board to take nearly all the remainder of his provisions. Timberlake's deposition constitutes the first recorded instance of the piracies of Thache, soon to be known as Blackbeard.[78]

Jamaican officials also continued seeking information about the piracies spawned months earlier by Hamilton's commissions. A day after Timberlake's deposition, the council offered Joseph Eels *nolle prosequi* in exchange for detailed testimony about Leigh Ashworth and the capture of the *Lovely Mary of Rochelle* the previous April. Eels, the ship's carpenter, had signed onto the sloop *Mary* intending to fish the wrecks, but he began to worry when Ashworth intercepted a small French vessel and asked its crew if they knew of any larger vessels nearby. Eels confronted Ashworth, asking about his intentions, to which Ashworth responded, "Don't trouble your head," as if he were hiding something. Eels then confirmed many of the details of the captures of the *Lovely Mary* and *Marianne*, after which he focused his deposition on the fate of the cargo of the sloop *Dolphin*. Eels explained that he had returned to Jamaica aboard the *Dolphin*, which had been loaded with goods intended for its owners, Daniel Axtell and Jasper Ashworth. Eels revealed how he went to Axtell's home at Port Royal around midnight and presented to him a letter from Leigh Ashworth, and that two days later Eels and some of Axtell's slaves unloaded the dry goods at Manatee Bay (a small harbor west of Kingston), using a canoe to bring them into Port Royal under the cover of darkness. The remainder of the valuables were kept on board the *Dolphin* at Manatee Bay, where Francis Fernando seized it. Skipping over the robbery of the *Dolphin* that occurred soon thereafter, Eels revealed that about two months later he joined the crew of another vessel bound for the wrecks and worked as a courier ferrying letters from Axtell and Jasper Ashworth to Leigh, who remained at Providence. Eels's testimony constituted enough proof that Axtell and Jasper Ashworth had been involved financially in piracy, leading to their arrests.[79]

Despite offering clemency to Eels in exchange for his testimony, the council reneged. They placed Eels in jail and slapped him with an impossibly high bail fee of £2,000. To grant a full pardon, the council mused, would "destroy his evidence," or compromise his self-serving testimony. Eels, of course, could not pay his bail and remained in jail.[80] After several unsuccessful requests for his release, on March 19 Eels was set free after offering to stand as King's evidence in the *Dolphin* case, and by putting up his Port

Royal property and slaves as collateral for the unpaid bond.[81] Eels's treatment at the hands of the council, however, could not have inspired confidence among common sailors, who would be able to use him as an example of the differential application of justice for ordinary men. Many sailors decided that the better course of action was to remain at Providence.

Providence Bound

What of those pardoned by Vincent Pearse? The paper trail confirms that at least 27 of the 209 pardoned mariners participated in the Jamaican piracies of 1715–16. Among those from the list who attracted the most attention of the council were Leigh Ashworth and Benjamin Hornigold—Ashworth primarily for his involvement in the capture of the *Lovely Mary of Rochelle*, and Hornigold, whose reputation as a pirate preceded him, for taking the *Marianne* and a few other ships. Fortunately, the names of Francis Fernando's crew on the *Bennet* have been preserved, almost in their entirety, thanks to a document describing the distribution of the prize money from the *Nuestra Señora de Belen*. Charles Vane and Charles Whitehead received a full share of fifty-five pounds of silver. They are joined by Richard Earle, John Sutton, and Matthew Reveare, about whom next to nothing is known beyond their brief appearance as members of Fernando's crew.[82] Fernando eventually abandoned the *Bennet* and went into hiding while the vessel remained at Providence. For a time, Benjamin Hornigold sailed the vessel, and four others can be identified as members of the *Bennet*'s reconstituted crew under him: John Martin (quartermaster), Richard Newland (Noland), Pearse Wright, and Robert Brown.[83]

Given the prominent role of Henry Jennings in the robberies, it is no accident that five of his crew from the *Bersheba* later accepted a pardon from Captain Pearse, most notably Othenias Davis, Jennings's quartermaster. John Cockram (Cochran), the *Bersheba*'s surgeon, is likely the same man who married the daughter of Harbor Island planter Richard Thompson two years before and had accompanied Benjamin Hornigold on several of the first pirate voyages fitted out in the Bahamas.[84] Francis Lesley, probably still a teenager, somehow made his way from his home at Barbados to assume a position in Jennings's crew. Joining those three was Nathaniel Hudson, a mariner who split his time between Jamaica and New York.[85] Rounding out the group was Jamaican mariner Francis Charnock, one of the men who chastised quartermaster Alan Bernard for "sitting with his fingers in his mouth" rather than helping to capture the *Lovely Mary of Rochelle*.[86]

Although it did not attract a lot of the council's attention, the crew of the sloop *Francis and Sarah* included ten men who accepted the pardon. Commissioned by Hamilton in December 1715 under Captain Charles Chapman, the *Francis and Sarah* was not initially named as an accessory to piracy. However, by July William Quarrel assumed command of the *Francis and Sarah*, intending to dive for sunken gold that eluded the vessel's owners months before. Quarrel returned to Jamaica on October 17, submitting a deposition indicating that bad weather had forced him to shelter at Providence, where twenty-eight of his men (all named in the deposition) seized a canoe and abandoned him.

In November, however, Domingo Guerrero, the captain of a Spanish sloop, arrived in Jamaica with evidence to indicate that Quarrel's crew had been up to much more than he had let on. Around mid-August, Quarrel encountered Guerrero in his sloop, the *Nuestra Señora de Regla*, while in the Florida Strait. Several other English sloops were anchored nearby, one of them under the direction of Benjamin Hornigold, who, in conjunction with Quarrel, captured Guerrero's sloop, confiscated his goods, and detained Guerrero at Harbor Island. Guerrero insisted that Quarrel's crew played an equal role in his capture and shared the spoils from his ship equally with Hornigold's. Quarrel protested his innocence, and the British captains of several other ships in the Florida Strait at the same time affirmed that Hornigold, not Quarrel, had robbed Guerrero.[87] Despite one briefly successful escape attempt, Quarrel spent several months in jail as a suspected pirate before being released.[88]

Ten of Quarrel's men, though, certainly became pardoned pirates. Most notable perhaps was Josiah Burgess, a Bermudian who would be captaining his own ship a year later. The others include Joseph and Thomas Pearce, who were possibly brothers and from Jamaica. Joseph, we know, chose to live permanently in the Bahamas, as did Anthony Kemp. David Sword was an "old experienced pirate" who was known to have chronic injuries and remained at Providence for at least another two years. Little is known about the remaining five: David Ross, Rowland Harbon (Harbin), John Waters, Richard Richards, and John Ealing, although Ealing accepted a pardon from South Carolina governor Robert Johnson several months after receiving one from Pearse, perhaps just for good measure.[89]

In addition to those who appear in the council's records, it is likely that a significant number of other Jamaican mariners gravitated into piracy by joining the crews commissioned by Hamilton, or as crewmen on noncommissioned ships involved in conducting wrecking operations in the Florida

Strait. We may never know for sure, but it is possible that Anthony Jacobs, who appears on Pearse's list, is the same "Capt. Jacobs" mentioned as the pirogue captain who apprehended stolen snuff from a Dutch crew out of New York in the spring of 1716. Henry Glinn and John Augur had been captaining Jamaican vessels for several years before turning pirate, and each man would have been in a position to join one or more of the Jamaican crews. William South, a native of St. Andrews Parish, seems to have been acquainted with Leigh Ashworth and later became a privateer in the War of the Quadruple Alliance. Benjamin Turnor, William Williams, James Mowat, John Hipperson, Samuel Addey, George Chissem, and William Austin all have backgrounds indicating that they were natives of Jamaica or later made their homes there. In a word, many of the era's pirates must have derived from the estimated eight hundred sailors constituting Archibald Hamilton's supposed anti-piracy force.

Jamaica's contribution to the golden age of piracy cannot be overstated. Although the Bahamians had taken the lead two years before by conducting revenge attacks on Spanish ships, Jamaicans, with the consent of their governor, took the initiative to deprive Spain of the vast quantities of bullion resting on the ocean floor off the Florida coast. Under the cover of Archibald Hamilton's questionable commissions, Jamaican captains also made opportunistic strikes against Spanish and French ships. When Jamaican officials tried to rein in the vessels, they acted too late, realizing that Hamilton had unleashed forces no one could control. Although unspoken, a degree of class conflict underlay the Jamaica Council's delayed attempt to investigate and punish the sailors at the behest of Spanish and French ambassadors. A "rigorous" prosecution, culminating in several proclamations issued in August 1716 declaring the men pirates, instilled panic in the maritime community. Many sailors understandably chose to stay away. At the same time, Jamaican merchants who funded and incentivized the wrecking/piracy expeditions received clemency for their testimony and only had to return money and goods that were traceable to the wrecks and the several prize ships. Feeling betrayed, at that juncture many mariners at Providence fully committed to going rogue, and whatever inclination they might have had to refrain from attacking British ships was gone. The so-called golden age of piracy subsequently reached its zenith, causing British officials to contemplate offering a royal pardon.

CHAPTER 4

The Pardon and Its Discontents

From the captain's log of the HMS *Phoenix*:

February 23, 1718: Moderate and Fair bore away for Providence att 10 this morning was off that harbour; where lay several ships & sloops with colors of all nations flying I then brought to and sent my lieutenant a shoar with a flagg of truce & his Majesties Royal proclamation of the Act of Grace

February 24: Ditto yesterday in the Afternoon my lieutenant returned aboard and informed me that he was receiv'd by a great number of pyrates with much civility to whom he read the publick the proclamation and they accepted the same with a great deal of joy all their commanders did the like and sent me information that a sloop called the Lark was att anchor at Bushes Key with a design to go upon the account again whereupon I made sail thither.... After I had fired several shott at her she bore down to me so I sent my lieutenant on board and took possession of her she had but 16 men wch pretended she for going into the harbour to surrender themselves to me and to accept of His Ma[jesties] Pardon in the evening prov'd little wind and continued all night so that I did not gett into the harbour til 7 this morning att which time I anchored in 3 fathom & was saluted by two of the pirates ships; their commanders and ringleaders came on board and informed me that my taking the sloop had very much alarmed all the pirates in general believing the men taking in her would be executed therefore the commanders assured me that setting at liberty would be a very great means to induce these people to surrender and accept the Act of Grace; which I accordingly did and this confirm'd them all of his Majesties goodness toward them

February 25: Squally with rain here we found 5 ships 3 of them from 18 to 36 guns also 9 sloops which were traders with these pyrates but pretended they never did it till the Act of Grace was Published one of the Dutch man of 36 guns & another of 26: one an English pink one a Bristol galley & the other a French ship of no force

February 26: Squally weather a great number of pirates came on board and surrender'd themselves and accepted his Majesties most gracious Pardon and took my Certificates for their Protection to carry to governments

February 27: Fresh gales several pyrates came on board to surrender themselves

February 28: Ditto a sloop came in from Carolina several pirates took certificates

March 1: Hard gales and squally att 10 last night our anchors came home and the shipp sailed aground att midnight hove off again itt being then high water and the wind abated the pyrates sett one of the ships on fire hoisted all our colours and att noon fired 15 guns being her Royal highness Princess of Wales birthday.[1]

Captain Vincent Pearse's logbook entries recounting his first week at Providence give the impression that it is a precise, accurate account of what transpired when he offered the pardon to the roughly five hundred pirates assembled there. We learn about details such as the weather; moderate and fair conditions gave way to rain and wind that caused the unmoored *Phoenix* to run aground, requiring the captain to wait for high tide to free the vessel. We know that the ships he encountered in Nassau harbor, captured prizes that pirates had turned into warships, were heavily armed and derived from several nations. Nine other vessels, he alleged, had been trading with pirates while pretending otherwise. Pearse also reveals that he sent First Lieutenant Richard Symonds ashore ahead of him to explain the Act of Grace and evaluate the pirates' reaction to it, which he described as being "very civil." Some of the pirates, we learn, were willing to rat out their accomplices. One pirate gang that manned the sloop *Lark* had been acting suspiciously, and Pearse's deft ability to project force while displaying magnanimity seems to have won over about half the pirates, who clamored for pardons in the days that followed. Law and order, it seems, had come at long last to the Bahamas, as witnessed by the ceremonial firing of a can-

Governor Robert Johnson of South Carolina, Pardon of Pirates, April 7, 1718. South Carolina Miscellaneous Records, 1716–1721, 33, South Carolina Department of Archives and History. While there are no surviving copies of the pardon certificates given by Vincent Pearse and Woodes Rogers, they probably resembled this one given by South Carolina governor Robert Johnson. In it, Johnson invokes the Act of Grace to grant pardons to pirates Daniel Arrowsmith and Francis Charnock. The etching in the bottom right corner indicates that Thomas Reynolds, James Gratricks, and Robert Hawks received pardons at the same time. Charnock and Gratricks received a pardon previously in the Bahamas from Vincent Pearse. Courtesy of the South Carolina Department of Archives and History and familysearch.org.

non celebrating the birthday of Princess Caroline of Ansbach, the wife of the future George II.

If only it were that simple. Pearse's sometimes terse entries conceal what was in reality a complex and contested process. What Pearse does not reveal is that, by the time of his arrival, the pirates of Providence had already known about the royal proclamation for about two months. During that span of time at least two delegations—one from Bermuda, another from Jamaica, and possibly a third from South Carolina—had offered the pardon, prompting about two dozen men affiliated with Henry Jennings to surrender in Bermuda.[2] Although he alludes to it occasionally, the pardon had a divisive effect on the pirate community. Pearse managed to convince 209 men to surrender to him, but at least that same number flatly refused. Some of the recusants quietly slipped away from Providence when the *Phoenix* appeared on the horizon, and others, notably led by Charles Vane, promptly "resumed their course of life" as pirates.

What Pearse chose not to reveal is that his own actions threatened to undermine the mission. As others would allege, Pearse was a reluctant pirate hunter who preferred watching pirate sloops through his looking glass rather than give chase to them on the high seas. On one occasion, he lobbed cannon fire from the *Phoenix* toward the town of Nassau, and in the process almost caused the inhabitants to rise up against him. On shore, Pearse not only ate and drank with pirates but also traded with them. Intent on lining his own pockets, Pearse bought silk, indigo, and brandy to sell on his return to New York. He also confiscated money that legally belonged to the pirates by virtue of the Act of Grace, and he absconded with building materials intended for the construction of the home of the newly installed governor, Woodes Rogers, who was expected to arrive in a few short months. Pearse even outfitted a sloop laden with a personal cargo of flour and confiscated goods, and sent it to St. Augustine to trade with the Spaniards, netting him over 2,100 pieces of eight. Little wonder, then, that many of the pirates of Providence did not trust him or the authority he presumed to represent.

Coming to a better understanding of the pardon therefore requires us to step away from Pearse's logbook and correspondence, which provide only a one-sided account of what may have happened. A more holistic assessment of this critical moment in history reveals that many of those who accepted the pardon were not pirates per se. Rather, they were among the many captains of merchant vessels conducting a brisk trade in piratically obtained goods, which had been criminalized by a 1717 Anti-piracy Act. While Captain Pearse, like many colonial administrators and naval officers, would take credit for his role in eradicating piracy, its demise owes much to these sea captains, who assumed the risk of confessing to piracy in order to restore their reputations and return to honest seafaring work. Much is also owed to the agency of certain "commanders and ringleaders" of pirate gangs, who took a leap of faith by accepting the pardon and by hoping that colonial governments would honor it. It helped that these were also men of some standing and reputation, including Francis Lesley, Thomas Nichols, Josiah Burgess, and Benjamin Hornigold. By their example, many of the common sailors who manned their ships followed suit. Piracy remained attractive to those who aspired to a life of adventure, dreamed of getting rich quick, or embraced their roles as outlaws. Those who took the longer view of the situation, however, realized that they had much more to gain by making an honest living and submitting to authority. As it turned out, the pardon was their means of returning to a normal life, and one can surmise that many accepted it almost with a sense of relief.

The Golden Age of Piratical Trade

By the summer of 1716, the pirate community faced no local opposition in the Bahamas, and therefore it was in a position to unleash its reign of terror. At the time of Pearse's arrival, upward of two thousand pirates were operating in the Caribbean and greater Atlantic Ocean, and some estimate that eight hundred to a thousand of them (mostly but not exclusively British subjects) made their home base in the Bahamas.[3] One of the key developments at this time was the pirates' increasing willingness to attack British ships. Certain pirate commanders who were reluctant to attack their countrymen, namely, Benjamin Hornigold and Henry Jennings, saw their influence wane while the more radicalized and aggressive commanders, such as Sam Bellamy and Edward Thache, took their place. Pirate attacks peaked in 1717–18 and included some of the era's most dramatic episodes, which made household names of the captains who conducted them. Notably, in March 1717 Samuel Bellamy and his accomplice Palsgrave Williams captured a heavily armed British slave-trading vessel named the *Whydah*. Together, they harassed shipping while traveling northward along the North American coast before Bellamy met his demise thanks to an April storm off Cape Cod. Williams and his crew dodged the storm by sheltering in the Gulf of Maine.[4] Meanwhile, Edward Thache had come to the attention of British authorities around December 1716, after which his attacks in Caribbean waters intensified. He joined ranks with Stede Bonnet and, around November

1717, captured a French slave ship, *La Concorde*, which he famously rechristened as the *Queen Anne's Revenge*, his flagship.

By May 1718 Blackbeard was at the height of his power, commanding *Queen Anne's Revenge* manned by 150 crew and sporting 36 guns, the flagship of a four-vessel fleet with an estimated 250 pirates. That month, Blackbeard's fleet famously blockaded the harbor at Charles Town, South Carolina, for more than a week as his crew picked off the occasional ship, seizing goods and passengers. Using prominent Charlestonian Samuel Wragg as a hostage, Thache even sent several of his men ashore to purchase medicines, and by that point Blackbeard had become the most wanted man in all of the Americas. Soon after the blockade at Charles Town, Blackbeard ran his ship aground at Beaufort Inlet in North Carolina, where his diminished crew surrendered, accepted pardons, and, for a brief while, seemed to give up piracy.[5]

Pirate attacks on the high seas such as these captured the most attention of the British and colonial press, as well as that of governing officials charged with eradicating piracy. The same is true of modern historians, who relish the opportunity to reconstruct the genealogy of pirate crews, track their movements throughout the greater Atlantic world, and tally the number and value of the ships they captured. While important, a more subtle transformation in Atlantic trade networks was occurring simultaneously, whereby the Bahamas, which merchant vessels largely ignored, became a magnet. From virtually everywhere in British America, sea captains sailed to the Bahamas in order to salvage what they could of the remains of the 1715 Spanish *flota* and trade with the pirates at Providence, whose purchasing power had vastly increased due to the success of their robberies. For their part, merchant captains saw an opportunity to obtain silver and gold specie, of which there was a chronic shortage in the colonies. Merchant captains also eyed valuable cargoes of sugar, indigo, distilled spirits, and tropical commodities like cocoa and logwood, which pirates had accumulated in abundance and could sell at lower prices since they did not bear the costs of production.

Pirates, meanwhile, needed buyers for their cargoes to make their risky efforts worthwhile. Pirates also required food, building materials, and other staples lacking in the Bahamas, where agriculture languished because of infertile soils and, in part, because its population devoted much of its efforts to seafaring. A kind of symbiosis therefore developed between the merchant sea captains and the pirates, who formed trade partnerships that were fundamental, not incidental, to piracy. Colonial governors understood this dynamic; in Jamaica, Governor Nicholas Lawes surmised that even more pirates would have accepted the pardon "were the pirates not supplyed with necessarys, and received intelligence from shoar."[6] The pirates, too, admitted to the importance of the provisions trade. As Wingate Gale, commander of the Bahamas' guard ship *Delicia*, revealed, "The pirates themselves have often told me that if they had not been supported by the traders from thence [Rhode Island, New York, Pennsylvania, etc.] with ammunition and provisions according to their directions, they could never have become so formidable, nor arriv'd to that degree that they have."[7]

Evidence for the Bahamas trade and salvaging activity derives from Naval Office shipping returns compiled irregularly and imperfectly in many colonies. Although a preexisting trade between the Bahamas and other colonies did exist, Queen Anne's War had largely disrupted those networks, and few ships bothered to sail there prior to 1715. Toward the latter part of that year, however, one notices a discernible uptick of ships sailing to and from the Bahamas. Because commerce with pirates was technically illegal and salvaging rested on shaky legal ground, it is reasonable to assume that many more undocumented vessels were active in the Bahamas. We will probably never know the full magnitude.

Spearheading this effort were sailors from Bermuda, who descended on the Bahamas even before Jamaican wrecking crews arrived there. On October 19, 1715, for instance, Bermuda skipper John Keele cleared outward for the Bahamas in a sloop, indicating that he could have arrived in the area at least six weeks before Henry Jennings and the Jamaicans. Keele invites suspicion because his vessel was laden with "only provisions for their voyage," meaning that he carried no goods for trading.[8] Most Bermuda ships followed suit, clearing outward only with supplies to sustain their crews for the voyage. What this would seem to suggest is that the vast majority of outbound Bermuda ships intended primarily to fish the nearby wrecks. At the same time, however, some captains clearly intended to trade with the pirates. Joseph Skinner, for instance, departed Bermuda around January 19, 1716, with beef, flour, bread, peas, Indian corn, and wine, presumably because the Bahamas lacked essential foodstuffs and he could find ready buyers there. Bermuda captains also sometimes stocked their ships with tableware, onions, cabbages, beer, cider, butter, and pork.[9]

Rather quickly, it became evident that voyages to the Bahamas could be lucrative. Bermudian skipper George Frith arrived home on February 23, 1716, with five hundred board feet of wood and forty pounds of "old iron." Two weeks later, Jonathan Williams returned from Turks Island with eight hundred bushels of salt, which was produced on the island and therefore should not arouse suspicion. However, Williams's cargo also included cacao, lime juice, and more "old iron," indicating that he stopped at Providence on his return voyage to purchase goods that could only have been had by trade with pirates. More telling was the April 2 arrival of Edward North, captain of the *William and Martha*, and Jeremiah Burch, who commanded the sloop *Elizabeth*. Evidently working as partners in a joint venture, the two captains returned from Providence with cargoes of 545 pieces of eight each, likely the fruits of ongoing salvage activities.[10]

Spurred by the availability of silver, by the summer of 1716 Bermudians began sending small fleets to the Bahamas. On June 28, four sloops arrived from the Bahamas, captained by seasoned veterans Daniel Tucker, John Fowle, William Hutchings, and Jeremiah Burch. Tucker's trading ventures netted him 1,775 pieces of eight, six gold ryals, and four small silver cups valued at twenty-five shillings apiece. Fowle, Hutchings, and Burch, meanwhile, possessed smaller but appreciable sums in the range of 400 to 500 pieces of eight. A day later Richard Leacraft, master of the sloop *Content*, arrived bearing 1,200 pieces of eight, and on June 30 Edward North came in with a whopping 1,800 pieces of eight. On July 9 Daniel Harrison declared a cargo of 1,684 pieces of eight and eighteen pounds of silver bullion. In addition to silver and gold, their cargoes included gunpowder, cartouche boxes, hourglasses, and the ubiquitous "old iron" salvaged from wrecked ships.[11]

For the better part of two and a half years, the Bermudians conducted what can only be described as a mad scramble for the Bahamas. Between February 1716 and Governor Rogers's arrival as governor in late July 1718, Bermuda's naval office recorded eighty-six return voyages from the Bahamas and the adjacent Florida coast. Bermuda's focus on the Bahamas seems to have peaked around April 1717, when a fleet of twelve ships returned from there within an eight-day span. By that point, many captains were devoting almost all their attention to the Bahamas. As the number of voyages increased, the declared cargoes of returning vessels gradually diminished in value. The April 1717 fleet, for instance, netted only twenty to forty pieces of eight for each ship, with some captains returning home empty handed. Increasingly, this became the norm, as vessels limped home with "only provisions" or "only ballast." Those few who assembled a cargo for the return voyage had to be satisfied with modest hauls, such as one by captain George Wells, who arrived home on June 4 only with "old iron" and "old junk." Still, Bermuda captains were sometimes able to acquire valuable commodities like indigo, claret, and brasiletto wood, as did one captain who acquired two and a half tons of the dyewood in May 1718.[12]

Although untold numbers of vessels came primarily to fish the wrecks, many ship captains preferred trading with the pirates. Because of its proximity to and proprietary connections with the Bahamas, South Carolina factored significantly in the trade to the islands. What is more, postwar trade between Charles Town and Spanish St. Augustine brought South Carolina shipping into close proximity to the wrecks, which naturally attracted treasure seekers. By December 1715, one British naval officer observed that Charles Town (still in the midst of an Indian war) was surprisingly "so thin of men" because many local mariners had gone south to dive on the wrecks. A year later South Carolina's Commons House of Assembly had become concerned that the wrecks diverted too many seafaring men away from normal commercial activity, and it briefly considered (but did not pass) a measure to "discourage" the treasure seekers.[13]

Whereas food constituted the bulk of South Carolina's outgoing cargoes, incoming vessels carried a preponderance of tropical commodities and small amounts of salvaged iron. Sometime in the first half of 1717, for instance, Benjamin Sims returned from the Bahamas with turtle shells. Neal Walker and Joseph Cockram, both Bahamians, arrived with dyewoods, cotton, cocoa, and sugar. Later that summer, Captain Robert Wishart arrived with wood, oil, and cotton, whereas Bostonian Robert Gamesby entered South Carolina from the Bahamas carrying dyewood. Captain Richard Smith, another Bahamian, carried dyewoods, cotton, and sugar to South Carolina, returning home with ale, cider, rum, and European goods.[14]

In the meantime, New England merchants and ship captains resumed their interest in the Bahamas. Rhode Islander George Maycock, sailing out of Boston, was among the first to trade there after the pirates had made their presence known, departing in June 1714 with a cargo of lumber. A year later, Peter Sergeant carried rum, flour, and butter to the Bahamas, and a steady trade continued for the span of two years. Between June 1714 and midsummer 1717, fourteen vessels cleared outward from Boston to the Bahamas, joined by six more from Salem during roughly that same span of time. The *Boston News Letter* reported an additional six outbound and ten inbound voyages to and from the Bahamas that do not appear in naval office records, indicating a trade that was even more robust than official records imply. As with South Carolina shipping, New England captains stocked their sloops with the fruits of local agriculture and industry. Rum, distilled from molasses into its drinkable form in New England, figures prominently, constituting the cargoes of six of these ships. A similar proportion trafficked in locally brewed beer and cider. New England vessels also carried lumber, shingles, oats, flour, bread, horses, onions, pork, and codfish, all staples that could not be produced locally in the Bahamas.[15]

New York's shipping returns tell a similar story of acceleration of the Bahamas trade. Between May 1716 (when records are extant) and Vincent Pearse's return to New York in May 1718, only two sloops cleared outward for the Bahamas, both in April 1718.[16] Yet New York port authorities cleared eighteen ships inward from the Bahamas during that span of time, suggesting subterfuge or perhaps that skippers navigating homeward from Caribbean destinations made impromptu stops there. For the New Yorkers, salt appears to have been the most frequently acquired commodity, which was carried home in six of the vessels. Three more vessels managed to obtain dyewoods, such as lignum vitae, boxwood, and brasiletto. In addition, one vessel returned loaded with oranges and hides. A few of the cargoes bear witness to salvaging activities or ongoing trade with those who had fished the wrecks. In March 1717 New York mariner John Tickell arrived home with "old iron" in addition to brown sugar. Most telling, two months later, Captain John Mutlow of the sloop *William and Thomas* of New York returned home with "the appurteness from a wrecked vessel at Harbour Island," indicating that his crew had worked at least one of the area's shipwrecks. A year later, John Veare came home from the Bahamas with "some Appertences taken from a Wreckt vessel there" in addition to some rum and three enslaved Africans.[17]

What is perhaps most striking about the inbound New York voyages, however, is that a few ships returned home with unsold European goods and other commodities, perhaps indicating that the Bahamas market may have actually become glutted because so many traders were arriving there. In July 1716 New York skipper William Glover returned home with unsold gunpowder, tobacco, and provisions, and in November that same year, Nicholas Dent came into port with a parcel of shoes he could not sell in the Bahamas.[18]

Shipping returns from each of these colonies indicate conclusively that a significant number of the men who accepted the royal pardon had been involved in the Bahamas trade. Nathaniel Hudson, who had served as Henry Jennings's quartermaster on the *Bersheba*, conducted one trading voyage in July 1717, guiding the sloop *Endeavor* of Jamaica from the Bahamas to Bermuda.[19] Hudson evidently felt safe enough to leave Providence to trade, despite being named in several depositions as an accomplice of Henry Jennings, still a wanted man. Naval records also provide snapshots of the pardoned New Englanders. From the port of Salem, William Harris made one voyage to the Bahamas in July 1716. The Boston newspaper also indicates that one captain named Noland cleared outward from Boston to Providence, most likely Edward, a Bahamian.[20] Three New Yorkers likewise appear on Pearse's list. In addition to William Pinfold and John Mutlow, John Stout also engaged in the Bahamas trade, as evidenced by the April 1718 clearance of the sloop *Catherine and Elizabeth*.[21] Two mariners who frequented Charles Town, South Carolina, appear in the records. Richard Divelly was among those ferrying goods to St. Augustine in the fall of 1716. Robert Wishart, who commanded a sloop owned by two Bermudians, made at least two voyages from Charles Town to the Bahamas in 1716–17.[22]

Captain Robert Wishart's case deserves special notice because he is the lone individual on Pearse's list to face smuggling charges derived from the Bahamian trade prior to accepting the Act of Grace. Although Wishart's origins are unknown, he was living in South Carolina by 1714, was married to a widowed woman named Jane, and had business connections in Bermuda and Kingston, Jamaica.[23] Wishart and his wife Jane appear in the historical record regularly as litigants, primarily in suits related to the estate of Jane's previous husband, Joseph Merry. Between 1714 and 1716, Robert and Jane initiated two lawsuits on behalf of Merry's estate, evidently to recoup debts owed to him. At the same time, four South Carolinians sued the Wisharts for debts that Merry had owed before his death. In the end, the Wisharts had to petition the Commons Assembly of South Carolina to pass a private bill to help resolve the disputes over Merry's estate.[24] There was no indication, as of yet, that Wishart was criminally inclined.

Wishart's slide into criminality derived from his captaincy of the sloop *Providence* of Bermuda. In the fall of 1716 Wishart cleared outward from Charles Town to the Bahamas, declaring "only ballast and provisions" as his cargo. Cargoes of this kind were rather common in South Carolina and should have aroused the suspicions of customs officers, who had to ponder why a ship captain who made his living by trade would venture out with nothing to sell. In February 1717 Wishart returned and pulled the same stunt again, declaring "ballast only" as his cargo.[25] Several months later, it was revealed that Wishart engaged in trickery, stopping at an undisclosed location on the North Edisto River (some forty miles south of Charles Town) to unload a cargo of olives, Madeira wine, European goods, oil, needles, and some Latin and Spanish books, all of which must have been obtained from pirates. Only after dispensing with these goods did he bother to enter his sloop with the proper naval authorities. In September Wishart was summoned before the vice-admiralty court, and after he failed to appear four times, the sloop and contraband were condemned and sold at auction that October.[26]

While the admiralty records purposefully do not reveal the identity of the informant who turned in Wishart, all signs point to Colleton County planter Richard Floyd, who owned in excess of 900 acres in close proximity to the North Edisto River. As Floyd later alleged in a lawsuit for assault he filed against Wishart seeking £200 in damages, on October 12 (just as the sloop and its cargo were being condemned) Wishart "did beat, wound, and evilly entreat" Floyd, so much so that "his life was despaired of." Floyd also mentioned "other enormities" that threatened the peace, including disparaging words Wishart directed at George I, the recently installed king whose legitimacy many disputed. As with his vice-admiralty case, Wishart ignored three summons to court, and Floyd probably never collected his £200.[27]

Wishart, however, is the exception that proves the rule. The vast majority of ship captains who traded in the Bahamas while it was in the thrall of pirates faced no legal consequences for doing so. In fact, what is striking is the number of mariners who probably should have appeared on Pearse's list as accomplices to piracy but did not. Take, for example, Peter Sergeant of Boston, who made three suspicious voyages to the Bahamas. In June 1715 Sergeant conveyed rum and food to the islands and never bothered to appear before customs officials on his return to Boston. A year later, Sergeant departed from Salem, only to disappear from the naval records for more than six months, indicating that he spent an extended amount of time trading in the Bahamas, or that he returned promptly but under the radar. Sergeant surfaced again in early 1717, arriving in Salem with dyewoods that likely derived from piracy. Captains Thomas Foster of Boston and Eleazar Moses of Salem each made two similarly suspicious round trips to the Bahamas in 1716. In addition to these repeat offenders, ten other New England–based captains conducted one recorded voyage to the Bahamas during the time it was under the control of pirates.[28]

As with Massachusetts, New York features a number of local mariners whose activities should arouse our suspicions. Most notable was Samuel Vincent, whose multiple voyages to South Carolina probably included illicit stops in the Bahamas. In the spring of 1717 Vincent commanded the sloop *Elizabeth* of Bermuda, which he sailed from New York to the Bahamas, returning home on June 5, when he declared a cargo of brasiletto wood.[29] On the return voyage, sometime in late May, Vincent was apprehended by the pirate Palsgrave Williams off the coast of New Jersey. Williams detained four of Vincent's men and confiscated some of the goods from the *Eliza-*

beth. One witness to those proceedings, however, indicated that a degree of familiarity existed between the two men. Williams reportedly encouraged Vincent to return to the Bahamas with provisions, suggesting that he might make a good profit there. A few days later, Vincent was at Sandy Hook on Long Island, where he agreed to carry Williams's boatswain, Richard Caverly, to New York City in exchange for some gold dust. Caverly was a wanted man by that point, and New York authorities arrested Vincent for "assisting" pirates.[30] Vincent got lucky; New York officials freed him within a week, and he departed again for South Carolina.[31]

Samuel Vincent was the most conspicuous suspect from New York, but two others are John Tickell and Jacob Phoenix, who traded off captaining the sloop *Wolf*. How these two men evaded suspicion is anyone's guess, for the *Wolf*'s owner was William Pinfold, a ship captain in his own right who traded in the Bahamas and later accepted the pardon. In March 1717 Tickell returned to New York after a voyage that had taken him first to St. Thomas (itself known to be a pirate nest) and then to Providence, sporting a cargo of "old iron" and brown sugar. Phoenix directed the vessel to the Bahamas that fall, arriving in New York in November with a more lucrative haul of lignum vitae wood.[32] John Fred, a veteran of the logwood trade, was another New York captain who knew Bahamian waters well.[33] Fred, who commanded the sloop *Ulster* of New York, sailed to Providence on July 4, 1718, presumably to sell a cargo of lumber. It just so happened that Fred arrived at the same time as Woodes Rogers, the newly installed governor. Rogers immediately suspected Fred of trading with Charles Vane and identified thirty-six hogsheads of sugar and some iron cable on Fred's ship that Vane had purportedly sold to him. Fred appeared before an ad hoc admiralty court that assembled on September 1 and declared his innocence, pleading that he had been apprehended by Vane and forced to load sugar against his will. John Fred also got lucky; Governor Rogers never found any witnesses to testify against him, so Fred went free after relinquishing the sugar and cables.[34] Fred nevertheless managed to limp home a month later with some of his cargo.[35]

Multiple reasons explain why many ship captains who traded with pirates in the Bahamas did not appear on Pearse's list. For most, it was probably a simple matter of timing. Pearse's stint at Providence occupied roughly six weeks, and anyone who was not present at that time easily could have avoided suspicion. Others avoided detection by remaining under the proverbial radar, conducting clandestine voyages outside the purview of naval officers and frequenting smaller ports that had no Crown presence. Quite a number more must have been smugglers, like Robert Wishart, who made a habit of unloading valuable goods at out-of-the-way rivers and coves before declaring cargoes as "ballast only" when they arrived in port.

Importantly, ship captains represented only the tip of the iceberg in the Bahamas trade, for the merchant community was equally involved as the owners of cargoes and the very ships these men commanded. In addition to their wealth, the merchants could rely on their political influence to protect themselves. Their numbers were legion, and to criminalize the merchants' activity in these key port towns would be to indict virtually the whole of society. The Bahamas trade flourished, then, because everyone was seemingly engaged in it and authorities tended to look the other way. In South Carolina, for instance, the sloop *Mary*, which roamed regularly between the Bahamas, the wrecks, and St. Augustine, was owned by none other than William Rhett, the colony's collector of customs. Other prominent South Carolinians had a hand in suspicious business as owners of vessels, including William Gibbon and Andrew Allen, partners of a leading mercantile firm. French Huguenot merchants Isaac Mazyck and Benjamin Godin sent one of their sloops to the Bahamas on at least one occasion.[36] Prominent New York merchants also owned vessels engaged in the Bahamas trade, including Stephen Richards, owner of the *Catherine and Elizabeth*, which made at least one voyage under the command of Captain John Stout. Nicholas Dent and Gilbert Ash, as well as two of New York's leading Jewish merchants, Lewis Gomez and Abraham de Susa, owned Bahamas-bound vessels.[37] Naval officers in the colony of Massachusetts did not record the names of vessel owners at that time, so we do not know the scope of the merchant community's involvement.

In Bermuda the owners and captains of Bahamas-bound vessels derived from some of the archipelago's oldest and most illustrious families: Frith, Tucker, Jennings, Courant, Trimingham, Joell, and Outerbridge. Shipping often assumed the dimensions of a family affair, and many partnerships consisted of close relatives. Consider George Frith, master of the sloop *Industry*, one of the first to return from the Bahamas after the wreck of the Spanish *flota*. George Frith owned a share of his vessel, but its co-owners included relatives Thomas Frith Sr. and Jr. Likewise, the sloop *St. George* constituted a family partnership. While Daniel Tucker served as captain and owned a share of the sloop, at least three relatives owned it along with him.[38]

The case of Bermuda is singularly important because of the involvement of one family, the Bennets. Benjamin Bennet served as lieutenant governor from 1701 to 1713 before being replaced by Henry Pullein. When Pullein died in 1715, Bennet resumed duties as acting lieutenant governor, and it was through his correspondence that British officials in London learned much of what was transpiring in the Bahamas. Despite representing royal authority in the colony, Benjamin Bennet had a direct financial stake in one of the ships conducting trade in the Bahamas. The vessel in question was the sloop *Benjamin*, which Bennet owned in conjunction with John Trimingham (a future governor) and two others. On May 9, 1716, the *Benjamin* cleared outward for the Bahamas under the command of Captain Daniel Harrison carrying only provisions for the crew, a sign that they intended to fish the nearby wrecks. Exactly two months later, the sloop returned home bearing 1,684 pieces of eight and eighteen pounds of silver bullion, as well as a parcel of "old iron," a share of which Bennet must have claimed. Harrison made one more voyage to the Bahamas that October, but there is no record of its return home, possibly due to a gap in the naval records.[39]

The governor's son, John Bennet, likewise had a financial stake in wrecking and trade in the Bahamas, as the owner of two sloops: the *Anne* and the *George*. Bennet's involvement began in April 1716, when he sent the *Anne* to the Bahamas carrying only provisions for the voyage. Two months later, the *Anne* returned from Turks Island with a load of salt, indicating perhaps that the crew had no success salvaging shipwrecks. In the summer of 1717 the *Anne*, under the command of William Richardson, set out for the Bahamas again carrying only provisions and seemingly returned empty handed. On October 1 Bennet sent Captain Richardson again, this time to the Florida coast in the *George*. On December 9 the *Anne* sailed again to Providence under the command of Benjamin Stovall. This time, however, the *Anne* was on a special mission, for on board was the owner himself, John Bennet, whom his father commanded to offer a pardon to the pirates. Although Bennet was on government business, these voyages also yielded profits. The *George* returned home from the Florida coast on January 10, 1718, with 280 pieces of eight. When the *Anne* arrived in Bermuda six days later, it had on board one hogshead of indigo and a like quantity of claret.[40] Although it is possible that the Bennets traded legally for these products, circumstantial evidence would seem to indicate that father and son engaged in commerce with the very same people to whom they offered pardons.

The Pardon

The strategy of offering clemency to pirates was nothing new in Britain. Going as far back as the reigns of Elizabeth I and James I, pardons had been granted to reformed pirates who agreed to work as pirate hunters.[41] In an attempt to curtail the Caribbean buccaneers, Governor Thomas Lynch (ca. 1671–74 and 1683–84) of Jamaica offered thirty-five acres of land to all who would cease their activities, in effect encouraging mariners to become planters. King James II issued a general pardon for pirates in 1685, and King William III adopted a similar policy in 1701. Intended to suppress the activities of the "Red Sea men," the 1701 pardon specifically excluded Henry Every and William Kidd, whose crimes were thought irredeemable.[42] In the midst of Queen Anne's War, Governor Thomas Handasyd of Jamaica offered a pardon to pirates who had gathered at the San Blas Islands (offshore from modern Panama) under the leadership of one Captain Michael (Mitchell), who made several requests for it in advance.[43] Handasyd's offer, which circulated in the fall of 1709, gave the pirates sixty days to turn themselves in and take the oath of allegiance, forgiving all crimes except high treason and "willful murder." In Handasyd's view, the ploy worked, as he boasted that a hundred penitent seamen ("sorry miserable creatures," he called them) had returned to Jamaica.[44]

Because pardoning had been a long-standing tradition, it is possible that some of the men who engaged in piracy following Queen Anne's War believed that their crimes ultimately would be forgiven. In a deposition taken before the Jamaica Council, Sarah Fernando (the wife of suspected pirate Francis Fernando) recalled a conversation that took place around the spring of 1716 between her husband and the merchant Thomas Bendysh. With Bendysh pressuring him to take more ships and Fernando resisting him, Bendysh was reported to have said, "You can take anybody ... We shall have an act of grace in two months."[45] That same expectation clearly had an impact on the mariner Stephen Smith, one of the many Jamaicans who fled to the Bahamas during the council's inquest. Writing to acting governor Peter Heywood in September 1716, Smith described his descent into piracy as an "accident," claiming he was "forced to go a pirateing for to gett a living which is much against my will. Could I but have a pardon," Smith pleaded, "I would directly come in, and bring a great many more English men along with me."[46] Captain Bartholomew Candler of the HMS *Winchelsea* believed that many suspected pirates went to Providence specifically to wait for a pardon. In a letter written in July 1717, Candler reported the demise of Sam Bellamy and most of his crew off Cape Cod, noting that the survivors (presumably Palsgrave Williams's crew) "have gone to Providence expecting [His Majesty's] pardon."[47] The idea of clemency even informed the thinking of the newly appointed governor of Jamaica, Nicholas Lawes. In a letter to the Board of Trade written that same summer, Lawes offered a "carrot and stick" approach. "To reduce the pyrates," Lawes argued, "[His Majesty's] clemency, accompany'd with a number of proper ships of war, to cruise in those parts, is the most, if not the only effectual means."⁴⁸

British officials in other branches of government were of like minds. That same year, the navy committed more of its ships to American waters to suppress piracy, Vincent Pearse's *Phoenix* included. Meanwhile, Parliament passed a new piracy act as part of the 1717 Transportation Act (4 Geo 1 c.11), which established the means for transporting felons to the American colonies. It effectively granted pardons to those who completed terms of indentured servitude (the death penalty awaited those who failed to comply). As for piracy, the 1717 Act renewed the 1698 act passed under William III and clearly stated that it applied to the colonies. As with the 1698 legislation, the 1717 Piracy Act took an expansive view of what it meant to be a pirate. In addition to outright robbery on the high seas, anti-piracy legislation criminalized all forms of providing aid and assistance to pirates, making no distinction in law between the "principals" or sea robbers and those who acted as "accessories." Article 9, for instance, states that a person could be judged an accessory "by setting them forth and by aiding abetting receiving and concealeing them and their Goods." Article 10 goes even further, denoting "every Person and Persons who knowing that such Pirate or Robber has done or committed such Piracy and Robbery shall on the Land or upon the Sea receive entertaine or conceale any such Pirate or Robber or receive or take into his Custody any Shipp Vessell Goods or Chattells which have been by any such Pirate." In other words, those who outfitted pirate ships and traded with pirates were breaking the law. Likewise, anyone who withheld information about pirates, fed or sheltered them, or had any favorable correspondence with pirates could be deemed an accessory.⁴⁹

On May 31, 1717, the Board of Trade drafted a report on the suppression of piracy, which they composed after having "discoursed with most of the considerable merchants and others concerned in H.M. Plantations in America." In addition to recommending an enhanced naval presence, the board urged the king "to pardon the said pirates provided they come in and surrender by a certain time to be limited."⁵⁰ The board passed along its recommendations to the secretary of state and the Privy Council, which began drafting a pardon that summer, copying much of the wording from King William's of 1698. Working collaboratively that summer, the Privy Council and Board of Trade completed a final draft, which they enacted on September 5, 1717. By virtue of the royal proclamation, the pirates had a full year to turn themselves in, meaning September 5, 1718. Those who failed to do so would be prosecuted as pirates according to law. All crimes committed before January 5, 1718, would be forgiven, a grace period of four months necessitated by the slow transmission of news in the eighteenth century. The act specified that pirates could surrender themselves to one of the secretaries of state in Great Britain or Ireland, but it also allowed them to surrender "to any governor or deputy governor of any of our plantations or dominions beyond the seas." In addition to clemency, the proclamation offered monetary awards for those involved in the "seizure or discovery" of pirates, for which it established a price schedule granting the most money for the apprehension of pirate "commanders" and correspondingly less for inferior officers.[51]

While the immediate intent of the pardon was to eradicate piracy, King George's policy was part of a broader campaign to win the allegiance of his subjects, many of whom were avowed Jacobites, or supporters of the exiled house of Stuart.[52] The king's accession to the throne had been controversial, as the German from Hanover replaced Anne, the last Stuart monarch. Spurred by his coronation in October 1714, protests broke out in more than twenty towns in the south and west of England. Jacobite demonstrations and plots continued to plague the early years of George I's reign, and historians identify the years 1715–22 as being particularly volatile.[53] In 1715 a full-scale rebellion took place under the direction of the Scottish Earl of Mar, whose goal was to install James Edward Stuart (James II's son, who lived in exile in France) as the rightful "King James III." At one point, the Earl of Mar had twenty thousand fighters under his command, and the earl's army scored important victories in Scotland before losing a decisive battle at Preston that November. The Jacobite cause temporarily collapsed, and many of the ringleaders were arrested and sentenced to death. While some notable rebels were executed, in July 1717 George I convinced Parliament to pass the Act of Indemnity, which offered clemency to Jacobites who, in a manner similar to the one laid out in the Transportation Act, agreed to relocate to the American colonies.[54] For King George this was a victory, signifying to skeptical subjects that he was in fact a merciful ruler.[55]

It was in this context that George I issued the piracy proclamation. The Act of Indemnity had been somewhat controversial because some thought it treated the Jacobite rebels too leniently.[56] Interestingly, when news of the piracy proclamation hit the London newspapers beginning in mid-September, it passed with hardly a whiff of critical commentary, perhaps a sign of widespread support among the British people. Most editors simply printed the full text of the proclamation, or reported sparingly on its passage and some of its provisions.[57] News of the pardon trickled slowly into the Americas and seemingly did not reach the colonies until November, mostly by word of mouth. The *Boston News Letter* published a complete version of the text on December 9, 1717, and colonial governors started receiving official copies from naval captains in December and into January 1718.[58]

At first, pirates who received word of the pardon appeared skeptical, partly because its transmission came through unofficial channels. For instance, in November 1717 Josiah Burgess apprehended a Bristol vessel captained by a man named French. When Burgess boarded his ship, Captain French showed him an unofficial copy of the pardon and asked Burgess and his men if they would consider coming in to surrender. Burgess and his crew answered that they would not do so, observing that the printed copy lacked the royal seal. For this reason, they believed it to be a "sham" and continued plundering French's ship.[59] A few weeks later, on December 5, Henry Bostock, master of the sloop *Margaret* of St. Christopher's, was taken by Edward Thache near Crab Island, in the Bahamas. Bostock reported his encounter when he arrived home on December 19, in a deposition that is memorable for its description of Thache's beard and stature. Bostock, however, also reveals that news of the pardon had been traveling by word of mouth among seafarers, who received it skeptically. When Bostock revealed that "an Act of Grace was expected out for them," Thache and his crew "seemed to slight it" while boasting of plans of a Christmas heist near Cuba.[60]

How news of the pardon arrived at Providence, and the manner by which pirates began to take it seriously, originates in Bermuda. In early December Lieutenant Governor Benjamin Bennet received official copies of the Act of Grace and deputized his son, John, to make a voyage to Providence to explain its contents. Sailing on board his sloop *Anne*, Bennet departed on December 9, 1717, arriving at Providence around mid-December.[61] Bennet first showed the proclamation to Thomas Nichols, who proved to be the epitome of the contrite pirate. Nichols described the pardon as "very welcome news," so he summoned all the pirates "to the beat of a drum" and read it "publickly to his own gang and to the other pyrates on the island of Providence." With Bennet by his side, Nichols "exhorted" the pirates to "lay hold" of the pardon.[62] During Bennet's stay at Providence, around the end of December or first of January, the former privateer Matthew Musson also arrived on behalf of Woodes Rogers, who had been appointed royal governor of the Bahamas a few weeks earlier. Musson's charge was to find a suitable house for Rogers to occupy. Therefore, by early January, the pirates were well aware of the pardon and the governor's imminent arrival.[63]

These circumstances catalyzed a first wave of surrenders, which occurred in January in conjunction with Bennet's return voyage to Bermuda. It is clear that some of these mariners were eager to leave their criminal pasts behind them. Francis Lesley, the young Barbadian planter's son, expressed his relief in a brief letter directed to Lieutenant Governor Bennet. Thanking him for sending the "most welcome news," Lesley avowed his "hearty desire" to "partake of your excellency's clemency." Echoing Lesley, Thomas Nichols wrote three days later, extending his "hearty and grateful thanks" to Governor Bennet for sending his son to deliver the proclamation. "Some of us as well as my self," Nichols wrote, had embraced the pardon, and Nichols finished by complementing the "particular marks of friendship" Bennet's government had shown the pirates, "which can never be forgotten."[64]

This first wave of surrenders centered on the authority of Henry Jennings, who was among the first to turn himself in. Born into a prominent Bermuda family, Jennings owned a "considerable estate" there and had significant property holdings in Jamaica. Jennings also had increased his wealth by virtue of the money he had forcibly taken from the coast of Florida, as well as from the capture of at least one French ship. He would have known the Bennets well, and perhaps he trusted the governor to honor the pardon. As with Jennings, many of the other mariners who surrendered first appear to have been from Bermuda or had preexisting ties to the colony. The process unfolded beginning January 13, when Bermudian John Tynes accepted the pardon from Lieutenant Governor Bennet, followed by Henry Jennings and two more men two days later. Between January 13 and February 10, fourteen men surrendered before Bennet at Bermuda. Eight more mariners trickled in between March and July, two of whom had earlier accepted a pardon from Vincent Pearse.[65]

Although some of the pirates needed little coaxing to get them to surrender, others were more reluctant, because the pardon made it unclear whether they could keep the money and goods they had obtained illegally.[66] Francis Lesley, for instance, chose not to return immediately to Bermuda, pleading that "I hope to partake" in the governor's clemency, but only after wrapping up "my affairs in this place [Providence] which will soon be over."[67] Thomas Nichols also delayed surrendering, stating that "some present affairs prevent me," another thinly veiled reference to securing his money and effects.[68] In fact, Jennings and many of those who surrendered first had left their goods at Providence, wanting to speak with Lieutenant Governor Bennet about the status of their property before taking the chance of losing it. The pirates made their wishes known directly to Bennet, who later reported hearing that many of the pirates wanted to surrender "but were afraid to bring their effects with them for fear of being seized." "They do declare," Bennet continued, "that they never will surrender without the assurance of enjoying what they have gotten, otherwise they say we have ventured [risked] our noses for nothing if we accept [His Majesty's] most gracious pardon." Pirates feared being left "destitute" and needed to keep some of their wealth if they were "to return to their families" and resume "an honest way of living."[69]

Because the royal proclamation was silent on several key questions about the scope of the pardon, colonial governors and naval captains had to improvise in order to implement it. Lieutenant Governor Bennet gave an expansive reading to the pardon, and he established a policy of not confiscating pirate goods but requiring the pirates to pay import duties on enumerated items.[70] Another question that arose was if the act of murder would be forgiven. The Board of Trade raised these and other questions with the Privy Council in February 1718. The council responded by affirming that all murders that occurred in the act of piracy were to be forgiven. As for the question of pirate goods, they tried to distinguish between a pirate's "proper goods" and those that had been taken through robbery.[71] Proper goods, they argued, should not be confiscated. Those that had been taken in the act of robbery, however, could be subject to forfeiture if the legal owners prosecuted and won their cases in a court of law.

The problem, of course, was that it was difficult to distinguish between legally and illegally obtained goods. Prosecutions were also unlikely because it was hard to identify the legal owners of pirate goods, since many would have been foreign nationals, or British subjects scattered throughout the Americas and Britain. Also, most goods could easily be stripped of any identifying markers, making it difficult to distinguish the original owners. Finally, the fact that pirates hailed from any number of colonies, as well as Great Britain, made tracking down them and their goods difficult. Simply put, adjudicating these cases was impractical, and most pirates were able to get away with their effects.

Around the same time Jennings and his companions left for Bermuda, the Jamaican government devised its own plans to convince the remaining pirates to surrender. On January 3 official copies of the royal proclamation arrived in Jamaica, where it was reproduced and "affix'd in the most frequented places" on the island. Soon thereafter, Governor Peter Heywood deputized two sloops to carry the proclamation so that they could "give notice to what pirates they could meet with." One sloop, captained by a man named Cook, encountered a pirate squadron off the coast of Cuba led by Benjamin Hornigold. Cook reported that Hornigold and the others expressed their intention to accept the pardon, but he managed to convince only one pirate captain and five "private men" to surrender themselves. Navy captain Thomas Durrell apprehended the six men, along with their sloop and goods, when they appeared in Port Royal. After consulting with Governor Heywood, he freed the six pirates to honor the royal proclamation but confiscated their effects, departing from the more lenient procedures Bennet implemented simultaneously in Bermuda. In the meantime, Jamaican officials were unsure what to do about Hornigold, who had robbed a Dutch sloop, it was learned, on January 8, merely three days after the expiration of the Act of Grace. Perhaps fearing that the pardon might not apply to him, Hornigold slipped back to Providence.[72]

The second sloop sent by the Jamaican government received orders to go directly to Providence, and the governor handpicked two men to carry out the mission. One was Nathaniel Hudson, a mariner who bounced between New York and Jamaica and had once served as Henry Jennings's quartermaster on the *Bersheba*. Hudson had also spent considerable time at Providence, so he knew the pirates well and might be able to convince them to surrender. Joining Hudson was William Smith. Born in Bermuda, Smith was also a wandering mariner who eventually settled in New York and became a prominent sea captain and merchant (explained in more detail in chapter 7). Armed with a copy of the royal proclamation, Hudson and Smith left Jamaica in late January, arriving at Providence about February 1, 1718. The following day, to the beat of a drum, he summoned the pirates to the home of Peter Miller, where John Bennet had conducted a similar ritual six weeks earlier. Standing atop a cask of wine, Hudson "read his majesty's said proclamation to all the pyrates then present," estimated to be three to four hundred persons. Hudson "exhorted" the men to accept the pardon, "which was so graciously offered them."[73]

Now having been informed twice, the Act of Grace remained a divisive issue among the pirates. Some individuals, like Hornigold, had attacked shipping after the January 5 expiration of the clemency deadline, so they probably feared that surrendering would lead nowhere but the gallows. Others expressed a deep-seated distrust of their government and simply seem to have preferred life as a pirate. One such individual was John Augur, who was on hand to hear Hudson's exhortations on February 1. Augur refused the pardon, saying that "the king is an old man and can't live long," implying that it would no longer be in effect if the monarchy soon changed hands. Augur argued that if they accepted it, they would lose "all wee have taken" and be forced "to work" unless they could cut a better deal with the government.[74]

Along with Augur's reported words, an article published about three months later in a London newspaper captured that same divisive spirit. "Two parties," it was reported, had formed at Providence. One had accepted the Act of Grace and, as a sign of their loyalty to the Crown, had raised the Union Jack above the fort. In defiance, leaders of the other party pulled down the British standard and replaced it with the death's head, or the Jolly Roger, and had even seized the vessels that had been sent there to offer the pardon. "They had held several consultations in what manner it was best for them to obtain the King's Pardon," the author continued, stating that the leading pirates "had come [to] a resolution to strengthen the island" so that they would not be surprised by a man-of-war. With a show of force, the pirates might "thereby obtain a general pardon with liberty (without being obliged to make any restitution)" so that they could "retire with the best of their effects" and leave Providence and go to "the neighbouring British plantations."[75] Although this anonymous letter probably reflected hearsay and embellished the purported seizure of vessels, it nevertheless captured the same fears pirates had expressed to Lieutenant Governor Bennet about the status of their property.

Into this turmoil stepped Captain Vincent Pearse. Born in Chatham, Kent, but raised in London, Pearse had a privileged upbringing. His father, Thomas Pearse, was a commissioner of the Navy Board, a position his brother (also named Thomas) later held.[76] Pearse was relatively young and untested when he assumed command of the *Phoenix* in October 1715, in the midst of the Jacobite rising of that year. The tense political situation contributed to the rough start Pearse experienced when he assumed command of the vessel. One of the first tasks before him was to recruit sailors, so he sent his first mate, John Daniel, with a drum into the streets of London, having him cry out "God save King George" at passersby. As made his way up Tower Street, an angry mob formed and shouted "God damn King George" back at Daniel. A scrum ensued, in which the proprietor of a local coffeehouse kicked and destroyed the drum. Pearse lost valuable time trying to prosecute the man who assaulted his first mate.[77] About a month later, Pearse received orders to sail to the river Elbe and inspect ships departing from Hamburg that were suspected to be carrying arms and ammunition to Jacobite rebels in Scotland. From there, the *Phoenix* sailed to the Scottish port of Leith in order to convey supplies to the army fighting against the rebels. The *Phoenix* bounced around several home stations for the next year before winding up at Sheerness, a port in the Thames estuary.[78] There, Pearse's carpenter accidently destroyed thirty pounds of gunpowder when he let seawater into the *Phoenix* in an attempt to "sweeten" the wooden hull. The carpenter's ensuing court-martial must have also caused Pearse to wonder if commanding a navy vessel was more headache than it was worth.[79]

In April 1717 Pearse received orders to sail to New York, where the *Phoenix* finally arrived in August. For the next two months, Pearse guided convoys of merchant ships for their protection as they sailed to Britain, making one stop at Annapolis, Maryland, and another at Virginia before returning to New York on October 30.[80] On January 25 Pearse received a letter from navy secretary Josiah Burchett, in which he included six copies of the royal proclamation. Two days later, he attended a meeting of the New York Council, whose members asked Pearse what might be the most effective means of publicizing the pardon. Pearse recommended that he sail to the Bahamas so that he could speak directly with the pirates. On that recommendation, the council ordered Pearse to sail there as soon as possible, expecting him to return in late March.[81] On February 5 Pearse hired a pilot, one Benjamin Bill of New York. Bill was a seasoned ship captain who had been sailing to the Bahamas since at least 1702, and he knew those waters well. On February 6 the *Phoenix* departed from New York.[82]

Pearse arrived at Providence at ten o'clock on the morning of February 23. A motley crew awaited him, as indicated by the "colors of all nations" flying on the vessels anchored there. Seemingly tentative at first, Pearse sent Lieutenant Richard Symonds ashore with a white flag of truce. When Symonds stepped on shore, he was met by "some hundreds" of pirates, who conducted him to the ruins of the old fort, where a Union Jack was flying. The first men to speak with Symonds were Josiah Burgess and Matthew Musson, who asked him "What news?" and inquired if the ship on the horizon was a man-of-war. Symonds reported that it was the *Phoenix* commanded by Vincent Pearse, and then he displayed six copies of the royal proclamation he had lodged in his pocket. Symonds asked the assembled pirates if they would accept the pardon, to which they responded in the affirmative. At the same time, the pirates informed Symonds that "they had accepted of them [pardons] before," clearly invoking the preceding Bermudian and Jamaican missions to Providence. Burgess and Musson then granted the *Phoenix* permission to anchor in Nassau harbor. Symonds returned to the *Phoenix* later that afternoon, and Pearse summarized the encounter by stating that the pirates had received Symonds "with much civility" and expressed "a great deal of joy" about the offer of clemency.

In addition to expressing their intent to surrender, Burgess and Musson played a key role in thwarting a plot headed by John Augur, the same man who previously refused the pardon. A few days before Pearse's arrival, Augur had stolen the *Lark* from Francis Lesley, assembling a crew of about fifteen men who anchored the sloop near a small key several miles from Nassau. Burgess and Musson informed Symonds of the sloop's whereabouts and the criminal intentions of its crew, which compelled Captain Pearse to make a show of force to bring them in. That evening, Pearse guided a sloop in the direction of the *Lark*, which surrendered after Pearse fired cannon shots at it. Pearse returned to Providence with his prize the following morning. The pirate leaders convinced him to release Augur and his crew, thinking that a merciful gesture would compel many others to accept the pardon. Pearse complied.

The formal process of pardoning the pirates began on February 24, when Pearse finally arrived on shore at Nassau, making his temporary headquarters at the home of Josiah Burgess. The first to surrender were Burgess, Thomas Nichols, Francis Lesley, and Benjamin Hornigold. The four pirates theatrically delivered their swords to Pearse as a means of acknowledging their acceptance of the Act of Grace. Pearse reciprocated by returning their swords. After this exchange, their crews accepted pardons, a number of men that Pearse described as "a great many" pirates. Also present at that time was John Lewis, the Jamaican mariner who had robbed the Marquis de Navarres nearly three years earlier. Unlike the others, Lewis refused to deliver his sword to Pearse. When asked why he did not do so like the other pirate commanders, Lewis reportedly said, "He could not tell whether he should be safe in surrendering himself." Lewis, it turns out, had good reason to be fearful. The Act of Grace applied specifically to all piracies that occurred after midsummer (June 24) 1715, which could potentially exclude him because Lewis's crime had occurred around May 10 that year. For this reason, Lewis was reluctant to confess to piracy, rationalizing that his crime was merely a "breach of trust."[83] Although Lewis eventually accepted a pardon from Pearse, his status remained questionable. For several more days, contrite pirates continued to appear before Pearse, who granted more pardons.

By March 4, Burgess, Nichols, Lesley, and Hornigold had surrendered, along with 114 men said to form their "company." Pearse reported the good news to Secretary Burchett in a self-congratulatory letter he penned that same day. However, the naval captain did not have much good to say about the reformed pirates, describing them as a "parcel of unthinking people" who would have gone pirating again had he not arrived just in time. Pearse complained that, since he lacked sufficient force to bring them in, he had to resort to verbal "persuasion," and he reported the alarming news that he had just missed an opportunity to confront the pirate Edward Congdon, commander of the sloop *Dragon*, who had left eighteen days before to join ranks with Edward Thache.[84]

In the weeks that followed, more pirates trickled into Nassau to accept pardons. It is probable these included a number of ship captains and their crewmen who traded with pirates but who, in Pearse's words, "pretended they never did until the act of grace was published." After receiving their certificates from Pearse, the majority seem to have slipped away, hopping aboard vessels destined for other colonies. On a couple of occasions, the *Phoenix* sailed to protect outbound convoys of merchant ships, whose captains feared being taken by pirates lurking nearby. Although 209 men eventually surrendered to him, Pearse nevertheless was unable fully to suppress the piracy impulse. On March 18 Pearse reported that sixteen pirates had gone away on a sloop "with a design to go pirateing again." A day later, two dozen more men took a boat to join them, with circumstantial evidence indicating that the men in question formed part of Charles Vane's gang. On March 21 Pearse received reports that these pirates had taken a sloop from Jamaica, so he sent his pinnace to attack them. After exchanging some small arms fire, the pirates got away. Pearse called Nassau's inhabitants to a meeting on March 22, asking for their assistance in catching the runaway pirates. Pearse got little cooperation, causing him to complain that the people "seemed more inclined to help them [the pirates] than to reduce them."[85]

During the final leg of his stay, Pearse continued to grapple with rogue pirates. Perhaps not coincidentally, his logbook becomes somewhat muddled and difficult to follow. On March 24 Pearse spotted a pirate ship, which he was able to distinguish because it was flying a red flag—symbolizing they would offer "no quarter" to those who opposed them. Pearse also claimed to have been keeping company with a certain Jamaican sloop, which betrayed him by slipping away and turning pirate again. Somehow, this same Jamaican sloop managed to capture the *Lark* near Harbor Island, returning on March 31 to anchor east of Nassau. On April 1 Pearse reported that a small boat "with several hands on board" came into Nassau harbor. Pearse tried to intercept it by firing his guns, but it managed to make it ashore. On April 2 Pearse claimed that pirates had taken two trading sloops, and that same evening, the *Lark* was spotted flying a black flag. With these two pirate sloops still on the loose, the time had long passed since Pearse was expected to return to New York. So the *Phoenix* weighed anchor on April 9, sailing with a convoy of five sloops, four of which he said were "bound for the wrecks."

Sailing to New York, Pearse managed to stage one more show of force against the pirates. On April 10, near Abaco Island, the *Phoenix* captured a sloop trailing behind his convoy. Although it bore the name *John and Elizabeth*, Pearse was convinced that the vessel was actually a French ship that pirates had taken months before, and he found that it was carrying a cargo of Dutch cowhides stolen by Benjamin Hornigold. After seizing the vessel, Pearse put its captain, John Sipkins, along with several crew and passengers, on board the *Phoenix*, placing one of his own men on board to steer the *John and Elizabeth* to New York. After a stop in Virginia, the *Phoenix* and its prize arrived in New York harbor on May 19.[86] Pearse had completed his mission, but the drama surrounding his capture of the *John and Elizabeth* had only begun.

Pearse the Pirate Accomplice?

Back in New York, on June 2 Pearse wrote a lengthy letter to Secretary Burchett describing what had transpired in the Bahamas. He was proud to report the "voluntary" surrender of 209 men, enclosing a three-page list of their names that forms the basis of this book. At the same time, Pearse acknowledged that more than three hundred others had not accepted the Act of Grace and that the elusive Charles Vane and an unruly gang of about forty-five men had gone on the account again. In attempting to catch Vane, Pearse complained that he got no help from the people of Nassau. "I several times summoned the inhabitants together in His Majesty's name & used all the arguments possible to prevail with them to assist me in suppressing the said pirate," Pearse wrote, confiding that "they always rejected all methods I proposed." Not only had the inhabitants been unwilling to catch Vane, Pearse believed that they also "entertained and assisted them with provisions and necessaries." On several occasions, the inhabitants had displayed an outward hostility to government, and Pearse lamented not having a second man-of-war at his disposal, which he believed would have enabled him to prevent Vane "as also the rest from going out again." In that same letter, Pearse recounted his capture of the *John and Elizabeth*. He described it as "a French ship taken October last and now loaded with hides piratically taken from the Dutch since January 5," undoubtedly a reference to Benjamin Hornigold's last reported heist. The hide-filled sloop had been "in possession of some people who had been pirates," and Pearse intended to initiate a prize case against the *John and Elizabeth* "according to law."[87]

What Pearse did not reveal, however, is that on May 27 the New York Council had launched its own investigation of the *John and Elizabeth*.[88] Importantly, the council interviewed the crew and passengers aboard the *John and Elizabeth*, many of whom were New Yorkers who had accepted the pardon. The deponents included John Sipkins, the New Yorker who served as the sloop's captain, along with his pilot, Benjamin Bill, William Smith, Nathaniel Hudson, William Connor, and Thomas Nichols, all of whom had local ties. Rounding out the group was the Bermuda mariner Samuel Tynes, the vintner Peter Miller from Providence, and Thomas Odell, a former New Yorker who fled the colony to evade charges of counterfeiting money. Altogether, their words paint an unflattering portrait of Vincent Pearse, accusing him of being a lazy pirate catcher who conducted his own clandestine trade on the side. In their view, Pearse seized the *John and Elizabeth* on trumped-up charges to conceal his own wrongdoing.

In the eighteenth century, it was common knowledge that Royal Navy captains conducted illicit trade on the side while they were supposed to be on duty.[89] Vincent Pearse was no exception, and before leaving New York, he placed on board the *Phoenix* two hundred barrels of flour that he intended to sell. Pearse's clerk, Edmund Barret, also carried a barrel of flour and an unknown quantity of butter. The plan was to sell the cargo at St. Augustine, where Pearse believed it could be disposed of "for the best advantage."[90] After arriving at Nassau, Pearse sought to amass an even larger and more valuable cargo by trading with pirates. To facilitate these exchanges, Pearse frequented a tavern operated by one Alexander Leggatt, which served as a community hub. By eating and drinking with pirates, Pearse gained familiarity with them, and he began asking around for bargains. On one notable occasion, Pearse allegedly inquired if "he could get a piece of brocade" silk, prompting a search that eventually led to Charles Vane, who reportedly sold him some for around 300 pieces of eight per yard. In just a few days, Pearse obtained more unidentified goods that he intended to sell to the nearby Spanish.[91]

To conduct the trading voyage to St. Augustine, Pearse tapped his pilot, the New Yorker Benjamin Bill, and assembled a crew by calling on nine of his sailors from the *Phoenix*. To complete the company, Pearse and Bill recruited six other mariners—all reformed pirates, mostly New Yorkers—at Nassau. On March 10 Pearse had Captain Bill load his flour and other goods on board a sloop named the *John and Elizabeth*.[92] One of the key questions involves the origins and ownership of the sloop. The original *John and Elizabeth* of New York was a fifty-ton, six-gun sloop built in Connecticut in 1714. It was owned by four of the city's most prominent merchants: Justus Bosch, Abraham De Peyster, William Walton, and Nathan Simpson. Bosch had been a city council member and mayor. De Peyster at that time was a member of the colony's council, and importantly, he was the same man tasked with recording the depositions during the *John and Elizabeth* investigation. Since March 1716 John Sipkins had captained the *John and Elizabeth* and, in its last recorded voyage, cleared outbound from New York to Jamaica around mid-August 1717.[93] Sometime that fall, Thomas Nichols, who commanded a pirate sloop called *Baymen's Revenge*, seized the *John and Elizabeth* and all of its cargo. Sipkins, however, managed to keep his clearance papers and ship register, and he made his way to Providence. Pearse made copies of those papers, which Captain Bill used to give the appearance that the sloop in question was the *John and Elizabeth* of New York.[94]

The actual identity of the sloop was the subject of disagreement among the deponents. Nathaniel Hudson, William Smith, and Samuel Tynes insisted that the vessel was in fact the *Lark*, which Pearse had seized the day he arrived at Providence and restored for his own use.[95] Conversely, Thomas Nichols and William Connor claimed that the sloop was a French ship, the *St. Jacque*, taken by Connor and Edward Congdon the previous October. Nichols and Connor claimed they conducted the *St. Jacque* to Providence in November. Around mid-January, Sipkins purchased it from Congdon for £130 and negotiated a verbal agreement with Connor and Nichols to relinquish whatever interest they had in the vessel as members of Congdon's "company." Nichols and Connor may have asked for no money because by that time they had already resolved to accept the pardon and wanted no further share of their prizes.[96] As fellow New Yorkers, the deponents appear to have sympathized with Sipkins for losing the *John and Elizabeth*. William Smith, for instance, referred to Sipkins's recent "misfortunes," and Connor justified relinquishing his share of the vessel on the grounds that Sipkins "had suffered enough already."[97] Whichever story one believes, the vessel captained by Bill and loaded with Pearse's goods was not the original *John and Elizabeth* of New York, and Pearse knew it.[98] In fact, Pearse's own correspondence indicates that the reconstituted *John and Elizabeth*, at about 110 tons, was more than twice the size of the original vessel. It sailed to St. Augustine with its crew of sixteen men around March 14.

While Bill and his crew headed for St. Augustine, Pearse continued bargaining for pirate goods. One allegation was that Pearse loaned the pirate John Lewis his pinnace so that he could transfer some brandy from Peter Miller's home to the *Phoenix*.[99] Pearse later bought a "negro" slave from the pirate William South, as well as an anchor from another group of pirates. Pearse reportedly offered Richard Newland £200 for the purchase of a captured Dutch vessel named the *Nightsramble*, although Newland refused him and sank the ship.[100] Along with purchases of these kinds, a witness testified that Pearse had confiscated some bricks and tiles designated for the construction of a church, which was to be erected when Governor Rogers arrived.[101] Pearse also allowed Thomas Nichols and William Connor to load a thousand pounds of indigo onto the *Phoenix*. Pearse, it was alleged, was to have "a considerable part [of the indigo] at a reasonable rate"—in other words, a bribe.[102]

In addition to trading with pirates, Pearse antagonized the people of Nassau, and he may have contributed to their uncooperative and belligerent attitude. Sometime in late March, Pearse fired several of the *Phoenix*'s "great guns" toward the town, with one shot landing on shore. As one deponent put it, these shots caused "consternation" among the townspeople, who grumbled, "We believe that the man of war instead of making peace is come to make war."[103] By shooting his great guns into town, Pearse stirred a conspiracy against him. According to Nathaniel Hudson, a "confederacy" formed between pirates who had accepted the pardon and those who had not, and they had resolved to burn the *Phoenix*. Hudson later credited John Sipkins and Thomas Odell for thwarting the plot by standing firm in their support for Pearse, ordering Sipkins's men to go on board the *Phoenix* to help defend it.[104]

Meanwhile, Captain Bill and the erstwhile *John and Elizabeth* made it safely to St. Augustine, where they sold Pearse's cargo, netting him (as it was said) in excess of 2,100 pieces of eight and three gold ryals.[105] On the return voyage, however, on March 28, Charles Vane, who commanded two sloops and another canoe, confronted Bill's sloop. Vane detained the *John and Elizabeth* and its crew for about three days, robbing them of the money earned from the sale of goods at St. Augustine. During their detention, three men from the *Phoenix* decided to join Vane's crew. Pearse's men later blamed Captain Bill for not fighting back, insinuating that Bill's crew had been overly familiar with Vane. Other deponents thought they had no choice but to surrender because Vane offered no quarter to anyone who opposed him.[106] While Vane confiscated Pearse's share of the money, he restored to Benjamin Bill 110 pieces of eight and gave Thomas Graham (one of the pardoned pirates who formed part of the crew) eighty pieces of eight that they had earned from the sale of their own cargo.[107]

When Captain Bill limped back to Providence around April 1, Pearse was furious. He called Bill on board the *Phoenix*, where he conducted an interview, asking Bill "how he came to lose the said sloop in so shameful a manner." Despairing, Bill said "he wished he had been killed" and blamed Thomas Graham for falsely claiming that Vane would have offered them no quarter if they resisted.[108] In retribution, Pearse confiscated a chest that held the 300-odd pieces of eight that belonged to Bill and Graham. Pearse's seizure of the chest of silver caused "further exasperation" among many of the pirates on shore, contributing to the unrealized plot to burn the *Phoenix*.[109]

During his stay in Providence, which lacked a proper customs officer, Captain Pearse issued let passes enabling vessels to depart from Providence legally with their cargoes. It was alleged that on April 3 Pearse drew up one such let pass for John Sipkins, permitting him to load a cargo of cowhides on board the *John and Elizabeth* and sail to Holland. Although Pearse never confessed to issuing one to Sipkins, two of the deponents, Thomas Odell and William Smith, reproduced the text of the let pass:

> Permit the John and Elizabeth, John Sipkins master loaden with hides to pass for Holland without any let hindrances or molestation given under my hand on board his [Majesty's] ship Phoenix in Providence harbor no proper officer being appointed as yet for this port this third April 1718.[110]

Astonishingly, in separate depositions, each man reproduced the same words verbatim, while a third deponent, Thomas Nichols, managed to perform the same feat by recalling the wording of Sipkins's purchase agreement with Edward Congdon.[111] How and why these mariners were able to do this is subject to speculation. One theory is that the men colluded and rehearsed their stories while in detention. It is also possible that it exposes the extent to which persons of intelligence filled the ranks of mariners. Although these deponents were literate, memorization is a key component of oral cultures. It stands to reason that eighteenth-century mariners who still had one foot in an oral culture were able to activate that skill. Importantly, their power of recall may constitute evidence that mariners had to memorize agreements in order to protect themselves—that is, to keep track of their wages, the terms of purchase agreements, and the composition and quantity of their cargoes, which were subject to inspection. Perhaps, then, Odell and Smith committed Sipkins's let pass to memory because of its unconventional nature and their mistrust of Pearse, and because they anticipated needing to do so to conduct the voyage to Holland.

Further illustrating their complicated relationship, Pearse had to hire some of the very same pirates he had just pardoned to replace the *Phoenix*'s three crewmen who had abandoned him to join Charles Vane. In addition to hiring Benjamin Bill again as his pilot, Pearse added Bahamas native Benjamin Sims as a second pilot. Although never implicated for piracy himself, Sims knew the pirates of Providence intimately and might have been an accessory. Pearse also hired the pardoned pirate Thomas Graham, who sailed with Benjamin Bill to St. Augustine on the *John and Elizabeth* and had expressed unwillingness to fight Charles Vane. Graham eventually left the *Phoenix* to serve on the HMS *Shoreham*, but Griffith Williams, who served as one of the ship's carpenters, filled his spot.[112]

The *Phoenix*, sailing with a convoy of sloops, departed Providence on April 8. The rechristened *John and Elizabeth* sailed a day later under the command of John Sipkins and caught up to the *Phoenix* on April 10. Despite having given Sipkins a let pass, Pearse seized the sloop, forced its crew onto the man-of-war, and placed his gunner and a few men on board to sail the captured sloop to New York. Making their way north, Pearse stopped at Virginia, picking up nine hogsheads of tobacco. One deponent revealed that Pearse had engaged in some shady behavior during their stop there, alleging that he paid customs duties on only five of the hogsheads and quarreled with Virginia's customs collector, even brandishing his sword when the collector tried to arrest him. Several of the deponents also questioned why Pearse gave preferential treatment to the pirate John Lewis, with whom he interacted "with much familiarity." Lewis had free reign to come and go as he pleased from the *Phoenix*, and some observed that Lewis spent much of his time holed up with Pearse in his cabin, where Lewis even slept. Others mentioned that the two frequented a tavern together in Hampton, Virginia.[113]

Returning to New York on May 19, Pearse continued bestowing favors on pirates like John Lewis, allowing him to go fishing with some of his subordinate officers. At New York City, Pearse also allowed Lewis to haul ashore a cabinet that was rumored to have "much gold" in it.[114] Meanwhile, William Connor and Thomas Nichols unloaded seven hundred pounds of indigo, some of which was believed to be Pearse's. Connor and Nichols apparently sold the indigo in New York City. In contrast to the treatment those men received, Benjamin Bill, John Sipkins, and some of the other mariners taken from the *John and Elizabeth* were forcibly detained on board the *Phoenix* for about eight days. Only on May 27 did Pearse release them.[115] Between May 27 and June 9, the former crew and passengers from the *John and Elizabeth*, as well as three of Pearse's crew from the *Phoenix*, gave their depositions before the council.

Pearse's correspondence and logbook, and the depositions taken in New York, seemingly depict two alternative universes, and we may never know exactly what transpired during the *Phoenix*'s important mission to the Bahamas. If we are to believe Pearse's side of the story, the mission was a resounding success. Despite facing stiff resistance from a motley crew of "young, resolute, wicked fellows," Pearse was able to convince 209 pirates, many of whom had evaded the law for several years, to give up a life of crime. Pearse deftly applied force when necessary to apprehend the *Lark* and the *John and Elizabeth*, confiscating piratically obtained hides from John Sipkins, a confessed pirate who had also accepted the pardon. If, however, we are to believe some of the mariners who testified against Pearse, we may conjure the image of an unscrupulous ship captain who traded with pirates, and cozied up to them when it suited his interests, only to turn on the pirates in order to silence them.

Predictably, Pearse's side of the story prevailed. The *John and Elizabeth* was condemned and the hides were sold, benefiting Pearse and the crew of the *Phoenix*, who were to receive shares of the monies raised. Although Pearse claimed that the sloop had been condemned in vice-admiralty court in New York, no records of those proceedings survive.[116] Ultimately, the rechristened *John and Elizabeth* fell into the hands of New York merchant Henry Lane, the same man who provisioned the *Phoenix* for the voyage to the Bahamas. That summer, Lane allowed Pearse to store supplies on board the *John and Elizabeth* while Pearse's crew was careening the *Phoenix*. Clearly, a degree of familiarity existed between the two men, who guarded the secret of the sloop's true identity.[117] Perhaps it was to Pearse's advantage that New York's attorney general, who also presided over the vice-admiralty court, was Lewis Morris. A preeminent landholder and merchant, Morris also served in the New York Assembly and later became the governor of New Jersey. In just a few short years, Morris would become Pearse's father-in-law.[118] And, while Sipkins lost his ship and the cowhides (which Sipkins eventually confessed had come from Benjamin Hornigold), he and the other suspected pirates faced no real repercussions for their actions.[119] Sipkins, after all, had been employed by Councilor Abraham De Peyster, whose investigations gave the New York government ample reason to exonerate them because Pearse had set them up. Sipkins, Connor, Nichols, Smith, and the rest quickly resumed their careers as merchant ship captains and, in time, even managed to become respectable.

While the details surrounding Pearse's activities can be called into question, his 1718 mission to the Bahamas nevertheless was a critical turning point in the war on piracy. Although the offer of pardons was not a singular event, and piracy and illicit trade continued, Pearse managed to gain the submission of a large number of pirates, including highly influential individuals such as Hornigold, Cockram, Williams, and even, briefly, Charles Vane. Pearse's mission also proved to be a turning point in the lives of the pirates themselves. At this critical juncture, those offered the pardon faced a choice: prolong a life of crime or fall in line with imperial goals. Pirates who surrendered—as well as those who traded with them—tended to possess the most social, political, and economic capital, which is why their lives generated more evidence in the paper trail. These men chose to surrender because they had much more to gain by resuming legitimate seafaring careers. Historians typically credit governing officials and merchants on both sides of the Atlantic for the relatively quick eradication of piracy within the following decade, but the pirates themselves made choices that facilitated its demise, enabling British trade and imperial expansion to flourish in coming decades. Importantly, the 1718 mission proved to be a key turning point in the history of the Bahamas, as the pardoning of the pirates, as well as their reformed behavior, helped disperse the truly hardened criminals and facilitate the institution of a royal government under Woodes Rogers.

CHAPTER 5

"Pirates Expelled—Commerce Restored"

Peter Goudet was a marked man. Literally. When Vincent Pearse compiled his list of pardoned pirates, he carefully drew a cross next to the names of twenty men who had "gone out a pirateing again."[1] Among them was Goudet, whose surname might have rung a bell for Pearse. Born in London in 1698, Goudet descended from French Protestant immigrants who had arrived in the city roughly a decade before. John Goudet, the future pirate's father, operated a prosperous mercantile business in the parish of St. Swithin London Stone. In 1697, however, the elder Goudet came under suspicion for illegal trading with the French during wartime. Parliament later impeached Goudet in a celebrated case, still cited by legal scholars, that received ample coverage in newspapers and pamphlets.[2] Although much about Peter's childhood cannot be known, it is clear that, despite his father's troubles, he received a good education. How he ended up as a pirate in the Bahamas is also unknown, but Pearse's etching implies that he sailed with Charles Vane and was probably involved in apprehending the erstwhile sloop *John and Elizabeth*.

Despite his reputation as a pirate, Goudet embarked on an improbable career as a Crown bureaucrat in the Bahamas. Early on, he earned the trust of Governor Rogers, who occasionally employed Goudet to keep the colony's accounts.[3] In 1723 Goudet received a formal appointment as clerk to Rogers's successor, Governor George Phenney, and soon emerged as one of the Bahamas' "principal inhabitants." Goudet received appointments simultaneously as the colony's treasurer, the fort's storekeeper, and collector of customs, a post he held for several years.[4] In 1729 Goudet was elected to the Bahamas inaugural legislative assembly, representing the island of Providence where he made his home.[5]

As he embarked on a career in government, Goudet established himself in the mercantile business and started a family. Throughout the early to mid-1720s he owned three vessels, but Goudet never captained his own ships, nor does he ever appear to have gone to sea much. Instead, he employed local mariners to guide his vessels, favoring South Carolina as a destination for trade, although occasionally venturing to Bermuda, Pennsylvania, and Jamaica. He traded mostly in local commodities like salt, logwood, brasiletto, and turtle shells. On return voyages, his captains typically brought home flour, beef, butter, and other foodstuffs produced in the mainland colonies. As his role in government increased, however, Goudet appears to have retreated from the shipping trade by selling all but one of his sloops.[6] In 1728 he wed Mary Hariott, and they had at least two children. By the early 1730s, Goudet also owned roughly ten slaves. While he continued to self-identify as a merchant, his slaveholding indicates that Goudet had redirected his efforts toward planting indigo and cotton.[7]

Although he achieved a measure of success, Goudet appears to have gradually become disenchanted with life in the Bahamas and stumbled into several controversies that left him dishonored. Losing his position as customs collector in 1729 may have prompted this downward spiral. Perhaps seeking a fresh start, Goudet relinquished his treasury duties in 1731 and received a position as the collector of customs for the newly established port of St. George, Winyaw Bay in South Carolina, where he spent the better part of 1732–33.[8] He did not do his job well. A naval officer who conducted a visitation there in 1734 complained that records at Winyaw Bay "were not duly kept" by the previous naval officer, implicating Goudet as the collector working under his direct supervision.[9] In fact, Goudet left only scant traces of his presence in South Carolina, including a brief mention in the colony's newspaper.[10]

On his return to Nassau in November 1733, Goudet found himself embroiled in a property dispute involving a town lot and building that served as the colony's jail. Goudet had presumably purchased it several years before from another inhabitant, and even established occupancy. Colony officials, however, questioned Goudet's "pretended title" and asked him to relinquish the property. Goudet refused and challenged them to sue him in court. A few weeks later, the recently installed governor, Richard Fitzwilliam, and his council charged Goudet with piracy, also accusing him of inciting a mutiny among the troops stationed at the fort. Goudet died sometime before September 18, 1735. Despite his recent troubles, Goudet, the owner of two town lots and two "back lots" in Nassau, remained among the five wealthiest Bahamians at the time he died.[11]

What does a pirate do when he retires? How does a former pirate lair transform itself into a functioning civil society under the rule of law? Although Peter Goudet became the most visible of the pardoned pirates who remained in the Bahamas, his story is not unique. Of the 209 men on Pearse's list, about fifty made homes in the Bahamas. A few were lifelong inhabitants, but many others, like Goudet, had arrived there only recently. Some left after a few years, typically to evade creditors. Most who remained worked as common seafarers, operating trading vessels while also trying to eke out a living raking salt, fishing wrecks, angling, hunting sea turtles, harvesting dyewoods, and scavenging for ambergris. Like Goudet, they owned ships, married and raised families, paid taxes, and some even held minor positions in government. And while a celebrated handful returned to piracy, the vast majority avoided serious legal entanglements for the remainder of their lives, which in many cases were tragically short. Some former pirates, in fact, turned on their own kind and were instrumental in reforming the colony. It was with some justification, then, that Woodes Rogers had the Bahamas adopt for its motto the Latin phrase *Piratis expulsis commercia restituta*—pirates expelled, commerce restored.

As Rogers recognized, though, the transformation of the Bahamas and its people was a gradual process. Piracy steadily declined after the institution of royal government in 1718, but much remained the same for many years after. The inhabitants, seafarers to the core, at times were reluctant to volunteer for public works projects, like restoring Nassau's dilapidated fort. Nor were they inclined to establish plantations, as the colony's promoters had intended as a means for transforming the Bahamian economy. British pirates may have been (mostly) expelled, but peace with the Spanish colonies was tenuous. Warfare broke out again in 1719, and many of the pardoned pirates answered the call as privateers, conducting retaliatory raids that cost some of them their lives. Spanish *guardacostas* harassed the Bahamas regularly for decades to come, sometimes targeting ships manned or owned by former pirates. Even for those who largely avoided illegal activity, the shadow of piracy lingered. Peter Goudet, for one, suffered the indignity of having the charge of piracy trotted out against him many years after the fact when it conveniently suited those to whom he stood opposed. As in other ways, Goudet was not alone, with even the colony's high-ranking councilors facing such charges on two noteworthy occasions. Although the arrival of Governor Rogers was a pivotal event in the history of Bahamas piracy, eradicating it was a drawn-out process indicating the gradual nature of the Bahamas' cultural transformation.

Expulsis Piratis

The arrival of Woodes Rogers in the Bahamas was unquestionably a transformative event in the colony's history. His life is well documented. Born around 1679 in the port town of Poole in Dorset, England, Rogers grew up in a seafaring family. His father was a prosperous merchant ship captain who owned several vessels and specialized in the North American trade, particularly the cod fishery based in Newfoundland. The Rogers family later moved to Bristol, and he spent the next several years at sea, most likely sailing to Ireland, the European continent, and perhaps Newfoundland. He was known to have been an avid reader of buccaneer William Dampier's account of his world travels, and, during the War of the Spanish Succession, Dampier later approached Rogers with a plan for conducting an ambitious privateering voyage. In 1708 Rogers received a commission placing him in charge of two ships, the *Duke* and *Dutchess*. Rogers famously circumnavigated the globe, targeting Spanish shipping in the Pacific and making attacks on land. On his return home, Rogers penned an account of his adventures, titled *A Cruising Voyage around the World* (1712), undoubtedly inspired by Dampier's earlier work. The book sold well, and Rogers was a celebrity even before becoming governor of the Bahamas.[12]

Bahamians such as John Graves had been pleading for the institution of royal governance since the turn of the eighteenth century, but credit for making that a reality goes to London merchant Samuel Buck, who in 1717 formed a partnership named the Bahamas Company and proposed resettling and fortifying the islands under royal rule. Rogers had proposed a similar venture for Madagascar, but by the summer of 1717 he entered into the Bahamas partnership and was actively lobbying to become its governor. Rogers received his appointment that fall, and he and the copartners spent the next several months preparing for the voyage. A small squadron of four merchant ships, a Royal Navy sloop, and two men-of-war departed England in late April 1718. After stops in Madeira and Barbados, the squadron reached the Bahamas on July 25.[13] That evening, the HMS *Rose* entered Nassau harbor, accompanied by the *Shark* sloop.[14] The pirate Charles Vane famously fired on the two Royal Navy vessels, and around midnight he set one of his prize ships on fire and cut the cables in an attempt to burn them. Vane meanwhile escaped, slipping away in the early morning hours of July 26 in a sloop "wearing a black flag" manned by ninety crew. Rogers had tried to stop them, but Vane's sloop "out sayl'd the two that I sent to chase them hence," which caused Vane to fire "guns of defiance" as he left Nassau harbor.[15] The governor and his entourage made landfall the next day. Captain George Pomeroy of the *Shark* perceived that the "marooners," as they called themselves, received the governor with "a great deal of seeming joy." Rogers similarly commented on the "many tokens of joy" the Bahamians expressed "for the re-introduction of government."[16]

Forming a government was the first of many tasks that befell Rogers when he arrived on shore to read publicly his commission as governor. In addition to the chief executive, the new Bahamas government was to consist of a twelve-man council, six of whom had been appointed from among the new settlers who had accompanied Rogers. The governor was to fill the remaining six vacancies with local inhabitants. The problem, as Rogers conceived of it, was where to find six trustworthy men in a colony overflowing with former pirates. "After I had made the necessary enquiries after the characters of the inhabitants," Rogers wrote, "I got information of a few that were the least encouragers of trading" with the pirates.[17] Six of these "least encouragers" of piracy completed the council.

Governor Rogers and the council met for the first time on August 2, when each of the twelve members swore the oath of allegiance to King George. They got down to business three days later, passing two resolutions: one to repair the dilapidated fort, and another to clear all the "brush and scrub" growing within a gunshot of it.[18] The work progressed slowly, however, due to an unspecified sickness that inflicted the colony and claimed the lives of two council members. Many of the soldiers from the independent company rapidly sickened, as well as some recently arrived settlers. By October eighty-six people were dead.[19] At the same time, Rogers never fully trusted the former pirates. He complained about their lack of a work ethic and their general unwillingness to submit to authority, claiming that they were "so addicted to idleness that they would almost choose rather to starve than work."[20]

Notwithstanding the stereotype of the lazy pirate, without their active assistance, transforming the Bahamas might have required a significantly greater amount of administrative effort, bloodshed, and property loss. John Cockram, for instance, drafted a map of all the Bahamas Islands and a more detailed sketch of Nassau harbor, which Rogers described as "indifferently well done."[21] However, one of the most overlooked, yet important, contributions from former pirates was an ad hoc court of admiralty that was called to determine the fate of one of Charles Vane's prize ships and some of his stolen cargo. Around July, Vane and his crew apprehended a French brigantine, the *St. Martin* of Bordeaux. Naval officers impounded the vessel on

August 7 and found on board wine, flour, and beef. In the meantime, they identified four sloops in Nassau harbor containing, collectively, 112 hogsheads of Vane's sugar. Two of these sloop captains had received pardons from Vincent Pearse in March. One was Robert Brown of Rhode Island, who had sixteen of the hogsheads on board his sloop, the *Eagle*. The other was William Harris of Charlestown, Massachusetts, whose sloop *Dove* contained twenty hogsheads. John Fred of New York, who had been trading with pirates for two years and never been caught, concealed thirty-six hogsheads on board the sloop *Ulster*, while New Englander John Draper had forty hogsheads on board the sloop *Drake*. A fifth vessel, the *Flying King* of South Carolina, also had sugar from it impounded, but Captain Joseph Parmenter escaped before standing trial.

Rogers likely learned about the contraband sugar from former pirates. One probable informant is Josiah Burgess, whom Governor Rogers appointed to a five-man commission authorized to seize and appraise the sugars. Another of the governor's accomplices was Othenias Davis, one of Henry Jennings's former crew. In addition to appraising the wine, flour, and beef from the *St. Martin*, Davis also conducted the sale of the goods, keeping track of incoming money and submitting invoices to members of the council. Although they were willing to assist in the apprehension of some of the piratically obtained goods, it is clear that neither Burgess and Davis, nor any of the other former pirates, wanted to subject the four sloop captains to the full force of the law. During the admiralty proceedings that followed on September 1–5, all four men were acquitted because no one at Providence was willing to testify against them. Captain Peter Chamberlain of the HMS *Rose*, who made a transcript of the proceedings, recorded in rote fashion that "no evidence appearing" rather than their innocence is what let them off the hook. The four men merely had to surrender the impounded sugar and return home with goods that were "properly theirs."[22]

Much like Vincent Pearse before him, Governor Rogers's success derived from his willingness to refrain from exercising the full extent of his power. Later, Rogers wrote to the Board of Trade asking them to "intercede" with the king "to procure [for the pirates] the same favors as Governor Bennet procur'd for those that surrendered to him at Bermuda."[23] Specifically, Bennet had provided the pirates with written certificates that served as "their security when they have occasion to visit any other settlement."[24] Such instruments were necessary for any mariner hoping to resume legitimate trading without facing arrest in other colonies. Importantly, Rogers realized that the pirates surrendered on the condition that they could keep the stolen goods they had accumulated over the last couple of years. Rogers learned this the hard way; Charles Vane defied the governor on his arrival specifically because Rogers at first would not guarantee that he could keep his prize goods.[25] As Rogers explained, he did not "seize many things that I might have laid my hands on because I would not quarrel at the time of my mens great sickness," fearing that the pirates would "send us all back again." By not taking full advantage of his position as vice admiral (a title he held simultaneously as governor), Rogers was able to "stop several here that would have been out a pirating afresh."[26]

As Rogers indicated, going easy on the pirates was not due simply to his discretion but rather because of the weakness of his infant government. For one thing, the widespread sickness of the soldiers made it increasingly difficult for the independent company to complete work assignments, much less defend the islands. Governor Rogers also lost the protection of the naval vessels that had accompanied him. Perhaps fearing for the health of his own crew, Captain Whitney's *Milford* left the Bahamas after spending only about three weeks there, departing on August 15. George Pomeroy of the *Shark* sloop joined him that same day, leaving behind only Captain Whitney and the crew of the *Rose*. Whitney later reported that Rogers had begged him to stay longer, stating that he was "not safe" due to the departure of the other man-of-war, uncertain health of the soldiers, and lack of a fort. Despite Rogers's plea, the *Rose* departed for New York on September 15, leaving the governor without a naval presence.[27]

To confront the pirates, Rogers had no choice but to rely on the services of the pardoned men. The immediate threat came from Charles Vane, who established a new base at Green Turtle Key, near Abaco Island. From there, Vane's small squadron, said to consist of three vessels and manned by ninety crew, continued to harass passing ships, seizing two that had recently sailed from South Carolina. Around mid-August Rogers received word that Vane had returned to Green Turtle Key with his prize ships, and he wanted to find some means of apprehending him.[28] Rogers was at first leery of appointing former pirates to do the job. "Should their old friends [pirates] have strength enough to design to attack me," he observed, "I much doubt whether I should find one half to joyn me." Nevertheless, he perceived that there were "severall good men [at Providence] that may be relied on." "Since I had no strength to do better," Rogers continued, he appointed Benjamin Hornigold to spy on, and perhaps capture, Vane. Governor Rogers indicates that Hornigold left Providence on August 17 and was gone a full three weeks. In the meantime Rogers heard no news from Hornigold, which caused him to question the former pirate's allegiances. "I was afraid he was either taken by Vane or begun his old practice of pirating again," Rogers thought, "which was the general opinion here in his absence." Evidently, few of the former pirates fully trusted Hornigold either.[29]

Rogers was pleasantly surprised, however, when Hornigold returned to Providence around September 6 with a seized sloop, a prisoner, and some useful intelligence. Hornigold reported that he had lurked near Green Turtle Key, spending most of his time "concealed" in an attempt to surprise Vane or some of his men. Although Hornigold could not apprehend Vane, he learned about the size of his squadron and identified the prize ships he had recently apprehended. Hornigold's prisoner was probably the commander of the sloop *Wolf*, Nicholas Woodale, who had been trading with Vane at Green Turtle Key and was caught with about seventy-five pounds' worth of stolen goods. Several weeks later, after learning that Vane had abandoned the area, Rogers again dispatched Hornigold, together with John Cockram, to retrieve stranded mariners and goods left on board one of Vane's prizes.[30]

Rogers understood that the former pirate's faithful adherence to his orders provided an important symbolic boost to his efforts to institute law and order. Yet Hornigold's actions also had a divisive effect on the pirate community, continuing the self-selecting process of differentiation between committed hard-core criminals and those who wanted to leave their pirating pasts behind. According to Rogers, Hornigold "disobliged his old friends [the pirates] by seizing this vessel [the *Wolf* sloop]," adding that it "divides the people here and makes me stronger than I expected."[31]

Following the unsuccessful search for Vane and the adjudication of the *St. Martin* of Bordeaux case, Rogers and his council finally were able to intensify their efforts to rebuild the fort. The biggest challenge was finding the building supplies and labor to do so. On September 20 the council issued an order requiring all able-bodied men to bring ten "straight sticks" of wood to the construction site. Eight days later the council issued orders for them to report to the fort to begin construction. Although the work assignment was technically mandatory, the council provided a loophole whereby anyone who donated ten pounds of silver plate to the government could earn an exemption.[32] It is not known if anyone benefited from this loophole, but it stands to reason that some of the pardoned pirates might have had the resources to avoid work, contributing to Rogers's unshakable perception that the inhabitants were "very lazy."[33] Reconstruction of the fort proceeded nonetheless, with most of the activity happening during a fourteen-day stretch in October.

More so than a devotion to the government, the lingering threat of Spanish attacks on the Bahamas ultimately compelled enough men to comply with the work order. The same day Rogers landed at Providence, a Spanish force eradicated an English settlement on Cat Island, with reports indicating that they spared neither women nor children. In recent months, at least three British sloops had suffered attacks in nearby waters, and their commanders had reported each incident to Governor Rogers, who took their depositions.[34] Word of these attacks promoted an "innate thirst of revenge on the Spaniard" that caused at least a critical mass of individuals to work on the fort with "zeal." Rogers perceived that a degree of reverse psychology contributed to that zeal, for by reconstructing the fort, "they forgot they were at the same time strengthening a curb for themselves." With the fort now in a "tenable" state, Rogers sensed that his infant government was stronger and that he was in a position to do more to eradicate the vestiges of piracy on the island.[35]

Early in Rogers's tenure as governor, Charles Vane posed the most significant threat to the colony, and rumors indicated that he and Stede Bonnet were planning to conduct a joint operation against it. Those attacks never materialized, but the colony did face a homegrown piracy threat, which famously led to the execution of eight men at Providence. That drama began in early October, when Governor Rogers outfitted three vessels and ordered their commanders to conduct a trading voyage to Cuba, where they might procure livestock and other provisions needed to feed the colonists and soldiers. Henry White, a former pirate who received his pardon in Bermuda, commanded the schooner *Batchelor's Adventure*. William Greenway meanwhile commanded the sloop *Lancaster*, and John Augur, another pardoned man who fomented the stillborn plot to attack Vincent Pearse, was placed in charge of the sloop *Mary*, a vessel owned by another reformed pirate, David Sword. The crews manning these vessels had recently all been pardoned for piracy by Governor Rogers. In addition to Augur, Barbadian Dennis McCarty and Englishman George Rouncifull received pardons from Vincent Pearse the previous spring.

The small fleet left Providence around October 5, first sailing to Green Turtle Key to hunt feral hogs. The night of October 6, mariner Phineas Bunce orchestrated a mutiny against the ship captains, and he recruited Augur and McCarty, who assumed leading roles. Meanwhile, Bunce and his followers marooned the loyal crewmen of the three vessels on Green Turtle Key, leaving them with few provisions. The pirates next sailed for Long Island, one of the smaller outlying Bahamian islands, and for several weeks terrorized the local population. Around late October, Spanish *guardacostas* attacked the pirates, killing three of them and wounding others, including the ringleader, Phineas Bunce. The pirates had little choice but to submit, and the Spanish commander, supposedly an Irish expatriate known as "Turn Joe," interviewed the prisoners and determined that some of them were forced men. Turn Joe accordingly gave them a Spanish launch, placing them in charge of conducting it, and the mortally wounded Bunce, to Providence. The remaining pirates, now under the direction of John Augur, limped to a key off the island of Exuma. Around November 4, the forced men and Bunce arrived before Governor Rogers to report what had happened. Bunce confessed everything and died the next day. Rogers immediately sent a vessel to Green Turtle Key to retrieve White, Greenway, and the other marooned men. At the same time, he sent Benjamin Hornigold and John Cockram to Exuma to find the stranded pirates. By mid-November, Hornigold and Cockram returned with thirteen captive pirates, and now the question was what to do with them.[36]

Timing was crucial to Rogers and the council's ultimate decision to try the men in a court of vice-admiralty. Soon after the apprehension of the suspected pirates, Governor Rogers learned that the pirate Stede Bonnet had been captured and that more than twenty of his crew had been tried and executed in South Carolina. Although Governor Rogers's commission as governor did not expressly grant him the power to execute pirates, the council determined it was the unwritten intent to allow Rogers the same authority exercised in a neighboring colony. The council's decision also hinged on the colony's ability to defend itself in the event the former pirates in their midst decided to attack in order to free their comrades. The recently repaired fort, although still somewhat lacking in material and manpower, nevertheless served as a bulwark against such an attack. Importantly, the guard sloop *Delicia*, commanded by the former pirate Josiah Burgess, had recently returned to Nassau harbor after an abortive effort to find Charles Vane. The *Delicia*'s sixty soldiers and sailors provided yet more of a deterrent to any former pirates who might forcibly object to the vice-admiralty proceedings. Delaying the trial, they mused, would only invite a jailbreak, so the proceedings began just a week later, on December 8.[37]

The trial and execution of pirates at Nassau in December 1718 is well known, but for the purposes of this study, it is important to emphasize the active and passive roles played by pardoned pirates. Here too, we find a division between those who actively assisted in the prosecution and others who were clearly ambivalent about executing men not so different from themselves. Those who most energetically served the anti-piracy cause were Hornigold and Cockram, who apprehended the prisoners before the bar. Also, Josiah Burgess served as a member of the vice-admiralty court and thus positioned himself to condemn his former accomplices. Conversely, two of the reformed pirates on Pearse's list served as witnesses in the trial, and each appear to have tried exonerating or lessening the sentences of the accused. For instance, on December 10 Thomas Terrill testified on behalf of John Hipps. Previously other witnesses had testified that he was a forced man, and Terrill reinforced this perception by describing Hipps as an "honest man" who once suppressed a mutiny while aboard a trading vessel. That same day, Benjamin Hornigold testified briefly on behalf of Dennis McCarty. Although he did not presume McCarty's innocence, Hornigold described him as contrite, noting that McCarty did not resist when he arrested him at Exuma. Rather, Hornigold reported, McCarty was the "first one taken" and appeared to "throw himself, and to have dependence, on the mercy of the Governor."[38] Mercy, however, would not be forthcoming for most of the prisoners. John Hipps was acquitted, and the young George Rouncifull was spared at the gallows, but eight others would die at the hands of the executioner two days later, on Friday, December 12.

Written descriptions of the ritually staged execution of the eight men reveal the tension present at that time. This no doubt derived from governing officials' fear for their safety; the roughly one hundred people in attendance were pardoned pirates who, as the author of the *General History* observed, avoided the "same fate" only by virtue of "his Majesty's Act of Grace."[39] The morning of the execution, the condemned were called individually before the Governor and Council, who asked them if they wanted to relieve their consciences of any "actions committed and yet unknown to the world"—a strategy to solicit confessions of other crimes. Interestingly, the council also asked the men if they knew about "any conspiracy against the government," whose representatives perceived that the inhabitants might revolt.

The execution took place at ten o'clock in the fort, where a makeshift gallows had been erected on a foundation of three barrels of wine. The prisoners were released from their irons, and the provost marshal escorted them to the top of the fort's ramparts, which faced the sea. Together, the prisoners and the crowd read "several select prayers and Psalms" that the prisoners themselves supposedly had chosen. From the top of the rampart, each prisoner descended a set of stairs, then had to walk back up to the gallows stage. A black flag flew above the gallows to mock the pirates' symbol of defiance. After the hangman placed nooses around their necks, the pirates stood on stage for forty-five minutes. Interaction between the condemned men and the crowd indicates a measure of intimacy between them. When John Augur ascended the rampart, someone gave him a small glass of wine, which he used to toast the "good success of the Bahama Islands and the governor." William Lewis, meanwhile, became visibly drunk in the forty-five minutes he spent on stage, sharing drinks with the pressing crowd and other condemned men.

In addition to singing more psalms together, the condemned pirates occasionally exhorted their "old consorts" among the spectators. Dennis McCarty, who kicked off his shoes above the rampart, gaily pranced to the gallows wearing long blue ribbons, asking the crowd to have "compassion" for him, insinuating that they should stage an uprising. At one point, McCarty reminisced, thinking about a time when "there were many brave fellows on the island, who would not have suffered [allowed] him to die like a dog." "However willing" the crowd might have been to save McCarty, they refrained, fearing "they saw too much power over their heads to attempt any thing in his favor." At the last minute, Governor Rogers reprieved George Rouncifull, largely because he knew the young man's parents from Dorset. After untying him and leading him away from the gallows, the butts of wine holding up the stage were pulled away, and the eight men fell to their deaths.[40]

Governor Rogers did not immediately perceive that the execution of the eight men had done enough to eradicate piracy from his colony. Summarizing the situation about two weeks later, Rogers alluded to five more alleged pirates he had seized and put in jail.[41] Two had been pardoned by Vincent Pearse: Pearse Wright and Thomas Bradley. Both men had been trading or vaguely "corresponding" with pirates. Around that same time, Rogers sent out "two small cruizers" manned with seventy persons to scour the waters for more suspects, but they were forced to return "for fear of being themselves taken" by pirates. Rogers exclaimed, "I hope I am now out of danger at least of the pirates," yet a month later Rogers entertained rumors of a pirate-instigated plot to "destroy me and my officers, and then deliver up the fort for the use of the pirates."[42] The plot never materialized, but at the end of January, Rogers received word that the pirate Edward Congdon had designs to come to the Bahamas to receive a pardon, taking advantage of an extension of the grace period the government had instituted the previous summer. The prospect of confronting Congdon, who commanded two ships with thirty-six guns apiece, put Rogers in a state of agitation. Although he was inclined to resist the pirates, Rogers feared that "I shall be forced to receive them at all hazards" due to the colony's poor state of defense and its lack of a man-of-war as a deterrent. Most of the inhabitants, he feared, "will joyn them or quitt [leave] me, and then they'll possess the place." Congdon never appeared. Meanwhile, Rogers and the council, citing the high cost of conducting more trials, decided to release Pearse Wright and Thomas Bradley, and possibly others who had been jailed for corresponding with pirates. Lacking a vessel to take them to England for trial, he was instead "forced to accept but moderate security for their good behavior."[43]

Like most colonial administrators, Woodes Rogers lauded his own efforts to suppress piracy, but he gave credit where it was due by commending some of the former pirates, whose decision to back the government was vital to its survival. Foremost among those was Hornigold, in whom Rogers expressed "full confidence" and whose actions had given "proof . . . to the world to wipe off the infamous name he has hitherto been known by." Rogers expressed equal admiration for John Cockram, and awarded both men by providing bounty money, as specified in the royal proclamation, out of his own pocket for capturing the pirates at Exuma.[44] Hornigold and Cockram also probably commanded the two unspecified cruisers Rogers sent out in late November on a continuing search for pirates. That the two vessels attracted the services of seventy-odd men speaks to the moral authority of the two former pirates, whose example must have convinced many other unsung men to leave piracy for good and assist in defending the colony. The pirates had been expelled in the literal sense, but more importantly in the figurative sense that ordinary seamen purged whatever tendency they had within them to be pirates. The colony, however, would have to confront an external threat before commerce could be restored.

War, Privateering, and Trade

It worked to Woodes Rogers's advantage that the Bahamas faced an existential threat from Spain concurrently with his efforts to purge the colony of pirates. Recall that Spanish *guardacostas* had struck at least three times in Bahamian waters in the summer of 1718, and that the specter of another attack motivated at least some former pirates to assist with the construction of the fort. That fall, Rogers had given special permission to a number of sloops to conduct trade in Spanish territories, particularly Cuba. The governor of Havana, however, refused to recognize the legality of the written passes Rogers had given the sloop captains and detained an unspecified number of Bahamian vessels in the Cuban capital. By December 1718 rumors of war abounded, and Governor Rogers perceived that the Bahamas lay in Spain's crosshairs. As Rogers stated, once Spain declared war, it would "begin with us," for Spain had never truly recognized British sovereignty over the islands.[45] Vessels arriving in the Bahamas perpetuated rumors of a massive Spanish offensive.[46] By March 3 Governor Rogers was writing plaintive letters to fellow governors in New York, Jamaica, and elsewhere, asking if they could spare men to help defend the Bahamas.[47] Rumors of war became a reality on March 31, when mariner Phillip Cockram (presumably the brother of John) arrived from Barbados with the official word that Spain had declared war on Britain.[48]

The War of the Quadruple Alliance (1718–20) derived from Spain's dissatisfaction with, and attempts to reverse, the terms of the 1713 Peace of Utrecht. To enforce the provisions of the treaty, France, Britain, the Dutch Republic, and the Austrian Hapsburgs formed the so-called Quadruple Alliance. Most of the actual fighting occurred in the Mediterranean, although in the Americas, France's capture of Pensacola in Spanish Florida in 1719, which stopped a planned Spanish invasion of South Carolina in its tracks, was one of the more noteworthy military maneuvers. In February 1720 a squadron of Spanish ships appeared in Bahamian waters, only to be repulsed by the colony's guard ship, the *Delicia*, assisted by the timely arrival of a British man-of-war, the HMS *Flamborough*. A peace treaty was signed at The Hague on February 17, 1720, but word of it spread slowly in the Americas, where privateering continued well into the spring after hostilities—officially, at least—ceased.[49]

Although several former pirates had been out the previous fall on "cruising" missions, the war effort began in the spring of 1719. In addition to hearing that war had been officially declared, the council learned that a large number of prisoners, all subjects of Britain including a number of Bahamians, were being "severely treated" in Havana. Thomas Walker of Providence had recently returned from the Cuban capital, where he pleaded with the Spanish governor to release them, including his son Charles, but to no avail. The council then determined that arranging for a prisoner exchange might work. Rogers promptly commissioned five local sloops to scour the area near the wrecks on the Florida coast, which continued to attract hopeful scavengers. The idea was to capture Spanish subjects and use them as collateral for the prisoner exchange.[50]

Bahamian mariners responded enthusiastically to the call of war. The council received petitions from many sloop captains, who were practically begging for privateering commissions.[51] Importantly, a significant number of individuals who received pardons from Vincent Pearse served as privateers. At least two served on board the guard ship *Delicia*, William Williams and Charles Whitehead, the latter as lieutenant.[52] Many undoubtedly lost their lives in the conflict, most notably Benjamin Hornigold and Josiah Burgess, who commanded their respective vessels. The circumstances of Benjamin Hornigold's death are mysterious. Commissioned in the spring of 1719, Hornigold departed Providence and was never heard from again. The author of the *General History* suggests that he died in a shipwreck, reporting only that he "was cast away upon rocks, a great way from land, and perished, but five of his men got into a canoe and were saved."[53] Captain Thomas Whitney, however, reported on July 3, 1719, that Hornigold had been captured by the Spanish near Cuba. It is reasonable to think Hornigold might have died in that encounter or was summarily executed after his capture, as punishment for the string of robberies he had inflicted on Spanish ships years before.[54]

Meanwhile, Josiah Burgess received a commission to captain the privateering sloop *Two Brothers*, which was scheduled to sail shortly after December 9, 1719.[55] Before voyaging, Burgess drafted a power of attorney and will, naming his fiancée, the "gentlewoman" Lydia Tarkenton, as his sole beneficiary. Burgess died sometime before June 1720, the victim of a shipwreck. The author of the *General History* colorfully described how his ship hit a reef near Green Turtle Key, claiming his life and that of George Rouncifull, the same young man Governor Rogers had pardoned under the gallows a few months earlier. As the story goes, Rouncifull, along with other surviving members of Burgess's crew, managed to climb into the sloop's pinnace in an effort to save themselves. Burgess, wounded and stranded on his sinking ship, called out to Rouncifull, pleading, "Will you go away and leave me to perish in this manner?" Out of devotion to his captain, Rouncifull jumped into the water and swam back toward Burgess in an effort to save him. Both drowned.[56]

Papers now lodged in the Pennsylvania probate records confirm some of the details of the *General History* account. Astonishingly, Philadelphia shipwright Nicholas Seley, who traveled to Providence in June 1720, witnessed the arrival of a canoe carrying seven survivors from Burgess's sloop. The "seven hands" who arrived on shore explained that Burgess's ship had struck a rock ten leagues from shore and that they had left Burgess behind thinking that he had been "lost in the said vessel." When he died, Burgess owned eighty-seven pounds' worth of movable property, including a silk suit, three swords, a silver tankard, and a "negro boy" named Nassau. Interestingly, roughly a quarter of the value of Burgess's modest estate consisted of books. In addition to several navigational treatises, Burgess's prized possessions included a copy of Plutarch's *Lives*, a collection of Shakespeare's plays, seven issues of *The Spectator*, and several works of theology. Burgess's engagement to a self-proclaimed "gentlewoman," along with his reading preferences, hint at the ambitions of an aspiring gentleman, cut tragically short by an accident at sea.[57]

The loss of some of the colony's most accomplished mariners is indicative of the dangers inherent to maritime travel during wartime. Perhaps in response to that danger, one detects an overall sense of panic gripping the Bahamas, which had the undesirable effect of stifling trade. On the home front, this sense of panic influenced the actions of governing officials, who questioned the loyalty of the French and German immigrants who had recently come to the colony with Governor Rogers. To ensure their loyalty, on May 11, 1719, the council had all the foreigners appear before them to take the oath of allegiance. A week later, the council ordered all the residents of Cat Island to relocate to Providence. Not only was their intent to remove the island's few residents from danger, but also the council feared having Cat Islanders kidnapped by the Spanish and forced to pilot their war ships to Providence. On May 26, governing officials received word that an attack of some 1,500 soldiers from Cuba was imminent. The council instituted an embargo on all shipping and ordered Harbor Islanders to ready their defenses.[58]

The Spanish attack did not materialize until February 9, 1720, when the council received intelligence indicating that the Spanish war fleet was on its way to the Bahamas. Rogers instituted another embargo on shipping, and within the next few weeks, the council ordered the construction of a stone lookout tower and the repair of the fort's breastworks. On March 19 the council ordered all able-bodied males from Harbor Island and Eleuthera to Providence to help man the fort. Even though peace had been restored in Europe, Providence remained at a high state of alert for several months, and the council repeatedly extended the shipping embargo, which was not lifted until May 1720.[59]

Governor Rogers relied on the services of former pirates to gather intelligence on the size and anticipated maneuvers of enemy Spanish squadrons. Rogers also sought out intelligence on the circumstances of Britain's French allies, whose strength in the Gulf of Mexico had been one of the reasons Spain refrained from attacking the Bahamas. John Cockram, along with New York privateer Samuel Vincent, provided one such service after a cruise to Hispaniola. Returning to Nassau on April 6, Cockram informed

Rogers that they had seen eight French ships in the Gulf of Mexico, evidently headed to Mobile, which had received an influx of soldiers. Cockram and Vincent were also probably the two men responsible for kidnapping near St. Augustine two Spanish friars, who testified before Governor Rogers that the French at Mobile were too strong, which caused the Spanish to redirect their military efforts toward Providence. That same day, William Williams, who had been a prisoner at Havana and somehow managed to escape, arrived in Nassau to confirm what others had said about the strength of French forces at Mobile and the likelihood of an overland French attack on northern Mexico.[60]

As was the case in previous wars, reliance on privateers was risky due to their propensity to turn to outright piracy. Some in fact came dangerously close to going rogue by attacking their own countrymen. Bahamian mariner (and pardoned pirate) William South learned this the hard way. Commissioned by Governor Rogers in the spring of 1719 as captain of the privateering sloop *Endeavor*, South and company went on a cruise to Cuba in search of enemy shipping. Nearing the coast, South spotted a vessel, which he took to be the enemy's, and approached it, only to receive a barrage of fire. He closed in on it, demanding to know why they fired on him, and discovered that its captain was none other than Leigh Ashworth. The two captains sailed together toward Havana, where they miraculously happened upon Charles Walker, a prisoner of the Spaniards who just escaped in a canoe. South took Walker on board, intending to bring him home to Providence. South invited Ashworth to accompany him there, but he refused, demanding that Walker serve the Jamaicans as a pilot. After an angry exchange of words, Ashworth forced Walker on board his ship (Walker eventually made it back to Providence a few months later). Ashworth also carried off a slave, presumably one belonging to South, who returned to Providence immediately to complain to Governor Rogers. Ashworth appears to have suffered no consequences for harassing a fellow British privateer.[61] In most instances, however, privateers simply ignored the peace treaty of 1720 and kept up their attacks on Spanish shipping in spite of the embargo.[62]

Despite Governor Rogers's contrary intentions, wartime Providence incubated a culture of piracy that spawned the final phase of pirate John "Calico Jack" Rackham's career. Rackham had once served under Charles Vane and had deposed him for being unwilling to attack a French man-of-war. After assuming command of his vessel, around May 1719 Rackham and company arrived at Providence. Although he presumably came in seeking a pardon, there is no direct evidence indicating that he did so.[63] Rackham drew no attention to himself until August 22, 1720, when a company he led—which included the notorious female pirates Anne Bonny and Mary Read—stole a sloop and alighted toward the Berry Islands. There, Rackham robbed a sloop captained by James Gohier, a member of the council, and spent a few days attacking fishing vessels around Harbor Island.[64] When news of the attack reached Providence, the council proclaimed Rackham, along with the government's longtime nemesis John Lewis and their companies, as pirates. At the same time, the council passed new regulations for tavern owners, incentivizing them to reveal any nefarious plots unfolding in their establishments.[65] In a few short weeks, Rackham's company turned south to unleash a war of terror near Jamaica, culminating in their capture, trial, and execution later that fall. John Lewis never again showed his face in the Bahamas.

Because of the dangers posed by enemy shipping and the monthslong embargoes instituted by the government, Bahamian commerce atrophied during the war. Pardoned pirates who remained in the Bahamas clearly endured some lean years before the restoration of profitable commerce. Perhaps in an attempt to commemorate those times, longtime Bahamian and pardoned pirate Charles Whitehead purchased a sloop and named it *Hard Times*. One of its first recorded voyages was in November 1721, when Whitehead directed the captain operating the vessel to proceed directly to Jamaica carrying only ballast, an indication that Whitehead had nothing of value to trade at that time.[66]

The Bahamas shipping industry in the 1720s remained, as it had been in prior decades, modest. Governor George Phenney, who replaced Woodes Rogers at the end of 1721, provides a snapshot of the colony's shipping capacity as it existed in the first half of the decade. In all, the island featured about seventeen vessels registered in the colony. Most were sloops, and small ones at that, averaging only about eight tons' burden each. In addition, the colonists had innumerable smaller vessels—canoes, turtle boats, pirogues—that were never registered and do not factor in official records. In most cases, such vessels probably served interisland commerce, as well as in local extraction activities. Perhaps unsurprisingly, since many Bahamians originated there, Jamaica was the favored destination of local mariners, with South Carolina and Bermuda as leading secondary destinations. Occasionally, Bahamian sloops ventured to Philadelphia and Barbados, and there is one recorded round trip to London. In late 1721 a Royal African Company ship landed at Providence with 295 enslaved persons, drastically altering the colony's demography and its slaveholding practices.[67]

Outbound Bahamas vessels typically carried locally harvested commodities. Among the most common trade items was brasiletto wood, which grew on several of the Bahamian islands. Salt was available at several keys off Exuma and Turks Island. Bahamians also grew indigo and harvested turtle shell. Although Bahamians did not yet distill molasses to make rum themselves, local mariners occasionally traded rum they acquired elsewhere. Traders sometimes carried citrus fruit, and on rare occasions they sold excess quantities of flour and other foodstuffs obtained from elsewhere. For the return voyages, Bahamian mariners typically stocked their ships with much-needed supplies of food. From South Carolina, they obtained beef, pork, rice, and corn, and in Philadelphia, ship captains obtained flour, bread, and cheese, as well as supplies of European goods, such as nails and candles. In all, the structure of the Bahamian economy remained much the same.

Shipping records bear the unmistakable imprint of the pardoned pirates. Nine individuals became captains in their own right. Of them, four men—arguably the most prosperous mariners—owned or co-owned the ships on which they sailed. In the year following the arrival of Governor Rogers, the most active merchant ship captain was William Williams. Born in Jamaica, and married to a woman from North Carolina, Williams's trading ventures reflected the regional networks he had established. Williams may have begun his piratical adventures in 1716, trading with Benjamin Hornigold and ferrying goods into South Carolina.[68] Within three years, he was operating two vessels. The first was the *Francis and Sarah*, registered in North Carolina in September 1716. The other vessel, the sloop *Endeavor*, Williams had registered at Providence. In May 1719 Williams arrived in Jamaica from Providence in the *Francis and Sarah*, bearing seal oil. For the return voyage in June, Williams carried rum. Williams returned to Jamaica on November 3 sailing the *Endeavor*, carrying coconuts. He returned to Providence about two weeks later, this time with rum. These voyages were perhaps the last of which he sailed in the two ships. After a nearly three-year absence in the shipping records, Williams appeared again in September 1722, but this time as the captain of the sloop *Bennet*, which he did not own. Once again bound from Providence to Jamaica, Williams's ship carried brasiletto, wood planks, and an unspecified number of "European goods." Like many of the mariners on Pearse's list, his presence in the shipping records diminished as time passed.[69]

In the first half of the 1720s, Providence's most active former pirate-trader was Thomas Terrill, whose piracies against Spanish shipping in conjunction with Benjamin Hornigold and John Cockram in 1713 first attracted the attention of British authorities. Terrill owned the sloop *Endeavor*, which was a Spanish "prize made free" in May 1720, perhaps indicating that Terrill had been a privateer in the recent war. He sailed the sloop himself occasionally, conducting one round trip to Philadelphia in the fall of 1720 and another to South Carolina two years later. From that point on, however, Terrill employed others to captain his sloop, and more properly, he ought to be regarded as a merchant. From 1722 to 1724, his vessels made four voyages to Jamaica, one to Pennsylvania, and one to London. In 1725 Terrill rid himself of the sloop, purchasing another one named the *Rebecca*, which made two more voyages to Jamaica.[70]

Peter Goudet, the owner of three vessels, also qualified as a merchant. Between 1722 and 1726, his boats made six voyages, principally to South Carolina, but also to Bermuda and Philadelphia.[71] Another prominent owner-captain was Daniel Stillwell, the very same man who escaped after being arrested in 1715 on charges of piracy. Stillwell owned a small sloop named the *Happy Return*, which made three voyages to Jamaica between 1722 and 1724. After a four-year hiatus, Stillwell reappeared in 1728 as the captain of the sloop *Three Sisters*, owned by another Bahamian, for two voyages to South Carolina. That Stillwell was now working for someone other than himself may indicate that he had fallen on hard times.[72] Finally, another pardoned pirate who rose to the rank of a merchant was John Cockram, who owned the vessel he sailed, the *Richard and John*, in partnership with his father-in-law, Richard Thompson of Harbor Island. The *Richard and John* made four voyages between 1718 and 1724, two to Barbados and one each to Bermuda and Philadelphia. Atypical for a Bahamian ship captain, Cockram specialized in the reexport trade, as his cargoes for the Barbados voyages featured European goods, beef, and flour that must have been acquired elsewhere.[73]

Meanwhile, Joseph Pearse and Richard Newland rose to the rank of captain some years after the pardon. Pearse surfaced in the records as a captain in September 1719 as master of the sloop *Mary and Pattie*, which he conducted to Jamaica on behalf of its owner from Bermuda. Around May 1724 he began working for merchant Samuel Lawford, owner of the sloop *Prince Frederick*. The thirty-ton *Prince Frederick* was unusually large for a Bahamian sloop, indicating the trading ambitions of its owner. That year alone, Pearse made one voyage to Jamaica and two more to South Carolina. As was common, ship captains who did not own their own vessels tended to bounce around, and in 1725 Pearse began a short stint as captain of the sloop *Rebecca*, making one round trip to South Carolina. Subsequent to that voyage, Pearse spent more than a year commanding the sloop *Elizabeth and Sarah*, owned by two prominent Bahamian merchants. Pearse directed the *Elizabeth and*

Sarah twice to South Carolina and once to Jamaica. In all Pearse conducted six voyages in these three ships, making him among the most well traveled of the former pirates.[74] Second only to Pearse in the number of recorded voyages is Richard Newland, who did not begin commanding ships until 1726. Like Pearse, he alternated between the *Elizabeth and Sarah* (formerly under the command of Pearse) and the *Carolina*, owned by Whetstone Rogers (Woodes's son) and John Colebrooke, whose partnership centered in New York invested heavily in developing a Bahamian rum distillery and indigo plantation.[75] In all, Newland made three voyages to South Carolina and two to Jamaica.[76] In addition to Pearse and Newland, former pirates Robert Hunter and George Raddon each served as captain at least once, mostly for voyages to Jamaica.[77] In addition to those who rose to the rank of captain, pardoned pirates Richard Ward, Joseph Mickelbro, and John Cullimore can be positively identified as crew members on one or more of these trading vessels.

Somewhat surprisingly, most of these mariners carried on without incident, generally avoiding legal entanglements related to the conduct of shipping. When they did run afoul of the law, it was mostly for petty violations that did not lead to extensive criminal proceedings. One who did occasionally get into trouble was Thomas Terrill. In December 1720 Terrill and one of the ship captains who worked for him, Thomas Petty, stood accused of failing to pay a duty on seal oil that the two had made together, which was believed due to the Bahamas proprietors. In turn, the council seized ten gallons of Terrill's rum and made him and Petty post a £100 bond for good behavior until their court appearance in May.[78] Exactly one year later, Terrill aroused suspicion again, this time for purchasing some stolen indigo from a Jamaican. Terrill pleaded his innocence, avowing that he had no knowledge of the indigo's origins. He petitioned to keep it, but surviving records do not indicate how either of these cases was ultimately resolved.[79] The final instance of a pardoned pirate engaged in lawbreaking is that of John Kemp, who received brief mention in the council's January 1729 minutes for smuggling French goods from Hispaniola. As with Terrill, Kemp's case made hardly a ripple in the colony's records.[80]

More commonly, the pardoned Bahamians were the victims of piracy, particularly in attacks instigated by Spanish *guardacostas*. Daniel Stillwell, for instance, on a voyage to South Carolina in June 1718, received a scare from the pirate William Greenway, who had recently led a mutiny on board a Jamaican wrecking vessel. Greenway's crew detained Stillwell for a short time, confiscating some of his trading goods, but not before paying him for what they took.[81] Stillwell was lucky; the Jamaican crew had spent considerable time at Providence in the previous weeks, and probably let him off easy because they knew him. A month later, Richard Ward and Joseph Mickelbro had an uncomfortable encounter with Spanish *guardacostas*. The two men formed part of the small crew of the *Dolphin*, then under the command of Thomas Bowlin. Setting out from Providence that July, the *Dolphin* headed for Cuba to trade livestock. As they approached the Cuban town of Porto Prince, a Spanish vessel seized the ship and placed the crewmen and livestock on the island. The Spanish commander kidnapped Bowlin and for over two weeks forced him to pilot the Spanish ship around the Bahamas so that he could spy on the English. On Bowlin's return to Porto Prince, the Spanish *alcalde*, believing the English men to be pirates, sent Bowlin and four other crew members back to Providence in a small boat, keeping Richard Ward behind as security for their return. After returning to Providence that September, Bowlin and the other four crew members gave depositions and sought letters from Governor Rogers "to prove themselves to be honest men" so that they could return to retrieve Ward.[82] John Cockram received a brief scare during a trading voyage to Mobile, where a Spanish ship lured him closer by raising French colors, only to replace them with a Spanish standard. The Spanish vessel fired shots at the English boat, but Cockram escaped unharmed.[83]

Spanish *guardacostas* sometimes merely harassed British shipping, but the commander Augustine Blanco posed the most serious threat to the Bahamas. Blanco was known to be a mixed-race individual from Barracoa who sailed with a privateering commission from the *alcalde* of Santiago de Cuba, both towns being notorious lairs for *guardacostas*. Although his crew featured mostly Spanish subjects, Blanco recruited sailors of other nationalities, including Richard Hancock, the "Scotch rogue" who served as Blanco's doctor. Blanco, once described as "an old robber among these islands [Bahamas] about twenty five years," had been involved in the invasions during Queen Anne's War, and it is probable that he instigated some of the small-scale attacks on Bahamian shipping in the summer of 1718.[84]

Blanco emerged as a persistent threat in the 1720s. In June 1722 he attacked Cat Island, seizing a fully loaded sloop. Blanco returned around August, this time making landfall. He and his crew spent upward of four weeks on the island, terrorizing the population, destroying property, and carrying away nine inhabitants. However, Cat Islanders managed to run one of Blanco's sloops ashore. Blanco escaped, but the inhabitants captured Hancock, along with several of his crew, and brought them to Providence. The prisoners stood trial for their crimes that fall, leading to the execution of Hancock and nine Spaniards. Undeterred, Blanco struck again almost three years later. In late March 1725 he apprehended the sloop *Snapper* while it was engaged in a salt-raking expedition and made landfall at Eleuthera, where he descended on the estate of Richard Thompson. In addition to kidnapping Thompson's son, Blanco stole goods and slaves valued at about 3,500 pieces of eight. Meanwhile, the crew of the *Snapper* escaped and soon reported the incident to Governor Phenney at Providence.[85] British authorities, however, never caught up with Augustine Blanco, who was still attacking British ships as late as 1729.[86]

Blanco's attacks directly impacted a few of the pardoned pirates. During the 1722 attack on Cat Island, for instance, Blanco's men struck the home of Alexander Campbell, destroying a boat he had recently built and ruining his stock of "callipatch" or salted turtle meat. Blanco also kidnapped Campbell, forcing him to pilot his sloop for a short time. Campbell later served as one of the star witnesses in the trial of Richard Hancock and Blanco's crew.[87] Similarly, Blanco's depredations directly affected the former pirate John Cullimore, who was among several men who escaped from Eleuthera and gave depositions before Governor Phenney in April 1725. Most of the pardoned Bahamian pirates did what they could to walk away from piracy, but pirates sometimes found them.

To "Be Honest and Live under Government"

Around 1721 the Bahamian governing council began meeting regularly in Nassau at a modest courthouse, descriptions of which do not survive. One thing that is certain about the building's interior is that somewhere affixed to one of the walls was a plaque of the Great Seal of the Realm under King George I. The Great Seal features a seated King George on a magnificent throne framed by a cloth canopy. Atop the canopy is a crown and small circular ensign, with two cherubs floating above the king's head. A robed woman to the king's right carries a battle standard in her right hand and a pike in her left, glancing sideways at the king—allegorically "the sword." On the king's left hand is another robed woman standing before a Union Jack. In her left hand are weighing scales, which balance evenly as she gazes at the king—metaphorically, "justice." After finishing its business there on February 11, 1722, the council adjourned for a span of more than two weeks, leaving the courthouse unoccupied. The night of March 1, a person—or, as it was guessed, a group of persons—broke into the building to defile it. When council members arrived the next morning, they discovered that someone had "irreverently, scandalously and maliciously [daubed] filth and ordure" on the Great Seal.[88] It was a polite way of saying they had smeared shit all over it.

When Governor Rogers arrived, his plea to the former pirates was to "be honest and live under government," something they were not accustomed to doing.[89] In spite of their reputation for lawlessness, a critical mass of the pardoned men did in fact obey the law, respect governing officials, and support their efforts to administer justice. The former pirates regularly looked to the institutions of the state to assert property rights, resolve disputes, and defend themselves from foreign threats. They also embraced institutions like the church, which conferred legitimacy on their marriages and children. Many were, in fact, family men. Charged with managing their own households, some former pirates readily embraced their responsibilities as subjects, serving the state in ways large and small, paying taxes, serving on juries, and occasionally by holding minor offices. At times, they chafed under what they perceived as the arbitrary exercise of power on the part of governing officials, who picked favorites when applying the laws of trade, and sometimes tried to line their own pockets through graft. Rather than stage a rebellion, most Bahamian protests were of a symbolic and individual nature, not unlike the smearing of "filth and ordure" on the Great Seal of the Realm.

Britons conceived of landed property as the foundation of one's rights and very identity as a "freeman," so it is unsurprising that the pardoned pirates who had the means to do so acquired land. In the Bahamas, several decades of proprietary neglect and foreign invasions meant that recordkeeping was negligible and disorderly, which clouded land titles. When royal governance came in 1718, the Bahamas proprietors relinquished their civil and military duties, but they retained the right to collect rents and other royalties in an attempt to generate income. The proprietors farmed out those responsibilities to the Bahamas Company, which, under the authority of the Governor and Council, was empowered to assign plots of land to individuals. The land assignments were technically twenty-year leases, subject to an annual quitrent of one farthing. The leases became perpetual (essentially fee simple title) once the landholder had made good on his or her payments. One condition of the leases was that the prospective landholder had to build a "suitable and tenetable" house on the property, a subtle attempt to keep residents at home working the land rather than remaining seaborne all the time, as was their tendency.[90]

Between 1719 and 1722, Governors Rogers and Phenney assigned land to

155 people, and the names of 127 of those individuals appear in the colony's records. Of the fifty pardoned pirates who remained in the Bahamas, eight of them (a rate of 16 percent) received town lots in Nassau. Typically, the lots were a quarter acre in size, reflecting their orientation to the sea rather than planting. The landholders figure among the more visible former pirates, such as Peter Goudet, Thomas Terrill, John Cockram, Charles Whitehead, William Williams, and John Cullimore. Robert Wishart received land at Providence but did not start improving his property until moving there with his family from South Carolina in 1723. Mariners Samuel Richardson and John Arturreal also received land. Most had come to the colony recently, and they presumably sought leases because they had no prior claims to property. Their situations were unlike those of some of the old settlers who accepted the pardon, like John Carey or John Bley, whose family had been at Providence for forty years and had been born there.[91]

As Britons believed that the family was a microcosm of the state, committing to married life and assuming responsibility for one's children was an important aspect of living "under government." Colonial promoters, in fact, feared the disorders inherent to societies that had a surplus of unwed males, and promoted family formation as a means for keeping the peace, growing the population, encouraging industry, and establishing civil society. Like many other colonies in their infancy, the sex ratio in the Bahamas skewed male, and one estimate holds that in the 1720s there were 1.35 adult males for every female. Still, the colony had enough women such that 80 percent of eligible men could potentially find a spouse.[92] Even former pirates had a sporting chance; the record positively identifies twenty-four of them who had wives.[93] Only one of the pardoned pirates, Alexander Campbell, appears to have been a lifelong bachelor.[94] A few of the former pirates (presumably those who were slightly older) married before their careers in piracy, such as John Cockram, who had married Catherine Thompson of Harbor Island sometime prior to 1714, and Robert Wishart, who was married to Jane by that time as well. Those who were slightly younger at the time of the pardon married in the decade or so that followed, including Peter Goudet, Edward Kerr, and John Edwards.

High mortality rates in the eighteenth century, however, meant that some of the pirates and their spouses married more than once, forming compound families of half- and stepsiblings. Approximately one-third to one-half of all Bahamian marriages featured at least one spouse who was a widow or widower.[95] The formation of former pirate Robert Brown's family is illustrative of this trend. Born in Cork, Ireland, Brown was married before he stumbled into piracy. He may have married his first wife, Sarah, before he left Ireland. At Providence, the couple had two children. Their son Thomas was baptized on January 8, 1722. On October 12 of that same year, the couple had a baby girl, whom they baptized almost a year later and named Sarah. Robert's wife Sarah died in October 1723, and Robert remarried spinster Esther Bossard a year later. They produced one son, born in July 1726 and baptized in September.[96]

It would be worth knowing more about the manner of woman who would marry a pirate. Unfortunately, like most women of humble status, their appearance in the historical record is fleeting, making the details of their lives unrecoverable. One partial exception to this rule, however, is the wife of Samuel Richardson, Dorothy, who was twice deposed by Governor Rogers and left a few clues about herself. The first deposition occurred in February 1721, when she protested that James Gohier, the agent for the Bahamas Company, denied her title to a plot of land. As Richardson explained, "she" had purchased the lot in question about four years earlier, at a time when there was no functioning government at Providence. Gohier would not recognize that purchase, so he refused to give her a patent. Richardson also alleged that Gohier had uprooted the seedlings of some orange trees "that she her self planted." Richardson succeeded in persuading Rogers to approve the land grant.[97] Mrs. Richardson appeared again in December during an investigation into the death of one of Gohier's servants named Bell, who had expired during his detention at the fort. Turned out by his master, Richardson sheltered and fed Bell for a few days before the authorities apprehended Bell and confined him to the fort. Richardson also reported a rumor that the fort's doctor had killed a man in Ireland, insinuating that foul play might have been involved.[98] Although both depositions are perfunctory, they depict a woman of industry and assertiveness, one capable of purchasing property, cultivating fruit, and even standing up to some of the leading men in the colony. Perhaps she liked to gossip, as it was a common way for women to influence the perception of neighbors when they were excluded from formal politics.[99] Finally, Richardson possessed a sharp mind despite being illiterate, as indicated by the bold "X" she inscribed next to her name on one of the depositions.

Like most Bahamians, the former pirates' families were modest in size, with two to three children being the norm. Pirates thus contributed to slow growth of the colony's population. According to the historians Craton and Saunders, in 1721 the entire population of the Bahamas was just under 1,000, with about 75 percent living at Providence. A decade later, when Governor Rogers (during his second term) conducted the colony's first census, the population stood at 1,388. Free children outnumbered free adults (486 to 446), which suggests that new births were a contributing factor to the increase in population. However, the population began to stagnate, probably the result of epidemics that struck the colony in the early 1730s. A census taken by Governor Richard Fitzwilliam in 1734 revealed that the population had actually declined in the three intervening years, from 1,388 to 1,378. This stagnation is attributable primarily to the attrition of the population at Providence, where the number of free adults fell from 633 to 538. Historians think that a combination of Nassau's population density and heavier port traffic made Providence more vulnerable to disease outbreaks than the out islands. In fact, as the population of Providence was declining, those of Harbor Island and Eleuthera were on the rise. With a healthier environment, Harbor Islanders and Eleutherans had larger families and lower death rates, resulting in modest increases in the two islands' free white population, from 346 to 397.

Remarkably, enslaved and free Africans experienced somewhat better health than white Bahamians, and certainly better than their enslaved counterparts in Caribbean plantation colonies. In 1721 nearly 28 percent of the colony's population (275 of 989) was listed as "negroes," which includes the enslaved as well as other African-descended people whose status is uncertain. By 1731 the percentage of Blacks was just over 32 percent, rising to above 35 percent in 1734. Initially, the increase in the enslaved population derived from the direct importation of enslaved persons from Africa in the early 1720s, most notably the 295 individuals who arrived on a single ship in 1721. With a higher percentage of enslaved males, the Black population was unable to sustain itself for at least a decade, but by the mid-1730s the sex ratio of enslaved persons began to even out, and more were living in family units. Thus, by 1734 the enslaved population featured a higher percentage of children.[100]

Like other white Bahamians, pardoned pirates embraced slaveholding, albeit at modest levels indicative of their financial circumstances and needs as mariners. Of the nine former pirates who owned slaves according to the 1731 census, six of them—Alexander Campbell, John Cullimore, Richard Legatt, George Raddon, Charles Whitehead, and Robert Wishart—owned just one slave. Another man, John Bley, owned two. The kind of work they did remains unknown, but we may perhaps look to Bermuda as another island colony that employed slaves in the maritime trades. As in Bermuda, male slaves might have staffed the crews of trading vessels, assisted with the loading and unloading of cargoes, and performed routine ship maintenance.[101] Enslaved women probably worked as domestics, doing the nursing, cooking, gardening, mending, and other tasks assigned them by the mistress of the household. Two of the pardoned pirates, Peter Goudet and David Champion, stand out for investing more heavily in slaves. Goudet's household included five "able negroes" and three "negro children," and a more detailed 1734 census indicates that he owned four enslaved men, two women, and three children. Champion, meanwhile, owned five adult slaves and two enslaved children. The greater number of adult slaves in these households suggests that Goudet and Champion may have directed their efforts at planting indigo or cotton, two of the main cash crops in the Bahamas. John Bley, who died many years later in possession of three enslaved men, identified as a "planter" toward the end of his life, making him yet another former pirate who turned to planting.[102]

By virtue of their slaveholding, pardoned pirates likely held attitudes toward Black people resembling those of Anglo-American settlers in plantation colonies.[103] They probably approved of the colony's first slave laws, a series of eight council resolutions passed on May 2, 1723. For example, one resolution required each slave to have a ticket indicating who their master was "when they go from their home." Like many slave codes, the 1723 resolutions prohibited slaves from assembling in groups of six or more, owning weapons, or uttering "threatening" words against white people—infractions that could lead to whipping. Enslaved persons were also required to "give way" to white people they passed in the streets, submit to biweekly searches of their homes for weapons, and obtain a pass from their master in order to participate in market exchanges. In recognition of the slave's humanity, the resolutions fined masters who used their slaves "in a barbarous manner" by cutting, maiming, or burning them.[104]

Although the Bahamas gradually instituted more draconian measures to control enslaved people, the colony retained some of its preexisting racial fluidity. The 1734 census indicates that there were seventy-seven free persons of color living in the colony, or about 5 percent of the population. Mary and Samuel Fox, for instance, were free people of color who had been born, baptized, and manumitted in Bermuda before settling in the Bahamas. Manumissions, while rare, occurred in the Bahamas as well. Sometime in 1721, on his deathbed, mariner Edward Holmes of Eleuthera set in process the manumission of his "mulatto" slave named Rachel, who was to be freed one year after his death. Four years later, Rachel appeared before the council demanding her freedom, presenting a written order drawn up by Eleuthera's justice of the peace. The council took the petition seriously, calling before them a witness, former pirate Daniel Stillwell, who affirmed that, about one week before his death, Captain Holmes had "designed her to be free."[105] Just as they embraced slaveholding, former pirates could sometimes be agents of manumission.

Along with conforming to the Bahamas' trends in family formation and slaveholding, the former pirates exhibited a surprisingly high degree of civic engagement. For instance, they paid taxes. In 1723 the council assessed heads of households to support the salary and maintenance of the colony's Anglican minister, Thomas Curphey. Nineteen former pirates appear on the assessment list. One of them, John Cullimore, took charge of the collection process by virtue of his position as one of Providence's constables. William Williams, meanwhile, joined a committee tasked with the physical construction of the church.[106] Although a small number of persons were later reprimanded by the council for being "in arrears" on their payments, none of them were former pirates, indicating that they had contributed to Curphey's salary.

The assessments give some indication of the relative levels of wealth of the former pirates. For perspective, consider that the wealthiest man in the colony, councilor William Fairfax, was assessed at four pounds. Thomas Terrill, who owned his own vessel and rose to the rank of the merchant class, was assessed at two pounds, making him perhaps the wealthiest of his peers. Others who had amassed respectable estates include John Cockram (assessed at one pound, four shillings), William Williams (one pound, one shilling), and Peter Goudet (one pound). More commonly, however, the assessments of former pirates tended to fall on the lower end of the spectrum. Ten of the former pirates were assessed at a modest four shillings, and two others, Joseph Pearse and Henry Shipton, were assessed at two shillings, making them perhaps the poorest of Providence's pirates. John Cullimore, assessed at zero, presumably received an exemption by virtue of his position as constable.[107]

In addition to fulfilling their financial obligations to the church, former pirates also served the state, as exemplified by the officeholding of Peter Goudet. After serving Governor Rogers informally as an accountant, his successor, Governor George Phenney, appointed Goudet as clerk of the Crown around August 1723. The clerkship entailed drafting correspondence dictated by the governor and taking minutes at council meetings. Goudet must have performed well, as Phenney kept him in that position for the duration of his governorship and steadily gave him more responsibility. By January 1, 1725, Goudet assumed duties as the colony's treasurer. One of the earliest surviving documents bearing his name is an account of the colony's cash reserves. His ledger tallied income, calculated in pieces of eight and derived from duties on trade goods and fines. It likewise enumerated expenditures for the construction of a church. That same day, Goudet also signed off on gunner John Allen's account of expenditures for the fort.

For the next four years, this became Goudet's standard routine. As treasurer, on a more or less daily basis he would have been responsible for collecting and keeping track of all monies raised, as well as making payments for supplies and for services rendered to the government. Goudet knew the relative value of Spanish silver and was able to convert it to British pounds sterling, which he performed the first quarter of each year, when he submitted the previous year's accounts. One of the problems he and the council dealt with regularly was raising public revenue in a colony that lacked a legislative assembly, which normally would have been responsible for passing tax bills. In some cases, raising and collecting public funds must have required deft political skill. In 1726, for example, the council negotiated with the inhabitants of Eleuthera and Harbor Island, who were reluctant to contribute to public works projects that disproportionately benefited the island of Providence. Nevertheless, they worked out a deal whereby they managed to raise in excess of 233 pieces of eight as "agreed by the inhabitants" of the two outlying islands. As the reconstruction of the fort was ongoing, Goudet was also responsible for distributing pay vouchers to those who labored at the fort, totaling in excess of 550 pieces of eight. Goudet managed to submit a balanced budget each year. Yet, having firsthand knowledge of the colony's finances, he must have been painfully aware of its diminishing revenue. In 1725, when Goudet first assumed treasurer's duties, the public revenue exceeded 1,770 pieces of eight. The next year it fell slightly, to 1,681, and then the colony experienced a drastic decline in 1727, when the colony took in a mere 423 pieces of eight, a figure that rebounded slightly in 1728.[108]

The institution of a legislative assembly in 1729 therefore must have seemed like a godsend in the Bahamas, whose government was finally brought in line with other colonies, as well as the British constitution. The people of Providence must have placed great trust in Goudet, electing him as one of their representatives. The Assembly met for the first time on September 29 and started working on legislation about a week later. Although Goudet served just one term in the Assembly, his fingerprints are everywhere on the colony's first laws. Goudet was appointed as one of four commissioners of highways, a body empowered to oversee the construction of new roads.

One bill Goudet worked on sought to prevent the "stealing and destruction of fruit and other provisions that are the produce of these islands." Along those same lines, Goudet was tasked with devising a bill to "prevent the destroying of wood by fire or otherwise," evidently aimed at arsonists. Goudet also helped craft two of the most important bills. As the colony's treasurer, he applied his expertise to devise the first law to raise public taxes. Goudet worked on another bill to regulate slaves—in which Goudet, as a slave owner, had a vested interest.[109]

Officeholding entangled Goudet in the government's chronic infighting and exposed him to accusations of misconduct. For example, in 1728, in the waning days of his tenure as governor, Phenney named Goudet as the Bahamas' deputy receiver of customs. In the meantime, the Crown appointed William Fairfax in that same position, leading to a dispute between the two men as to whose appointment was legitimate. When the dispute came before the council, it was determined that Goudet, who refused to step down, could remain in his position temporarily provided he paid security for good behavior. Whether or not he paid is unclear, but within a matter of months, Fairfax, not Goudet, was exercising duties as deputy receiver.

Having ridden Phenney's coattails into the office of treasurer, Goudet unwittingly became embroiled in the former governor's legal and financial troubles. As he left office in the fall of 1729, Phenney found himself indebted to one Edward Cale, who, as it turned out, had named Goudet as the executor of his estate. Phenney urged Goudet to "secure the effects" of Cale and provide him with information about the status of his finances, evidently in an attempt to evade the debt. Goudet refused to comply, and his secretive behavior led the council to believe that Goudet had a "design to convert the effects of the late Edward Cale to his own proper use"—in other words, stealing. At the behest of the council, Goudet eventually complied and submitted Cale's account book. Goudet, however, refused to appear before the council, and the matter seems to have been dropped.[110]

Meanwhile, Phenney also faced charges of illegally raising public funds without the approbation of a duly elected assembly, and then misappropriating the money. The Board of Trade conducted an investigation spanning more than a year, requiring Goudet to leave the Bahamas and appear in London before the board as a witness. Arriving in June 1731, Goudet defended Phenney's fiscal management, stating that "not having had power to call any Assembly, they were obliged to raise money for the public service without it." Goudet also affirmed that Phenney had spent some of his own money to obtain provisions for the colony, resulting in monetary compensation for the former governor.[111] Perhaps because of the testimony he provided, as well as the high quality of his bookkeeping, Goudet received an appointment as customs collector for the newly instituted port of Winyaw Bay, South Carolina.[112]

Goudet, of course, was not the only former pirate to serve the colony. Eleven or more served on grand juries at various points in the 1720s and 1730s. These include some of their cohort's most engaged citizens, like Thomas Terrill, Daniel Stillwell, George Raddon, Robert Brown, Peter Goudet, Charles Whitehead, and John Cullimore, but also men who appear in the historical record infrequently, like Adonijah Stanberry.[113] In addition to adjudicating cases that came before them in quarterly court sessions, the grand jury occasionally presented a written "address" to the governor, often flattering him with obsequious words of praise. These addresses also offer a window into the Bahamians' thinking about public affairs, as they denote the perceived shortcomings of the colony that the citizenry felt required the governor's intervention. For example, in their August 1722 address, the grand jury recommended the institution of an assembly, which in turn could raise taxes for the continuing repair of the fort, which they noted still lacked bastions. A year and a half later, in May 1724, the grand jury bemoaned the fort's lack of provisions and gunpowder. At the same time, they recommended having a small man-of-war dock there permanently as the colony's station ship, which by defending oceangoing traffic would improve trade. That December the grand jury lamented that the Bahamas could not afford placing an agent in London to lobby on its behalf (something done in many other colonies) and asked Governor Phenney to assume that role in ad hoc fashion through written correspondence with his superiors back home. In February 1726 the grand jury chastised the Bahamas Society, the joint-stock company involved in the settlement of the colony, for failing to provide enough supplies. A year later the grand jury asked that a "proper officer" be sent to the Bahamas to write property deeds and maintain land records. They also requested, again, an assembly so that tax money could be raised. The lack of an assembly was the most persistent of the colony's problems. That ten former pirates signed their names to the addresses indicates that they supported these initiatives, and they exhibited enough public spiritedness to diagnose the colony's shortcomings and offer remedies.[114]

In addition to serving on grand juries, former pirates appear as minor officers in the court, as well as jurors in a few noteworthy criminal cases. William Bridges and Adonijah Stanberry, for instance, served as jurors in a March 1719 court of oyer and terminer that convicted William Whalin of theft and of burning down a house in Nassau. Based on the testimony of several persons, including former pirate Thomas Terrill, the jury sent Whalin to the gallows.[115] John Arturreal and Charles Whitehead, meanwhile, were among the twelve men who adjudicated the case of a Bristol mariner who in February 1722 arrived at Nassau with no bill of lading, causing the jury to condemn it and sell the goods.[116] Arturreal and Whitehead thus played a small role in enforcing the British Empire's acts of trade. Likewise, on several occasions William Williams served as the clerk and deputy marshal for the court of quarterly sessions. Because he was fluent in Spanish, Williams also interpreted for Spanish prisoners on trial, including for the members of Augustine Blanco's crew rounded up in 1722.[117] Finally, former pirates also acquiesced to militia duty, with eight of them listed in 1727 as men "fit to bear arms."[118]

It was not, therefore, the reformed pirates who were the Bahamas' greatest malefactors. That distinction belongs instead to some of the Crown's high officers, whose graft and infighting cause one to question who the real pirates were. In December 1721 two factions among the governing council dredged up piracy accusations against councilors John Howell and Thomas Walker. The infighting spilled over into the early weeks of 1722 and perhaps compelled some unknown people to make their opinion of them known by smearing feces on the Great Seal the night of March 1. Although the councilors eventually made amends, the Bahamas continued to suffer from the bad behavior of governing officials. Councilor Peter Courant, for instance, was a bigamist who abandoned his wife and began living openly with another woman. After being fined, Courant and his lover fled the colony "to parts unknown." Only then did the council see fit to strip Courant of his office.[119] Councilors also sometimes weaponized accusations of Jacobitism.[120] Uttering words against the government seems to have been a habit, in particular, of the regiment's chief officer, Lieutenant Simon Ferrall. In a case that came before the council in 1726, soldiers accused Ferrall (also a councilor) of uttering slanderous words, behaving like a tyrant in the exercise of his office, and conducting himself generally in a manner "unbecoming of a gentleman." Several months later, the Court of General Sessions convicted Ferrell for his verbal outbursts, and he languished in prison for two years before successfully petitioning to be sent home.[121]

Finally, as noted above, Governor George Phenney suffered from repeated accusations of "maladministration." One accusation was that he skimmed from government coffers to line his own pockets, and on one occasion, he allegedly hanged a soldier for desertion after he received a pardon from the king. Phenney also labored under accusations that he orchestrated the exportation of the colony's supply of flour to maximize profits rather than ensure Bahamians could eat. His reputation suffered greatly because of his wife, who as a "sole trader" monopolized commercial activity at Providence, charging exorbitant prices for provisions. So offensive was the Phenneys' behavior that some accused them of driving away many of the colony's inhabitants. The Phenneys defended themselves successfully against most of the accusations, but the governor's health suffered and the couple returned to England in 1729, preparing the way for Woodes Rogers's second stint as governor (1728–32).[122]

Even more than conducting trade and engaging in civic duties, the most salient feature of life in the Bahamas was its brevity. Mariners may have assumed the risk of piracy because they knew that their time on earth was likely to be short. Privateering during the War of the Quadruple Alliance claimed the lives of Benjamin Hornigold, Josiah Burgess, and George Rouncifull. An untold number of others also must have died in the conflict, meaning that a critical mass of the pardoned pirates' lives ended by 1720. The island of Providence in particular suffered periodically from disease outbreaks, and we can assume these were responsible for claiming the lives of John Dalrimple (d. 1723), Robert Wishart (d. 1724), Daniel Stillwell (d. circa 1728–31), David Meredith (d. before 1731), and Jacob Roberts (d. before 1731).[123]

In addition to the attrition caused by death, a number of the former pirates left the Bahamas seeking greener pastures elsewhere. Thomas Terrill, for instance, moved back to Jamaica permanently in 1725 to be with his wife. Henry Shipton moved with his family to Jamaica, and in 1724 William Williams returned to Edenton, North Carolina, where he had lived before becoming a pirate and had met his wife. John Cockram left for an undisclosed destination in 1725 to dodge his creditors, and John Mounsey moved permanently to London in 1726.[124] Mounsey, a pauper, was later admitted to Bethlem Hospital—commonly known as "Bedlam," which housed the mentally ill—before dying there in 1732.[125]

When Governor Rogers conducted the first census of the colony in 1731, only fourteen of the pardoned pirates remained. Twelve of them appear in the census, and two others, Peter Johnson and Richard Newland, must have been absent at the time it was compiled. When Governor Richard Fitzwilliam conducted another census in 1734, only nine of the former pirates remained. Peter Goudet died a short time thereafter, leaving John Bley, John Cullimore, Anthony and John Kemp, Robert Shoar, Richard Newland, John Howell, and George Raddon.[126] George Raddon was still living in 1736, as is demonstrated by a tax list and deposition he gave that year. Bley, Kemp, Cullimore, and Shoar appear in a 1741–42 tax assessment list, although their careers as sailors had probably long passed them by.[127] Remarkably, Richard Newland was the lone former pirate still navigating vessels in the early 1740s. In 1742 he was the object of a prisoner exchange with Spanish authorities in Cuba during the War of Jenkins' Ear.[128] John Howell, now commonly referred to as "esquire," died in 1752 while still seated on the Bahamas Council.[129] The last man standing happened to be John Bley, who died around October 1758.[130] One is left to wonder if Bley, Howell, or any of the oldtimers ever discussed their past lives as pirates, regaling younger men with stories about Hornigold, Blackbeard, Rackham, and Vane, or boasting of the bravery and physical prowess of their youth.

The Long Shadow of Piracy

Although Bahamian authorities could with some justification boast that pirates had been expelled, that was not entirely true. In some ways, piracy provided a model for the extractive, exploitative Bahamian economy, which was subject to repeated boom-bust cycles.[131] The lingering specter of piracy can be discerned in the initial mistrust Governor Rogers exhibited toward the reformed pirates. The perception that the Bahamas was little better than a pirate nest also delayed the institution of an elected assembly for eleven years, for it was assumed that the colony lacked a sufficient number of persons fit for public office or capable of assuming their responsibilities as voters. The shadow of piracy also loomed in the conduct of Bahamian politics, whereby politicians sometimes weaponized the suspicious pasts of their rivals in order to impugn their character.

The political weaponization of piracy originates with the departure of Woodes Rogers, who left Providence in December 1720. The Crown named George Phenney to replace him as governor shortly thereafter, but Phenney did not arrive at Providence to occupy his position until November. For the span of several months, the Bahamas lacked a chief executive, so councilor and commissioner of customs William Fairfax stepped in as acting "deputy governor." Fairfax's presumption of authority stoked the resentment of James Gohier, who felt that he had a rightful claim to the deputy governorship by virtue of his position as the president of the council. Gohier, who was also the colony's chief justice, refused to recognize Fairfax's authority. He published a libel against Fairfax, warning the inhabitants that his motive was to institute martial law and deriding him as an "enemy of the people."

Fairfax retaliated against Gohier by removing him from the office of chief justice and accusing him of smuggling. Fairfax also made an enemy of Gohier's friend, Thomas Walker, another member of the council. Walker was the captain of the colony's guard ship, the *Delicia*, and had been shot at during Gohier's arrest, sometime in August.[132]

As a result of Fairfax's contentious deputy governorship, factions formed within the council. On one side were Gohier and Walker, who refused to recognize Fairfax's authority. On the other side were Fairfax and his friend John Howell, who played a key role in stripping Gohier of the chief justice position. These factions came to blows on December 10, 1721, when James Gohier leveled a battery of accusations of "maladministration" against William Fairfax. Fairfax retaliated that same day. He had learned that, despite his reputation as an anti-piracy crusader, Thomas Walker was overly familiar with the pirates and had even traded with them in the past. Fairfax convinced mariners Thomas Terrill and Peter Courant to appear in council, where they alleged that Walker maintained in his possession a bejeweled gold crucifix that pirates Daniel Stillwell and Benjamin Linn had robbed from Spaniards in 1714. In his defense, Walker conceded that he had obtained the crucifix in the process of apprehending Stillwell and Linn at Harbor Island in January 1715, arguing that he kept it in his possession as compensation, for he had spent his own money capturing the pirates. In Walker's mind, he had earned it.[133]

The two factions sparred in council for more than a week. William Fairfax defended himself four days later, rebutting many of the accusations made against him. Thomas Walker testified on December 17, affirming many of the accusations Gohier had made against Fairfax.[134] To retaliate for the piracy allegations made against Walker, he and Gohier dredged up old accusations that John Howell had been a pirate, as it was common knowledge that he had served as Benjamin Hornigold's surgeon four years earlier and accepted a pardon. Their objective was to have Howell removed from the council, so when that body met again on December 19, they called before them twelve witnesses to testify about Howell's past, including several pardoned pirates.

Possessing the most firsthand information was Richard Newland, who was present when Howell first joined Hornigold's crew. Newland explained that he had sailed with Hornigold as his quartermaster about the year 1717, when they took a Jamaican ship near Portobello. In the process of robbing the Jamaican vessel, and needing a surgeon, Hornigold forced Howell on board his ship. Newland affirmed that Howell expressed his dislike for the "piratical manner of living" and claimed that Howell attempted repeatedly to escape. One of Hornigold's consorts, a French pirate named Bondavis, was also in need of a surgeon and tried to persuade Hornigold to give up Howell. Hornigold apparently left the choice up to Howell, who decided to remain with Hornigold, preferring to serve an English, rather than French, pirate captain. Newland remained unsure, though, if Howell ever received a share of Hornigold's plunder. Pardoned pirates Robert Brown, Pearse Wright, and Edward Carr confirmed much of what Newland said, indicating that Howell was in fact a forced man who tried to escape. Several other mariners who were not pirates confirmed Howell's innocence, and William Fairfax predictably described his friend as a "gentleman" of "good character."[135]

Despite hurling serious accusations against each other, Fairfax, Gohier, Walker, and Howell all maintained their positions on the council. Howell's witnesses had evidently convinced the entire council that he was indeed a forced man who never received a share of plunder. Walker died four months later, which may have diffused some of the council's internal dissension. However, Walker's "crucifix case" surfaced again when the object in question could not be located during the estate inventory conducted after his death. The council called his widow before them, who testified that she had given it to another island resident, Parabow Skinner, to sell on her behalf. The "crucifix case" remained unresolved for almost four years, when in April 1726 Mrs. Walker and Skinner appeared before the council. The two testified that they managed to sell the crucifix, worth an estimated fifty pounds, for seven pounds, six pence "and no more." Unwilling to deprive a needy widow, the council allowed Mrs. Walker to keep the money.[136]

Of course, piracy was more than a phantom menace, for there were real pirates who had to be dealt with. Richard Clark faced piracy accusations in June 1720 that were dismissed due to a lack of evidence, and John Rackham's company began its last stand as pirates about three months later. The colony faced another homegrown piracy threat in July 1722, when mariner Alexander Wyat conspired with Edward Jarvis and Gabriel Tompkin (two felons who had been transported to the Bahamas), Daniel McFarling (a soldier in the regiment), and Valentine Rodrigo, a Spaniard who apparently had become a naturalized British subject some years before. The night of July 10, the five men stole a boat anchored in Nassau harbor and sailed for Andros Island. On route to their destination, the erstwhile pirates sailed uncomfortably close to a sloop, whose commander alleged that their "resolute appearance terrified him," causing him to return to Providence. Governor Phenney immediately outfitted three sloops to apprehend the suspected pirates. One of the sloops caught up with Wyat, and its captain, Solomon Middelton, asked that they identify themselves. Rodrigo and Wyat (who was also fluent in Spanish) responded by saying they were "Espanoles" or Spaniards, an evasive tactic indicating they were up to no good. Middleton's forces overwhelmed Wyat's crew, and they surrendered. A three-day trial in vice-admiralty court took place in early August. As had happened almost four years before, the court convicted the suspects and sentenced them to hang. Unlike the 1718 convictions, however, the council pardoned all five men.[137] The pardons not only indicate an unwillingness to execute pirates who did not do anything but also show that homegrown piracy had receded as an existential threat.

The specter of piracy nevertheless continued to hang over the heads of some of the few men who managed to live a long time, and it surfaced again after the arrival of Governor Richard Fitzwilliam. Born in Ireland, in 1715 Fitzwilliam received an appointment as comptroller of customs at the port of Carrituck, North Carolina, and moved into a similar position in Virginia two years later. He served for a time on the Virginia Council and held the position of surveyor of customs for the Southern District of America (encompassing colonies southward from Pennsylvania) from 1727 to 1731 before receiving an appointment as governor of the Bahamas in January 1733. Known as a "firebrand," Fitzwilliam was embroiled in many conflicts in Virginia, yet he maintained employment with the Crown despite repeated accusations of malfeasance. Bahamians, some of whom became familiar with Fitzwilliam during his stint as surveyor of customs, must have looked on with trepidation when he finally appeared in the Bahamas in early 1734.[138]

In addition to being "vain, self-centered, stubborn, inflexible, and greedy," Fitzwilliam harbored a deep mistrust of legislative assemblies. After just a few months in office, he developed a particularly unfavorable opinion of the Bahamas Assembly, describing its members as "a sett of headstrong, simple, ungovernable wretches." "The power of holding Assemblys," Fitzwilliam wrote, "has been very prejudicial to the inhabitants, because they are too few and ignorant to have any such previledge or power invested in them."[139] Fitzwilliam could speak of this with some authority, for, predictably, the inhabitants had tried to undermine his capacity to govern. Shortly before his arrival, someone absconded with the minutes of the council and hid those along with most of the colony's legislative statutes, presumably to "prevent [the laws] being put in execution." Fitzwilliam also accused certain Bahamians of publishing a pamphlet detailing the "grievances" of the inhabitants, and he alleged that some were conspiring to provoke a mutiny among the soldiers in the regiment.[140]

To attack those he perceived as his antagonists, Fitzwilliam dredged up old accusations of piracy, indicating that Bahamians still whispered about the pasts of some of the pardoned men in their midst. Fitzwilliam identified as his chief irritant the Assembly speaker John Colebrook, along with two or three other persons "who have heretofore been pirates."[141] One of Colebrooke's former pirate coconspirators was Peter Goudet. On February 22, 1734, Fitzwilliam arrested Goudet on charges of piracy, though he described his transgression as "using practices tending toward the disquiet of the government and raising mutiny in the garrison." While Goudet was in prison, the governor had his house searched to discover his motives and identify his "secret abettors."[142] Fortunately for Goudet, who was a few months from the grave, the charge of piracy did not stick. However, that did not stop Fitzwilliam from trying to level the same accusation against others. That November Fitzwilliam singled out Charles and John Walker, the sons of the late anti-piracy crusader Thomas Walker.[143] As in Goudet's case, the charges never amounted to much, probably because they had committed no piracies in the first place. Within a few short weeks, they were sailing again. In fact, Charles Walker later assisted Governor Fitzwilliam in putting down a mutiny among the soldiers, so it would appear that the Walkers eventually earned his trust.[144] Fitzwilliam, though, compiled a mounting list of infractions and was removed as governor in 1737.

The pirates eventually died out, taking their stories and memories of the old days with them. But in some ways the Bahamas never escaped the long shadow of piracy. In 1737, 600 pieces of eight were discovered in the home of John Sims, described as a "mulatto" who died intestate. After considerable hand-wringing and consultation with government officials experienced in matters of estate law, Bahamian authorities seized it on the suspicion that the Spanish silver had been obtained years before in some act of piracy. Around that same time, another cache of silver and gold turned up on the property of Benjamin Sims, whose pig had unearthed it while rooting around an orange tree. Sims claimed that the 1,000 pieces of eight were his and had been buried in a jar for safekeeping by his brother, who died before revealing its location. Fitzwilliam asserted that the property belonged to the Crown, but Sims refused to hand it over and managed to keep it for himself.[145]

Stories of buried treasure persist, and the colony's motto, "Pirates Expelled—Commerce Restored," remained in use until the Bahamas achieved its independence in 1973. With the passage of time, the memory of pirates has become sanitized and safe. Green Turtle Key's inhabitants, mostly of African descent, celebrate a local variation of junkanoo, or street parade, each New Year's Day featuring an effigy of "Old Bunce." Described by historians as "half Guy Fawkes, half mummery monster," Old Bunce is a trickster whose role is to "provoke amusement and exact tribute" from onlookers. Old Bunce undoubtedly preserves the memory of Phineas Bunce, the ringleader of the pirates executed at Providence in 1718.[146] Stroll around the city of Nassau today, and one will find numerous trinket shops selling pirate paraphernalia. One can visit the Pirate Experience, a museum of sorts featuring life-sized dioramas of golden-age pirates, including one of John Rackham, Mary Read, and Anne Bonny. Patrons who read the placards will discover the "Attractions of Piracy" (rum, riches, women, and the warm seas of the Caribbean) and learn to answer the question "Why Did the Pirates Disappear?" (war ships, the gallows, and Governor Rogers). Thirsty visitors can even down a pint of ale at Pirate Republic Brewery. Situated near the harbor, in the exact spot where pirates roamed the earth, the taproom's nautically inspired decor enables patrons to envision them, and perhaps entertain the notion that pirates are with us still.[147]

CHAPTER 6

A Pirate's Life No More

Even as a dead man, James Fasset caused trouble. After receiving his pardon, Fasset, a Philadelphian, hung around Providence for a couple more months. He and one of his accomplices, Edward Berry of Jamaica, claimed ownership of a sloop, most likely a vessel that had been seized during the course of their piracies. They named it the *Rogers*, perhaps to flatter the Bahamas' new governor, who was expected to arrive soon. On July 10, 1718, the *Rogers* arrived in South Carolina, where Fasset and Berry had the sloop registered before returning to the Bahamas a couple of weeks later to deliver three chests of glass. Fasset and Berry again went to South Carolina that fall, arriving just in time for the trial and execution of the pirate Stede Bonnet and his crew.[1] In the midst of those proceedings, pirate ships appeared off the bar of Charles Town harbor, causing South Carolina authorities to hastily assemble a defense force. Fasset answered the call of duty by joining the crew of the sloop *Revenge* (which had been Bonnet's flagship) under Captain Fayrer Hall. On November 14 Fasset's ship caught up with the pirate Richard Worley, commander of the *New York Revenge*, killing him and many of his crew in an hours-long firefight.[2]

Following his confrontation with Worley, Fasset drifted to Boston. Being illiterate, he never rose to the rank of captain or master of a vessel. Instead, he worked as an ordinary sailor under Captain Henry Timberlake, master of the sloop *St. Christophers*, which regularly made round trips to the Caribbean island of that name.[3] During his time in Boston, he befriended a local butcher named Mark Potts, whom he named as the executor and benefactor of his estate in a will penned on August 1, 1720. In addition to leaving Potts all of his supposed property, Fasset bequeathed to him any outstanding wages that might be due to him.⁴ For a couple of years, Fasset kept a low profile. His only legal entanglement was the arbitration of a debt dispute with another local mariner.⁵

Around March 1723 the relationship between Fasset and Potts deteriorated. Witnesses later testified that the two men had come to verbal blows while having dinner at a local tavern. Potts, it seems, refused to serve as Fasset's executor yet retained some of his legal papers. In turn, the illiterate Fasset asked Potts to return the papers, fearing that Potts might take advantage of him. Potts denied having the papers, and the verbal sparring escalated. Potts said that Fasset "deserved to hang," undoubtedly invoking Fasset's reputation as a pirate. Fasset called Potts a "rascal" before backing off, saying that Potts was "not worth his anger." Scheduled to sail again in about six weeks, Fasset hastily searched for another executor, prevailing on Boston clothier George Skinner, who agreed to serve as his power of attorney. Outward bound to the island of St. Christopher's on April 24, Fasset slipped overboard and drowned in Boston harbor.

Because Fasset and Potts had a last-minute change of plans, the administration of Fasset's estate was up in the air when, a day later, George Skinner appeared in Boston before probate judge Samuel Sewall. Skinner informed Judge Sewall that Fasset had drowned the night before and asked for a letter of administration to settle Fasset's estate, noting that he had "no relations in these parts" who could assume that role. Sewall honored Skinner's petition and at the same time ordered him to search for Fasset's body so that he could receive a "Christian buriall." Skinner appeared again two days later stating that he had it "on good information" that some of Fasset's belongings were lodged in the home of George Hargrave, a Philadelphia mariner who had recently moved to Boston. Still under the perception that Fasset had died intestate, Judge Sewall granted Skinner letters of administration empowering him to represent Fasset's estate. Three days later, Skinner initiated a debt case against a local mariner who allegedly owed Fasset £500. Surprisingly, on May 6, George Barwick appeared before the probate court to prove Fasset's original will in which he named Potts the executor. Between May 26 and June 10, Judge Sewall deposed three men who knew Fasset and had conversed with him about his estate just before he died. On June 17 Judge Sewall ruled that the original will superseded the verbal arrangement Fasset had made with Skinner. Sewall drew up letters of administration, giving Potts one year to settle Fasset's estate.⁶

The estate inventory compiled several months later indicates that Fasset was living hand-to-mouth and owned essentially nothing. His movable possessions consisted of a "parcell of tools & instruments," a pillow, blanket, and a rug valued at three pounds. In addition, Fasset's executors received twenty-two pounds in cash from Captain Timberlake for back wages, making the combined value of Fasset's estate the miniscule sum of just over twenty-five pounds. Fasset's earnings, however, were offset by more than eight pounds of debt he owed to three Bostonians. Court and filing fees gobbled up almost another ten pounds, and it cost four more pounds to pay for the futile four-day search for Fasset's body. Thus, by the time his estate was settled, Fasset was worth a measly four pounds.

What does a pirate do when he retires? Fasset's short post-piracy life offers important clues about the fate of the vast majority of mariners who left Providence. Like Fasset, most returned home to ply their craft as mariners, and some rootless individuals bounced around various colonies trying to earn their livelihoods. In some cases, pardoned pirates volunteered as pirate hunters, while others took up privateering during the War of the Quadruple Alliance. Fasset's inability to receive payment for his services, however, is indicative of how the former pirates' humble status sometimes disadvantaged them in the face of government bureaucracies and before the law. That Fasset's own friend believed he "deserved to hang" likewise illustrates that some individuals faced stiff odds in shedding their reputations as pirates. Indeed, a few noteworthy individuals never managed to transition to honest seafaring work. As was the case in Providence, former pirates from other colonies tended not to survive long, leaving it up to friends or widows to settle their affairs. Former pirates who succeeded in shedding their pasts tended to live longer and inhabit communities that offered sufficient opportunities for conducting honest trade. Boston, Massachusetts, was one such community, perhaps incentivizing Fasset's decision to relocate there prior to his death. Altogether, the experiences of these men indicate that there was no single way to be a pardoned pirate.

Diaspora

One of the principle strategies pirates employed to slip back into mainstream society was through dispersal. Typically, when a pirate crew decided to end its predations and part ways, small groups of individuals would catch passing vessels bound for various destinations in Britain, Ireland, or the colonies. Consider, for example, Henry Every's crew, which fanned out in small numbers to the Bahamas, South Carolina, Pennsylvania, and Massachusetts. The former crew of Howell Davis and Bartholomew Roberts did much the same two decades later. In addition to the forty-odd individuals who shipwrecked at Craignish, Scotland, smaller numbers deposited themselves in Virginia, Anguilla, and St. Thomas. Because relatively few such individuals were ever arrested, historians rightly presume this was a successful strategy. Speculatively, some former pirates were returning home, while others—those with fewer preexisting attachments to place—probably sought a fresh start elsewhere. Many resumed seafaring careers, while a select few became planters, artisans, or innkeepers. At the time of the pardon, Captain Pearse indicated that roughly half of the pirates fled when he appeared, and during his stay at Providence, he continually referred to instances of pardoned pirates catching the first available ship to other colonies.[7] By returning home, the pardoned pirates formed a kind of diaspora that spanned virtually all of Britain and its American colonies. But it was a diaspora of a different kind, one requiring secrecy and a willingness to shed, rather than embrace, one's identity as a pirate.

It is possible to track the homeward journeys of some of these mariners in the immediate aftermath of the pardon. As the Act of Grace technically required pirates to surrender to a duly instituted government, many of those who carried Captain Pearse's certificates believed that they needed to obtain further protection by receiving one from a colonial governor. Perhaps due to its proximity, as well as the preexisting ties many mariners had established there, South Carolina was a leading destination for the pardoned men. Mariners also sensed that South Carolina's governor, Robert Johnson, was inclined to honor the pardon, something they could not take for granted in some other colonies. In fact, two weeks before Captain Pearse arrived at Providence, eleven men had accepted pardons from the South Carolina governor, and news probably spread through word of mouth.[8]

No fewer than nineteen of the men on Pearse's list made Charles Town their first stop. The first to appear was the Jamaican mariner Francis Charnock, who accepted a pardon on April 13, less than a week after Pearse's departure from Providence.[9] Others began trickling into town over the next couple of months. Othenias Davis, Bostonian Samuel Boyce, Bahamians Thomas Reynolds and Samuel Richardson, and Englishmen Marmaduke Gee and James Gratricks appeared before Governor Johnson to accept the pardon on June 30.[10] Ten days later, Thomas Emly, John Ealing, Bahamian Richard Legatt, and Jamaican Edward Berry did the same.[11]

Others who ventured to South Carolina did not ask for another pardon, preferring instead to resume their trading careers as quickly and inconspicuously as possible. Most notable among them was Leigh Ashworth, the Jamaican responsible for pirate attacks against French shipping two years earlier. Since that time, Ashworth had quietly avoided Jamaican authorities by hiding at Providence. By December 1717 he began captaining a schooner named the *Success*, which was owned by William Gibbon and Andrew Allen, partners of one of South Carolina's most influential mercantile firms. That these eminent Charlestonians chose to employ Ashworth reflected his preexisting ties to South Carolina, and also that his reputation remained largely intact. After making at least one round trip between South Carolina and the Bahamas, it was reasonable for Ashworth to return to South Carolina after receiving his pardon from Vincent Pearse. There, he found employment on another vessel, the pink *Anne* (a narrow-stern, three-mast ship), which left Charles Town harbor around June 1. On June 14 Ashworth arrived in Jamaica, perhaps for the first time in over two years.[12]

Following Ashworth's example, other pardoned men funneled through Charles Town in an attempt to quickly resurrect their reputations as honest traders. Barbadian Thomas Chandler, for instance, had been singled out by Vincent Pearse as one of the twenty men who had returned to piracy after accepting the pardon. Nevertheless, he found employment there as master of the pink *Robert and Sarah*, departing South Carolina around mid-July for Barbados.[13] He remained active as a mariner for at least another seven years.[14] Philadelphia captain Daniel Carman followed a similar path in resuming normal trading, stopping in South Carolina before returning without incident to Philadelphia in late July. Pardoned pirates who ultimately settled in the Bahamas made similar voyages. Henry Shipton, for instance, sailed to South Carolina shortly after the pardon and found a position captaining a vessel he guided to Boston in early June.[15]

A select few mariners called South Carolina their home, or at least gravitated there for several months after receiving the Act of Grace. South Carolina mariner Robert Wishart, the convicted smuggler, made a beeline for Charles Town after receiving his pardon, arriving in late March 1718. Still in command of the Bermudian sloop *Endeavor*, Wishart arrived carrying "only ballast," an indication that his return home was not a trading voyage. By midsummer, Edward Berry and James Fasset arrived, and, after making one return trip to the Bahamas, they remained there for the duration of the fall.[16] Thomas Reynolds followed them, and he also stuck around long enough to engage in the fight against Stede Bonnet and Richard Worley before returning permanently to the Bahamas. Finally, Boston mariner Richard Rawlings gravitated to Charles Town and joined in the fight against Bonnet.[17]

A smaller number of pardoned pirates made their first stops in Virginia.

Because the colony's governor, Alexander Spotswood, was one of the British Empire's most devoted anti-piracy officers, Virginia proved to be somewhat less welcoming. For instance, Jamaican William South landed there around April 13 in the schooner *George*. It is not known if he sought a pardon from Governor Spotswood, but it is clear that his freedom was precarious because he immediately came under suspicion for illegal trading. Spotswood and his council directed the naval officer to impound the *George* and had South taken in for questioning. Ultimately, South was released, but the fate of his allegedly illegal cargo is unknown. Boston skipper John Jackson and James Kerr arrived in Virginia sometime before early May. They too came under suspicion for wrongdoing when the captain of a Maryland vessel appeared before the council to complain that Jackson and Kerr had lured one of his crewmen onto their boat, intending to abscond with him. Once again, the council took punitive action, requiring Jackson and Kerr to post bond for good behavior and appear before the council to answer some questions.[18] Finally, two of the mariners who sailed with Vincent Pearse's convoy appeared in Virginia as members of the Royal Navy. Thomas Graham joined the crew of the HMS *Phoenix* under Vincent Pearse. When the *Phoenix* arrived at Virginia in late April, Graham transferred to the HMS *Shoreham* and wound up spending another year in naval service. Griffith Williams, meanwhile, somehow made his way to Virginia and joined the *Phoenix* as its carpenter, serving for several months.[19]

Pardoned men from New England who found their way home concealed the fact that they had been trading with pirates in the Bahamas. Boston captain John Richards upheld a ruse whereby, instead of subjecting himself to the naval officers in Boston, Richards landed his ship at the smaller port of Marblehead, which had no naval officer. The newspaper indicated that he had entered inward "from Jamaica," suggesting that Richards neglected to mention his stopover in the Bahamas. Similarly, John Mitchell of Charlestown normally would have entered his vessels at the port of Boston, but when he departed from the Bahamas, he sailed for the New Hampshire port of Piscataway, arriving around mid-April. Piscataway at that time also lacked a naval officer, so Mitchell would not have to reveal his complicity in the pirate trade. As with the others, the newspaper bluntly reported that he had arrived "from North Carolina," indicating that he also concealed his whereabouts. In addition to these New Englanders, Bahamian John Bley, who had ties to the region, sailed from the Bahamas directly to Newport, Rhode Island. When he arrived in early April, the Boston newspaper reported that Bley had carried with him "two of the pirates who surrendered" but did not reveal that Bley too had received a pardon. After spending a short time in Rhode Island, Bley sailed for Boston and from there set out on a trading voyage to the Leeward Islands before returning to the Bahamas.[20]

In all, 27 of the 209 men on Pearse's list from colonies other than the Bahamas appear somewhere in the historical record within roughly four months of the pardon. Additionally, approximately ten others sailed in a convoy with Vincent Pearse to New York, the subject of the next chapter. Bostonian Abraham Adams found his way home, as did his contemporary across the harbor, William Rouse of Charlestown. Henry Berry, meanwhile, eventually reached Newport, Rhode Island. Given the prevalence of Jamaicans, it is unsurprising to see mariners John Dunkin, Thomas Williamson, William Austin, John Crew, John Johnson, and Nicholas Woodale appear in Jamaica's Anglican Church registers.[21] Two names on Pearse's list pop up in Edenton, North Carolina: Richard Richards (originally from Boston) and Thomas Stoneham, a carpenter who undoubtedly was intimately acquainted with the town's mariners. Cornelius Mahon and William Hasleton returned to Barbados, and John Smith appeared in Bermuda before embarking on a life as a maritime nomad in the following decade.[22] Like Smith, a few of the mariners' homes are hard to pin down, indicating the mobility inherent to their trade. George Sinclair, for example, in the mid-1720s owned and sailed vessels registered in Bermuda and Jamaica, indicating his continuing ties to both colonies. He traded regularly in the Bahamas and South Carolina, where he possibly died in 1730.[23]

In addition to those who are easily identifiable from Pearse's list, many others are enigmatic because their appearance in the historical record is brief. For example, could Thomas Trouton and Packer Adams be the same men who apprenticed as Thames watermen in London more than a decade earlier?[24] It is conceivable that after learning to pilot vessels in their home port, the two men started making ocean voyages. Adams, for one, spent more than one year in the navy, enlisting on the HMS *Blandford*, which saw service in the Caribbean toward the end of Queen Anne's War.[25] Similarly, Richard Kaine was a shipwright from Charles Town, South Carolina. Given his proximity to the Bahamas and the likelihood that he knew some of the pirates, it is no stretch to imagine that he is the same man.[26] A few other individuals with uncommon names offer the tantalizing prospect of the geographical scope of the origins, and ultimate destinations, of the pirate community. Thomas Clies possessed an uncommon surname that is concentrated in the village of Breage, Cornwall, adjacent to the minor port of Porthleven. Two infant boys named Thomas were baptized in the local church in 1687 and 1689, undoubtedly cousins. Given the Cornish seafaring tradition and the uniqueness and concentration of that surname, one of them likely became a pirate.[27] Characteristic of commoners who lived three centuries ago, as of this writing forty of the men on Pearse's list cannot be identified conclusively in the historical record, making their pardons the only definitive proof that they had ever existed.

Many of the pardoned pirates are difficult to locate because they died within a few years after leaving the Bahamas. Some of their deaths are easy to confirm. Francis Lesley, for instance, was buried in his home parish of St. Michael's, Barbados, in November 1718. Peter Mallet (or Melotte) also died in 1718, as revealed by a memorial to him in the church at Charlestown, Nevis, that is still partially legible. In addition to indicating that he was a native of New York who married into a local family, the inscription reveals the year of his death and that he was buried "att sea."[28] William Rouse of Charlestown, Massachusetts, died in January 1721.[29] As was the case in the Bahamas, a gradual attrition occurred whereby the men on Pearse's list either died in the 1720s or disappeared from the historical record.

John Mitchell's untimely demise shortly after the pardon illuminates the expansiveness of his entanglements as a sea captain and provides a unique opportunity to observe how his widow, Elizabeth, coped with her loss. Mitchell, whom Pearse identified as one of the pardoned men who turned pirate again, quickly made his way to North Carolina, where he had sailed regularly in years past. He must have died before June 3, when his widow Elizabeth, along with William Montfort of Boston and Joseph York of Gloucester, Massachusetts, named mariner James Nichols as their power of attorney, granting him authority to initiate a lawsuit against a North Carolina merchant named Edward Mayo. The men involved in the lawsuit were co-owners of the sloop *Hannah and Mary*, which Mitchell had captained since 1711. Mayo was the object of the lawsuit because he had been named the executor of the estate of the deceased Ann Jennings, who owed the co-partners of the sloop more than eight pounds in specie for a debt contracted in 1715. Whereas the men could sign their own names to the power of attorney, Elizabeth consented with a mark. Because of her illiteracy and gender, Mitchell required the assistance of her deceased husband's business partners and friends to engage with the court system in a distant colony.[30]

Although Mitchell was prepared to take action immediately after her husband's death, over four years passed before her attorneys initiated the lawsuit in a North Carolina court. The reason for that delay probably stemmed from a protracted property dispute she had to resolve with a Charlestown neighbor.³¹ Beginning in September 1722, the Chowan precinct court summoned Mayo several times, but Mayo refused to appear. A notation on a March 1723 attachment indicates that Mayo justified his absence on the grounds that more than three years had expired since the debt had been contracted, and therefore it should be invalidated. Mitchell and Montfort countered, arguing that debts had no expiration date. Mitchell and Montfort convinced the court to summon Mayo again in May 1723, and at that point the paper trail runs cold, suggesting that Elizabeth Mitchell never saw the eight pounds of specie she was owed.³²

As a coda to Elizabeth Mitchell's story, it is reasonable to suspect that she endured poverty in her final days. Sometime before 1727, Mitchell moved to nearby Malden to live with her eldest daughter. That October, the town of Malden issued a summons to the sixty-five-year-old Mitchell to appear in court to answer the charge that she had been "absenting herself from the public worship on the Lord's day." Mitchell failed to appear in court, which fined her. Mitchell filed an appeal two months later, asking the court to rescind the fine. She explained that she was "necessarily detained" nursing back to health her eldest daughter, who suffered from a "broken breast," or abscess of the mammary gland associated with lactation. In addition to her advanced age, Mitchell pleaded that she lived two miles from the church, and, because she had no horse to ride, attending services regularly was difficult for her.³³ Presumably, a sympathetic judge waived the fine. But the shame and potential financial burden imposed on Mitchell was an inconvenient distraction for an old woman nursing a sick daughter. We are left to wonder how many other pirate widows had to endure poverty and social ostracism, but one can suspect that Mitchell's circumstances were not unique. For a pirate, leaving behind a widow was an occupational hazard.

Rogues

While pardoned pirates generally refrained from wrongdoing and drew little attention to themselves, a conspicuous minority had a difficult time transitioning to legitimate seafaring work. For some who accepted pardons merely for trading with pirates, the temptation to continue doing so was strong because, for three months following Pearse's visit, there was still no government in the Bahamas. The more committed pirates gravitated into their old trade, indicating that their acceptance of the pardon was a mere pretense to keep the authorities momentarily off their backs. Because of antipiracy efforts in the Americas, the remaining pirate captains sought new targets and safe harbor elsewhere, particularly in West Africa and the Indian Ocean, where the golden age of piracy was for a short time sustained. Finally, the roster of pardoned pirates includes one outright murderer, indicating that a life spent cultivating the image of ferocity sometimes led to its actualization.

Vincent Pearse's departure from Providence in April 1718 created a power vacuum in the Bahamas, which was temporarily filled by the pirate Charles Vane, whose crew continued to attack shipping before Governor Rogers's arrival in late July. Because Vane had made several captures that summer, this presented ample opportunities for those seeking to profit from the clandestine trade in stolen goods that had attracted otherwise honest sea captains to the region for the past three years. Instead of returning home after the pardon, two New England mariners remained in the Bahamas and profited from Vane's continued aggressions: Robert Brown of Newport, Rhode Island, and William Harris of Boston. Although there were other sea captains who undoubtedly traded with Vane, his capture of the French brigantine *St. Martin* of Bordeaux ultimately attracted the attention of the authorities and could have landed Brown and Harris in jail, if not subjected to a death sentence as accessories to piracy.

Vane allegedly captured the brigantine around July 4, and its cargo of wine, beef, flour, and sugar attracted several customers, including Robert Brown of Rhode Island. He made at least one prior round trip between Newport and the Bahamas, so it was no coincidence that Brown was present when Pearse arrived in 1718 offering pardons.[34] Unlike those pardoned pirates who fled, Brown remained at the Bahamas for the span of several months, and when Governor Rogers arrived at Nassau in late July, he received information that Brown had on board his sloop sixteen hogsheads of Vane's sugar. Rogers impounded the cargo of the *Eagle*, along with those of four other sloops, and held admiralty court proceedings in early September to condemn the stolen goods.[35]

When questioned by the admiralty court's officers, Brown insisted that he was the victim of, rather than an accomplice to, piracy. Brown explained that on July 4 near Eleuthera, his sloop was taken by Edward England and Charles Vane, who stole in excess of £100 worth of goods from him, put some of the stolen sugar on board, and anchored it in Nassau harbor, unsure of what the two pirates ultimately were going to do with it. Brown claimed that he had been unable to return to his sloop before Governor Rogers arrived. As there were no witnesses willing to testify against him, the admiralty court let Brown go, requiring him to hand over the stolen sugar. Brown departed from the Bahamas on September 8, and it is unlikely he set foot there ever again.

William Harris's story resembles that of Brown. Although he typically sailed out of Boston, Harris enjoyed connections with merchants in Saybrooke, Connecticut, who owned the sloop *Dove* he commanded in 1718. Prior to the formation of the Bahamas pirate lair, Harris commonly traded between Connecticut, Boston, and the West Indian island of St. Christopher's.[36] The *Dove* was floating in Nassau harbor when Governor Rogers arrived, and it was swept up in the same dragnet that led to the apprehension of Brown's sloop, revealing that he had on board twenty hogsheads of stolen sugar put there by Vane. When questioned, Harris concocted an alibi resembling Brown's. Because their stories aligned so perfectly, Governor Rogers and the rest of the admiralty court knew that Harris and the others had been trading with Vane, but, again, the lack of witnesses compelled the court to release Harris but confiscate the sugar.[37]

Following the close call in the Bahamas, Harris continued to toe the line between legal and illicit trading. On his next voyage, Harris returned to St. Christopher's, where the naval officer impounded his vessel. On January 3, 1719, a prize court declared his entire cargo to be contraband, confiscating the frigate in the process. Harris, along with two merchants with a financial stake in the vessel, petitioned the Privy Council to reverse the charges. The council rendered a decision about a year later, carefully distinguishing the contraband goods from the ones Harris traded legally. They determined that over £187 worth of beef, butter, pork, tea, and spice were legal and therefore partially reversed the judgment rendered at St. Christopher's. However, the Privy Council identified upward of eighty-nine pounds' worth of candles, cards, and starch as contraband, so they affirmed their confiscation, "together with the ship, furniture, and tackle."[38] In losing the ship, perhaps Harris finally learned his lesson, for his career spanned at least another decade and not once did he again invite the suspicion of naval authorities.

In addition to those who continued trading for stolen goods, a small number of pardoned pirates embraced their outlaw status and never willingly gave up a life of crime. The most obvious example is Charles Vane, who accepted a pardon but remained a thorn in the side of Vincent Pearse and Woodes Rogers. After eluding Rogers at Nassau, Vane continued to attack shipping in the Carolinas, and there were rumors of him seeking to link up with Edward Thache and Stede Bonnet that persisted into the fall. Around August 1718 Vane briefly sailed in conjunction with Charles Yates, and the two focused their attacks on shipping in the Carolinas. One of their captures netted a cargo of enslaved Africans, which Yates put on board his vessel. Yates, however, had a change of heart and decided to turn himself in. He landed at Charles Town, South Carolina, on September 10, giving up the enslaved persons and asking for clemency. Governor Johnson accepted the surrender of Yates and eight of his crew, who received pardons that same day.[39]

Vane's demise is well known. After being deposed in favor of John Rackham, Vane acquired a vessel and sailed with a few loyal crew members, only to be shipwrecked somewhere off the coast of Honduras. Vane survived on a deserted island until a passing British ship spotted him in the early months of 1721. Vane appealed to the crew to rescue him and tried to conceal his identity by assuming another name. However, one of the crew recognized Vane (who was well known in Jamaica and in the Bahamas), and he was taken to Port Royal, Jamaica, to stand trial for piracy. The trial occurred on March 22, 1721. Somewhat ironically, three men who served Vincent Pearse on board the *Phoenix* three years earlier were on hand to testify against him, implicating him in the March 1718 capture of the sloop *John and Elizabeth* of New York. The captains of two vessels that Vane had taken in 1718 were also at Port Royal to testify against him. Vane, naturally, pleaded his innocence, but the court found him guilty. He was hanged on March 29, precisely three years to the day he attacked Benjamin Bill and the sloop *John and Elizabeth*. His body was placed in a gibbet and left to rot just east of Port Royal on Gun Key.[40]

Charles Vane must have been a charismatic individual endowed with natural leadership qualities, a reputation that persists in modern renderings of him on film and in video games. At least three of the men who accepted pardons from Vincent Pearse fell under his spell and briefly returned to piracy. John Mounsey surrendered with Charles Yates in South Carolina and lived at Providence for a number of years before returning to England.[41] Another pardoned man in Vane's circle was the Jamaican Nicholas Woodale, who traded with Vane and was caught around September 1718 ferrying some of his goods.[42] This feat earned him a brief mention in the *General History*. Woodale, however, never received a second pardon and probably lived quietly in Jamaica for another thirteen years.[43] A third pardoned man, Arthur Van Pelt, also served with Vane. Van Pelt, however, nearly was hanged for piracy in Virginia when Robert Fletcher, captain of the sloop *Providence*, brought Van Pelt and two others to the colony and failed to declare his ship before the naval officer. Fletcher, meanwhile, attempted to pass off the pardoned pirates as "ship wrecked men" he had saved from the coast of South

Carolina. Virginia authorities considered Fletcher to be a shady character and remained unconvinced of his story. The Virginia Council conducted an investigation, getting the three pirates to confess that they had formed part of Vane's crew. Van Pelt and the other men were tried in December, found guilty, and sentenced to hang.

However, further inquiry revealed that the pirates had abandoned Vane at the same time Yates's men surrendered in South Carolina. They had seized Fletcher in order to pilot them into Charles Town harbor, intending to surrender there, just as Yates's men had done. Fletcher instead took them to Virginia, but they insisted that their intention all along had been to accept the pardon. Ultimately, the Virginia Council made Van Pelt and his accomplices the object of their "mercy," reversing their convictions but recommending them for service in the Royal Navy because they did not want former pirates "straggling about the country."[44] Such was the lure of Vane's brash and uncompromising defiance of authority that some men were tempted to forego the second chance at an honest life offered to them by the Act of Grace.

Of course, Vane's crew was not the only one that quickly reverted to piracy. Notably, at least three of the men pardoned by Pearse engaged in the mutiny of the *Buck* sloop, which spawned the piratical careers of Howell Davis, Walter Kennedy, and Bartholomew Roberts. That saga begins in 1718 in London, where the copartners involved in resettling the colony formed a small squadron of supply ships. The *Buck*'s twelve-man crew, which included future pirates Howell Davis and Walter Kennedy, navigated the vessel to Providence in July 1718. About six weeks into his tenure as governor, Woodes Rogers sent the *Buck*, along with the sloop *Movil Trader*, on a special mission to Cuba and Hispaniola to fetch supplies needed in the struggling Bahamas. In order to provide more defensive manpower, Rogers supplemented the crew with about thirty pardoned pirates. Around October, near Hispaniola, Howell Davis led a mutiny, and the *Buck* quickly turned to piracy. After attacking several ships in the Caribbean, Davis and the crew of the *Buck* sailed to Maio in the Canary Islands, where they captured three ships, including a Liverpool vessel that they appropriated and renamed the *King James*. From there, the *King James* rampaged along the coast of West Africa in early 1719. Preying on vulnerable slave-trading ships, the *King James* supplemented its crew by recruiting disgruntled sailors working in the slave trade, including Bartholomew Roberts. South of Sierra Leone, the pirates captured an Ostend (in modern-day Flemish Belgium) vessel, the *Marquis de Campo*, which they renamed the *Rover*. At the Portuguese-controlled island of Principe, Howell Davis was killed in a firefight, after which the crew, now swelled to over a hundred pirates, named Bartholomew Roberts as its captain.

After preying on West African shipping, in the summer of 1719 the *Rover* headed to Brazil, capturing a valuable Portuguese prize ship, after which the crew separated at Salvation Island. Roberts and over half of the men jumped in a sloop in order to continue their piracies. Walter Kennedy and forty-seven of their men assumed command of the *Rover* and sailed for Barbados. There they captured and assumed command of the *Eagle*, a New York vessel. Small groups of men siphoned off at Anguilla, St. Thomas, and Virginia. Meanwhile, Kennedy and forty-two others sailed the *Eagle* across the Atlantic in an attempt to reach Ireland. However, a storm in the Irish Sea forced its crew to ground the *Eagle* at Craignish in Argyll, Scotland, around December 1719. About half of the men absconded and were never heard from again. Argyll officials did, however, apprehend twenty-one of the suspected pirates, leading to the convictions and executions of ten of them in Leith, Scotland. Two of the *Eagle*'s crew, Walter Kennedy and James Bradshaw, later turned up in London, where they were convicted in July 1721.[45]

Three of the individuals who came ashore at Craignish appear on Pearse's list, and they must have been among the thirty pardoned pirates recruited at Providence to supplement the crew of the *Buck*. John Clark, from Bangor in Ireland, in an early deposition tried to conceal his involvement in the mutiny, but he issued a gallows-side mea culpa in which he confessed to being a pirate before Governor Rogers's arrival there.[46] The second pirate identifiable on Pearse's list was "Doctor" Archibald Murray, a former accomplice of Charles Vane who served as a surgeon. Murray, the son of a Scottish laird, spared himself by turning King's witness against his accomplices. Presumably, he returned to civilian life somewhere in Scotland. Meanwhile, Francis Charnock appears to have bided his time in London using an alias before returning to his home in Jamaica.[47]

Upon the institution of royal governance in the Bahamas, pirates seeking to continue their lives on the account had gravitated to liminal, marginalized spaces in the Indo-Atlantic littoral where state authority was weak. It is therefore likely that the crew of the *Buck* sloop encountered other former pirates on the coast of West Africa, their new hunting grounds. One such individual was the Philadelphia mariner Richard Taylor, who remained a terror of the high seas for five years after accepting the pardon. Born about 1685, Taylor may have once served in the Royal Navy. By 1716 he was captaining the sloop *William's Endeavour* of Philadelphia, on which he made multiple round trips to Barbados and Antigua. On homeward voyages, Taylor clandestinely stopped in the Bahamas to trade with pirates, fish the wrecks, and engage in piracy himself, concealing his activities from Pennsylvania authorities. He was at Providence when the Bermuda delegation led by John Bennet explained the Act of Grace to the pirates.

Initially, Taylor responded enthusiastically, arriving voluntarily in Philadelphia on February 21, 1718, with five crewmen who received a pardon the next day. Nevertheless, Taylor seems to have found it difficult to sever ties with Providence, for he returned there almost immediately to receive a second pardon from Vincent Pearse. He was still sailing Bahamian waters that summer, now in command of the sloop *Elizabeth and Mary*. Taylor happened to be at Providence when Woodes Rogers arrived, and on August 4, 1718, Taylor volunteered information about a recent Spanish attack on the settlements at Crooked Island and Cat Island.[48] Perhaps it was a renewed sense of devotion to king and country that compelled Taylor four days later to volunteer for service on the *Shark Sloop*, then stationed in Providence, as an able seaman and steward to the ship's surgeon.[49]

If it at first appeared that Taylor had changed his ways, he relapsed into piracy just a few months later. In Philadelphia rumor spread that Taylor and his crew had been hanged in Virginia along with those from Blackbeard's ship, but in reality Taylor had joined up with Edward England, and he may have been working by his side for a series of attacks that December near Barbados and the Leeward Islands.[50] Having lost their safe haven at Providence, and with colonial governments and naval captains breathing down their necks, England and Taylor were among those who fled seeking new targets and safe harbors elsewhere. They wound up off the coast of West Africa and joined up with Howell Davis, Thomas Cocklyn, and the French pirate Olivier Levasseur (La Bouche). Mostly working in conjunction with these pirates, England began targeting shipping near the Gambia River around March 1719. The *General History* and contemporary British newspaper reports identify England as the man responsible for the capture of about ten British vessels that spring. Taylor, meanwhile, assumed command of his own vessel, the *Speakwell*, which was involved in the June 1719 capture of the slave ship *Heroine*.[51]

After their string of successes, England supposedly allowed his company to vote on their next move, and the majority favored trying their luck in the Indian Ocean. As their predecessors had done a generation earlier, around the fall of 1719 the pirates headed for Madagascar and the adjacent island of St. Maries to resupply, careen, and rest. At least two witnesses testified to Taylor's presence at Madagascar around that same time, each indicating that he had been the quartermaster of the *Dragon*, commanded by Edward Congdon. The witnesses declared that one of the Madagascar natives delivered a parcel of letters to the pirates, and the task of reading them publicly fell to Taylor. As it turned out, Commodore Matthews left the letters behind in an attempt to communicate with another naval officer. On reading the letters, Taylor learned that the two men were plotting to conduct clandestine trade with the pirates of Madagascar rather than hunting them down. "Damn my blood," Taylor remarked, noting that the two naval officers were "more upon the trading account." Nevertheless, Taylor remained wary, urging his compatriots to "stand by one another and take care of ourselves."[52]

At Madagascar, Thomas Cocklyn died, and Taylor assumed command of his ship, the *Victory*. Working in conjunction with La Bouche, Edward England captured a Dutch ship that he kept for himself, renaming it the *Fancy* in honor of the legendary Henry Every. In November 1720, near Bombay, England captured a British East India Company vessel named the *Cassandra*. Taylor assumed command of it a few months later.[53] Taylor remained active in piracy for about another two years. The *Cassandra*'s biggest prize was the Portuguese ship the *Nossa Senhora de Cabo*, which Taylor captured off the coast of Madagascar. Owned by the Portuguese viceroy of India, it was rumored to be valued at over one million pounds sterling.[54] According to one eyewitness, around April 1721 Taylor and his crew, consisting of 112 white and 40 Black men, voted to determine their next move. Overwhelmingly, they chose to give up piracy and depart for the West Indies, where they hoped to benefit from the Act of Grace.[55] Nevertheless, Taylor and his crew seem to have remained in the Indian Ocean for a while longer, returning to Madagascar before finally embarking for the West Indies around November 1722.[56]

Luckily for the historian, two of the pirates' victims penned memoirs that provide a glimpse of Taylor in action and give some insight into his character. Slave ship captain William Snelgrave provided a memorable account of his capture near Sierra Leone by Cocklyn, Davis, and La Bouche. Snelgrave relates how he was forced to have dinner with the three pirate captains on Davis's ship when a fire broke out on the main deck. As the pirates were "mostly drunk," pandemonium ensued, and even the captains did not know what to do. Snelgrave credited Taylor with saving all persons on board, saying that he "spared no expense to extinguish the fire in the hold," and despite being scalded he "never shrank until it was conquered." Because of his bravery and resourcefulness, Snelgrave opined that Taylor was "as brisk and courageous a man as I ever saw."[57] Jacob de Bucquoy, one of the Dutch crew members who remained a captive on the *Fancy*, knew Taylor well because he shared a cabin with him. He depicted Taylor as a mercurial man who at times "got angry easily and his fury made him out of control." Physically threatening, Bucquoy believed that Taylor was simply a "brute." Yet in moments of danger Bucquoy admitted that his "calm, his presence of mind, his personal courage in grave circumstances gained him the admiration of his companions."[58] As the historian Peter Earle observes, Taylor's mercurial personality, a mix of rage and calm, "was fairly typical of many of his pirate captain contemporaries."[59]

Following their successes in the Indian Ocean, Taylor and his crew returned to the Caribbean, arriving off the coast of Panama in April 1723. There, the *Cassandra* encountered Captain John Laws, commander of the HMS *Mermaid*. When confronted by a royal navy vessel, Taylor and his company finally decided to give up a life of crime. On behalf of the 107 crewmembers, Taylor wrote a petition to Captain Laws asking for an "island Act of Grace" issued by the Jamaican government.[60] Taylor explained that they had not committed an act of piracy for about one year and that they were ready to "render ourselves serviceable to our King and country and by our future actions make amends for the ill we have committed." Taylor proclaimed that he had not intentionally violated the pardon he had received several years before. Rather, he stumbled into it by associating with "those who had left Providence" who had "partly forced and deluded" him into returning to his old course of life.[61] Captain Laws initially responded favorably to Taylor's offer, writing back that the newly installed Jamaican governor, the Duke of Portland, had recently pardoned fifty pirates brought in by naval captain Digby Dent.[62] Captain Laws could not, however, pardon the men himself, so he sent a second petition from the pirates directed to the Jamaican governor. When the Duke of Portland's response arrived a few weeks later, Taylor and his men were disappointed to hear that Portland believed pardoning the pirates to be "wholly inconsistent with the honor of the English nation, and my character."[63]

Rejected by Portland, Taylor reached out to the Spanish governor of Panama, who offered them clemency if they agreed to convert to Catholicism and become Spanish subjects.[64] Taylor and his crew accepted the deal and even commenced selling valuable jewels and other commodities to enthusiastic local buyers.[65] Captain Laws tried one last time to convince Portland to change his mind, but the Jamaican governor held his ground, issuing a final warning to the Panamanian governor not to associate with pirates. What happened next is uncertain, but Taylor presumably assisted the Panamanian governor in ousting some English logwood cutters in the Bay of Honduras, crept back to Jamaica to retrieve his family, and moved with them to Cuba. There Taylor is said to have carried on for the rest of his days as a petty trader.[66]

Like Taylor, the New Englander Palsgrave Williams violated his pardon by joining the pirates who sailed to West Africa. After accepting the pardon, Williams joined the crew of William Moody, who continued to terrorize Bahamian and Carolinian waters into the fall. Later joined by Olivier La Bouche, Moody sailed for West Africa and was soon deposed by La Bouche as the commander of his ship. Williams appeared next in the spring of 1719 when he served as La Bouche's quartermaster, which he believed was a demotion relative to the position he had enjoyed under Sam Bellamy. Snelgrave records a story that illuminates Williams's jealous reaction to the demotion. The incident began when the pirates rifled through Snelgrave's possessions and found a chest with three used coats. Snelgrave advised the three pirate captains, Cocklyn, Davis, and La Bouche, each to take one for themselves rather than add them to the common pile of goods that were to be distributed by the quartermaster. This elicited a protest from Williams, who said he would cut Snelgrave "to pieces" for advising the captains to take the coats. Snelgrave was taken aside by a mariner named Elliot, who advised him to "be sure [to] call him captain." Williams "loved" the title, and the men called him as such to humor him. Snelgrave made amends with Williams sometime later and counted him as a good friend.[67] Although there are some reports of Williams eventually returning to Rhode Island to live the remainder of his life quietly, historians have probably confused him with his son or grandson, who went by the same name. Not once did the elder Williams appear again in Rhode Island, perhaps dying somewhere off West Africa or in the Indian Ocean.

While some pirates simply disappeared, the demise of John Lewis uniquely stands out because he is the lone individual on Pearse's list to be executed for a crime other than piracy—murder. Lewis, recall, first came to the attention of the authorities in 1715 when he cast away the Marquis de Navarres and absconded with the marquis's goods. Lewis appeared that summer in South Carolina before disappearing for the better part of three years. Lewis, who had a wife in New York, seems to have hidden at Providence in 1717–18. His name appears on a list of men who accepted the pardon in South Carolina in February 1718, indicating that Lewis was among those who fled Providence after receiving word of the Act of Grace, seeking pardons from nearby governors. Lewis promptly returned to Providence and received a second pardon from Pearse that March. Lewis then accompanied Pearse on the HMS *Phoenix* on its return voyage to New York. For a while, Lewis's status was uncertain, as the pardon applied only to those acts of piracy committed after midsummer 1715, and Lewis's robbery of the Marquis de Navarres had occurred a few months before that date. It is possible that Lewis spent some time in jail. In the meantime, Lewis's wife, Ann, petitioned Governor Robert Hunter directly, asking him to consider her husband's case. Hunter took up the petition with the council on October 28, and the council unanimously agreed to pardon Lewis, believing that doing so lay "within the meaning" of the Act of Grace.[68] After receiving three pardons, Lewis at last was a free man.

The War of the Quadruple Alliance offered Lewis the chance to serve king and country, and in the summer of 1719 he joined the crew of the privateer sloop *Three Brothers*, which was fitted out in New York under the command of Bermuda's John Cracraft. The privateers, however, were overzealous in the undertaking. On September 6, somewhere off the coast of North Carolina, the *Three Brothers* seized the vessel of one of Britain's allies, a French freighter, *L'Amité* of Dunkirk. Cracraft took the prize ship to Bermuda to have it condemned, landing around September 27. John Lewis can therefore be traced to Bermuda that fall, and he was certainly on hand for vice-admiralty proceedings that October. Lewis left Bermuda shortly after December 10, when he borrowed fifty pounds from a female innkeeper in the town of St. George.[69]

Lewis next appeared in the Bahamas. One man by that name enlisted as a captain's steward on the HMS *Flamborough*, which had been stationed at Nassau, and he served from March to July 1720.[70] Following his brief stint in the navy, Lewis somehow made his way to North Carolina, where he encountered the privateer Othenias Davis. In Core Sound, which comprises part of the Outer Banks, Lewis absconded with Davis's schooner and returned with it to Bahamian waters, plundering a Rhode Island vessel on August 6 near Abaco Island. Then about two weeks later off Andros Island, Lewis attacked the ship of Bahamian Neal Walker, taking two enslaved men, a foresail, and provisions. This brazen act in turn caused Governor Rogers and the council to proclaim him a pirate (along with John Rackham for different crimes) a few weeks later.[71] In the meantime, his wife Ann died in New York, and by 1721 he settled permanently in Pembroke Tribe, Bermuda, an area encompassing the town of Hamilton.

After dodging prosecution for piracy for over five years, it appeared that Lewis finally began adjusting to a normal life. He married for a second time, to the widow Mary Smith Joell of Pembroke Tribe, daughter of Samuel Smith, a preeminent member of Bermuda's governing council. Mary's first husband was the privateer William Joell, who died in action in November 1719.[72] Although they were married only for a short time, the couple produced a daughter named Mary, and Lewis became the stepfather of a young son by Joell. Perhaps because of his years spent privateering and engaging in piracy, Lewis had enough money to purchase two slaves. Lewis was also in a position to loan money. This led to one routine court appearance whereby Lewis sued a local merchant for eighty pounds. Lewis appeared in court again with his wife Mary in her capacity as executor of the estate of her late husband, again seeking restitution for debt. In addition to appearing in court as a plaintiff, in December 1721 Lewis served as a juror, indicating that people in Bermuda trusted him.[73]

For reasons that are not entirely known, Lewis's life rapidly spiraled out of control in the early months of 1722. That February, Lewis engaged in fisticuffs with his wife's former brother-in-law, Thomas Joell. Lewis initiated two lawsuits against Joell, one asking for ten pounds as compensation for assault and battery and another for ninety-nine pounds in damages. Bermuda's court records both cases as being "withdrawn," so the parties may have reached an accommodation.[74] Then, on March 19, Captain Francis Landy, a longtime Bermuda mariner and privateer, entered Lewis's home. Some kind of argument ensued, and Lewis took out a rapier, stabbing the unarmed Landy once in the back and delivering a fatal blow to the chest. Lewis fled the scene of the crime and went into hiding for a few weeks, leading everyone to presume he was guilty.[75]

Eventually, John Lewis was apprehended and stood trial from June 4 to 7. "On trial for his life," Lewis pleaded not guilty, but he faced stiff odds. Fifteen persons volunteered to stand as King's evidence against Lewis, including Richard and Rebecca Joell, Mary Lewis's former in-laws. Their willingness to do so suggests that some kind of dispute between the Smith-Lewis and Joell families lay at the root of Lewis's troubles. Witness testimony does not survive, but extant court minutes indicate that fourteen of the fifteen witnesses implicated Lewis. The judge delivered his charge to the jury on June 6, framing their deliberations in a manner that guaranteed a conviction, recommending that they not "meddle" in matters of law but simply determine "whether the charge in the indictment be proved." The judge recapitulated the charges against Lewis as if they were established matters of fact, describing how Lewis delivered two rapier cuts to Landy's body. The judge also appealed to the jury's emotions, asking them to remember

Landy's widow and fatherless children. The jury returned with a guilty verdict the morning of June 7, and Lewis was hanged a week later.[76] Like other widows, Mary Lewis suddenly found herself without an income, and the state appears to have seized some of Lewis's property. In January 1723 she petitioned the Bermuda court, asking for the return of two of Lewis's "negroes." She never remarried and probably remained reliant on her father's largesse to feed her family. Compared to other widows, she was lucky, as her father's estate was valued at over 1,100 pounds sterling at the time of his death in 1729. In his will Samuel Smith bequeathed property to his grandchildren and to Mary Lewis. But there was a catch: she was to receive them only on the death of Smith's second wife Miriam, a young woman roughly Mary's age who lived at least until the year 1769. Mary Lewis therefore probably never enjoyed full use of the property.[77] Such were the drawbacks of being a pirate's widow.

Pirate Hunters, Privateers, and Navy Men

While a few noteworthy individuals relapsed as rogues, more commonly the pardoned men resumed some form of legitimate seafaring. In South Carolina the continuing predations of Stede Bonnet, Richard Worley, and James Cole offered the opportunity for a select few to join directly in the fight against piracy by joining the crews involved in their capture. At least two more individuals served as privateers in the War of the Quadruple Alliance, and a handful of others enlisted in Royal Navy service. Most others presumably carried on as ordinary seamen, and only a select few rose to the rank of captain and made seemingly respectable lives for themselves after the pardon.

The establishment of royal governance in the Bahamas dramatically altered the calculus for pardoned pirates and any of their accomplices who might have been tempted to return to their old course of life. Gone were the freewheeling days when merchants and ship captains could trade in the Bahamas with pirates and expect to get away with it. By virtue of the Act of Grace, a bounty system went into effect on September 6, 1718, whereby crews that killed or captured pirates would receive financial compensation from the Crown. These incentives, combined with the stiffened resolve among merchants and governing officials, contributed to a kind of feeding frenzy atmosphere in colonial ports like Charles Town, South Carolina, where the pirate threat remained imminent. When news arrived that several pirates were cruising off Charles Town harbor, governing officials led by Governor

Robert Johnson acted. At long last, the war on piracy had come to South Carolina.

The story of pirate Stede Bonnet's capture, trial, and execution has been told many times before and therefore will not be recounted in detail here. Nevertheless, it is worth recalling that around the first of September 1718, South Carolina officials received word that pirates had been spotted nearby, the presumption being that it was Charles Vane. Colonel William Rhett assembled and commanded a small squadron of vessels, which Governor Johnson empowered to capture or kill any pirates they could encounter. After receiving word that Bonnet was careening his ship in the Cape Fear River, Rhett directed his squadron northward. Arriving at Cape Fear on September 26, they sailed upriver and caught up with Bonnet the following day. Bonnet surrendered after a firefight, and Rhett's victorious men returned to Charles Town on October 3 with prisoners and several recovered prizes, including Bonnet's flagship, the *Revenge*. Awaiting his trial before the vice-admiralty court, Bonnet escaped from a Charles Town jail on October 24 and fled to Sullivan's Island, where a posse commanded by Rhett recaptured him and returned to Charles Town on November 6. Between October 28 and November 8, twenty-eight members of Bonnet's crew were tried, found guilty, and executed. Bonnet stood trial on November 10 and received the same sentence. After several delays, Bonnet was hanged at Charles Town on December 10.[78]

Given the number of former pirates who gravitated to South Carolina after the pardon, it is unsurprising that two of them fought against Bonnet. The Jamaican Edward Berry served with about sixty others on board the sloop *Sea Nymph* under Captain Fayrer Hall, a relatively prominent local mariner who had close ties to the Bahamas because he had been engaged in the clandestine trade there.[79] Richard Rawlings of Boston, meanwhile, was one of the seventy men on the sloop *Henry* commanded by John Masters, which carried William Rhett, the squadron commander.[80] Berry and Rawlings therefore were firsthand witnesses to the epic battle of September 26–27. Because the river was too shallow at low tide, the *Henry* and *Sea Nymph* got stuck on sandbars the evening of September 26. Bonnet sent some of his men in canoes to investigate, and the pirates prepared for their defense. Berry and Rawlings would not have slept that night, because Rhett had ordered the men to stand guard in case the pirates attacked. Bonnet sailed downriver the next morning to attack Rhett's squadron, which stood its ground by sailing toward them. Once again, because of the low water levels, all three vessels stuck. The *Henry* was only a pistol shot away, and the five-hour firefight took place mostly while the sloops were beached. During the firefight, both sides taunted each other. The pirates were said to have "whiffed" their bloody flag and derisively waved their hats at the pirate hunters, who responded with choruses of "huzzahs." Both of the South Carolina sloops sustained massive damage. Rawlings must have thought himself lucky to survive; ten men from the *Henry* died, and another fourteen were wounded.[81] Although the author of the *General History* believed that the *Sea Nymph* had been "of little service" in the engagement, the sloop nevertheless sustained two deaths and had ten of its men injured, indicating that Edward Berry too had done a fair share of the fighting.

Amid the trials and executions of Bonnet and his crew, another alarm was raised in Charles Town when two pirate vessels, supposedly commanded by William Moody, were spotted outside the harbor. The pirate had recently taken two ships bound to South Carolina, and the citizenry feared that he might blockade the harbor as Blackbeard had done several months before. Therefore, Governor Robert Johnson impressed four vessels and issued a proclamation asking for volunteers and "promising 'em all the booty to be shared."[82] Upward of three hundred men answered the call. Four had received pardons from Vincent Pearse. John Mounsey, John Dunkin, and Edward Bead served under Fayrer Hall, who once again commanded the *Sea Nymph*. James Fasset, meanwhile, joined the crew of John Masters, captain of the *Revenge*, formerly Bonnet's flagship. Governor Johnson himself led the squadron this time, and on November 14 they caught up with the pirates in the harbor. The commander was killed in the ensuing firefight, and both vessels capitulated.

As it turned out, William Moody had made his escape, and the pirate who died in the first encounter was actually Richard Worley. Possibly a Jamaican, Worley was among those who had sailed on the *Bennet* with Francis Fernando and shared part of the plunder derived from the capture of the *Nuestra Señora de Belen* in early 1716.[83] Worley later drifted to New York, where his short reign of terror as a pirate captain began as commander of the sloop *New York Revenge*. The second ship that surrendered was the *Eagle*, which Worley comically renamed the *New York Revenge's Revenge*, and placed one James Cole on board as its commander. As with Stede Bonnet's crew, Worley's surviving men stood trial for piracy, leading to the conviction and execution of another twenty-six men that December.[84]

The names of the men who fought in these engagements survive precisely because of the legal instruments used to claim the bounty money provided for by the Act of Grace. Receiving bounty money was a slow process, sometimes dragging out for years. Seamen of modest means could not wait that long, and their professions required them to scatter regularly around the Atlantic and Caribbean. Having Crown officers distribute monetary rewards to each individual mariner was therefore next to impossible. So, about a month later, articles of agreement were drawn up in which the mariners relinquished their rights to the bounty in lieu of immediate cash in hand provided to them by their captains. In turn, ship captains were to receive the entirety of the bounty money; this was compensation for their trouble filling out the required paperwork, the delay in acquiring compensation, and the risk involved should the Crown renege on its promises. James Berry, for instance, received five pounds of South Carolina current money for waiving his rights to Fayrer Hall for the capture of Bonnet. Richard Rawlings received two pounds from John Masters of the sloop *Henry* for that same engagement.[85] Mounsey, Dunkin, Bead, and Fasset received fifty shillings (worth roughly two and a half pounds) from Hall and Masters for killing Richard Worley.[86] From the perspective of the ordinary seaman, it was probably a good deal, as the British Treasury was still mulling over the captains' petitions for compensation in 1723.[87]

In addition to the bounty money, the captors of pirates could also expect to receive shares of the plunder. Obtaining and distributing it fell within the purview of the quartermasters, and for this reason William Keith (*Henry*) and John Stevenson (*Sea Nymph*) appear in South Carolina admiralty court prize actions relating to Stede Bonnet's capture. The spoils from capturing Bonnet were perhaps less than the sailors were anticipating, since several individuals were on hand to enter a libel, or protest, to reclaim their stolen goods. As a compromise, Bonnet's captors received salvage fees derived from the sale of the impounded goods but had to relinquish the rest to their rightful owners. Prizes awarded for the capture of Worley's ships were perhaps more lucrative. Again, the quartermasters John Mason (*Mediterranean Galley*), Lionel Wood (*King William*), John Smith (*Revenge*), and John Howard (*Sea Nymph*) appear on all the legal paperwork pertaining to the sale of the prize goods. The condemned sloop *New York Revenge* netted £530 at auction, and presumably the four quartermasters distributed the proceeds accordingly. Moreover, goods confiscated from the *Eagle* (alias *New York Revenge's Revenge*) netted in excess of £150 at auction and £190 derived from the sale of the goods seized from the *New York Revenge*. In each case, the purchasers put down small sums of promise money, but the four quartermasters had to initiate court cases in February 1719 in order to collect the remainder.[88] It is not known if any of the remaining money was collected, and given the tendency of mariners to move on, it is unlikely that they received the full share of what was due to them.

Financial incentives no doubt played a role in convincing former pirates to serve as privateers during the War of the Quadruple Alliance. Two of the pardoned pirates who fled Providence eventually commanded privateer vessels, and two more served as crewmen. The most noteworthy was the ubiquitous Leigh Ashworth. Not much is known about his final stint as a privateer, although it is certain he returned to Jamaica in the summer of 1718 and received a commission from its governor the following spring. Ashworth appeared off the coast of Cuba in early May when he encountered two Bahamian privateers, William South and Thomas Porter, and engaged them in a brief firefight, after which he absconded with South's doctor. Ashworth's aggressiveness toward friendly shipping verged on piracy, so it is clear he retained some of the tendencies he had acquired in the past few years. He soon disappeared from the historical record, so he may have died during the war, or sometime before his parish church at Port Royal began keeping records in 1723.[89]

Ashworth probably assumed an aggressive posture toward his own countrymen because of the intense rivalry to capture prize ships. Othenias Davis provided stiff competition. Although his name is unsung in the annals of piracy and privateering, Davis was unquestionably the war's most successful pirate turned privateer. Davis first received a privateering commission from Governor Rogers on March 20, 1719. He commanded a twenty-five-ton sloop dubbed the *Movil Trader*, initially owned and operated by pirate accomplice Thomas Porter. When Davis assumed command of the vessel, he purchased a half share in it, and he and Porter agreed to split the proceeds of their privateering venture equally. At least three other pardoned pirates joined their crew: Marmaduke Gee, Richard Richards, and Peter Johnson.

Their first voyage was to the northern coast of Cuba, and it took Davis just one month to capture a prize, a Spanish sloop named *Nuestra Señora de Candelaria* (or *Assumption*). Davis intercepted the vessel somewhere between Havana and Key West, and its cargo featured three Black and six Indian slaves. The *Movil Trader*, meanwhile, continued to cruise the Gulf of Mexico for another three months, resulting in the seizure of another Spanish sloop, *La Ninfal*, on July 22. As with their previous capture, the cargo of *La Ninfal* included two Indian slaves. Instead of returning to Providence, Davis and Porter quickly made their way to Charles Town to initiate prize cases in the South Carolina Court of Vice-Admiralty. Predictably, in a time of war, the court condemned the two vessels as legal prizes, awarding them, as well as the slaves on board, to Davis and Porter.[90]

The prompt adjudication of their prizes must have convinced Davis and Porter to change their places of residence. The two men identified themselves as mariners from Providence but began styling themselves as being "from Providence... but now residing in South Carolina." Almost immediately after finishing their cases in vice-admiralty court, the two men received a second privateering commission from Governor Johnson, and they readied themselves for another "voyage beyond the seas."[91] After departing from South Carolina, Davis and Porter captured one more prize, the Spanish ship *St. Anthony*. Instead of returning to Charles Town, the privateers took the *St. Anthony* to Edenton, North Carolina, where it was condemned on September 12, 1719. The *St. Anthony* proved to be a much bigger prize than their previous two captures, as it was a 150-ton ship with a cargo of 107 tons of cocoa, 40 bales of silk thread, and an undisclosed amount of other goods. With each ton of cocoa worth £120, it was a valuable haul.

Biding his time in North Carolina, Davis's fortunes took a turn for the worse when, sometime in the summer of 1720, John Lewis appeared in Core Sound in the Outer Banks and absconded with the *Movil Trader*. Perhaps the loss of their ship, combined with the high value of the prizes derived from the *St. Anthony*, spawned infighting among the *Movil Trader*'s crewmembers. That summer Davis initiated four lawsuits in order to reclaim goods and money derived from it. Two of those lawsuits were directed at his own mariners. Robert Hawkins appeared before the Edenton court on June 21 in order to answer Davis's accusation that he owed him £1,000. About a month later, Peter Johnson received a court summons for the exact same amount. In addition to stealing from their captain, the *Movil Trader*'s crewmembers fought among themselves for the spoils. In one instance, Davis served as the attorney for mariner Robert Ingersoll, who accused Richard Richards of detaining from him £300 worth of cocoa and silk. Finally, Davis sued Edenton planter John Shackleford on July 29. Davis had apparently placed twelve tons of cocoa in his possession for safekeeping, but Shackleford lost it and owed him £1,440. The court's decisions on these cases are not known, but they were filed as "suits dismissed," indicating that Davis was promptly paid or that the court believed Davis's accusations were unfounded.[92] Following the loss of their ship, Davis's crew dispersed. Thomas Porter parted ways with Davis, appearing in Providence again before settling in the Danish colony of St. Thomas. Marmaduke Gee returned to London, while Peter Johnson made his home at Providence. Richard Richards appears for the last time in the historical record in Davis's suit against him. Davis received brief mention in a September 5, 1720, proclamation issued against John Lewis but then disappears from the historical record, indicating perhaps that he died soon thereafter.[93]

As was the case during prior wars, several pardoned pirates volunteered for short-term service in the Royal Navy. Two individuals, in fact, enlisted on vessels that had assisted with the installation of Woodes Rogers as the Bahamas' royal governor. John Crow served for about eighteen months on the *Milford*, joining on January 17, 1719, during the ship's brief sojourn at Jamaica, where he received a discharge on June 2, 1720. Meanwhile, Robert Bass piloted the *Shark* sloop for three months it spent in Jamaican waters in 1720. Three individuals served on the HMS *Flamborough* under Captain John Hildesey, whose appearance in the Bahamas around February 1720 helped deter a Spanish invasion. John Dalrymple enlisted as a pilot in the fall of 1719 and remained in that station roughly until the time of the thwarted Spanish invasion. William Williams replaced him and served in that capacity for four months. Thomas Stoneham, who can be spotted occasionally in Edenton, North Carolina, and nearby Virginia, enlisted on the HMS *Pearl* and was involved in the November 1718 attack against Edward Thache. Arthur Van Pelt, who frequented the same area, joined the *Pearl* for a three-month stint in the spring of 1719.[94]

Domesticated Pirates

William Williams had enough of sailing, and of the Bahamas. When the colony's court of quarter sessions summoned jurors to appear on February 27, 1724, something triggered Williams, leading him to absent himself in contempt of court. Perhaps Williams was mad that Governor Phenney had called up the militias the day before to work on the ongoing reconstruction of the fort at Nassau. Maybe jury duty caused hardship for those who raked salt for a living, as March was prime season. Whatever the case, Williams emerged as the "ringleader" of a group of jurors who steadfastly refused to serve in court, verbally cajoling several others to follow his lead. A day later, Williams and Charles Whitehead (both pardoned pirates) were taken into custody and called before the council to answer some questions.[95] The matter seems to have blown over quickly, but shortly thereafter Williams took his entire family to Edenton, North Carolina, where his wife Frances was born and raised. Arriving no later than October 1724, Williams and his wife transformed themselves into innholders, selling rum, wine, beer, and eggnog to a clientele of wandering mariners, local tradesmen, and planters from the countryside.[96] The Williams family were fixtures of St. Paul's Church in Edenton, which occasionally utilized their inn to lodge indigent persons and, in one instance, host a funeral.[97]

It was a quieter life than he once led, but one not without incident. In the spring of 1726 Williams and his wife appeared before the court to answer charges of innholders Bartholomew and Martha Scott for slander. Frances Williams accused Martha Scott of stealing a pair of silver shoe buckles from her, and Scott believed Williams made the accusation to ruin her reputation and give the inn operated by Williams a competitive advantage.[98] William Williams also found himself on the receiving end of a debt lawsuit when mariner John Bole sued Williams to recover in excess of £100 worth of goods he received but had not paid for.[99] A year later, a tailor named John Miles stole some butter and rum from Williams, sparking another lawsuit that was eventually settled in Williams's favor.[100] Finally, nearing the end of his life, in July 1732 Williams sued one William Mullers to recover a thirty-pound debt, in a case that was ultimately dismissed.[101] In the meantime, Williams served the local government in minor capacities, as constable, provost marshal, and court arbitrator.[102]

In May 1730 Williams drafted a brief will, directing his wife and executor Frances to sell his "two houses and lots" in Edenton. Frances was to receive her widow's third, and the remainder of the funds were to be distributed equally between their four children. Williams died shortly before December 20, 1732. Although he had worked as an innholder for the final eight years of his life, Williams identified himself as a "mariner" in his will, indicating that he remained a sailor at heart.[103] Like many persons, Williams died in debt, owing a local merchant in excess of twenty-two pounds in cash and nine barrels of pork. When the merchant tried to collect his debt from Frances Williams four years later, he discovered that she had "removed her self out of this government" to a destination unknown.[104]

Unlike many of his peers, William Williams managed to acquire a new trade that did not entail lengthy sea voyages and was lucrative enough to enable him to purchase two properties. He was also lucky enough to die with a wife and four kids by his side. For a pardoned pirate to live long and maybe prosper, certain preexisting conditions had to be met. First, it helped if he came from a good family, one that was financially competent enough to own property he might inherit someday. It was also advantageous to receive at least a basic education, as literacy and numeracy were essential skills for entering the officer ranks of trading vessels. A family's honor and reputation also mattered; a good family name promoted one's ability to establish credit, forge business connections, and even find a spouse of like status or better. Where one was born or made a home had repercussions too. A thriving port town offered ample employment opportunities for mariners, whereas one might languish in a backwater community with relatively little shipping traffic. The human density of a town, and even its climate, might play a role given that some British colonies were demonstrably healthier than others were. Prospering as a mariner therefore was contingent on simply living long enough, something relatively few of the pardoned pirates managed to do. Although the historical record self-selects for aged, propertied individuals, it nevertheless affords the historian an opportunity to observe ordinary people—even pirates—going about the routines of everyday life.

John Perrin of Virginia was among the minority of pardoned pirates for whom the wheel of fortune seemed to spin in his favor. His grandfather, also named John, arrived in Virginia as an indentured servant sometime before 1642, and numerous relatives joined him to settle in Henrico and Gloucester Counties.[105] By the time John (the pirate) was born in 1689, the family had become reasonably prosperous landowners there, inhabiting a peninsula on the north side of the York River that bears the family name to this day. He must have received an education, possibly enabling him to assume the captaincy of a vessel at the precocious age of nineteen.[106] As there is no direct evidence indicating that he participated actively in sea robbery, he probably accepted the pardon as an accessory to piracy, having (as was alleged) funneled Benjamin Hornigold's stolen merchandise to South Carolina in 1716. He also made several suspicious southward voyages, indicating that he continued trading with pirates there. He no doubt encountered Vincent Pearse during one such voyage dating to February 5, 1718, when he cleared outward from Virginia to the Bahamas on the sloop *Lucy*.[107]

With his pirating days behind him, Perrin had little trouble reconstituting his career as a merchant sea captain. He never again ran afoul of the law; the only extant court records in which he appears were for routine debt cases, in which he was most often the complainant.[108] Perrin probably sailed irregularly throughout the 1720s, but he seems to have reached the peak of his career by the mid-1730s, when he presided over a small trading empire. By then Perrin, who had ceased going to sea himself, had become the owner of five vessels, one of which specialized in the tobacco trade to Bristol, England, the family's ancestral home. He advertised his services regularly in the *Virginia Gazette*. In one instance, he boasted of virtues of his snow *John and Mary*, which he described as "a new vessel, well rigg'd & fitted" capable of holding "about 240 hogsheads" of tobacco for a voyage to Bristol. His process involved placing advertisements for freightage on the *John and*

Mary in December or January, while the various captains under his employ scoured Virginia's rivers until they filled its hold. The vessel typically sailed for Bristol around March or April, returning the following fall. The *John and Mary* made at least five such voyages from 1736 to 1745. Concurrently, Perrin dabbled in the Madeira wine trade. One of his vessels, the schooner *Sarah*, conducted two such voyages between 1745 and 1748, in which he exchanged items such as corn, peas, and tobacco for wine.[109] Perrin likewise regularly sent these vessels, along with his sloops *Diamond*, *Dolphin*, and *Abington*, to Barbados and other Caribbean destinations. Typically, the captains working in his employ exchanged corn, peas, ham, and lumber products for sugar and molasses.[110] Perrin's trading probably ceased by 1751 due to his advancing age.

No longer engaged in active seafaring, Perrin probably occupied much of his time enhancing the estate he inherited from his father and growing his own tobacco. Although we will never know for sure how much Perrin profited from trading with pirates, tradition holds that in 1716 he began construction on a brick plantation house on Sarah's Creek at Gloucester Point later known as "Little England," which directly overlooks Yorktown.[111] Perrin's newfound wealth may have enabled him to build it. A deed Perrin composed in 1747 illustrates the combination of land and sea businesses that occupied much of his life. In it, Perrin indicated that he owned an unspecified number of vessels, half shares of which he bequeathed to his son John, who also became a ship captain and merchant. Tellingly, he also gave him "22 negroes," indicating his aspirations for producing tobacco.[112] Yet Perrin continued to refer to himself as "Captain" for the remainder of his life, suggesting that he identified most with the sea. Perrin and his wife Mary had at least one other child, a daughter named Sarah who died young. John Perrin died in 1752 at the age of sixty-two, making him one of the longest-living pardoned pirates. He was interred in the family cemetery near the estate, and a century ago the inscription on his tombstone was still visible. "Little England," which housed French troops during the siege of Yorktown, still stands, and in 1970 it was added to the National Register of Historic Places.[113]

Prosperous former pirates residing in the backwaters of North Carolina and Virginia, however, are rare. Perhaps it is mere coincidence, but an unusual concentration of reasonably successful pardoned pirates lived in Boston or other nearby ports in New England. Arguably, the most prolific of the New England mariners was William Harris, the same captain who had his sloop impounded by Governor Rogers in August 1718 and barely dodged conviction for trading with Charles Vane. After returning to the New England area that fall, Harris cautiously stuck close to home and did not sail again until July 1719 on a short voyage to Connecticut. A year later Harris assumed command of the ship *Donington*, making the long voyage to London, possibly his only transatlantic trip. For a span of about seven years, Harris's name disappeared from the Boston newspapers, indicating that he may have put long-haul sailing on hold. Harris reappeared, however, in 1727, making one voyage to St. Christopher's. Harris's career peaked from 1729 to 1733, when he conducted approximately fourteen voyages, half of which were to North Carolina. Harris tended to stay close to home by working the coastal trade in North America, also sailing occasionally to Connecticut (twice), Philadelphia, and once to Antigua in December 1730. In January 1734 Harris cleared outward from Boston to Jamaica for what appears to have been his final voyage.[114]

Samuel Boyce rivaled Harris in terms of the number of voyages he made in the 1720s. Boyce got back into action in October 1718, when he assumed command of the schooner *Phoenix*, bound for Madeira. In 1719–20 he made two voyages to Antigua, and in 1720–21 he engaged in a yearlong voyage that took him first to Curaçao, then to the Bay of Honduras. Boyce's voyages tended to be lengthy; a 1722–23 voyage to Madeira and back took him seven months, and a voyage to London that commenced in September 1724 kept him away from home upward of ten months. In July 1725 Boyce departed from Boston to the West Indies, perhaps his last long-distance trip.[115]

In contrast to Harris and Boyce, other New England mariners appear to have been in the final stage of their sailing careers at the time of the pardon. William Rouse of Charlestown, Massachusetts, for instance, came home after receiving the pardon from Pearse, and he sailed for Newfoundland around May 12, 1718, for presumably his final voyage. Approaching his mid-fifties, Rouse had spent decades at sea, and his brush with pirates in the Bahamas, combined with the quick turnaround to Newfoundland, sickened him. Fearing that his demise might be imminent, Rouse wrote a will immediately on his return home, one indicating he was "infirm of body but of sane and disposing mind."[116]

Like Rouse, Bostonian John Richards's career as a sea captain was in its twilight. After the pardon, Richards spent upward of a year in command of the ship *Samuel*, making one voyage to St. Thomas in the summer of 1718 and another to Nevis that winter. Between 1720 and 1724, Richards made four more voyages, including a transatlantic trip to Portugal. Although he lived another nine years, Richards does not appear to have sailed again, perhaps relying on income derived from the rental of wharfage property he owned in Boston.[117] Fellow Bostonian Abraham Adams also retreated from active seamanship within a couple of years of being pardoned. Adams made at least one more voyage around 1719–20 in a sloop named the *Hopewell*, whose captain stiffed the crew of their wages. Adams and three other sailors had to sue him in vice-admiralty court in December 1720, and the haggling over wages might have convinced Adams finally to give up the life of a mariner.[118] Meanwhile, James Brown of Rhode Island remained actively trading between the Caribbean and closer destinations like New Jersey for about five years, and then he died in December 1723.[119]

As for the common sailors who owned little property, the historical record only allows fleeting glimpses of life after the pardon. In 1721 Henry Berry of Newport sued a fellow mariner who beat him with a "wooden handspike," asking £150 in damages for assault and battery.[120] In 1723 a Montserrat merchant casually mentioned John Hipperson in the postscript of a letter, indicating a rumor that he had turned pirate again proved to be unfounded.[121] Those who avoided all future legal entanglements appear mostly in church records, capturing them at key moments in their lives. In the parish of St. Michaels Barbados, for instance, Cornelius Mahon married Patience Hasleton in May 1723. His bride, a widow, had been married into the family of a fellow pardoned pirate, William Hasleton, who died and was buried in the cemetery of that same church in 1728.[122]

Given the preponderance of Jamaicans, it is no coincidence that many of their names appear in the island's Anglican Church records. In some instances, they capture moments of great joy, such as the marriage of John Crew and Jane Potter in Kingston in July 1722, and that of Edward Berry and Rachel Ryley, who wed in the same parish in January 1723. Francis and Mary Charnock baptized their daughter Elizabeth at Kingston in September 1724, but sadly, Mary and Elizabeth died less than two years later. Jamaican church registers confirm the pattern seen in the Bahamas, where pardoned pirates died off gradually over the next decade. John Dunkin passed away in 1723, followed by Edward Berry two years later. Richard Hawks and Griffith Williams died in Kingston in 1727, and by that time scarcely any of the pirates from Pearse's list can be found in the island's church records.[123]

Pardoned pirates who owned property spent their twilight years expending considerable energy defending it and ensuring that their families would be provided for when they were gone. For instance, in his will William Rouse arranged to pay ten pounds to three executors—all friends from Boston and Charlestown—to ensure that his last wishes were honored, relieving his wife Mary of that burden. In addition to leaving Mary the customary widow's third of his estate, Rouse's instructions were to sell off his real estate and three slaves to raise enough cash so that Mary could provide for their children, many of whom had not yet reached the age of majority. Although Rouse claimed to be "infirm of body" when he wrote the will in June 1718, he managed to survive for another two and a half years and summoned the energy to make property transactions, no doubt in an attempt to shore up his family's finances. Four days after writing his will, he sold the Charlestown wharfage property he had purchased in 1709, which netted him twenty-nine pounds. Then, in May 1719, Rouse purchased a house and lot in Concord for in excess of forty-two pounds. It was a bizarre move considering his infirmity and long-standing commitment to his home in Charlestown. Perhaps his health briefly improved and he contemplated retiring to the countryside to raise his family. Rouse was undoubtedly pleased that he lived long enough to celebrate the wedding of his oldest daughter, Catherine, who married Charlestown mariner Solomon Phipps in October 1720. To honor the occasion and give the young couple a head start in life, Rouse gave Catherine seventy pounds' worth of "household goods," a down payment on her inheritance that Rouse deducted from the bequest made two years earlier. Rouse finally succumbed to his afflictions and died in January 1721.[124]

The inventory of Rouse's property taken on January 26, 1721, gives some indication of his financial position and the way he might have viewed himself. With real and movable property valued at just over £968, Rouse had done fairly well by the standards of the day. His estate consisted of the "mansion house" and adjacent wharfage in Charlestown, as well as four acres of pastureland with two cows and three acres designated as an orchard. Because he had not sailed regularly for at least two years, Rouse owned only one "small boat." The two cows he owned appear in the record as "dried," indicating they were past their prime as producers of milk. Importantly, Rouse owned three enslaved men, all designated as "negroes" and valued at fifty pounds apiece. In addition to being a status symbol for New England town dwellers, who sometimes employed slaves as domestics, it is likely that the three men tended his small herd of livestock and maybe assisted in operating his wharf. In terms of movable property, Rouse's home featured many of the tools of everyday life, such as tables, chairs, and andirons. The Rouses obtained some decorative items too, including curtains, table linens, several wall hangings, and a "Japan table," indicating the appeal of goods inspired by East Asian designs.

In particular, Rouse's personal effects reveal the image he wanted to project before the public. He owned one sword, a sign of gentlemanly status, as well as two coats and three jackets that would have distinguished him from common seamen and laborers. The two periwigs he owned sent much the same message. Rouse retained some objects indicating his occupation as a mariner, including a quadrant (used for determining latitude) and two looking glasses. Rouse also owned one cane, enabling us to envision that a hard life at sea left him hobbling from a sore knee, hip, or back. Finally, the most valuable movable property was 165 ounces of silver plate valued at over ninety pounds sterling. We do not know how he acquired that much silver, but it is tempting to think he might have done so by trading with pirates.[125]

Rouse's attempt to acquire the symbolic trappings of gentility, however, belied the precariousness of his financial situation. Moreover, Mary Rouse still had at least four minor children at home to raise, requiring her to divest of some of the family property. In April 1721 Rouse's executors sold the pastureland to two mariners for £175.[126] Three months later they discovered to their utter horror that Rouse died owing money to creditors in London, most likely for a case dating to 1715 derived from his stint as captain of the *King of Spain*. Rouse's executors preemptively declared his estate insolvent to shield Mary from her dead husband's creditors. This enabled her to sell fifty pounds' worth of personal property earmarked for her children's maintenance.[127] Mary outlived her husband by at least sixteen years, and she remained in the house until 1737, when their youngest child, William, reached the age of majority. Mary Rouse sold the home to her eldest surviving son, John, also a sea captain. At sixty pounds, she gave him a good deal. The remainder of the Rouse estate was valued at £600, which was distributed to Mary and her other surviving adult children.[128]

William Rouse did not live long enough to see his youngest children grow to adulthood, and he never laid eyes on any of his grandchildren. Rouse's oldest son and namesake William (the first) had preceded his father in death six years earlier. Daughter Ruth died in February 1722, a victim of the smallpox epidemic that prompted the first vaccination controversy in colonial America.[129] Several of Ruth's siblings appear to have died around that same time, including Joseph (b. 1708), Peachie (b. 1712), and Elizabeth (b. 1714). Only four of Rouse's eight children lived to adulthood: Catherine, John, Mary, and the youngest, William (the second). Solomon and Catherine Phipps welcomed at least six children into the world during the decade spanning 1723–33. John Rouse married sometime before 1727 and had at least three children of his own. Daughter Mary wed Stephen Ford Jr., the son of a longtime family friend, in 1731.[130] Like most families, the Rouses experienced their share of calamities, but the ability of some of their children to survive and form families ensured William Rouse's legacy of blood descendants and property, something that many pardoned pirates never managed to do.

Other Boston mariners gradually refrained from active seafaring but resurfaced occasionally conveying property and filing or defending themselves against routine lawsuits. William Harris, for instance, sued a ship captain for unpaid wages in 1729.[131] Likewise, Samuel Boyce resurfaced in 1725 as a petit juror in the Court of Common Pleas, and he appeared again in 1727 as a deponent in a lawsuit involving the estate of a fellow mariner.[132] That same year, shipwright William Copp sued Boyce for £200 in a dispute over some property Copp's wife inherited on Prince's Street, where Boyce made his home.[133] In 1729 Boyce and his wife Abigail, in their capacity as executors of the estate of her deceased former husband, received permission to sell his real estate in order to cover debts that were more than fifteen years in arrears.[134] Samuel cashed in soon thereafter, selling a lot on Prince's Street to another local mariner for £330.[135] Samuel and Abigail appeared for the last time in November 1736, when, in consideration of thirty-two pounds, they relinquished their rights to a chunk of their land on Prince's Street to the town of Boston, intended for the construction of a new alley.[136]

Meanwhile, Captain John Richards retired from seafaring and divested of his Boston property in order to retire to his place of birth, Lynn. His legal squabbles in Boston were minimal; Richards appears twice in the Suffolk County records as the plaintiff in two lawsuits, petty debt cases that netted him a combined forty-four pounds.[137] Richards began preparing for his retirement in November 1727, when he sold one of the family's properties in Salem to another mariner for £370.[138] The family remained in their home on Ship Street in Boston, but in September 1731 they sold it and some wharfage to Thomas Hutchinson, father of the infamous lieutenant governor whose policies spurred the populace to revolt against their king in 1775.[139] Finally, in September 1732, Richards made the move to Lynn. As his wife Mary's name appears nowhere in the estate documents, it is likely that she died in the preceding months. Perhaps in Mary's honor, he purchased one hundred acres of pastureland and a small island in Humphrey Pond that had once been part of the estate of Benjamin Allen, Mary's father.[140] It was a homecoming of sorts. The son of a yeoman, Richards returned to his roots in the countryside. Unfortunately, Richards did not enjoy the bucolic life for very long, as he died in October 1733.[141] Richards's daughter sold some of the property a year later, while her two younger siblings remained in Boston to start families.[142]

The ultimate fate of the individuals who comprised the pirate diaspora features a range of experiences indicating that there was no singular way to rebound after receiving a pardon. Some individuals struggled to live within the bounds of the law, whereas others jumped at the chance once again to serve as privateers during the War of the Quadruple Alliance. In many cases, their lives were short. Therefore the image of a pirate growing old, sparring in court, conveying property, and bequeathing it to his children is perhaps at odds with pirates who adhered to the creed "A merry life, but a short one." As the experiences of William Williams in North Carolina, Virginian John Perrin, and several mariners in Boston indicate, however, pirates who were lucky enough to survive managed to accomplish these very things. In this, they resembled successful mariners and other tradespeople, whose goal was to achieve economic competence, earn the respect of their peers, and have something to show for it when their time had passed. If their individual circumstances were favorable, these goals were within reach. But success was contingent on several factors, including one's inheritance, education, industry, and no doubt some luck. If Boston provided one context where these factors were met, a tightly knit cohort of pardoned pirates from New York City proved that a common mariner—even a former pirate—could live long, prosper, and rub shoulders with the city's mercantile and political elite.

CHAPTER 7

The Respectable Pirates of New York

William Smith probably realized he had fallen in with the wrong crowd. When the erstwhile sloop *John and Elizabeth* limped into New York harbor in May 1718, Smith and other members of the crew spent a week confined in the hold of the HMS *Phoenix* at the behest of Captain Vincent Pearse. Leveling charges of piracy against the *John and Elizabeth*'s commander, John Sipkins, Pearse also pondered what to do with the sloop and the 1,978 contraband rawhides on board, allegedly acquired from the pirate Benjamin Hornigold. When Smith and his companions gained their freedom on May 27, they faced a barrage of interviews conducted by the New York Council. With the charge of being an accessory to piracy hanging over his head, Smith sat for three interviews. The first came on May 31, in which he divulged hearsay circulating around John Lewis, who had robbed the Marquis de Navarres three years earlier. Smith also acknowledged that he served as Captain Sipkins's mate on the sloop *John and Elizabeth*, recounting Pearse's seizure of the vessel near Exuma. Evasively, the Bermudian Smith identified himself as being from North Carolina and explained that he became familiar with the pirates because they had captured him and taken him to Providence.[1]

Sensing that Smith had not divulged everything he knew, the council summoned him again on June 3. On that occasion, Smith finally confessed that he had bought rawhides from Hornigold in the past, but he avowed that those on board the *John and Elizabeth* had been purchased legally. In an attempt to deflect attention from his own misdoings, Smith leveled countercharges against Captain Pearce, insisting that Pearse had given Sipkins a let pass to sail with the hides to Holland. Smith even recalled the exact wording of the pass, adding that Pearse had issued similar documents to other sloop captains.² Because of the seriousness of these accusations, the council called Smith before them one last time six days later. In a lengthy interview that must have occupied the better part of a day, Smith now identified as being "late of Jamaica," a confession indicating his proximity to piracy. Smith provided detailed descriptions of his mission to Providence with Nathaniel Hudson to announce the Act of Grace, while also revealing John Augur's plot to attack Pearse and resume his pirating ways. Smith also attempted to exonerate Sipkins by identifying him as one who helped foil Augur.

At the same time, Smith leveled more accusations against Captain Pearse. He explained how Pearse fraternized with John Lewis, evaded customs officials in Virginia, and even traded with pirates for indigo. For Smith, it might have been the worst three weeks of his life. Had the New York Council decided to press the case, it might have nipped in the bud a promising career as a ship captain, because the former Bermudian had already established a presence in New York and Connecticut and had made the acquaintance of one of the city's premier merchants, Justus Bosch. Although the vice-admiralty court of New York eventually condemned the rawhides, Smith and his companions walked away unscathed, probably because councilman Abraham De Peyster, who transcribed the interviews, owned a quarter share in the *John and Elizabeth* and had known Sipkins personally for a number of years.³

It was thus no accident that William Smith evaded justice, or that he and some of his accomplices became pillars of the New York maritime community. Perhaps like no other colonial port city, in New York there emerged a cohort of tightly connected pardoned pirates who forged business partnerships with one another and developed long-standing working relationships with some of the city's most eminent merchants. Consequently, these former pirates thrived in ways that few of the pardoned men could. They tended to live longer than their counterparts in other colonies, spending enough time on earth to raise families and amass generational wealth. They married well, in some cases to daughters of the city's respectable Dutch *burghers*, whose comfortable financial positions enabled them to funnel generational wealth to their sons-in-law. Although none of them rose to the rank of gentleman, their modest success secured their legacies and the respectability of their families, some of whom remain in New York to this very day. William Smith surpassed them all, becoming a merchant of some eminence and a church trustee, and leaving grandchildren who would one day marry into the family of a U.S. president. Untangling the social networks of the New York mariners reveals how they stumbled into piracy and how they climbed their way back to respectability.

New York in Transition

The Dutch origins of New York are well known, but it is worth briefly revisiting its historical development, which had a direct bearing on the lives and identities of the mariners who called it home. Dutch claims to the region derive from Englishman Henry Hudson's 1609 voyage, and in 1621 the Dutch West India Company (WIC) was established. The new company (conceived as a monopolizing trading company like its counterpart in the East) founded the colony of New Netherland, anchored at the tiny town of New Amsterdam that sprang up at the southern tip of Manhattan. The colony grew slowly at first but accelerated during the 1650s, attracting an ethnically and religiously diverse European population by the time of the English conquest in 1664. Both the Dutch and English regimes trafficked in enslaved persons from Africa, contributing further to New York's diversity. The commercial orientation of the colony's capital, New Amsterdam, also emerged in the early years of Dutch rule. Amassing beaver furs, along with farm produce and lumber derived from the colony's interior, New Amsterdam's merchant community traded regularly with the mother country, as well as the West India Company's other possessions, such as Curaçao.

The English conquest amplified some of the city's defining features, particularly its ethnic diversity and commercial orientation. As the terms of capitulation allowed continued trade with and emigration from the Dutch Republic, postconquest New York experienced a continuing trickle of Dutch immigrants, particularly in the wake of the short-lived 1673 reconquest. The English, however, comprised the bulk of the immigrants, which also included enslaved Africans, French Huguenots, and a small number of Jews. Despite occasional epidemics and outmigration, New York's population rose steadily, and its growth accelerated after the turn of the eighteenth century. Between 1703 and 1712, New York's white population grew from 3,700 to over 4,846, primarily because of "opportunistic migration by individuals" from the British Isles. The gradual influx of British subjects permanently altered the city's demography, and by 1730 they constituted a majority of its population. Ethnically Dutch citizens comprised just under 40 percent.[4]

The growth of the English population had a corresponding effect on the city's culture, as British practices gradually supplanted those of the Dutch. To be sure, Dutch architectural styles persisted well into the eighteenth century, and the Dutch language continued to be the principal means of communication for the Dutch at home and in church. But the generation that came of age in the early eighteenth century faced growing pressure to adjust to British culture. For instance, the English calendar of celebrations became institutionalized, which included the birthdays, accession days, and coronation days of British monarchs. New Yorkers also celebrated Guy Fawkes Day, in which wine and bonfires provided both amusement and patriotic indoctrination by commemorating the foiling of the infamous 1604 Gunpowder Plot. The English language superseded all others in business and politics, and it was employed exclusively in the city's first newspaper. New York's English governors, meanwhile, promoted English language and culture by establishing grammar schools and one charity school, all under the tutelage of Anglican schoolmasters.[5]

Meanwhile, the city became an important cog in the imperial trade system because of its favorable position within not one but two trading networks. New Yorkers retained the right to trade with the Dutch Republic and its colonial possessions, and those connections never withered. The city's expanding number of trading vessels continued making regular voyages directly to Holland, and the Dutch colony of Curaçao remained an important destination for the acquisition of sugar, rum, and occasionally slaves. Building on a foundation of Dutch commerce, New York amplified its trade with London, and especially British colonies in North America and the West Indies. Barbados and Jamaica attracted the most traffic from New York among the West Indian colonies. Flour, bread, and beaver furs constituted New York's leading exports, and city merchants imported manufactured goods, wine, and rum that could be reexported or sold locally. In a word, the import/export trade dominated the city's economy. In the first quarter of the eighteenth century, roughly 40 percent of all heads of households identified as merchants or worked in the maritime trades.[6]

One important consequence of this mercantile activity was the increasing disparity between rich and poor in the city, where by 1703 the top 20 percent of taxpaying New Yorkers owned 69 percent of the city's wealth. The historian Thomas Archdeacon finds that, notwithstanding the massive fortunes obtained by a few of the most prominent Dutch merchants, Englishmen appear disproportionally among the mercantile elite. For the city's wealthiest merchants, diversification proved to be one of the secrets of their success. The most enterprising merchants also invested in ships, which enabled them to earn more money carrying goods for others. Although not as wealthy, ship captains fared well in this economy, frequently amassing estates valued in roughly the top quartile of the New York City population. A few of the city's ship captains managed to enter the ranks of the merchant class by taking advantage of their knowledge of trade and connections to mercantile communities throughout the Atlantic world. Common sailors, however, occupied the lower rungs of New York society, owning estates valued at less than half of those of their captains. Thus, it behooved an ambitious mariner to rise in rank.[7]

Of the pardoned pirates, most of those identified as New Yorkers came to the colony after 1703. In fact, only three men from Pearse's list were born or raised in New York. Peter Mallet (Mellotte/Marlet) descended from French Huguenots who arrived in Staten Island (still technically a part of Dutch New Amsterdam) around 1662. The son of a blacksmith who later migrated to Piscataway, New Jersey, Peter was born in the 1680s at Staten Island but spent most of his adult life in Nevis. There he married a woman named Martha, and the couple had one daughter.[8] John Sipkins, meanwhile, descended from the city's Dutch population. Sipkins's father, Jan Sipken, was a soldier from Amsterdam who probably came to the colony during the brief Dutch reconquest. Sipken evidently liked what he saw in New York, so he stayed, a decision probably influenced by his courtship of a local woman, Else Borger. Sipken and Borger married in October 1674 and produced at least six children. John Sipkins was their fourth born, baptized as Jan Sipken on June 10, 1688, at the Dutch Reformed Church.[9] The family lived in the North Ward, the city's least affluent neighborhood, inhabited principally by tradesmen. His father's occupation was as a "sloopman" who tended to boats, thus making John Sipkins one of many children who followed their fathers' line of work.[10] At the time John was born, the family lived on King Street (modern Pine Street), which runs parallel to Wall Street one block to the north.[11] In addition to having five siblings as playmates, as a child John might have enjoyed the company of about a dozen or so other children who lived nearby. Sometime in the early 1690s, however, the family moved a couple blocks south, but still in the city's North Ward.

Unlike most pirates, enough records exist to establish the Sipken family's place in New York society. John's father supported Jacob Leisler's rebellion of 1689–91 and played a small part in it by serving as the fort's gunner under Leisler's short-lived government.[12] While never wealthy, Jan Sipken earned enough money to appear respectable. In 1688 he made a contribution of 100 florins toward the construction of the new Dutch church. City-wide tax lists compiled between 1695 and 1699 reveal that Sipken, a property owner, was consistently assessed at just over twenty-five pounds, meaning that the family was nearly of middling wealth (or around the fortieth percentile of estates).[13] John Sipkins probably watched the ongoing construction of the new church (completed in 1696) from his own yard, as the family home abutted the new churchyard on the east side.[14]

Although he was generally an upright citizen, the elder Sipken did occasionally get into trouble, or nearly so. In 1696 the Court of General Sessions accused him of "entertaining negroes" and allowing "unlawfull gaming" during a late-night escapade at his home.[15] Sipken appeared in court a year later, when a financial dispute in a lower court led to a decision that went against him. This compelled Sipken to appeal to the Supreme Court to have the decision reversed. Still, Sipken retained a degree of status in the community, doing a stint as a juror for that same Supreme Court, and receiving a government contract in 1700 to complete work on a sailing vessel, perhaps to install its guns.[16] Sipken unfortunately died sometime before the conduct of the city's 1703 census, perhaps during a yellow fever epidemic that ravaged the colony in 1701–2.[17]

John Sipkins would have been about thirteen years old when he lost his father. At the relatively young age of twenty-three, John was captaining vessels, so it is plausible that, as a boy, he learned how to navigate boats at his father's side. In March 1711 the Boston newspaper reported that Sipkins had been cleared outward for Curaçao, a likely destination for a New York mariner of Dutch origins. Sipkins made at least a couple more round trips to Curaçao in the years that followed, but he ventured occasionally to Jamaica, St. Christopher's, St. Thomas, and Campeche.[18] He made one trip to Holland that included a stop at the English port of Cowes on the return home. Sipkins crossed the Atlantic Ocean once more, sailing to Madeira to retrieve wine.

Importantly, in the course of his navigations, Sipkins became acquainted with the Bahamas. Around January 1712, sailing homeward from Curaçao, Sipkins's ship got blown off course in the Florida Strait, forcing him to make an emergency landing at Providence. Although a skilled mariner, Sipkins experienced more than his share of bad luck at sea. On the homeward voyage from Cowes in 1715, for instance, Sipkins encountered a storm in the North Atlantic, which resulted in a lengthy twelve-week ocean crossing and forced him to make an unscheduled landing at Marblehead, Massachusetts. From Marblehead, Sipkins sailed to Newport, Rhode Island, arriving there in March 1716. As fate would have it, at the same time another captain named Territ Lester arrived there from Providence, and he gave a detailed report about the ongoing efforts in the Florida Strait to salvage the wrecked Spanish plate fleet. As Lester and Sipkins were at Newport at the exact moment and sailed together from there to New York, there can be little doubt that this encounter kindled in Sipkins an interest in the goings-on in the Bahamas.[19]

The other native New Yorker, close in age to Sipkins, was John Stout. His father, who went by the same name, was a mariner from Jamaica who seems to have retained his principal residency there, even after marrying a New York woman named Amerantie (Amerancey) and purchasing land in Staten Island.[20] Perhaps because of this arrangement, the Stout family is elusive, and there are no records indicating when the couple wed or when their children were born. One can estimate, however, that the couple married sometime around 1690 and that John, their oldest son, was born before 1693. Family tradition holds that John was born in Jamaica, so one possible scenario is that he came to New York as a young boy. Stout had one younger brother, Harman, who also became a ship captain and sailmaker.[21] Given his father's profession and continuing identification of Jamaica as his home, the younger John Stout probably only rarely saw his father. John Stout Sr. died in 1699 on a voyage from Jamaica to New York. Although sickening, Stout had the presence of mind to compose a brief letter directed to another ship captain from New York, whom he named as the administrator of his estate. Stout's letter makes no mention of his family's needs, but he empowered his administrator to find buyers for his cargo of sugar and hides, as well as the three-quarter share of the sloop he owned. Stout was also traveling with a considerable amount of Spanish coins.[22] We are left to speculate if Stout's family received the portion they were due.

Perhaps because of his father's sometimes dangerous profession, it was not a foregone conclusion that Stout would follow in his father's footsteps. In January 1706, and with the blessing of his mother, John Stout entered into a six-year apprentice agreement with a New York barber.[23] In addition to trimming and shaving beards and hair, Stout would have also learned how to pull teeth and perhaps do other invasive procedures, as barbers at that time were more like barber-surgeons. Stout finished his apprenticeship, for he was admitted as a freeman of the city in 1717, listing his trade as "barber."[24] But he must not have liked the work; within months he was a ship captain, indicating that he probably went to sea after finishing the apprenticeship, perhaps applying the barber skills he had acquired to groom and provide medical care for crewmen. Given that his mother approved and paid for the apprenticeship, it is reasonable to speculate that John's quest for a trade that suited him created some strain between him and his mother.

Uncharacteristically, Stout's seafaring career can first be traced to his part ownership of a vessel, the sloop *Speedwell*, which sailed from New York to Curaçao in November 1715. Soon thereafter, Stout purchased a share in a second sloop, the *Antelope*, which made at least one voyage to Jamaica in 1717.[25] That Stout had enough financial means to make such investments as a young adult may indicate that his family was relatively well off; family lore indicates that the elder Stout was a "gentleman" and "merchant," so perhaps his father had left him some money, which he invested to good effect.[26] At the same time, Stout became a captain in his own right, assuming command of the sloop *Catherine and Elizabeth* in 1717. Like many other ship captains at that time, Stout developed an interest in the Bahamas trade. In January 1718 he left New York on a voyage to South Carolina, but the rumor of profits to be earned in the Bahamas diverted him there at the exact moment of Vincent Pearse's arrival. Stout probably accepted the Act of Grace because, although no pirate himself, he had been caught red-handed trading with the pirates of Providence.[27]

Sipkins and Stout knew each other, and the two would have shared some formative experiences growing up in New York City. First, they probably spoke at least some Dutch, since both men had at least one parent of Dutch origins. Furthermore, both men would have been impressionable boys during King William's War, when privateers fitted out there to strike against their inveterate foes, the French. They probably retained vague recollections of Captain Kidd, the Madagascar trade, and the permissive attitude toward piracy exhibited by Governor Benjamin Fletcher.[28] It is possible that both men had opportunities themselves to engage in wartime privateering, specifically during the latter stages of the War of Spanish Succession. Of the two, Stout is the likeliest candidate to have served as privateer, perhaps with Captain Benjamin Bill of New York, who in 1713 commanded a prize vessel named the *Gryphon*.[29] If Stout was in fact a member of Bill's crew, privateering may have been another possible source of the money he used to purchase shares of his sloops.

It is significant that Stout and Sipkins began their careers at a time when New York merchants were investing more heavily in the slave trade, which increased steadily during the decade preceding 1718. Both men might have perceived that enslaved Africans were becoming a noticeable presence in New York, and they undoubtedly heard firsthand accounts of one of the city's most alarming and consequential slave rebellions. On the night of April 6, 1712, a group of about twenty slaves set fire to a building in the city's North Ward. During the mayhem that ensued, and armed with hatchets and knives, they killed six white men. New York authorities quickly rounded up dozens of suspects, and thirty-nine individuals stood trial. Twenty-one enslaved persons were convicted, and all received death sentences that were carried out in barbaric fashion. Predictably, New York governing officials quickly passed a series of laws aimed at curtailing the limited freedom of mobility and assembly that the city's slaves had hitherto enjoyed.

John Sipkins was at sea during the rebellion and subsequent trials, but on his arrival home later that summer, he must have been horrified to learn that the epicenter of the rebellion was at Maiden Lane, in a North Ward neighborhood close to where he grew up. Sipkins undoubtedly knew that one of the enslaved men who had been executed belonged to the merchant William Walton, who later employed Sipkins as master of the sloop *John and Elizabeth*. Sipkins was no doubt aware that three slaves belonging to merchant Rip Van Dam and one to William Thong had also been executed, as both men employed Sipkins's and Stout's close acquaintances as ship captains.[30] Later in their careers, neither Sipkins nor Stout appear to have traded for slaves, and perhaps the memory of the 1712 rebellion made them leery of importing yet more enslaved Africans into the colony.

Judging by the date at which they married, Sipkins and Stout were probably slightly older than the other New Yorkers on Pearse's list. The oldest was perhaps Sipkins, who married Deborah Alsop of Newtown, Queens, in February 1711.[31] For Sipkins, it was a smart match. Deborah Alsop was the daughter of Richard Alsop, whose family traced its lineage to the first English migrants from New England who settled on Long Island while it was under Dutch rule.[32] The Alsops were Presbyterians who probably fled to New Netherland in order to worship as their consciences, and not New England's Puritan divines, dictated. The Alsops remained dedicated to their Presbyterian faith; Sipkins and Deborah Alsop married at the Presbyterian Church at Jamaica, Queens. Three years later, John Stout married Abigail Bill, the daughter of mariner Benjamin Bill. Captain Benjamin Bill was a Bostonian who came to New York sometime before December 1694, when he wed Geesje Van Fort.[33] Abigail, their eldest child, married John Stout in June 1714.[34] Although not a pirate himself, Benjamin Bill's personal, maritime, and commercial networks provided the foundation of the pirate ring that coalesced in New York.

Two Degrees of Benjamin Bill

Descended from early settlers of the Massachusetts Bay Colony, Benjamin Bill was born in Boston in 1674 and moved to New York before his marriage in 1694. By the turn of the eighteenth century, Bill became a fixture in the trade with Curaçao.[35] Between 1705 and 1707, he conducted no fewer than six voyages to the Dutch island, seeming to flaunt the dangers inherent to long-distance trade during wartime.[36] Bill also briefly worked as a slave ship captain, conducting one round trip from Jamaica to West Africa in 1702.[37] During the War of Spanish Succession, Bill became a trusted news source, and his wartime observations of the enemy sometimes found their way into the *Boston News Letter*. For instance, in November 1705 Bill arrived home from Curaçao and reported that a French privateer had taken three New York vessels. After another homeward voyage the following May, Bill delivered the bad news that the French had retaken the island of St. Christopher's and that the enemy had plans to conquer the Leeward Islands and Jamaica (ambitions the French never realized). During the spring of 1707, Bill himself was on the receiving end of an attack by French privateers. Bill appears not to have sailed for another three years, possibly because of this hardship.[38]

Around 1710 Bill returned to the sea and refocused his trading operations to the islands of Barbados and Jamaica, making occasional stops at nearby Boston and one trip to Madeira. Because he was a well-traveled seaman, Bill established business relationships with some of the city's leading merchants, such as Augustus Jay (grandfather of the revolutionary John Jay) and Walter Thong.[39] Bill was therefore in a position to introduce them to his son-in-law John Stout and the younger generation of mariners within his orbit. By 1717, and now in his forties, Bill retreated from long-haul maritime duty, settling down on his recently purchased estate at Staten Island.[40]

In the course of his navigations, Bill became familiar with the island of Providence. His first recorded presence there was in December 1702, when Governor Ellis Lightwood commissioned Bill, along with two other sea captains, to inspect the cargo of a sloop that Lightwood seized on suspicion of illegal trading.[41] Although it is probable that he returned there again several times, Bill's next confirmed visit to Providence was almost fifteen years later, when in May 1716 he returned to New York from the Bahamas.[42] Bill was not involved in any wrongdoing, but he was present on the island at the exact moment the pirates under Benjamin Hornigold seized control of it. It is therefore highly likely that he knew firsthand of the theft of Spanish silver that took place on the coast of Florida, and of the Jamaican pirates' recent seizures of French and Spanish ships, the spoils of which they shared at Providence. Bill also would have known that the pirates needed provisions and that opportunities were to be had for those willing to trade with them. So when Captain Vincent Pearse needed a pilot to guide the HMS *Phoenix* to Providence, he chose Benjamin Bill, who knew Bahamian waters and the pirates and contraband traders who had gravitated there.

Why Captain Bill agreed to accept the assignment is unknown, but it is possible he felt that his presence at Providence might enable him to intervene on behalf of his son-in-law, John Stout, as well as several of Stout's acquaintances who he knew had been trading with the pirates. On January 10, 1718, about four weeks before Pearse sailed, Stout departed New York as master of the sloop *Catherine and Elizabeth*. New York shipping records indicate he was cleared outward to South Carolina with a variety of foodstuffs. However, South Carolina shipping returns reveal that Stout never appeared there, and it is reasonable to suspect that Bill knew that Stout's real intention was to sail to the Bahamas.[43]

John Stout's presence in the Bahamas enables one to establish the connections between him and a handful of fellow mariners who were close to him in age and engaged in illicit trade with the pirates. Foremost among them was William Pinfold. Born in London in 1683, Pinfold grew up a short walk from St. Paul's Cathedral. Pinfold's father, Richard, was a haberdasher or hatmaker. The Pinfolds appear to have been reasonably prosperous, judging by Richard's ability to take on two apprentices during the 1680s. William, however, spurned his father's trade, choosing to go to sea.[44] He must have immigrated to New York sometime after the turn of the eighteenth century. Unlike most young mariners, he possessed enough financial means to purchase shares of sailing vessels. He partnered first with John Stout, who was half owner of the sloop *Speedwell*. The *Speedwell*'s only recorded voyage, to Curaçao, occurred in November 1715.[45] Suspiciously, its captain never cleared the ship inward at New York, and its absence from the shipping returns suggests he was making undocumented voyages to the Bahamas. Pinfold's associations, in turn, enable one to widen the scope of the New York pirate-trading ring to include John Sipkins and John Mutlow. Pinfold's connection to these men possibly derived from his partnership with the merchant William Walton, who for more than two years had kept Sipkins in his employ as master of the sloop *John and Elizabeth*, in which Walton owned a quarter share. About a year after the pardon, Pinfold and Walton together purchased a sloop named the *Hampsted* and hired John Mutlow to conduct it to Curaçao.[46]

The merchant Justus Bosch, meanwhile, provides a critical link between the maritime circle that formed around Benjamin Bill and William Smith. The son of a sword cutter from Leiden who moved to New Amsterdam in 1660, Justus Bosch was a prominent merchant who also served on the New York City Common Council.[47] Along with Abraham De Peyster, William Walton, and Nathaniel Simpson, Bosch owned a share of the sloop *John and Elizabeth* at the time John Sipkins was its master, which implies that he also knew Pinfold, Mutlow, Stout, and, of course, Benjamin Bill. In addition to his mercantile business in New York City, Bosch owned a one-eighth share of an iron foundry in Connecticut. His business dealings there possibly enabled him to make the acquaintance of William Smith, who began sailing a Connecticut ship in 1715. Another possible scenario is that John Sipkins introduced Bosch and Smith, for Sipkins had been sailing Bosch's vessel around the time Smith appeared on the scene in New York.

A wanderer in his youth, the Bermudian Smith appears to have drifted first to Boston, then sailed out of Connecticut from 1715 to 1717. Before he traded with pirates, Smith had been attacked by them, suffering at the hands of Olivier La Bouche and one of his accomplices named Main in the spring of 1717.[48] He returned to Bermuda that summer in order to conduct one voyage to Barbados and Antigua. Smith happened to be in Jamaica in January 1718 and was one of two men commissioned to sail for Providence in order to inform the pirates of the Act of Grace.[49] The extent to which Smith traded with the pirates cannot be discovered, but his tendency to alter his story about his whereabouts—simultaneously claiming to be a resident of North Carolina and Jamaica—suggests that he had been making clandestine stops at Providence. The fact that Jamaican officials nominated him to spread news of the pardon is indicative of the same. Justus Bosch nevertheless must have taken a liking to Smith, for in 1719 the two entered into business together as co-owners of the sloop *Anne*, which Smith captained for the span of eighteen months.[50] Meanwhile, Smith fell for Bosch's daughter Gerritje (Charity), and the two married in September 1720 at the Dutch Reformed Church. Bosch's partnership with Smith continued for another decade as co-owners of three sloops.

Having established the central cast of characters who formed New York's ring of pardoned pirates and their merchant backers, we should also consider several other men among their number whose connections were tangential. First, there were William Connor and Thomas Nichols, two New York mariners who, unlike their peers who merely traded with pirates, actively engaged in piracy. Nichols commanded a pirate sloop dubbed the *Dragon*, with

Connor serving under him as one of his crew. Their only confirmed feat of piracy was the October 1717 capture of the French ship *St. Jacque*, which the two men brought to Providence and claimed to have sold to John Sipkins. Both men later joined Sipkins as crewmen of the *St. Jacque*, now renamed the *John and Elizabeth*, and with him gave depositions before the New York Council. As their stories never lined up, it is impossible to know exactly what the two men had been doing.[51]

However, circumstantial evidence suggests that Connor, Nichols, and Sipkins had a preexisting relationship. Curiously, in October 1717 Sipkins was reported to have been captured by pirates. At the same time, the Boston newspaper glibly reported a story emanating from New York that "Nichols a pirate" had suffered a shipwreck near the island of Caicos. The same story related that all the shipwrecked men had survived and that they had "since got three sloops a pirateing."[52] One possible scenario is that Nichols and Connor cajoled Sipkins into relinquishing his sloop, on which they sailed for Providence. Whatever their relationship, Nichols and Connor accepted pardons around the same time as Sipkins and wound up together on the so-called *John and Elizabeth*. After their pardons, Connor and Nichols briefly owned together the sloop *William and Thomas*. Connor remained active at sea for a number of years. Not incidentally, Connor was also acquainted with John Stout, whom he employed to captain a sloop he owned for a 1721 voyage to Barbados. Of the New York mariners pardoned for piracy, only John Martin and Daniel Jones seem to have had no connection to the pirate ring emanating from Benjamin Bill.

New York mariners operated within an ecosystem in which trading with pirates was deemed acceptable. Consequently, the New York pirate ring had close connections to other ship captains who traded with pirates, but they avoided being caught by Pearse—the men who should have been on Pearse's list but were not. William Pinfold again provides a telling example. By 1717 Pinfold was the sole owner of the sloop *Wolf*, employing both John Tickell and Jacob Phoenix as its master. Between July 1717 and April 1718, the *Wolf* made a number of suspicious voyages to the Bahamas. For an October 1717 voyage, the *Wolf* had been cleared for Barbados, but on the homeward voyage it stopped in the Bahamas and did not return to New York until March 24, 1718. Pinfold's presence at the Bahamas when Pearse arrived indicates that he probably joined Captain Phoenix for that voyage.[53] Similarly, William Smith was an acquaintance of the mariner John Fred, who had been caught trading with Charles Vane when Woodes Rogers arrived at Providence. Smith and Fred never partnered in business, but the two men bought beer from the same North Ward brewer.[54] Because of the city's relative degree of intimacy, it is improbable that Smith and Fred could have done business with the same brewer and not known each other.

The New York pirate ring features individuals who rose to the rank of captain or who owned shares of vessels, indicating their place in the upper strata of maritime workers. While these men are the most visible in the historical record, it is probable that a number of common sailors who constituted their crews received pardons as well, but they left little to no trace in the archives. Pearse's list features a number of individuals who had distinctively Dutch names, which hints at their origins in New York. Garret Peterson, for instance, was in all likelihood a New Yorker of Dutch descent, for the forename Garret (Gerrit in Dutch) is common in New York but exceedingly rare among the British population there or elsewhere. It is also tempting to think that one James Peterson might have been a relative, for the Dutch Reformed Church records feature several baptisms of "Jacob Pieterszen," who like many of their generation tended to Anglicize their names. Cornelius Derickson, who died at Providence shortly after Woodes Rogers's arrival, was also likely a New Yorker. Likewise, variants of the surname "Peters" (or Pieters, Pieterszen) occur commonly among the New York Dutch, and the presence of two men by that name—Chris and William Peters—may indicate a similar origin. Unfortunately, the lives of New York's Dutch mariners who occupied the lowest echelons of society remain elusive.

Given Benjamin Bill's prominent role as Captain Pearse's pilot and temporary commander of the erstwhile sloop *John and Elizabeth*, the composition of the New York contingent that accepted the Act of Grace was no mere coincidence. Bill knew the geography of the Bahamas, and his presence at Providence in the spring of 1716 would have given him considerable insight into the prospects of trading with the pirates assembled there. Through his son-in-law John Stout, Bill was only two degrees removed from Stout and other younger mariners, who had become close because they worked for the same merchants. Similarly, the composition of the hastily assembled crew of the would-be *John and Elizabeth* was no coincidence. John Sipkins was a known commodity in New York maritime circles, so individuals such as William Connor, Thomas Nichols, and William Smith naturally sought him out in an attempt to extricate themselves from Providence. If it is true that Vincent Pearse double-crossed them by seizing the sloop and the hides as they were bound to Holland, they must have received a rude awakening having to answer for charges of piracy after receiving their pardons. Perhaps only Sipkins's relationship with Abraham De Peyster saved them from facing trial and execution. Everyone involved with the *John and Elizabeth*, it seems, wanted to put the past behind them.

Family and Fortune

Despite their close brush with the law, the New York pirates rebounded quickly. None faced subsequent accusations of piracy, nor is there any hint in the historical record that their reputations suffered because they had accepted pardons. Those who were not already married found spouses, and a lucky few remained healthy enough to stay exceptionally busy at sea. Over the course of their careers, these pirates amassed property they had either earned or inherited from their families and in-laws. Like most propertied individuals, they defended their estates in court and sometimes ensured that a paper trail existed to guarantee title to them. New York's former pirates engaged in these actions because they took the long view of their situations, the goal being to pass on their legacies to their widows and children.

New York's pardoned pirates enjoyed certain advantages in life that positioned them for success as sea captains. One might describe them as promising young men. First, their families had enough means to provide them with at least some education; Stout, Smith, and Nichols were verifiably literate. As for the status of their fathers, Stout, Pinfold, Sipkins, and Smith were the sons of skilled tradesmen. William Smith's father, for instance, was a cordwainer (shoemaker) from Bermuda who when he died in 1711 left William his entire estate in Devon Tribe, which he was to receive after his mother's death. The Smith family was also an exceptionally large one. One of Bermuda's administrative jurisdictions (similar to a parish or county) is "Smith's Tribe," where Smith's grandfather owned land. Smith therefore had countless relatives he might call on in the event he ran into hard times. In other words, he had a safety net should his adventures in New York backfire.

Precisely because they came from respectable families and acquired a trade, New York's pardoned pirates tended to marry well. In some instances, they coupled with local women from moderately prosperous families with landed estates. Such was the case with John Sipkins's wife, Deborah Alsop, whose father, Richard, owned several different properties in Queens County. When Richard Alsop died in 1718 he left Deborah fifty pounds in cash, plus a share of his movable property.[55] Similarly, William Pinfold married into a prominent English family from Queens. Elizabeth Lawrence, his bride, was the daughter of John Lawrence, also a descendant of the first English families that settled on Long Island while it was under Dutch rule.[56] In addition to owning extensive properties on Long Island, John Lawrence was a rather prominent New York politician. In the 1690s he served on the New York Council and the Supreme Court, and he even did a couple short stints as mayor. William Connor, meanwhile, married a well-to-do widow named Elizabeth Bayley in early 1721. Bayley's first husband, John, went by the title "Esquire" and served as a lower court judge. When he died in 1719 he bequeathed to Elizabeth a town lot in Rye that included orchards, pastures, and floodlands, as well as another tract of land at Throgmorton's Neck in Westchester County. Connor came into possession of this estate by virtue of his marriage to Elizabeth, which may explain why he did not go to sea again after 1721.[57]

As was common, New York's pardoned pirates often married the daughters of seamen and tradesmen. John Stout's wife, Abigail Bill, best illustrates this trend. Her father, Captain Benjamin Bill, was never rich, but he managed to acquire a respectable estate through seafaring and other activities. From 1695 to 1699, tax assessments of her father's East Ward property indicate that Bill's family had a modest estate assessed at just over ten pounds.[58] But Benjamin Bill was one of the most capable mariners of his generation, and his steady employment in the coming decades suggests that he was able to provide a dowry when Abigail and John married in 1714. Two years later, Bill purchased farmland at Staten Island from John Stout, a transaction that may indicate the Bill family benefited reciprocally from their son-in-law's wealth. Bill continued to sell property at Staten Island for the better part of a decade after his relocation there.[59]

John Mutlow, meanwhile, married Elisabeth Blom (Bloom) in August 1716.[60] Elisabeth's father, Arent Fredrickszen Blom (or Aaron Bloom), was a rather prosperous turner, or woodworker, specializing in the lathe. Elisabeth's brother, Teunis (Anthony), was a mariner who once served on a privateer vessel, which may explain how Mutlow and Blom first made their acquaintance.[61] In the mid-1680s the Blom family lived on New Street in the city's North Ward.[62] The 1695 city tax list indicated that their property was assessed at over forty pounds, somewhat more than many of their neighbors. The same tax list indicates that the Blom family also owned a "house etc" in the West Ward valued at over seventy pounds, a property that might have included his workshop, but which he appears to have sold around the turn of the century.[63] Impressively, Blom also owned three houses and lots on Queen Street, in the city's posh East Ward. Blom died in 1709, and five years later his widow Hester sold all the family's real estate for a whopping £600. Elisabeth was to have shared her father's estate with her siblings on her mother's death, but it is possible that her mother instead gave it to her as a dowry when she wed Mutlow two years later.[64]

Of any of the former pirates, William Smith attracted the spouse with the greatest financial means, when in September 1720 he married Gerritje (Charity) Bosch, daughter of Justus Bosch. A merchant by trade, Bosch may not have inhabited the most elite rank of that profession, but he was an aggressive businessman who had a hand in other economic activities.[65] This aggressiveness sometimes led Bosch to skirt the law, which may explain his willingness to associate with a reformed pirate. For instance, in 1705 Bosch formed a partnership with two other men in an attempt to purchase land in Connecticut from the Mohegan Indians, which Connecticut officials nullified.[66] Bosch maintained an interest in Connecticut, however, leading him to purchase a one-eighth share of an iron foundry in the town of Farmington. When Charity and William married, Bosch provided his daughter with a £200 dowry. In 1725 he purchased two hundred acres of land in Westchester County, New York, where he intended to retire. In addition to co-owning sloops with his son-in-law during the 1720s, Bosch owned a home on Pearl Street in New York City's wealthy East Ward. In 1730 the Bosch house was valued at thirty pounds for tax assessment purposes—respectable, but nowhere near the value of the homes of the upper echelons of New York's mercantile community. Still, at the time of his death, Bosch was wealthy enough to leave each of his six sons £500 and his two youngest daughters £200 each, all derived from the sale of unspecified real and personal property. Bosch, in other words, was a wealthy man with an estate that must have exceeded £4,000 in value.[67]

Another sign that the pardoned pirates married into prosperous families is that some of them owned slaves. As the city's 1703 census reveals, at that time the Bill family owned one enslaved woman, whereas the Bloms owned one enslaved woman and her male child.[68] Across the East River in Queens, the Lawrence family owned five slaves, three of whom were male, indicating they worked the family farm. As the Alsops were also farmers, it is no surprise that at the time of his death in 1718 Deborah's father Richard owned an enslaved man.[69] Having grown up in the presence of slaves, the future brides of the pardoned pirates would have felt entitled to own them as adults and would have expected them to relieve them of child-rearing and household chores. It is reasonable to assume most former pirates owned one or more slaves in order to meet their wives' expectations, and perhaps their own.

No doubt because they married into respectable, even locally prominent New York families, the pardoned pirates managed to resume their careers as merchant ship captains largely without incident. John Stout, for instance, sped home quickly after receiving his pardon, arriving in New York on March 24, 1718. In just two weeks, Stout was again at the helm of the sloop *Catherine and Elizabeth*, which he guided to the Bahamas, indicative of the sustained appeal of doing business there. Stout loaded his ship with rum, distilled spirits, shoes, and hats, evidently anticipating that these commodities were in short supply there. In similar fashion, when William Pinfold returned to New York, he immediately sent his sloop *Wolf* to South Carolina under the command of John Tickell, who carried provisions and wine. Because Tickell never appeared before the customs officers in either port, it is plausible that he instead went to the Bahamas. William Connor and Thomas Nichols, owners of the sloop *William and Thomas*, hired another skipper to guide their ship to the Bahamas in late October to trade provisions and lumber.[70] For his part, William Smith promptly got back into the carrying trade, venturing on the sloop *Ann* (which he co-owned with Justus Bosch) to Bermuda, from which he sailed to Barbados with a cargo of cabbages. His next voyage took him to Saltatuda to pick up a load of salt before returning to New York in March 1719.[71] And, after laying low for about a year, John Mutlow and William Pinfold ventured together to Jamaica on the ship *Hampstead*, of which Pinfold was a co-owner.[72]

One former pirate had his career cut short because, like many of his peers, he died young. After the condemnation of the sloop *John and Elizabeth*, John Sipkins seems to have refrained from sailing for a year, venturing once to Curaçao in May 1719, and sending his sloop *Deborah* once to the Bahamas six months later.[73] Sipkins probably returned to the Bahamas around December 1720 for what tragically became his final voyage. Homeward bound in January, Sipkins's ship wrecked near the bar of Matanzas, the barrier island adjacent to the town of St. Augustine, Florida. While it is possible he was the victim of a storm, the more likely scenario is that he had been chased by Richard Holland, an Irishman who went rogue by attacking British shipping at the behest of the Spanish governor of Florida.[74] Sipkins's wife Deborah must have received the news of her husband's demise by February 2, 1721, when she received a letter empowering her to administer the estate of her deceased husband, who left no will. Sipkins appears to have died without issue, and Deborah remarried in May 1722.[75]

Two of the New Yorkers, meanwhile, probably withdrew from maritime work to pursue other trades. This was not uncommon. As Daniel Vickers's work on Salem, Massachusetts, has revealed, mariners often transitioned between seafaring and landed employment in order to make ends meet. Vickers also finds that their careers at sea could be relatively brief, a short phase in a multifaceted career, often prompted by advancing age or the inability to rise to the officer ranks. Thomas Nichols may have fit this mold, as he never returned to the sea after October 1718. One possible explanation is that he moved to Rye, New York, in Westchester County to become a fuller, or cloth maker. Throughout the 1720s, a fuller by that same name bought and sold several properties in Westchester. In 1724 he married Jane Hosier, a Quaker widow with three children from Flushing, Queens. A year later, Nichols became a Quaker himself by joining the Friends Meeting at Flushing. Nichols died in 1734 and left his property to his mother and three stepsons, indicating that his wife predeceased him. Although he identified as a fuller in each of his property transactions and in his will, a 1725 court case referring to "Capt. Nichols" suggests that some people still knew him as a sailor.[76]

Nichols's partner, William Connor, stuck with his trade as a mariner for a few years but then retreated to Westchester County, perhaps to live the life of a farmer. On July 19, 1721, just a few months after marrying the widow Elizabeth Bayley of Rye, Connor's name appeared in the paybook of the HMS *Phoenix*, commanded by none other than Captain Vincent Pearse. The *Phoenix* returned to New York that year, and Connor signed on as an ordinary sailor. He served until November, mostly while the ship remained in New York.[77] Around that same time, Connor was half owner of the sloop *William and Sarah* of New Jersey, captained by his old acquaintance, John Stout, who in November 1721 conducted the vessel on one voyage to Barbados.[78] Never again did Connor captain or own a vessel.

In contrast to the more elusive figures, several of the pardoned pirates became fixtures of New York's maritime community. William Smith, the transplanted Bermudian, was perhaps the most prolific sailor, enjoying a career that spanned at least another sixteen years after the pardon. Prior to his marriage, he joined Justus Bosch in the ownership of the sloop *Anne*, a vessel they purchased in Connecticut. Smith guided the *Anne* on four voyages that took place between March 1719 and August 1720. After a maiden voyage to Saltatuda, Smith went twice to Curaçao and once to Jamaica, typically carrying provisions, grain, and lumber. Smith's marriage to Charity Bosch on September 10, 1720, interrupted him for a span of about eighteen months, although Smith and Bosch kept the *Anne* busy by sending it out with other captains.[79]

In early 1722 Smith resumed sailing after rechristening the sloop as the *Hannah*, which made six runs that year, four to the Bahamas. When Smith arrived in New York from the Bahamas that February, he reported the news that Governor Phenney and more troops had arrived there, indicating a sustained interest in Bahamian affairs. Typically, Smith hauled provisions and grain, sometimes returning with indigo. In one instance, he returned with elephant tusks deriving from the Bahamian direct trade with Africa. Although he was sailing again, Smith relinquished his duties occasionally to other captains, perhaps because he and Charity were starting a family.[80] By 1723 William Smith was at the peak of his career as a ship captain. Together with Bosch, he purchased a schooner named the *Mary and Anne*. Between June 1723 and June 1726 Smith made fourteen round trips, mostly to Curaçao but occasionally to Jamaica and Barbados, and once to St. Thomas. In addition to their schooner, Smith and Bosch also owned the sloop *Speedwell*, which made only one recorded voyage to Curaçao.[81]

Smith's career flourished in part because of the nepotism he enjoyed in partnership with his wealthy father-in-law. However, by the mid-1720s Smith widened his range of business connections, indicating that some of the city's leading merchants, as well as those in other ports, valued his acumen as a ship captain. One such partnership was with the brothers Mordecai and Daniel Gomez. Born in the West Indies, they were the sons of Luis Moses Gomez, a Sephardic Jew whose family settled in New York sometime before 1705.[82] Smith began working for the Gomez brothers in the summer of 1726, when he assumed command of their schooner, the *Jacob*. Between July 1726 and May 1728, Smith made six voyages on the *Jacob*, four to Jamaica and two to Antigua. Typically, Smith carried lumber, provisions, whale oil, and tar, exchanging them for tropical commodities like sugar, rum, cotton, and coconuts.[83] Existing ledgers also indicate that Smith conducted business on behalf of other leading merchants, such as Peter Jay, Christopher Bancker, and Peter Vallet, owners of the goods consigned on Gomez's ship for a 1726 voyage. As captain, one of Smith's responsibilities was to carefully distribute quantities of Spanish silver to the merchants who employed him, for which Smith received small sums on top of the fees he charged for captaining the ship.[84] Later, Smith leveraged his expertise in the Jamaica and Antigua trades to assume the command of the ship *Prince William*, owned by New York merchants Paul Richard, Robert Livingston, Moses Levy, and the brothers David and William Clarkson. Between November 1728 and February 1730, Smith made five voyages in the *Prince William*, mostly to Jamaica but with one stop at Antigua.[85]

As a measure of the esteem in which others held him, Smith's observations about geopolitics and trade—acquired in the course of his navigations—sometimes found their way into local newspapers. Following one trip to Antigua, Smith related information he received about Spain's 1727 assault on Gibraltar.[86] After one voyage to Jamaica in 1729, Smith reported that flour had been selling there for between twenty-three and thirty shillings per barrel, a much better rate than on the Spanish Main, where captains were having a hard time unloading their cargoes. Smith also revealed that word on the streets in Port Royal was that Britain and Spain would soon be at war, anticipating an event that would take another decade to transpire.[87]

In the twilight of his captaincy, Smith found opportunities to partner with yet other New York merchants. Beginning in October 1729 Smith commanded the ship *Francis*, which he owned with three New Yorkers. In the span of about ten months, Smith conducted four voyages, three to Antigua and another to Curaçao. At the same time, Smith invested in the sloop *Mary Anne*. His partner in that venture was the Antigua merchant Samuel Archibald, a connection he must have forged in his many visits to the island in the previous decade.[88] In 1732 Smith joined with Antigua merchant Henry Bonnin as the proprietors of the New York–built sloop *Revenge*, a provocative name perhaps intended to pay homage to Smith's youthful dalliance with piracy. The *Revenge*, captained by Smith's brother-in-law Albertus Bosch, sailed exclusively to Antigua between 1732 and 1737.[89]

Smith's final stint as a captain was on the brigantine *Nonsuch*, which he began sailing in 1730. At the helm of the *Nonsuch*, Smith conducted a combined twelve voyages to Curaçao, Jamaica, and Madeira. His final voyage was a transatlantic round trip to Lisbon, Portugal, which commenced in December 1734. The brigantine's owners consisted of three New York merchants, including Abraham De Peyster Jr., the son of the man who had interrogated Smith in June 1718.[90] In the sixteen years since, Smith's career had flourished. Once a relatively unknown migrant from Bermuda, Smith had carved out a niche for himself in New York mercantile circles through his association with Justus Bosch. By the time he stopped sailing in 1735, Smith was no longer reliant on Bosch and had earned enough money to enter the ranks of the merchant class.

Ownership of trading vessels enabled Smith to retire from active seafaring and devote his attention exclusively to mercantile activity. After he stopped sailing, Smith invested in three vessels that primarily traded to Jamaica between 1738 and 1747. One was a sloop built in New York in 1738 and named the *Charity*. In addition, Smith purchased two brigantines, also built in New York. In 1742 he acquired the *William* and a year later the *Mary and Anne*. Shipping registers from Jamaica specify the ownership of these vessels as "William Smith & Co.," indicating that he had partners who owned shares but Smith was the principal owner. Smith never sailed these vessels himself. Instead, he relied on Bermudian turned New Yorker Josias Smith (presumably a relative) to guide the *Charity*, along with his son, John, who occasionally assumed command. Aside from his relatives, Smith employed a revolving cast of local ship captains, especially James Jauncey of Bermuda. Jauncey, who started working for Smith in 1741 as commander of the *Charity*, married Smith's daughter Mary two years later, thereby following in the footsteps of Smith by immigrating to New York and working for his father-in-law. By the mid-1740s Smith relinquished his ownership of the *Charity* to his son, John, who by then had founded a mercantile business of his own. He also partnered with his son-in-law, James Jauncey, in the ownership of the *Mary and Ann*.[91]

Each of Smith's vessels typically conducted about three round trips to Jamaica annually. Smith dealt mostly in flour, along with other locally produced commodities ranging from lumber to ham. For example, in May 1744 James Jauncey arrived in Jamaica in the *Mary and Anne* carrying over forty-two tons of flour and biscuits, along with seven and a half tons of "grain" (presumably wheat). On top of that, Jauncey's ship was laden with unspecified amounts of beef and candles, along with vegetable oil, lumber, and rice. Somewhat curiously, Smith's vessels often departed Jamaica laden only with ballast. One possible reason is that the sale of foodstuffs netted enough cash to return home with empty ship bottoms, or that he directed his captains to purchase sugar and molasses elsewhere. That Smith occasionally dealt in rice may indicate that his ships stopped in South Carolina on the homeward voyage. Of course, Smith occasionally purchased goods available in Jamaica. On one voyage in January 1747, his son John brought home a ton of fruit, osnaburg cloth, copper, and unspecified "prize dry goods." A few months later the sloop *Charity* arrived in New York with molasses. By the late 1740s Smith appears to have begun retreating from active business, relinquishing day-to-day management to his son and son-in-law.[92]

Although he never owned any vessels, John Mutlow became a prolific ship captain, remaining employed into the early 1730s. A year after his 1719 voyage to Jamaica on the *Hampstead*, Mutlow was placed in charge of the pink *Charlotte*, owned by Henry Cuyler, along with Moses Levy, Jacob Franks, and Nathan Simpson, some of New York's most distinguished Jewish merchants. In September 1720 Mutlow guided the *Charlotte* to Amsterdam with a cargo of furs, dyewoods, and brown sugar, along with a parcel of letters written by New York merchant Philip Van Cortlandt to his contacts in Holland. After his return to New York, Mutlow briefly commanded the sloop *Friendship*, on which he made two voyages to Curaçao.[93] Then, in November 1723, Mutlow began a nearly five-year stint on the sloop *Burnet*, whose owners included Henry Cuyler, Joseph Robinson, Walter Thong, and Rip Van Dam, who at one point was the wealthiest merchant in New York and served as the colony's acting governor in 1731–32. During those five years, Mutlow made twelve voyages in the *Burnet*, specializing in trade to Curaçao, St. Thomas, and Barbados. In addition to those key ports, Mutlow occasionally ventured to Suriname, and his final voyage on the *Burnet* in 1728 was to Madeira. As with most New York vessels, the *Burnet* typically carried locally produced provisions and lumber, which he sold in exchange for tropical commodities like sugar, cotton, coconuts, and lime juice.[94] Mutlow finished his career in the employ of Rip Van Dam, conducting Van Dam's sloop *Duke of Portland* twice to Jamaica and once, in his final recorded voyage, to Madeira.[95] As one of the acting governor's preferred ship captains, it is clear that Mutlow too experienced no hardship because of the taint of piracy.

Finally, John Stout sailed for about five years after the pardon. On his return home from the Bahamas in March 1718, Stout remained in command of the sloop *Catherine and Elizabeth* for the span of about three months, conducting another round trip to the Bahamas. In the spring of 1719, now in command of the sloop *Elizabeth*, Stout returned to the Bahamas twice more before abandoning it as a destination. In September 1719 Stout guided the *Elizabeth* to St. Thomas, conducting trade with several of the island's Dutch merchants, perhaps facilitated by his passing knowledge of their language.[96] In early 1721 Stout assumed command of the sloop *Monmouth*, which he guided to the Bay of Honduras to retrieve logwood. In November 1721 Stout entered the employ of another pardoned pirate, William Connor, half owner of the sloop *William and Sarah*, on which he sailed once to Barbados.

Because he had relatives in New Jersey, Stout sometimes frequented the port of Perth Amboy, twice conducting the sloop *Mary* from there to Barbados. Stout specialized in the trade in bread, flour, and beer, perhaps purveying the alcoholic beverage because his brother, the sailmaker Herman Stout, owned land and a brewery in New Jersey. During his captaincy, Stout forged relationships with several merchants from Barbados and New York, including his brother Herman, with whom he owned a one-third share of the sloop *Monmouth*.[97] Although he probably lived into the early 1730s, Stout retreated from deep-sea navigation after 1723, perhaps focusing instead on local commerce between New York and New Jersey that was outside the purview of naval officers.

In addition to engaging in the routine trade in local produce and tropical commodities, two of the pardoned pirates, William Smith and John Mutlow, played a substantial role in the New York slave trade. From its inception, New York had imported enslaved persons, but the colony developed little direct trade with Africa. Consequently, New Yorkers relied on the reexportation of slaves from the West Indian colonies, especially Jamaica, Barbados, and Curaçao. Compared to the colonies that had developed plantation systems, the number of imported slaves was small, but steady nonetheless. In 1718, a peak year for slave imports, 475 enslaved persons arrived from the West Indies. For the years 1719–30, New Yorkers conducted 323 voyages whereby they imported 1,580 enslaved individuals from the West Indies, or roughly 150 slaves per year. Typically, ship captains dealt in small cargoes of slaves averaging about five persons per voyage. In some instances, ship captains returned to New York with just one slave, and the single largest importation of slaves from the West Indies during that span of time was a 1722 voyage in which thirty-four enslaved persons were landed.[98]

Given that they had married into slaveholding families and worked at the behest of slave-trading merchants, Smith and Mutlow probably never questioned the morality of enslaving human beings. Smith's venture into slave trading began in August 1723, when he arrived in New York from Jamaica with twelve enslaved persons. During the ensuing decade, Smith made fifteen more voyages to the West Indies in which he returned to New York with slaves, typically small cargoes of five or fewer. Smith's largest haul derived from a 1731 voyage to Antigua, in which he returned with twenty-four enslaved persons. Over the span of his career, as captain and owner of vessels, Smith imported 132 slaves, or over 6 percent of the total brought to New York from 1723 to 1739.[99] While not as prolific a slave importer, John Mutlow conducted five voyages to the West Indies in which he returned home with a combined total of thirty slaves.[100] Smith became a slave owner himself, and although an inventory of Mutlow's property does not exist, it is probable that Mutlow also owned one or two slaves. If questioned, New York's mariners might have justified the enslavement of human beings on the grounds that their services were needed for the routine maintenance of their families, and that, as a form of property, slaves were a valuable investment that would benefit the next generation.

Pardoned pirates had good reason to be mindful of the next generation, for they were, in fact, family men. William and Elizabeth (Lawrence) Pinfold, for instance, had two sons, Richard and Edmund, and two daughters, Elizabeth and Deborah. Neither of Pinfold's sons became mariners, possibly because William is thought to have died at sea. Richard identified as a "yeoman" and lived on his paternal estate at Hellgate Neck, which his father had purchased in 1719.[101] Pinfold's descendants remained locally prominent in Queens, including one grandson who served in the Continental Army during the American Revolution.[102] Likewise, John and Elizabeth (Blom) Mutlow produced five children, John (b. 1719), Margaret (b. 1721), Roberd (b. 1723), Arent (b. 1725), and Daniel (b. 1731).[103] Three of them tragically died in rapid succession between August 24 and September 15, 1731, probably victims of a smallpox epidemic that ravaged the city that year.[104] Two of them lived until adulthood. Margaret (Gretie) married in 1756. Arent (Aaron) was a mariner like his father but died sometime before 1748 when he was still in his early twenties.[105]

John and Abigail (Bill) Stout, meanwhile, had four children, Amerantie (b. 1715), Benjamin (b. 1717), John Jr. (b. 1720), and Catherine (b. 1722). John Jr. became a sailor like his father, while Benjamin became a noted tavern keeper in New York. The Stouts' daughters also lived into adulthood and happened to marry two brothers, Jacob and Tuenis Somerendyck. All of their unions produced children, and the Stout family name continues in the region to this very day.[106] For their part, William and Charity (Bosch) Smith had four children, three of whom lived to adulthood. Their only son, John, pursued his father's line of work, briefly captaining ships before setting up shop as a merchant in the 1740s. Their daughter Mary (b. 1722, d. 1788) followed in her father's footsteps in a different way by marrying a Bermuda ship captain, James Jauncey, who settled in New York. Their second daughter, Annika, was born in 1727 but lived for only about six months. Charity gave birth to another daughter in 1731, also named Annika. Charity died in November 1742, and William married again in 1744 to Sarah Het, the daughter of René Het, a French merchant from Newtown, Queens. Even beyond his fifty-third birthday, Smith continued to produce children by Sarah, who had Blanche (b. 1745) and Sarah (ca. 1747). Sarah (Het) Smith died in 1747, possibly due to complications from childbirth.[107]

Although Smith and Mutlow were English, and Stout had an English father, each of them looked to the Dutch Reformed Church to enact rituals signifying important milestones in their lives. All three men were married in the Dutch church, and Mutlow and Stout baptized all their children there. Of the three men, John Mutlow appears to have been the most devoted to the Dutch church. In February 1725 he, along with his friend William Glover (a mariner who was also caught up in the controversy surrounding the sloop *John and Elizabeth*) and their wives, who were sisters, became full church members by professing their faith before the congregation.[108] Neither Stout nor Smith took that step.

William Smith never joined the Dutch church because he was, at heart, a Presbyterian. When it came to religious worship Smith was flexible as a younger man, and he acquiesced to the Dutch church perhaps to please his wife and in-laws. As he aged, Smith gravitated toward the Presbyterians. Records indicate that Smith only baptized his daughters by Charity (Mary, Annika 1, and Annika 2) at the Dutch church. It is possible that Smith deferred to his wife's preferences for the baptism of their daughters while choosing to baptize his son elsewhere. Because fires set in New York during the American Revolution destroyed many old church records, we do not know when or where Smith's son, John, was baptized. The leading possibility is the First Presbyterian Church in New York, on Wall Street. William was a long-standing member of that church and owned a pew there. As an adult, John Smith worshipped at the same church, which suggests he had in fact been baptized as a Presbyterian.

William Smith was keenly devoted to the Presbyterian Church. From 1744 to 1748 he served as one of its trustees, a small elected body that attended to the church's temporal affairs. Existing minutes of their meetings indicate that he attended just three times in February and March 1747; perhaps he was tired of the work or simply slowing down due to his advancing age. Others who served with him include William Smith the attorney (William's brother-in-law) and Peter Van Brugh Livingston, the future revolutionary leader whom Smith later named as one of the executors of his estate. Smith was on hand to deliberate the minister's request for a raise, the collection of poor relief, and the repair of the church building. Significantly, William remarried at the Newtown Presbyterian Church in Queens, but he baptized his daughter Blanche at the Wall Street church in 1746.[109]

Regardless of their level of piety, the churches fulfilled the purpose of cementing ties between families through the sponsorship of their children's baptisms. Baptismal records indicate that three of the pardoned pirates were immersed in networks formed through the Dutch church. In spite of his being an outsider from Bermuda—or perhaps because he was one—William Smith answered the call on several occasions to sponsor the baptisms of newborns in the Bosch family, who returned the favor when William and Charity began having children of their own.[110] Similarly, Dutch church records reveal the intertwining of John Mutlow, his friend the mariner William Glover, and the notorious John Lewis, the former pirate who was executed for murder in Bermuda in 1722. In addition to being mariners, what connected the three men were their wives, who were sisters. Sometime prior to 1713, Glover wed Margaret Blom, and Lewis at that time was married to Annetke (Ann) Blom. In 1716 Mutlow married Elisabeth Blom, and when they baptized their firstborn son, John, in August 1719, John and Elisabeth Mutlow called on the Glovers to serve as sponsors. Four months later, the Mutlows reciprocated by sponsoring the baptism of the Glovers' daughter. Because they both grew up in New York, John and Abigail (Bill) Stout perhaps had the most extensive network of family and friends to call on, as the baptisms of their children feature sponsors who, aside from Abigail's godfather, had no obvious familial connections.

As family men intent on passing their property to their descendants, it was incumbent on them to secure it with written legal instruments. Somewhat characteristically for mariners, New York's pardoned pirates sometimes neglected this aspect of their lives. Only one left an extant will, and rarely do they factor in the paper trail of recorded instruments like deeds, letters of administration, and conveyances. The most notable exception is William Smith, who made use of recorded instruments intermittently throughout his life and left a will. Although he had been in New York since 1715, Smith retained ties with Bermuda, his place of birth. In 1725 Smith witnessed the will of a man from Southampton Tribe. Six years later, in New York, William received a letter of administration for the estate of his deceased brother John. Although John lived in Bermuda, he was known to have "goods, credits, and rights" in New York City but died intestate, so it was up to William to settle his brother's affairs. In April 1732 New York officials again appointed him to administer the estate of one James Arbuthnot of Antigua.

The account book of James Gibson, a merchant from Perth Amboy, New Jersey, affords an intimate look at the ordinary affairs of a pardoned pirate. A dealer in all manner of goods, one of Gibson's regular customers was John Stout, who frequented Gibson's store for about three years between 1727 and 1730. In a series of purchases made from May to July 1727, Stout acquired lace, rum, tape, a cap, and some nails from Gibson, and he returned that fall to buy some more rum, mohair, nails, and some lace for his daughter Catherine, whose name Gibson recorded affectionately as "Catey." It is evident that one of Stout's main purposes was to provide sewing material for his wife, Abigail, and their daughter Catherine, who, although just five at the time, perhaps was beginning to learn at her mother's side. In addition to making numerous purchases of cloth himself, Abigail and Catey sometimes bought sewing materials from Gibson on their own accounts. In 1729 Abigail and Catey exchanged some linen for homespun, gartering, and poplin, and picked up some nails for John while they were in the store. Stout's son, John, also became a customer, buying from Gibson a coat, as well as some gingham and tape that were probably for his mother and sister. Gibson's account book therefore allows a glimpse into Stout's domestic life, indicating that he aspired to provide his family with some of the nicer things that the money he made at sea enabled him to acquire.[111]

Like most men engaged in business, New York's pardoned pirates occasionally landed in court. In some instances, their appearances were celebratory. John Stout (1717) and William Connor (1719) appeared in court to confirm their status as freemen of the city, a distinction that enabled them to vote and hold minor offices.[112] Most often, however, they appeared as defendants or complainants in minor debt cases. William Connor, for instance, sued a local man in December 1718 in the New York Mayor's Court for an undisclosed small sum. In July 1720, however, Connor was on the receiving end of a debt case, one he appears to have lost.[113] Connor's former partner, Thomas Nichols, also had to defend himself in two debt cases filed in the Westchester County Court of Common Pleas in 1721 and 1722. In 1724 Nichols appeared in the Supreme Court to fend off a lawsuit.[114]

The most litigious of the pardoned pirates, however, were John Stout and William Smith. Stout's first court appearance came in October 1715, when one Thomas Kearney sued him in the Mayor's Court for twenty pounds. Kearney won the lawsuit, and Stout had to pay an additional six pounds to cover Kearney's court costs. As that case foreshadowed, Stout appeared in the Mayor's Court exclusively as a defendant. In September 1716 one Tywitt Caleyeux sued Stout for an undisclosed sum. Then, on July 11, 1721, two men, Daniel Riche and Nicholas Hasher, filed separate cases against Stout. The Mayor's Court chose to interview Riche that day because he was "bound to sea," suggesting that he was a mariner suing Stout for his wages. Both cases continued for several months and were not resolved until October 31, when Stout went free thanks to a writ of habeas corpus.[115] In addition to the Mayor's Court, Stout also had to defend himself in the New York Supreme Court, when in October 1723 another man sued him for twenty-three pounds. That case appears to have dragged on for a full year, ultimately leading to a decision that went against Stout, who had to pay the full sum plus six pounds in court fees.[116]

In contrast to Stout, William Smith more frequently appeared in Mayor's Court as a plaintiff. In one case dating to February–March 1728, Smith sued a local man for an undisclosed sum of money. In another case dating to November 1729, the constable returned "non est inventus," indicating that the defendant could not be found, making it probable that Smith did not recoup the money he was owed. Smith did have one run-in with the law as a defendant, when in May 1732 a man and a woman sued Smith in his capacity as administrator for the estate of James Arbuthnot of Antigua. Smith allegedly withheld twenty-nine pounds due to them, which the court ordered Smith to pay. As the Arbuthnot case demonstrates, being named as an estate administrator could be more headache than it was worth.[117]

While most lawsuits originated for small debts, two of the pardoned pirates had legal entanglements that were more involved and therefore more interesting. The first was a case in the New York Supreme Court involving one Isaac Mense, who faced charges of counterfeiting and altering "York bills," as New York's paper money was commonly known. Mense was indicted on one count of counterfeiting in November 1724. The jury found Mense not guilty, but the colony's attorney general, James Alexander, initiated another suit against Mense in March 1725 on four related counts. While twelve prominent individuals stood as King's evidence against Mense, eighteen others testified on behalf of the defendant. One of them was Thomas Nichols, the former pirate. Nichols's deposition was not recorded, but his testimony must have been convincing enough to have Mense acquitted on two of the charges.[118]

In what was their first legal battle, William Smith and his wife, Charity, initiated two cases in the Mayor's Court that occupied them from November 1723 to January 1724. Unlike the routine debt cases, this one involved the family's honor, particularly that of Charity Smith. Around November, a man named John Golding published what Smith described as a "libel" against Charity. What Golding said about her is not known due to the ephemeral nature of most privately published broadsides. One possibility is that Golding spread some kind of rumor questioning Charity's sexual fidelity, which Smith also believed was an assault on his honor. Whatever the circumstances, William sued Golding for libel, asking £100 in damages. Together, William and Charity initiated a second lawsuit against Golding for an undisclosed sum. After filing their lawsuits, William and Charity may have had a change of heart, for the couple never entered a formal charge against Golding, and the court dropped the lawsuits for "want of a declaration." In the end, the Smiths had to cough up in excess of four pounds to Golding for having to fend off a frivolous lawsuit. Maybe Smith's past association with pirates, and Charity's marriage to one, was somehow alluded to in Golding's lost publication.[119]

Given that they engaged with the legal system on occasion to document their property and defend themselves in court, the fact that most of the pardoned pirates failed to leave a will is somewhat perplexing. It also makes it impossible to assess the value of their estates and to establish precisely when they died. John Sipkins was deceased by January 1721, the same year William Connor and John Martin disappeared from the historical record, suggesting that they also died just a few years after the pardon. The remainder of New York's former pirates, however, lived at least into the 1730s. John Stout died sometime before December 22, 1734, when Abigail Bill, named as Stout's widow, sponsored an infant girl's baptism.[120] Thomas Nichols, if indeed the same man who became a fuller in Westchester County, died that same year.[121] John Mutlow died sometime between 1732 (the last record of his presence) and November 1745, when, just before going to sea, his son Arent (Aaron) composed a brief will in which he bequeathed his small estate to his widowed mother.[122] Across the channel in Long Island, William Pinfold was probably long dead by August 1751, when his wife Elizabeth, known colloquially as "Widow Pinfold," was buried at the Newtown Presbyterian Church in Queens.[123]

The lone individual to leave an extant will was William Smith, whose last words reveal that he was perhaps the most successful of any of the former pirates. As shown by the will penned on February 18, 1752, Smith lived longer than any of his peers in New York. At age sixty-one, Smith conceded he was "infirm of body," yet he claimed to be "of sound mind and disposing memory." Importantly, Smith identified himself as "mariner and merchant" of New York, in recognition of his adopted city and his ascent into the ranks of the merchant class.[124] After retiring from active duty at sea around 1734, Smith operated a store out of his home on the south side of Queen Street on Hanover Square, now a small park in the city's Financial District. Located in the city's tony East Ward and near the waterfront, in 1730 his property was assessed at thirty pounds for tax purposes—modest in relation to the city's grandees, but respectable, and it is likely that he made improvements over the next couple of decades that enhanced its value.[125] The Smith home on Hanover Square became a well-known destination in the city, and nearby merchants sometimes casually referred to it when guiding readers to the location of their places of business. When Smith's son, John, established his own mercantile firm in 1750, he moved into the Queen Street home and sold his wares there, directing customers to "the house of his father, Mr. William Smith in Hanover Square."[126]

It is significant that John Smith identified his father using the honorific title "Mister," which was commonly employed to signify professional status or wealth and occupied a position merely one rank below that of "Gentleman."[127] The bequests Smith made in his will reveal that he deserved the title. Over the course of his career, Smith acquired not only the home on Hanover Square but also nearly two hundred acres of land in Greenwich, Connecticut, indicating Smith's diversification into farming and the lingering ties to that colony. First, there was a 120-acre tract that he had purchased from Justus Bosch, and adjacent to that was a seventy-acre tract with an orchard on which a home and barn stood. Smith also owned a small eight-acre tract. The property featured an unspecified number of horses, cows, sheep, and farm utensils. No farmer himself, Smith probably leased the properties and collected rents, intending to utilize the properties more as long-term investments. Perhaps as was to be expected for a man who occasionally trafficked in slaves, William Smith owned several enslaved persons at the time of his death. One "negro wench" lived with him at his home on Hanover Square, and an enslaved family, consisting of a man, a woman, and their two children, lived and worked at the Connecticut properties.

Smith's foray into Connecticut real estate ownership, along with the wealth he accumulated as "mariner and merchant," enabled him to provide well for his children. Doing so was every father's duty, but Smith had to be especially concerned because his two youngest daughters, Blanche and Sarah, were minors who were soon to become orphans. As his son and heir, John Smith received the property on Hanover Square, along with his father's female slave. Blanche and Sarah, meanwhile, received an equal share of the eight-acre tract in Connecticut. Smith directed his executors, his children John and Anne, along with his "beloved friend" Peter Van Brugh Livingston, to sell the properties within three months of his death and have the siblings divide the proceeds equally. In addition to real estate, Smith provided his children with cash. John received £250 of New York current money and a silver double tankard that family tradition holds once belonged to Justus Bosch.[128] Blanche and Sarah, meanwhile, each received £400, whereas Anne, who was about age twenty-one, received £600. Smith's eldest daughter, Mary Jauncey, had married a few years before and received no cash, which suggests she received a dowry in the neighborhood of £400–600 at the time of her marriage. In all, Smith left his children £1,650, a whopping sum that represented just a mere fraction of the value of his estate.[129] Smith died at three o'clock in the morning on April 20, 1752, and was buried beneath his pew at the First Presbyterian Church on Wall Street.[130] In accordance with his father's wishes, John Smith advertised the sale of the Connecticut properties at public vendue, and he did the same for the home on

Hanover Square. Extant records do not reveal if those properties sold, but James and Mary (Smith) Jauncey may have purchased the Hanover Square property, thus keeping it in the family.[131]

By virtue of their father's wealth and connections, the Smith family became eminent. In 1743 Mary, the oldest, married the Bermuda ship captain James Jauncey, who settled permanently in New York. Jauncey is noteworthy because he was a privateer during the War of the Austrian Succession (ca. 1739–48) and the Seven Years' War (1754–63). Success at sea enabled Jauncey to establish himself as a merchant, an occupation that further enriched the family. Mary and James Jauncey sent two of their sons to the College of New Jersey (now Princeton) and another son to King's College (Columbia University). When the United States declared independence in 1776, Jauncey remained loyal to the Crown and had his estate seized by New York authorities. James Jauncey fled to Britain, but his sons and wife stayed behind, and in 1790 the sons successfully petitioned to have their father's property restored to them.

The American Revolution, in fact, divided the family. Smith's daughter, Anne, married clergyman Benjamin Hoyt, who became a Continental Army chaplain.[132] Meanwhile, Smith's youngest daughters by Sarah Het, Blanche and Sarah, benefited financially through a provision in their grandfather René Het's will. Blanche Smith married the Yale-educated Presbyterian minister Jedediah Chapman in 1767 and had three children by him before dying in 1773. Reverend Chapman was an outspoken proponent of American independence, known for being "so obnoxious" to the Loyalists that British officials once put a bounty on his head. Sarah and Jedidiah's youngest son, Robert Hett Chapman (the pirate's grandson), was educated at Princeton and later served as the president of the University of North Carolina. Unfortunately, Sarah Smith died at age twenty.[133]

John Smith, meanwhile, continued in the tradition of his father by becoming a ship captain who later operated a profitable mercantile business. Also like his father, John Smith invested in farmland in Westchester County and elsewhere. In 1750 he married Mary Smith, daughter of Judge William Smith of Long Island, one of the leading men in colonial New York. For a short time, Judge Smith had been Captain William Smith's brother-in-law by virtue of his marriage to Sara Het. John and Mary had one daughter together, also named Mary, but Mary Sr. died at a relatively young age. John Smith remarried sometime before 1755 to Margaret Stephens of Westchester County, the daughter of a British army officer. John and Margaret had nine children together, often bestowing on them names invoking the memory of their ancestors, as with Justus Bosch Smith, the couple's sixth child.[134]

As improbable as it may seem, two of John Smith's children married into the family of John Adams, the revolutionary leader and second president of the United States. William Stephens Smith, born in 1755, graduated from the College of New Jersey and served with distinction in the Continental Army, fighting in the Battles of Long Island and Trenton, and even serving as a member of the Marquis de Lafayette's staff at Yorktown. After independence, Smith joined the staff of John Adams, the first U.S. ambassador to Great Britain. In London he met Abigail "Nabby" Adams, John and Abigail's eldest daughter. They married in London in 1786, returning to New York a couple years later. President George Washington appointed William Stephens Smith as the first U.S. marshal for the district of New York, after which he served as the district's supervisor of revenue. In 1800 his father-in-law, President John Adams, appointed Smith as the surveyor of the Port of New York. Smith also served one term as a congressman, representing his district in New York from 1813 to 1815 before dying in 1816. William's sister, Sarah (Sally) Smith, met Charles Adams after he had set up a law practice in New York. Abigail Adams, the first lady, described Sarah as an "amiable virtuous Girl, with every disposition to make him [Charles] a good wife." The couple married in 1795 and had two daughters. Charles's well-known struggles with alcohol contributed to the failure of his law practice and doomed speculative real estate ventures that impoverished his family. Charles died tragically in 1800 at age thirty from cirrhosis of the liver. Sarah moved into the home of John and Abigail Adams, and the former president and first lady provided for her as she raised the two girls, great-granddaughters of the pirate William Smith.[135]

That the grandchildren of a former pirate would one day marry into the family of the president of the United States indicates the degree to which piracy—and pirates—were interwoven in the fabric of colonial society. For New York in particular, it reveals that the men who accepted the Act of Grace paid no price for associating with pirates. In some cases, like that of William Smith, they thrived. The permissive attitude of New York governing officials and merchants as it pertained to piracy certainly played a role in their rehabilitation as upright ship captains. But so did their relative standing in the community before the golden age of piracy, as well as the strategic alliances they made with some of the city's leading merchants. As with their commercial partnerships, the pardoned pirates' marital choices reveal strategic thinking, for their unions with daughters from solidly "middling" or even locally prominent families provided them with the real and social capital that, in turn, expanded their opportunities in business. None of the New York pirates entered politics, and none would ever inscribe the words "Esquire" or "Gentleman" next to their names. However, unlike many of the pardoned pirates who toiled in obscurity and appeared fleetingly on history's stage, the respectable pirates of New York managed to secure their legacies by raising families, amassing property, and ensuring that their family names would endure, precisely because the infamy that might have been attached to them was quickly and conveniently forgotten.

CONCLUSION

Noncanonical Pirates

On May 9, 1724, an advertisement appeared in the *London Weekly Journal or Saturday's Post* announcing the imminent publication of a book titled *A General History of the Pyrates, from Their First Rise and Settlement in Providence, in 1717, to the Present Year 1724.* To entice prospective readers, it listed each of the book's chapters, most of which bore the name of pirate captains who had become newsworthy in recent years: Every, Thache, Bonnet, Vane, Rackham, and Roberts, to name but a few. In addition, the book promised detailed coverage of the "remarkable actions and adventures of the two female pyrates, Mary Read and Anne Bonny." The author, who styled himself "Captain Charles Johnson," seemed to be privy to inside information about the pirates, claiming to have derived his work "partly from their own journals and papers, partly from the author's intimacy with several of them, and partly from the confession of such as have been executed."[1] Captain Johnson's tome appeared in print five days later, but the author continued to revise and correct his work, issuing a second edition that September and serializing the book's preface in *Parker's London News* between September 9 and October 9, 1724.[2] A robust advertising campaign in London newspapers continued that fall, and by early February the book was selling in Dublin. Captain Johnson released a third edition in June 1725, undoubtedly inspired by the recent capture and execution of the Scottish pirate, John Gow, who received a new chapter of his own. The author persisted, issuing a two-volume fourth edition that appeared in 1726 and 1728 and included a number of additions and corrections.[3]

Audiences in the Anglophone world had been primed for stories of the pirates of Providence, because their exploits received ample coverage in newspapers and other publications. The earliest reports of postwar piracy tended to refer to pirates collectively and anonymously, simply referring to them as "the pirates" and neglecting to name their commanders. Gradually, however, the actions and characteristics of individual pirates came into sharper focus, and a few had become household names in Britain before the *General History* appeared. On June 1, 1717, Benjamin Hornigold and Edward Thache received mention for piracies they committed, and about a month later London newspapers chronicled the rise and fall of Sam Bellamy, focusing primarily on the capture and fatal wreck of his great prize ship, the *Whydah*.[4] By January 1718 news writers began adding the qualifiers "noted" or "famous" when mentioning the name of Thache, and it was about a year later that his alias—Blackbeard—came into widespread usage.[5] Newspapers also covered the capture, trial, and execution in South Carolina of the pirates Stede Bonnet and Richard Worley, but these were not the only source of pirate stories.[6] In April 1718 a magazine titled *The Political State of Great Britain* chronicled the surrender of Henry Jennings in Bermuda. Subsequent editions recounted the piracies of Thache, Vane, and Hornigold and offered a detailed account of Thache's demise off the coast of North Carolina.[7]

Meanwhile, trial transcripts emerged as a kind of genre of pirate literature. In July 1719 a transcript of the vice-admiralty trials of Stede Bonnet and his crew appeared in London as a lengthy pamphlet, and two years later Jamaica's lone publisher issued transcripts of the trials of John Rackham, Charles Vane, and their accomplices.[8] Then, in February 1723, the trials of Bartholomew Roberts's crew at Cape Coast Castle in West Africa, which led to the largest mass execution of pirates in British history, appeared with considerable fanfare.[9] Each of these publications provided raw material for the *General History*, whose pseudonymous author remained unknown for nearly three centuries but is now presumed to be the newspaper publisher Nathaniel Mist.[10]

Still in print, the *General History* established a "canon" of pirates, elevating the lives and actions of the "most notorious" criminals as the titular subjects of the book's chapters. In the process of canonizing them, the *General History* contributed to the perception that the phase of piracy following Queen Anne's War was indeed its golden age. Its pages are filled with stories and descriptive details that made these pirates legendary: the beard and devilish appearance of Thache; the gender deviancy of the female pirates Anne Bonny and Mary Read; the sociopathic cruelty of Ned Low and William Fly.[11]

If deviant, pirates in the *General History* nevertheless articulate a set of values, ably summarized by the historian Marcus Rediker. One of the pirates' underlying motives, for instance, was revenge against ship captains who treated them cruelly and arbitrarily, an implicit critique of the hierarchical culture of the Royal Navy and merchant marine. Envisioning a more democratic shipboard culture, pirates like Bartholomew Roberts devised articles of agreement that gave each man a vote on "affairs of moment" and equal shares of food and liquor. Pirate articles also provided financial compensation for the wounded and somewhat equalized the shares of plunder earned by officers and common sailors.

Charting their own course at sea, pirates developed a subculture of defiance that mocked authority and is memorably captured in a mock "play" performed by the crew of Thomas Antsis. Staged as a vice-admiralty pirate trial, the play features an "attorney general" character who insists on hanging the pirate not for his crimes but for drinking small beer (that is, weak with low alcohol content), stating that "sober fellows" were all "rogues." Equally incompetent is the play's "judge," who repeatedly insists on hanging the pirate before any testimony is taken. When the "prisoner" insists on presenting his side of the story, the judge preempts him and charges him with treason. The prisoner begs the judge to listen to reason, and the judge replies, "Raskal, we don't sit here to hear reason—we go according to law." Finally, the judge orders the prisoner's execution because he is hungry and wants to finish the trial. In addition to mocking legal authority vested in the state, pirate culture embraced death itself, represented by the skull and crossbones displayed on pirate flags and the motto attributed to Bartholomew Roberts that "a merry life, but a short one" was the only kind worth living.[12]

Although the idea of the radical pirate is compelling, it is important to realize that the "most notorious" pirates are only a subset of the general pirate population. In fact, the *General History* features a mere eleven men who accepted the Act of Grace before Captain Vincent Pearse, or less than 5 percent of the 209 total. Among them, only Charles Vane received a chapter devoted entirely to his exploits. Benjamin Hornigold's piracies receive mention, but these actions are set in a context emphasizing his rehabilitation after the pardon. The same applies to Josiah Burgess and John Cockram, who come into view most vividly in the book as Governor Rogers's trustworthy pirate hunters. The *General History* chronicles the October 1718 piracy of John Augur and one of his accomplices, Dennis McCarty, whose performance on the gallows remains one of the book's most entertaining episodes. George Rouncifull appears regularly in the 1718 pirate trials as the recipient of Governor Rogers's mercy. Palsgrave Williams, meanwhile, plays second fiddle to his more notorious accomplice, Sam Bellamy, in the chapter devoted to his career. Richard Taylor's capture of the *Cassandra* in the Indian Ocean and escape to Spanish America receive a few pages of coverage in the chapter devoted to Edward England. A few other pirates make only cameo appearances in the *General History*. Nicholas Woodale and Robert Brown of Rhode Island receive brief mention for trading with Charles Vane. Finally, the "Captain Clark" who met Governor Rogers at shore when he landed at Providence in July 1718 is probably the same man who washed ashore at Craignish, Scotland, about fifteen months later.[13]

What of the remaining 198 pirates on Pearse's list whom the author of the *General History* did not see fit to mention by name? By canonizing certain "most notorious" outlaws, the *General History*, through a process of exclusion, relegated the vast majority of pirates to "noncanonical" status. As with noncanonical biblical writings, the result has been to repress the memory of pirates whose experiences were unorthodox, or at least did not conform to the expectations of Nathaniel Mist, his readers, or eighteenth-century naval captains and governing officials. Noncanonical pirates unfortunately have not attracted the attention they deserve from modern historians, whose investigations tend to perpetuate the canon of pirates established three centuries ago. The appetites of modern readers and viewers, conditioned by Hollywood renderings of pirates on film, in video games, and in popular books, reinforce this dynamic, making it seem like the stories of canonical pirates are the only ones available to investigate. In other words, canonical pirates are important as historical actors, but noncanonical pirates barely penetrate our historical consciousness.

My purpose has been to bring to life the experiences of these forgotten noncanonical pirates. And what lessons do noncanonical pirates teach? First, uncovering the lives of ordinary people in the Atlantic world, especially well-traveled mariners, requires a research strategy that elaborates on the investigative methods typically employed in maritime historical research. While crucial, the writings of naval captains and governing officials, as well as contemporary newspapers, provide only a one-dimensional account of pirate actions, typically focusing on the most daring exploits of canonical pirates acting like . . . well, pirates. In contrast, intensive penetration of the administrative records from Britain and its colonies captures ordinary people engaging in everyday activities and enables a holistic reconstruction of their lives. In addition to investigating sources more intensively, tracking pirates throughout the Atlantic littoral requires an extensive research strategy, as many pardoned pirates left traces in the paper trails of multiple colonies.

Only by this means could we learn that the otherwise unremarkable James Fasset was part owner of a sloop registered in South Carolina, happened to be there to fight against the pirate Richard Worley, and resided in Philadelphia before migrating to Boston, where the probation of his will briefly caused a minor controversy. Just the same, it was possible to see how William Williams gravitated from the place of his birth, Jamaica, to North Carolina and the Bahamas before returning to North Carolina late in life to operate a tavern.

Although specific details about their childhoods remain out of reach, the available evidence allows for informed guesses about how these men gravitated to maritime work and into piracy. A few were slightly older men, but the vast majority were born around the year 1690 and grew up in or near port towns scattered widely throughout Britain and, in particular, its colonies. As such, they were familiar with the sea and the maritime trades. Importantly, they came into the world at a time when imperial rivalries intensified, resulting in the rise of an entire generation who knew nothing but ceaseless warfare. Therefore, as teenagers and young adults, mariners of this generation had ample opportunities to serve on privateering vessels, presumably during the latter stages of Queen Anne's War. At the same time, they were the beneficiaries of a maturing imperial trade system, which was their mainstay. Privateering, as such, should be viewed as an interruption in the mariners' more typical occupation as operators of merchant trading vessels. As we have seen, captains of merchant trading vessels often specialized in a few routes, enabling them to forge deep connections to multiple colonies. One of the critical components of the imperial trade system was the exchange of North American agricultural produce and lumber for tropical commodities harvested in the West Indies. It was no accident that the vast majority of pardoned pirates operated within this trading system and thus acquired familiarity with the waters that form an axis between Jamaica and the Bahamas.

Piracy in the postwar era unfolded somewhat differently in different places and changed over time, meaning that regional and temporal circumstances shaped the motivations of the pardoned men who gravitated into it. The earliest attacks emanated from the Bahamas, where the main motivation (beyond simply self-enrichment) was to revenge themselves on the Spanish, whose privateers had devastated the islands during the previous war. The destruction of the Spanish *flota* in 1715 drastically altered the dynamic, resulting in a mad scramble for the remains of the sunken treasure. If not the first Britons to appear on the wrecks, the Jamaicans clearly led the way, thanks to the approbation of their governor, Archibald Hamilton, and prominent members of the merchant community who funded the wrecking operations. Jamaican wrecking, however, spiraled out of control, as crews began attacking Spanish salvagers and seizing foreign ships. In turn, Jamaican mariners lost the backing of the merchant community and their political leaders. Perhaps to exonerate themselves, Jamaican officials launched an investigation into piracy that caused perhaps hundreds of Jamaican seamen to flee to the Bahamas to avoid prosecution. Once they established a base at Providence, the pirates intensified their attacks against Spanish and French shipping and eventually began attacking allied Dutch vessels as well as those from their own country. From that point onward, yet another dynamic developed whereby the captains of merchant vessels from North America and Bermuda, who had mostly avoided the Bahamas for a decade, began venturing there regularly. Sometimes they came in search of sunken gold, but more importantly to sell provisions to the pirates, who could pay in cash or with plundered tropical goods, presumably at a reduced cost. A "golden age of piratical trade" quickly ensued.

A few of the pardoned men such as Benjamin Hornigold, Josiah Burgess, Palsgrave Williams, and Thomas Nichols were confirmed pirate commanders. Many others formed their crews and thus were actively engaged in the armed takeover of merchant ships. A substantial number, however, appear to have engaged in piracy only vicariously through trade. This explains why Bermuda mariners conducted at least eighty voyages to the Bahamas and nearby coast of Florida between 1716 and 1718, sometimes returning with mass quantities of specie. Not to be outdone, North American skippers eagerly got into the action, seeking profits in the provisions trade. From New York, we see John Mutlow and John Stout suspiciously voyaging to the Bahamas when it was under the control of pirates, along with the likes of upstart merchant William Pinfold, whose decision to accompany his ship's captain on one trip resulted in his acceptance of the Act of Grace. South Carolina's Robert Wishart clearly dealt with pirates and even tried to get away with smuggling goods that derived from plundered Spanish ships. Captains from New England likewise engaged in the provisions trade with the pirates of Providence, attracting William Harris and others of his accomplices who managed to avoid detection. As defined by the 1717 Piracy Act, trading with pirates made them accomplices to piracy and thus criminals in the eye of the law.

Mariners who happened to be at Providence when Captain Pearse arrived bearing the Act of Grace thus were faced with an important choice that was, on one level, deeply personal: prolong a life of crime or fall in line with imperial goals. Pirates who had embraced their role as criminals or felt they had little to gain by surrendering chose the former. Those who accepted the Act of Grace, however, swallowed their pride and chose the latter, in most cases resuming their careers as mariners and ship captains engaged in intraimperial trade. Pardoned men did so because many of them possessed enough of the economic, social, and political capital that made it possible for them to do so. New Englanders such as John Mitchell and Abraham Adams had not only inherited property from their fathers but also accumulated estates of their own in the course of respectable careers as sea captains. New Yorkers William Pinfold, John Sipkins, and John Stout were in similar circumstances. In addition to possessing economic capital, these men also forged connections with leading merchants and tradesmen in their respective cities, and most were family men. In short, they were deeply embedded in local communities and institutions, so they humbly accepted the pardon rather than sacrifice all that was worthwhile in life. Rather than a composite snapshot of a "typical" pirate, Pearse compiled his list of 209 men thanks to a self-selecting process that disproportionately represents men who thought it worthwhile to live not just in the present but also with an eye toward the future. Intentionally or not, the pardon may have exposed a class divide within the pirate community, separating the somewhat richer men from the poorer mariners.

On another level, however, the collective decisions made by these pardoned pirates had broader implications for the future of the British Empire. Historians tend to attribute the rapid demise of piracy in the 1720s to the exertions of the British navy, the steel wills of colonial governors, and changing attitudes among the colonial merchant class, which saw more opportunity for profit by operating within the imperial trading system than by plunder. While these influences partly explain the demise of piracy, the surrenders of Henry Jennings in Bermuda and of Benjamin Hornigold, Thomas Nichols, Francis Lesley, and Josiah Burgess at Providence contributed to a new dynamic whereby respected pirate leaders provided examples for others to follow. The momentum they generated led to the pardons of more than two hundred men in the Bahamas, at least twenty in Bermuda, thirty-six in South Carolina, and undisclosed smaller numbers in other colonies. Pardoned men may not have constituted a majority of the pirates, but they represent a critical mass who were happy to step away from criminal activity and chart new courses for themselves—and the empire they served—with peace of mind. In retrospect, piracy did not so much decline but instead found expression in officially sanctioned privateering, which conveniently served imperial goals.

And what does a pirate do when he retires? One of the salient features of eighteenth-century life was its brevity, and it is noteworthy that many of the men on Pearse's list died within a few short years after the pardon. John Mitchell, Francis Lesley, and Peter Mallet, for example, may have never made it home alive after departing from Providence. Benjamin Hornigold, Josiah Burgess, George Rouncifull, and perhaps many others who are undocumented perished during privateering missions conducted during the War of the Quadruple Alliance. William Rouse died in January 1721, followed by Robert Wishart two years later. The majority of the pardoned gradually disappeared from the historical record as the decade of the 1720s waned. Maybe old pirates never die; they simply fade away.

Those who managed to live and abide by the pardon quickly resumed their maritime careers. Some became successful privateers like Othenias Davis, who received commissions in the Bahamas and South Carolina and nabbed at least three Spanish vessels during the War of the Quadruple Alliance. A considerable number of the pardoned men, around fifty, remained in the Bahamas, where they plied their trade as mariners but also appear to have scavenged for ambergris, harvested logwood, and perhaps raised fruit, indigo, or cotton. Minor offices in government attracted the likes of John Cullimore and John Cockram, whereas Peter Goudet rose to the position of treasurer and assemblyman. Most of the Bahamians married and produced families. The remainder of the pirates fanned out to their home ports or took up residence in new ones, following life trajectories not unlike those of the Bahamians. William Smith, the transplanted Bermudian who settled in New York, perhaps best exemplifies the aspirations of those who returned home to engage in honest seafaring work. After forging a business partnership with the merchant Justus Bosch, he married Bosch's daughter, Charity, and became one of the city's more successful ship captains. In time he began investing in merchant trading vessels and eventually retreated from active maritime work to become a prosperous merchant. In the course of his business career, he served as a trustee for his beloved Presbyterian Church on Wall Street and raised five children. Although he died in 1752, his legacy continued in the form of two grandchildren who married into the family of none other than President John Adams.

The example of pardoned men like William Smith calls for a nuanced reconceptualization of piracy—and of pirates. Historical debates about the political consciousness and motives of pirates are burdened by monolithic frameworks that depict them either as radical outcasts who formed a defiant subculture or as shrewd businessmen governed by the profit motive. Certainly, some pirates fit either of those descriptions. But the experiences of this particular subset of pirates suggest that most were rather ordinary sailors who drifted into piracy opportunistically, while at the same time underscored by their desire to make money. Pardoned pirates did not seek to revolutionize the social order because they were deeply invested in that social order. Of course, mariners constituted a subculture specific to their trade because of the way they dressed, walked, and talked. By focusing on what they did on land, however, it becomes evident that the aspirations of seamen were not so different from those of landed tradesmen, as evidenced by the way they formed families, participated in church rituals, and served in government. These aspirations likewise are revealed in the way pardoned pirates amassed moderately respectable estates and used institutions of government like the courts to ensure that their legacies could be passed on to their descendants. That so many of the pardoned pirates were able to slip back seamlessly into their trades and communities would seem to indicate that their contemporaries regarded them as rather ordinary.

Finally, the ordinariness of pirates calls for a reconceptualization of the colonial societies from which they sprang and the relationship between the maritime and terrestrial worlds. Together, colonies on land and seaborne activity comprised an organic, interdependent whole. Although metropolitan authorities never were able to micromanage the inner workings of this system, colonial producers always depended on the maritime community to ship their goods and sometimes provide protection at sea. Trade in terrestrial products, in turn, was the lifeline and justification for maritime work. Unsurprisingly, mariners and their contemporaries on land shared much of the same worldview, that of ambitious risk-taking by upstarts seeking to better themselves by any means necessary, even the rank exploitation of others. This entailed destroying indigenous communities and taking their land, enslaving Africans and forcing them to labor on plantations, and evading the law in order to trade freely with foreigners and adversaries. Within this theater of ambition, many strived, some thrived, and others failed. Piracy was so ordinary because it was a manifestation of the same impulses inherent to settler colonialism.

And yet, there is something extraordinary about the lives of noncanonical pirates, for they transformed an empire and were transformed by it. Through acts of piracy and providing support for the sea robbers, they provoked a response from metropolitan authorities, who initiated regime change in Jamaica and the Bahamas, passed anti-piracy legislation, and enhanced the naval presence in American waters. By accepting the Act of Grace and resuming their maritime careers, chastened, they contributed to the further development of the imperial trade system and, in some cases, the institutions of governance in their home communities. Their compliance also legitimized the Act of Grace and the myriad colonial officials charged with enforcing imperial mandates, and perhaps even solidified the position of George I, whose accession to the throne had been hotly contested. In the figurative sense, they may have been small men on a big stage, but writers ranging from Nathaniel Mist to myself thought them worthy of a book. Well-behaved pirates, it turns out, can make history.

On December 29, 1724, another advertisement promoting the sale of the second edition of the *General History of the Pyrates* appeared, but this time in the *American Weekly Mercury* of Philadelphia.[14] Established in 1719 by Andrew Bradford, the newspaper was the first to appear in the British North American colonies outside Boston. The advertisement had been placed by Bradford's father, William, one of colonial America's best-known pioneering printers. Over the course of his long career, Bradford became the public printer for the colony of New Jersey and in 1725 established New York's first newspaper, the *New York Gazette*. Bradford is also known as the man who trained the printer John Peter Zenger, whose acrid denouncements of Governor William Cosby resulted in a celebrated libel case that established precedent for freedom of the press. In 1723 Bradford directed a young upstart named Benjamin Franklin to Philadelphia to seek work with his son, Andrew, thus launching the career of colonial America's most celebrated printer.[15]

It just so happened that William Bradford's New York printing shop was situated in Hanover Square, only a few short steps away from the home of the pardoned pirate William Smith. The physical proximity of the two men invites speculation as to their relationship, both to each other and to the *General History*. Bradford might have sought out Smith occasionally in an attempt to buy the imported goods he sold from his home. Perhaps Smith was in the habit of stopping by Bradford's shop to purchase books or a copy of the newspaper. In the event the paths of these two men did cross, it is tempting to imagine that Smith purchased a copy of the *General History* and that they discussed it together. Bradford might have guessed that, as a mariner with connections in the Caribbean, Smith must have known some of the pirates and perhaps witnessed some of the events described in the book. Bradford surely would have plied Smith with questions about its authenticity or asked him to elaborate on certain points made by the author. It is enticing to think of how Smith might have responded to Bradford. Did he boast of knowing some of the world's "most notorious" pirates and confess candidly his own past lawbreaking? Conversely, did he deny knowing anything, or did Smith give shifty answers indicating that he perhaps knew more than he was willing to reveal? Did Bradford ever find out that Smith was a pardoned pirate? On such questions, the historical record is silent, but my hunch is that Smith would have remained coy. For a pardoned pirate to restore his reputation, it was perhaps best to let these things pass in silence. Smith probably chose to bask in the anonymity of being a "noncanonical" pirate because things worked out better for him that way.

APPENDIX

A LIST OF THE NAMES OF SUCH PIRATES AS SURRENDERED THEMSELVES AT PROVIDENCE TO CAPT. VINCENT PEARSE

Enclosed in Vincent Pearse to Secretary
Josiah Burchett, June 3, 1718 ADM 1/2282

* = *Denotes those identified by Pearse as having returned to piracy.*

Entries left blank denote those who cannot be
identified conclusively in the historical record.

ADAMS, ABRAHAM: Principal residence, Boston, Massachusetts. Son of a Boston innkeeper, Adams may have been captaining vessels by 1705, and made voyages to Antigua from 1708 to 1711. A voyage from Boston to South Carolina in November 1716 probably acquainted him with the Florida wrecks and opportunities for trading with pirates in the Bahamas. Following the 1718 pardon, he appears selling real estate he inherited from his father, and he sued a sea captain for back wages in 1720. He disappears from the historical record in 1723.

ADAMS, PACKER: Principal residence, London, England. Apprenticed as a Thames waterman/lightman in 1708. Because of his uncommon first name, he is probably the same man who from 1709 to 1711 served in the Royal Navy aboard the HMS *Sweepstakes*, which saw action in the Caribbean during Queen Anne's War. He disembarked at Barbados in 1711 and probably remained in the West Indies for several years until engaging in piracy.

ADDY, SAMUEL: Principal residence, Kingston, Jamaica. Probably the son of a Kingston tavern keeper of that same name who died in 1715.

ALLEN, ARTHUR: Principal residence, Bahamas. Served as a crew member on the sloop *John and Elizabeth* for a voyage undertaken to St. Augustine at the behest of Vincent Pearse in March 1718. Allen was later assigned land at Providence between 1719 and 1722.

ALLEN, JOHN: Principal residence, Boston, Massachusetts. Allen navigated regularly between Boston and Barbados in the early 1700s. He appears to have died in a whaleboat fight against Indians in 1724.

ANDREWS, JOHN:

ARROWSMITH, EDWARD:

ARTERILE, JOHN: Principal residence, Bahamas. As a "widower," he remarried one Mary Low in July 1721 and with her had at least two daughters, Anna and Rebecca. He served on a grand jury and a court of common pleas in 1722, and he appears on a list of men capable of bearing arms in 1727. He died sometime before 1731, when the first census of the Bahamas was conducted. As his surname is often spelled "Arturreal" in Bahamian documents, it is possible that he was a naturalized former Spanish subject.

ASHWORTH, LEIGH: Principal residence, Port Royal, Jamaica. Born in 1693 in Liverpool, he and his brother Jasper immigrated to Jamaica sometime before 1716, and both brothers established commercial connections in South Carolina. Ashworth achieved notoriety as a pirate in 1716 as captain of the sloop *Mary*, which was involved in capturing a French vessel. Ashworth was among the many Jamaicans who hid out in Providence from 1716 to 1718, when he returned to Port Royal after accepting the pardon. He served as a privateer in 1719 during the War of the Quadruple Alliance. He disappears from the historical record about that time, making it possible he died in the conflict.

AUGER, JOHN: Principal residence, Jamaica. He appears in the historical record as master of the sloop *New Tryall*, which sailed from South Carolina to Jamaica in May 1710. Skeptical of the pardon, he twice refused it before accepting the Act of Grace bestowed by Vincent Pearse, and then fomented a thwarted plot against the naval captain during his tenure at Providence. He was among the ringleaders in the October 1718 piracies that led to the conviction and execution of Auger and seven others that December.

AUSTIN, WILLIAM: Principal residence, Jamaica. While there are no records of Austin's maritime work, two men by that name appear in the Kingston Parish church registers in the 1720s, making it likely that he was one of them.

BARKER, JOHN: Principal residence, New York. A ship captain by that name made two trips to Antigua and one to St. Thomas between 1715 and 1716, putting him in the epicenter of pirate activity in the Bahamas and Jamaica. The vessels he sailed were owned by Justus Bosch, a New York merchant with close connections to other pirates on Pearse's list.

BARNES, HENRY:

BASS, ROBERT: Principal residence, Jamaica. Bass appears fleetingly in the historical record as a Royal Navy man during the War of the Quadruple Alliance. He enlisted at Jamaica on February 21, 1720 as a pilot for the *Shark* sloop, serving in that capacity for about two months before receiving a discharge at Port Royal.

BEACH, SAMUEL:

BEAD, EDWARD: Principal residence unknown. This is probably the same man who served on board the *Mediterranean Galley* in the fight against Richard Worley in November 1718, for which he received bounty money.

BERRY, EDWARD: Principal residence, Jamaica. Berry was probably baptized in St. Andrews Parish in 1689. After receiving a pardon from Pearse, Berry ventured to South Carolina to receive another pardon from the governor in July 1718. For a short time Berry partnered with pirate James Fasset as owners of the sloop *Rogers*, which made at least two voyages between the Bahamas and South Carolina. He remained in South Carolina to fight against the pirate Richard Worley in November 1718. Berry later took up residence in Kingston, Jamaica. He married in 1723 but died and was buried at Kingston on June 7, 1725, evidently without having children.

BERRY, HENRY: Principal residence, Newport, Rhode Island. He was a mariner who sued another Newport resident in 1721, seeking restitution for a beating he suffered while cutting logwood along the coast of New Spain.

BIRDSELL, THOMAS:

*BISHOP, RICHARD: Principal residence, New York. Instigated a petty debt case in the New York Mayor's Court in 1720.

BLEY, JOHN: Principal residence, Bahamas. Born in the Bahamas to one of the "old settlers," Samuel Bley, who arrived in the early 1680s. He was a merchant sea captain and occasionally served on the Bahamas grand juries. Bley was married and had four children still living at the time of the 1740 census. The Bahamas' longest living pirate, Bley died in 1752.

BOYCE, SAMUEL: Principal residence, Boston, Massachusetts. Boyce may have been born in Saybrook, Connecticut, around 1673, making him one of the older pirates. He was active as a mariner and captain from 1690 to about 1725, with many voyages to the West Indies and South Carolina. Boyce accepted a second pardon in South Carolina in July 1718. He was married to a woman named Abigail and had several children by her. Boyce owned property in Boston and died shortly after 1736.

BRADLEY, THOMAS: Principal residence, Bahamas. After the pardon, he was accused of trading with pirates and imprisoned for one month around December 1718, after which he disappears from the historical record.

BRIDGES, WILLIAM: Principal residence, Bahamas. Possibly descended from one of the old settlers. Served as a juror in the William Whalin theft/arson case in 1719. He was still living in the Bahamas in 1723, after which he disappears from the historical record.

BROWN, JAMES: Principal residence, Newport, Rhode Island. Possibly the same man who served as a privateer in the Indian Ocean in the 1690s and caught a ride back to the Americas on board Henry Every's vessel, the *Fancy*. He married Ann Markham, daughter of Governor William Markham of Pennsylvania, where for a time he took up planting. The family moved to New York, where he resumed sailing vessels, mostly to Rhode Island and nearby destinations. He died before 1726 and was survived by his wife and a daughter.

BROWN, ROBERT 1: Principal residence, Bahamas. Appears regularly in the Bahamian records in the 1720s as a juror and deponent. He was married twice and had several children by both women. He last appears in the historical record in 1726.

BROWN, ROBERT 2: Principal residence, Rhode Island. Possibly the brother of James Brown who may have seen navy service in 1707 when a man by that name enlisted on the HMS *Windsor* stationed in New England. At the time of the pardon, Brown commanded the sloop *Eagle*, later the subject of an admiralty court case on suspicion of trading with Charles Vane. He disappears from the historical record by 1731.

BRYAN, JAMES: Principal residence, Jamaica. Possibly the same man who married in 1709 in St. Catherine's Parish.

BURGESS, JOSIAH: Principal residence, Bahamas. Possibly descended from a Bermudian family by that name. Burgess came to Providence after abandoning the Jamaican sloop *Francis and Sarah* around September 1716. He was active in piracy from that point forward and emerged as one of the commanders who first surrendered to Pearse. After the pardon, Burgess cooperated regularly with Governor Rogers, dying in 1720 on a privateering voyage.

CALVERLEY, PHILLIP: Principal residence, Newport, Rhode Island. Possibly related to other piracy suspects sharing his surname. He appears elsewhere only once in the historical record, when in 1703 he was called before the Newport Town Council to pay a debt.

CAMPBELL, ALEXANDER: Principal residence, Bahamas. He was living on Cat Island in 1722, when he testified against Richard Hancock and others from Augustine Blanco's crew for piracy. Campbell appears for the last time in the historical record on the 1731 census of Eleuthera as the sole member of the household who owned one slave.

*CARMAN, DANIEL: Principal residence unknown. One man with that surname commanded a vessel that arrived in Philadelphia from South Carolina in July 1718. The timing and proximity suggest this was the same individual.

CARRILL, MARTIN:

CARYE, JOHN: Principal residence, Bahamas. Carye may have been a descendent of some of the Bahamas' "old settlers." He was involved in some of the piracies conducted in the Bahamas in 1713–14 and was married at the time. He does not appear in Bahamian records from the 1720s, so it can be presumed he died shortly after the pardon.

CHAMPION, DAVID: Principal residence, Eleuthera, Bahamas. Champion may have served in the Royal Navy after the Treaty of Utrecht, for a man by that name enlisted on the HMS *Roebuck* in October 1715 and was discharged at Martinique in March 1716. He appears on the 1731 census, along with his wife, two children, and seven slaves. He died before the compilation of the 1734 census.

*CHANDLER, THOMAS: Principal residence, Barbados. One of the older pardoned pirates, Chandler navigated vessels in Caribbean waters from 1701 to 1721. His last voyage occurred in 1721. He died in 1725 and was buried in St. Michael's Parish.

CHARLTON, JOHN:

CHARNOCK, FRANCIS: Principal residence, Jamaica. He was involved in the 1716 attacks against Spanish and French ships near Bahia Honda, Cuba. Accepted a second pardon in South Carolina in April 1718. After the pardon, Charnock joined the *Buck* sloop mutineers and was among the remnants of Howell Davis's crew that washed ashore at Craignish, Scotland. He hid in London for a while then returned to Jamaica. He was married to a woman named Mary and had one daughter, both of whom died before 1725.

CHICK, HENRY: Principal residence, South Carolina. Chick appears elsewhere in the historical record just once, when he enlisted at Charles Town on the HMS *Success* in August 1715, receiving a discharge there the following March.

CHISSEM, GEORGE: Principal residence, Jamaica. Appeared in South Carolina in 1709, where he signed two bonds to a local man, indicating trading connections there.

CHOW, WILLIAM:

CLAPP, JOSEPH: Principal residence, Bahamas. Appears on a 1728 list of inhabitants who left the colony. One source indicates he fled to Jamaica.

CLARK, JOHN: Principal residence, Bangor, Northern Ireland. One of the *Buck* sloop mutineers, who was arrested at Craignish, Scotland, and executed in 1720.

CLARKE, NABEL:

CLIES, THOMAS: Not identified conclusively in the historical record. Possibly from Cornwall.

COATES, JAMES: Not identified conclusively in the historical record. Likely a Jamaican, and one of the older mariners. Appears in 1693 as master of the pink *Robert*, bound for London.

COCKRAM, JOHN: Principal residence, Bahamas. Possibly born in Jamaica, Cockram married Catherine Thompson of Harbor Island before 1714, and he was involved in the earliest piracies against the Spanish in the postwar period. Known as the "doctor" on board the *Bersheba*, Cockram was also involved in the 1716 Bahia Honda attacks and provided a deposition for the Jamaica Council in its piracy investigation later that year. Following the pardon, Cockram assisted Governor Rogers in hunting down pirates. He remained a ship captain and was once recommended for the Bahamas Council. He fled the colony sometime before 1728, possibly for debt. He died before 1734. He and Catherine had at least one son named Phillip.

CODD, THOMAS:

CONNELLY, DARBY: Principal residence, Ireland. Age seventeen at the time of the pardon, Connelly probably drifted to Barbados for the next couple of years. In February 1720, at Barbados, he enlisted on board the sloop *Philippa* captained by Daniel Greaves, commissioned by the Barbadian government to repel a recent invasion of pirates, probably Bartholomew Roberts. Connolly's appearance on the *Philippa*'s crew list is the only time his name surfaced again after the pardon.

CONNOR, WILLIAM: Principal residence, New York. Commander of the pirate vessel *Dragon*. During Pearse's mission to Providence, he served on the *John and Elizabeth* and was deposed in New York in the 1718 council investigation. He surfaces occasionally in New York's Mayor's Court and continued his career as a mariner until 1721, when he married a wealthy widow from Westchester, New York, after which he may have taken up farming.

CREIGH, JOHN: Principal residence, Antigua. Captain of the sloop *New Sea Flower*, which sailed between Antigua and Barbados around 1705–6. Following the pardon, he may have remained at Providence, for one "John Cray" appears on a 1723 church assessment list.

*CREW, JOHN: Principal residence, Jamaica. Crew probably joined Charles Vane during Pearse's residency at the Bahamas. Following the pardon, enlisted on the HMS *Milford* and served for more than one year. He married at Port Royal in 1722, after which he disappears from the historical record.

CULLEMORE, JOHN: Principal residence, Bahamas. Cullemore was a longtime resident of the colony, appearing regularly in local records dating to the 1720s. He was married, had at least three children, and owned slaves. One of the Bahamas' more prominent residents, he was elected to the Assembly in 1734 representing Harbor Island. He lived at least until 1741, after which he disappears from the historical record.

DALRIMPLE, JOHN: Principal residence, Bahamas. Following the pardon, Dalrimple enlisted on the HMS *Flamborough* in October 1719 and remained in service through the thwarted Spanish invasion of February 1720. He had a house in Nassau and died in January 1723.

DAVIS, OTHENIAS: Principal residence, Jamaica. Served as the quartermaster of the *Bersheba* involved in 1716 piracies. Davis accepted a second pardon in South Carolina in June 1718. Following the pardon, he became half owner of the privateer vessel *Movil Trader*, which took several prizes during the War of the Quadruple Alliance. He engaged in admiralty and other court proceedings in the Carolinas between 1720 and 1721, after which he disappears from the historical record.

DAWS, ANDREW:

DERICKSON, CLOIS [CORNELIUS]: Not identified conclusively in the historical record. Derickson possibly was from London, where a man by that name was living at Elephant Court in the parish of St. Mary Whitechapel prior to 1718. A soldier by that name joined Woodes Rogers at Madeira on his voyage to the Bahamas and was listed among the deceased in October 1718.

DIVELLY, RICHARD: Principal residence unknown. Master of the sloop *Industry* of South Carolina, which he sailed to St. Augustine around April 1717.

DRYBRO, ROBERT:

*DUNKIN, JOHN: Principal residence unknown. Dunkin possibly arrived in the Americas via navy service. He later served in South Carolina in the attack on the pirate Richard Worley. What happened to him next is uncertain, although a man by that name died in Jamaica in 1723.

DWOOULY, DOMINIC:

EALING, JOHN: Principal residence, unknown but possibly Jamaica. Crew member of the Jamaican sloop *Francis and Sarah*, which he abandoned in September 1716 to join the pirates at Providence. He accepted another pardon in South Carolina in July 1718.

EARLE, RICHARD: Principal residence, Jamaica. Earle served under Francis Fernando on the sloop *Bennet*. He was involved in the 1716 capture of the Spanish vessel *Nuestra Señora de Belen* and received a share of the plunder.

EDMUNDSEN, WILLIAM: Not identified conclusively in the historical record. One man by that name appears in a book recounting a thwarted mutiny of a Rhode Island sloop off the West African coast in 1726.

EDWARDS, JOHN: Principal residence, Boston, Massachusetts. Edwards was one of the older pirates, as he was active in Boston's maritime community twenty years before the pardon. He had long-standing ties to the Bahamas. In 1698 he captained the *Bahama Merchant*, whose co-owners included one individual from Providence, where he received a commission to hunt down a pirate named Kelly but was accused of abandoning his vessel. He also served on a 1704 Boston expedition to salvage a shipwreck in the Bahamas led by James Roisie. He moved to the Bahamas permanently by 1727, when he married a woman from Eleuthera. He appears for the last time in the historical records in 1728.

EMLY, THOMAS: Principal residence unknown. He was possibly a commander of a sloop that voyaged from Rhode Island to Philadelphia in September 1711, so he could originate in either of those places. He accepted a second pardon in South Carolina in July 1718.

FASSET, JAMES: Principal residence, Boston, Massachusetts. Fasset's origins are unknown. After the pardon, he gravitated to South Carolina, where he engaged in the fight against pirate Richard Worley. He moved to Philadelphia, then Boston, where his death generated a dispute over the executorship of his estate, a story featured in chapter 6.

FEVERSHAM, GEORGE: Not identified conclusively in the historical record. One possibility is that Pearse mistranscribed the name of George Featherstone, who later served with the pirate John Rackham and appears elsewhere in Bahamian records.

FORBES, ADAM:

FRYERS, JOSEPH:

FURROW, JOHN:

GARRISON, CHARLES:

GATER, GEORGE:

GEE, MARMADUKE: Principal residence, London. Born in 1684, Gee resided in St. Mary Bermondsey parish and may have once apprenticed as a weaver. He married in 1713 and had one daughter. He appeared in Bermuda in 1715 to witness a power of attorney. Following the pardon, he accepted another one in South Carolina in June 1718 and served under Othenias Davis on the *Movil Trader* as a privateer. On returning to London, Gee and his wife had another daughter, baptized in 1724. Gee disappears from the historical record thereafter, although his wife was buried in 1731.

GLINN, HENRY: Principal residence, Jamaica. Before piracy, Glinn was the master of the *Mermaid Galley*. He conducted one slave-trading voyage from West Africa to Jamaica, arriving home in January 1711. He sailed the same vessel again in 1713. What happened to him after the pardon is unknown.

GOODSIR, JAMES: Principal residence, Bahamas. He is probably among the Jamaicans who stayed at Providence beginning in 1716. He remained at Providence at least until 1723, after which he disappears from the historical record.

GORMAN, EDWARD:

*****GOUDET, PETER:** Principal residence, Bahamas. Born in London, Goudet's association with piracy derives from his association with the pirate Charles Vane. After the pardon, Goudet became a colonial bureaucrat, including stints as treasurer and customs collector. He served in the Bahamas' inaugural assembly in 1729. In business he was a merchant trader who owned three vessels, and his ownership of about ten slaves indicates he also planted indigo and cotton. He married and had two children before working for a short time as a customs controller in South Carolina in the early 1730s. He returned to the Bahamas in 1733 and died a year later.

GRAHAME, THOMAS: Principal residence unknown. A crew member of the erstwhile *John and Elizabeth* who earned money trading at St. Augustine (ca. March 1718) for a voyage undertaken at the behest of Vincent Pearse. He enlisted on the HMS *Phoenix* for its return voyage to New York in April 1718, after which he disappears from the historical record.

GRAHAME, WILLIAM: Principal residence, Bahamas. Appears on the 1731 census with a wife and two kids.

GRATRICKS, JAMES: Principal residence unknown. Possibly from London; a man by that name inhabited the parish of St. Sepulchre, County Middlesex, marrying in 1708 and dying in 1725. He accepted a second pardon in South Carolina in July 1718.

HARBIN, ROWLAND: Principal residence, Jamaica. Abandoned the sloop *Francis and Sarah* at Providence in September 1716.

HARRIS, WILLIAM: Principal residence, Boston, Massachusetts. Harris was active as a mariner from 1699, making him one of the older pirates. He sailed regularly to the West Indies before accepting a pardon, probably for trading with pirates. Accused of trading with Charles Vane, Harris's sloop was the subject of a 1718 admiralty case conducted by Governor Rogers, after which he was caught once more for smuggling at St. Christopher's. Nevertheless, Harris continued sailing vessels until the early 1730s and died around that time.

HASLETON, WILLIAM: Principal residence, Barbados. Hassleton probably lived with his wife in St. Michael's Parish, where they baptized three children in the early 1700s. Possibly a relative by marriage of Barbadian and pardoned pirate Cornelius Mahon.

HAWKINS, HENRY: Principal residence unknown. A man by that name appears on the payroll of the HMS *Windsor*, which was stationed in the West Indies from 1709 to 1711.

HAWKS, RICHARD: Principal residence, Jamaica. He appears as a beneficiary of a 1725 will recorded in Jamaica, and a man by that name was buried in Kingston in 1727.

HAYS, EDWARD:

HILL, DANIEL:

HIPPERSON, JOHN: Principal residence, Jamaica. Baptized in August 1685 in St. Andrews Parish. After the pardon, Hipperson was accused of trading with pirates in January 1719 but was never prosecuted. Four years later he was the subject of a rumor indicating he had left St. Christopher's and again turned pirate, which proved to be unfounded. He disappears from the historical record around 1723.

HOLMES, MARK: Not identified conclusively in the historical record. Possibly from Rhode Island, as one "Captain Holmes" from that colony receives occasional mention in the Boston newspaper.

HORNIGOLD, BENJAMIN: Primary residence, Bahamas. Possibly born in Ipswich, Suffolk, England. Much remains unknown about his early life, but he emerged around 1713 as one of the instigators of Bahamian piracy against the Spanish. He may have joined the crew of Francis Fernando on the *Bennet*, which he later commanded. At one point the most notorious British pirate, Hornigold is best known for his association with Edward Thache. After the pardon, he accepted another one in New York, and he emerged as one of Woodes Rogers's most reliable pirate hunters, whose exploits are featured in chapter 5. He died while commanding a privateer vessel during the War of the Quadruple alliance.

HOUGHTON, ROGER:

HOWELL, JOHN: Principal residence, Bahamas. A doctor forced to serve under Benjamin Hornigold, Howell remained in the Bahamas and served on the council beginning in 1721. In December 1721 political opponents resurrected piracy charges against him, which were soon dropped. He served on the council many years afterward. Among the longest-lived pirates, Howell died in 1752.

HUDSON, NATHANIEL: Principal residence, Jamaica. Hudson appears to have had long-standing connections in New York and may have been sailing there as early as 1711. He served as the quartermaster of the *Bersheba* and was involved in the 1716 Bahia Honda piracies. He resumed sailing merchant vessels in 1717 and was once attacked by the pirate Sam Bellamy. Sent by the Jamaican government in January 1718 (along with William Smith) to announce the pardon, he joined the crew of the *John and Elizabeth* after Pearse's arrival and was later deposed in New York in the council's piracy investigation. He returned to Jamaica and appears as a debtor to a deceased Kingston merchant in 1724, at which point he disappears from the historical record.

HUNT, JOHN: Not identified conclusively in the historical record. However, there are contemporary mariners from Barbados, Jamaica, and Bermuda by that name who remain possibilities.

HUNT, WILLIAM: Not identified conclusively in the historical record. Two possibilities are men by that name who lived in Jamaica and Rhode Island around that time.

HUNTER, ROBERT: Principal residence, Bahamas. Hunter continued working as a mariner until his death around April 1725, and he once served as master of the ship *Benjamin and Mary*. He was married to a woman named Elizabeth, and they had one son who was baptized in January 1722.

JACKSON, JOHN: Principal residence, Boston, Massachusetts. Jackson was actively involved in maritime commerce from 1698 to about 1720, conducting voyages between Virginia and Newport, Rhode Island. He disappears from the historical record following a 1720 court appearance in Rhode Island.

JACOBS, ANTHONY: Principal residence, Jamaica. Jacobs probably served in the Royal Navy, enlisting on the HMS *Seaford* for a month in 1712. He was named as the captain of a pirogue involved in the 1716 piracies against Spanish shipping, after which he disappears from the historical record.

*JOHNSON, JACOB: Principal residence, Bermuda. Johnson continued as a ship captain for about a decade after the pardon. He served the Bermuda government in minor capacities; in 1719 he interpreted for French complainants in a prize case, and he held a position as customs searcher in 1724. Johnson disappears from the historical record in 1727.

JOHNSON, JOHN: Not identified conclusively in the historical record. Possibilities include contemporary mariners from Barbados, New York, and Bermuda.

JOHNSON, PETER: Principal residence, Bahamas. Johnson's life before the pardon is not conclusively known, although there was a Boston mariner by that name who once served as a privateer, as well as a crew member for the HMS *Seaford* who enlisted at St. Christopher's in December 1717 for a deployment that lasted until March 1718. After the pardon, he probably served as a privateer under Othenias Davis, captain of the *Movil Trader*. He appears again in the Bahamas in 1730, commanding a vessel owned by Woodes Rogers that made one voyage to Jamaica, after which he disappears from the historical record.

JONES, DANIEL: Not identified conclusively in the historical record. Possibilities include a "young commander" who sailed in consort with Stede Bonnet around August 1718, as well as the commander of the sloop *Dove*, which sailed between Philadelphia and Maryland around that same time.

KAINE, RICHARD: Not identified conclusively in the historical record. Possibly a Charles Town, South Carolina, shipwright who received protection from impressment in February 1716.

KEMP, ANTHONY: Principal residence, Bahamas. Kemp abandoned the *Francis and Sarah* at Providence in 1716 and remained there for the rest of his life. He last appears in the 1731 census, living at Eleuthera with a wife and four children.

KEMP, JOHN: Principal residence, Bahamas. Probably the brother of Anthony Kemp, John was involved in some of the first postwar acts of piracy emanating from the Bahamas. He had a wife and two children. A lifelong resident, Kemp disappeared for a while in 1728 under suspicion of smuggling, but he returned to the Bahamas in 1729. He is listed on the 1734 census, at which point he disappears from the historical record.

KERR/CARR, EDWARD: Principal residence, Bahamas. Deposed during investigation of Robert Howell for piracy in 1721, Kerr married in 1723 and had one daughter baptized in 1726. He last appears on a 1728 tax assessment, after which he disappears from the historical record.

KERR, JAMES: Not identified conclusively in the historical record. Possibly named as the supercargo for Woodes Rogers's 1718 trade mission to Cuba, which resulted in the piracies spearheaded by John Augur.

LAMB, THOMAS:

LAVOY, WILLIAM:

LEGATT, RICHARD: Principal residence, Bahamas. Leggatt may have seen service in the Royal Navy during Queen Anne's War. He accepted a second pardon in South Carolina in July 1718. He appears in Bahamian records in the 1720s, as well as the 1731 census indicating that he had a wife, two children, and one slave.

LESLEY, FRANCIS: Principal residence, Barbados. Son of John Leslie of St. John's Parish, Lesley was involved in Henry Jennings's 1716 piracies. Among the first to accept the pardon, for a short time afterward he conducted trade with Jamaica in the *Bersheba*. He died and was buried in Barbados in November 1719.

LEWIS, JOHN: Principal residence, Jamaica. Possibly the son of a Kingston merchant by that name, Lewis, born around 1691, was active as a commander of vessels from 1709 and served as a privateer during Queen Anne's War. He married in New York before 1712 and maintained connections there before the 1715 act of piracy whereby he absconded with the effects of the Marquis de Navarres. Pardoned also in New York, Lewis resumed privateering during the War of the Quadruple Alliance. He may have briefly returned to piracy in 1720, at which point he married for a second time in Bermuda, where he eventually was executed for the murder of Francis Landy, as chronicled in Chapter 6.

LYELL, ALEXANDER:

MAGGRIDGE, ROBERT:

MAGNESS, JOHN: Principal residence, Bahamas. Following the pardon, he operated Bahamas Company vessels, appearing in 1722 as a crew member of the pink *Althea*. After testifying against a Bahamian charged with expressing Jacobite sympathies, he disappears from the historical record.

MAHON, CORNELIUS: Principal residence, Barbados. Married in 1723 to a relative of William Hasleton. After being indicted for assault in 1725, he disappears from the historical record.

MALLET, PETER: Principal residence, Nevis. Born in New York City to French Huguenot parents, Mallet (also Melotte) spent his adulthood in Nevis. A ship captain working mostly Caribbean routes from 1706, Melotte died at sea in 1718, possibly on his return voyage from Providence. He was buried at Nevis, leaving a wife and daughter.

MANN, GEORGE:

MARSHALL, PETER:

MARTIN, JOHN: Principal residence, Boston and New York. From about 1714 onward, Martin worked as a ship captain specializing in routes to Campeche. After the pardon, he appears in New York, making runs to Jamaica and Curaçao. In 1720 the governor of Virginia employed him to hunt pirates and deliver a flag of truce to St. Augustine, and he disappears from the historical record two years later.

MCCARTY, DENIS: Principal residence, Barbados. Although his origins are obscure, he was probably a Royal Navy sailor who served on the HMS *Sweepstakes* from 1709 to 1711. The *General History* indicates that he had a wife and small child, so he may have been one of several men by that name who appears in the 1715 Barbados census. He was executed at Providence for piracy in December 1718.

*****MEREDITH, DAVID:** Principal residence, Bahamas. Meredith testified at the December 1718 pirate trials, and he does not appear in the historical record again until 1736, when he was reprimanded for failing to respond to the 1734 census. He had a wife and two children, and he died sometime before the 1740 census, which lists his wife, Ruth, as a widow.

MICKELBRO, JOSEPH: Principal residence, Bahamas. He appears just once after the pardon in a September 1718 deposition. He presumably died shortly thereafter, perhaps while serving on a privateer vessel during the War of the Quadruple Alliance.

MILLER, EDWARD:

*****MITCHELL, JOHN:** Principal residence, Charlestown, Massachusetts. Born in July 1664, Mitchell was probably among the oldest pirates to accept the pardon. His father was a ship captain, and John followed him in the same profession, specializing in routes to North Carolina in the 1710s. He receives mention in 1716 as one who stole salvaged silver from a Spanish encampment on the coast of Florida. He died shortly after the pardon, and his widow pursued a small debt case on his behalf in a North Carolina court until 1723.

MOODEY, JAMES: Principal residence unknown. Born about 1679, a mariner by that name frequented South Carolina in 1719, and another one appears in the Kingston Parish registers a decade later. He nevertheless stopped at Providence occasionally, once just months after the pardon and again in 1725.

*****MOODEY, SAMUEL:**

MORGAN, CHARLES:

MOUNSEY, JOHN: Principal residence, Bahamas and London. Mounsey briefly returned to piracy, joining Charles Yates, an accomplice of Charles Vane. He received a second pardon in South Carolina in September 1718 and later joined the crew of the *Sea Nymph* involved in attacking the pirate crews of Stede Bonnet and Richard Worley. He lived at Providence for about five years before returning to London, where in 1728 the Board of Trade interviewed him about the conduct of Governor Phenney. He was admitted to the Bethlem Hospital (or "Bedlam") in 1731 and died there the following year.

MOWAT, JAMES: Principal residence, Jamaica. Inventoried the estate of a Kingston man in February 1716.

*****MURRAY, ARCHIBALD:** Principal residence, Bangor, Northern Ireland. After the pardon, he was a mutineer from the *Buck* sloop that engaged in piracies under Howell Davis and Bartholomew Roberts. In December 1719 he was among those who washed up at Craignish, Scotland. He avoided prosecution by serving as King's evidence against his accomplices.

MUTLOW, JOHN: Principal residence, New York. Of unknown origins, he married Elisabeth Blom in New York in 1716 and became a notable sea captain. He was active until the early 1730s and presumably died around that time, leaving his wife and a surviving son.

*NEARNE, DAVID:

NEVILL, JAMES: Principal residence unknown. It is possible he served in the navy aboard the HMS *Shoreham*, from which he received a discharge in South Carolina in July 1716.

*NEWLAND, EDWARD: Principal residence, Bahamas. Appears just once in the historical record prior to the pardon, as the author of a power of attorney granted to another Providence mariner in June 1717. His whereabouts after the pardon are unknown.

NEWLAND, RICHARD: Principal residence, Bahamas. Engaged in piracy as the quartermaster for Benjamin Hornigold. Although his origins are unknown, he appears to have spent most of his adult life in the Bahamas and captained numerous vessels in the late 1720s and early 1730s. He appears occasionally in the Bahamas records as a deponent and grand juror, but there is no record of him having a family. He may have continued sailing vessels as late as 1742, when he was the subject of a prisoner exchange with Cuban officials.

NICHOLS, EDWARD: Not identified conclusively in the historical record. Possibilities include a man from Barbados and another from Jamaica who were contemporaries.

NICHOLS, THOMAS: Principal residence, New York. Ship captain since at least 1706. Nichols's lone confirmed piracy involved his command of the sloop *Dragon*, which presumably captured the French vessel *St. Jacque*, which was later converted to the erstwhile *John and Elizabeth* of New York. After the pardon, he co-owned a vessel with fellow pardoned pirate William Connor for a short time before settling down in Rye, New York, where he married and worked as a fuller (cloth maker). He had two daughters and died in 1734.

PARMYTER, EDWARD: Not identified conclusively in the historical record. Possibly related to two prominent families by that name, from Jamaica and New York, respectively.

PEARSE, JOHN: Not conclusively identified in the historical record, there are two contemporary mariners by that name living in Jamaica and Boston at the time who remain possibilities.

PEARSE, JOSEPH: Principal residence, Bahamas. Possibly a Jamaican by birth, Pearse abandoned the sloop *Francis and Sarah* in September 1716 at Providence and stayed there the rest of his life. He captained numerous vessels, was married to a woman named Martha, and had two sons. He disappears from the historical record after 1726.

PEARSE, THOMAS: Principal residence, Jamaica. He abandoned the sloop *Francis and Sarah* in September 1716 at Providence. After receiving his pardon he disappears from the historical record.

PERRIN, JOHN: Principal residence, Virginia. Born around 1689 to a locally prominent

Virginia family, Perrin commanded two sloops at the time he was apprehended in 1716 on suspicion of trading with the pirate Benjamin Hornigold. After the pardon, Perrin, who owned more than twenty slaves, emerged as a prominent tobacco shipper who also grew some of his own product. He died a wealthy man in 1752.

PETERS, CHRIS:

PETERS, WILLIAM: Not identified conclusively in the historical record. Possibly from South Carolina; a man by that name commanded a company involved in the colony's 1728 raid on the Yamasee Indians living near St. Augustine.

PETERSON, GARRET:

PETERSON, JAMES:

PINFOLD, WILLIAM: Principal residence, Queens, New York. Born in London to a relatively prosperous haberdasher, Pinfold came to New York sometime before 1714, when he married Elizabeth Lawrence. They had several children who became relatively prominent fixtures of Long Island. Pinfold sailed vessels until 1723 and supposedly died at sea.

RADDON, GEORGE: Principal residence, Bahamas. Raddon captained numerous trading vessels in the 1720s and served occasionally on grand juries and in other minor governmental capacities. He had a wife named Elizabeth, three children, and one slave, all of whom appear on the 1731 and 1734 censuses. Raddon was still living in 1736, after which he disappears from the historical record.

RAWLINGS, RICHARD: Principal residence unknown. Rawlings may have been from Boston, where a man by that name cleared a vessel arriving from Barbados in 1710. He was in South Carolina in 1718 and involved in the fight against Stede Bonnet.

REVEARE, MATTHEW: Principal residence, Jamaica. Crew member of the *Bennet* under Francis Fernando in 1716, he received a share of plunder derived from the Spanish vessel *Nuestra Señora de Belen*. What happened to him after the pardon is unknown.

REYNOLDS, THOMAS: Principal residence, Bahamas. Reynolds was pardoned again in South Carolina in July 1718. He was married to a woman named Ruth, with whom he had a daughter baptized in 1723.

RICHARDS, JOHN: Principal residence, Boston, Massachusetts. Born in 1677 in Lynn, Massachusetts, Richards served as a privateer in Queen Anne's War and was already known as a ship captain by the time he wed Mary Allen of Salem in 1705. A prolific sailor, Richards remained busy at sea through the mid-1720s. He owned multiple properties in Boston before selling them and moving back to Lynn around 1731. He died two years later, preceded in death by his wife and survived by three children.

RICHARDS, RICHARD: Principal residence unknown. Richards conducted one trading voyage between Anguilla and Barbados in the fall of 1715, after which he emerged as one of the men who abandoned the Jamaican sloop *Francis and Sarah* around September 1716. He served as a privateer under Othenias Davis in the *Movil Trader* and was last spotted in North Carolina in July 1720 fending off a lawsuit initiated by a fellow privateer.

RICHARDSON, SAMUEL: Principal residence, Bahamas. He accepted a second pardon in South Carolina in June 1718. Along with his wife Dorothy, he received land at Providence before disappearing from the historical record in 1723.

ROBERTS, JACOB: Principal residence, Bahamas. He appears infrequently in Bahamian records, being assessed a tax in 1723 and baptizing a son in 1725.

ROBERTS, WILLIAM 1: Not identified conclusively in the historical record. Possibly the same navy man who enlisted on the *Shark* sloop in November 1720, receiving a discharge at St. Christopher's the following April. There was also a contemporary ship captain from Boston sharing the same name.

ROBERTS, WILLIAM 2:

*ROGERS, EDWARD:

ROGERS, MICHAEL: Principal residence, Bahamas. Rogers may have originally come from Jamaica and served on two vessels that saw service in the Caribbean during Queen Anne's War. He had a wife and son, and he last appears on a 1728 list of men capable of bearing arms.

ROPER, FRANCIS: Not identified conclusively in the historical record. Possibly a planter from Nevis who was a contemporary of Peter Mallet.

ROSS, DAVID: Principal residence, Jamaica. Abandoned the sloop *Francis and Sarah* around September 1716 at Providence.

ROUNCIFULL, GEORGE: Principal residence, Weymouth, England. Born in 1693, Rouncifull is best known for being spared the gallows in 1718 because of Woodes Rogers's familiarity with his father. He supposedly died with Josiah Burgess while on a privateering mission in 1720.

ROUSE, WILLIAM: Principal residence, Charlestown, Massachusetts. One of the oldest pirates, Rouse was a prolific mariner whose career spanned more than three decades from 1689 to 1718. He owned significant properties and had a large family; his story appears in detail in chapters 1 and 6. Rouse died in 1721.

SAVORY, EDWARD:

SHIPTON, HENRY: Principal residence, Bahamas, possibly with origins in Jamaica. After receiving the pardon he sailed once to Boston and appears not to have engaged again in long-haul sailing. He had a wife named Ann and two children born in the Bahamas. He left the colony with his family around 1725 and moved to Kingston, Jamaica. They baptized a son there in January 1727, after which Shipton disappears from the historical record.

SHOAR, ROBERT: Principal residence, Bahamas. Shoar appears only once subsequent to the pardon, on a 1742 tax list. At the time, he was living alone.

SINCLAIR, GEORGE: Principal residence unknown. Sinclair (sometimes spelled "Sinklar") may have originally come from Barbados and served in the navy before joining Palsgrave Williams. After the pardon, he captained ships registered in the Bahamas, Bermuda, and Jamaica, appearing in the shipping lists of several colonies before disappearing from the historical record in 1730.

SIPKINS, JOHN: Principal residence, New York. Born in 1688 in New York, Sipkins was the son of a Dutch immigrant. He was a prolific sea captain from about 1711 to 1720, when he died at sea off Florida. His story is recounted in full in chapter 7.

SMITH, JOHN: Principal residence, Bermuda. Although contemporary mariners by that name are ubiquitous, it is probable that John was the older brother of William Smith. He was active at sea from about 1713 to 1731. Smith had ties to New York through his brother, who settled his local affairs when he died.

SMITH, WILLIAM: Principal residence, New York. Arguably the most successful of the pardoned pirates, Smith came from Bermuda to New York around 1715. Tapped in Jamaica to offer the pardon to pirates, which he also accepted, he was also a subject of the 1718 investigation of the sloop *John and Elizabeth* for trading with Benjamin Hornigold. After the pardon, he became a prolific sea captain and merchant whose career spanned another twenty-five years. He married Charity Bosch in 1720, and their grandchildren married into the family of President John Adams. He died in 1752 and was interred in the First Presbyterian Church on Wall Street. His story is recounted in full in chapter 7.

SOUTH, WILLIAM: Principal residence unknown. Possibly from Jamaica, South was arrested for smuggling in Virginia shortly after the pardon but released. South served in the Bahamas as a privateer in 1719, and he may have been making voyages to St. Thomas until 1730, when he disappears from the historical record.

SPENCER, WILLIAM: Not identified conclusively in the historical record. One contemporary ship captain by that name was operating out of Boston around the time of the pardon.

STACEY, EDWARD:

STANBURY, ADONIJAH: Principal residences, Bahamas and South Carolina. Stanbury probably circulated between the Bahamas and Port Royal, South Carolina, for most of his adult life. After the pardon, he remained at Providence until at least May 1719, when he served as a jury member. He next appears as a member of the South Carolina militia, in a 1728 raid led by John Palmer against the Yamasee Indians living near St. Augustine, Florida, at which point he disappears from the historical record.

STILLWELL, DANIEL: Principal residence, Bahamas. Originally from Jamaica, Stillwell was one of the "strangers" who began conducting pirate raids against the Spanish in conjunction with Benjamin Hornigold around 1713. He was married to a woman named Sarah, although there is no evidence to indicate they had children. Following the pardon, he resumed sailing vessels and probably died shortly after 1728, the year his wife died.

*STONEHAM, THOMAS: Principal residence, North Carolina. Stoneham was probably a carpenter by trade who lived in Edenton, North Carolina. After the pardon, he enlisted on the HMS *Pearl* at Virginia prior to the vessel's deployment against Blackbeard. He appears in some routine debt cases in Edenton and disappears from the historical record after 1723.

STOUT, JOHN: Principal residence, New York. Stout was the son of an English Jamaican sea captain and a New York woman of Dutch descent. Although not wealthy, the family was financially secure. He apprenticed as a barber and later took to sea. He owned several vessels and continued sailing for about five years after the pardon. He had several children with his wife Abigail (Bill) and died sometime in the early 1730s.

SUTTON, JOHN: Principal residence, Barbados. Sutton had been captaining trading vessels since at least 1702, sailing Caribbean and North American routes. He served under Francis Fernando on the *Bennet*, engaging in the Jamaican piracies of 1716 and receiving a share of the plunder derived from the *Nuestra Señora de Belen*. His whereabouts after the pardon have not been identified.

*SWIMSTONE, MICHAEL:

SWOORD, DAVID: Principal residence, Jamaica. Described as "an old experienced pirate," Swoord (Soward) was known to be hobbled by an old wound. After the pardon, he appears twice as a victim of piracy, first at the hands of John Augur, and later by John Rackham. He disappears from the historical record in 1720.

TAYLOR, RICHARD: Principal residence, Philadelphia, Pennsylvania. Born about 1685, Taylor had probably captained merchant vessels and spent time in the navy before turning to piracy. He accepted a pardon in Philadelphia a few weeks before receiving one in the Bahamas. Seemingly cooperative with Governor Rogers, Taylor returned to piracy and was active off West Africa and the Indian Ocean between 1719 and 1722. In the Indian Ocean, he assumed command of the *Cassandra*. He gave up piracy in 1723 and surrendered to Spanish authorities in Panama. Taylor is thought to have lived out his final days in Cuba or elsewhere in the Spanish colonies.

TENNET, JOHN:

TERRILL, THOMAS: Principal residence, Bahamas. One of the instigators of postwar piracy in the Bahamas along with Hornigold and Stilwell. Following the pardon, he received land at Providence, continued sailing trading vessels, and appears regularly in Bahamian records engaging in routine business until 1726. Then he moved to Jamaica, presumably to join his wife.

THOMPSON, JOSEPH: Principal residence, Harbor Island, Bahamas. Possibly related to eminent Harbor Island planter Richard Thompson. Following the pardon, it is possible he briefly returned to piracy, for his name is mentioned in conjunction with William Moody and a vaguely detailed attack near Jamaica in December 1718. He nevertheless returned to the Bahamas, married, and had at least one son. He appears on a 1728 militia list, after which he disappears from the historical record.

TISSO, WILLIAM: Principal residence, Barbados. Born in 1700, William would have been a teenager at the time of the pardon. Three generations of men by that name appear in Barbados records. It is possible that the family had business connections in Rhode Island.

TOWNSHEND, MARTIN:

TROUTON, THOMAS: Principal residence, London. He apprenticed as a Thames waterman/lightman in 1706.

TURNER, DAVID: Principal residence unknown. He is mentioned in conjunction with the pirate Sam Bellamy and described as a "North country man." If indeed this is the same man, he must have left the *Whydah* before it sank in April 1717.

TURNOR, BENJAMIN: Principal residence, Jamaica. Turnor accepted a second pardon in South Carolina in July 1718. He appears to have married and started a family in Kingston during the 1720s.

VALENTINE, RICHARD:

VAN PELT, ARTHUR: Principal residence unknown. Possibly a New Yorker of Dutch ancestry. After the pardon he briefly returned to piracy, sailing with Charles Yates. He was picked up in St. Thomas by a ship captain who brought Van Pelt and two others to Virginia. He was convicted of piracy there in December 1718 but reprieved on the condition that he join the navy. He enlisted on the HMS *Pearl* in April 1719, received a discharge in New York in July, then disappears from the historical record.

*****VANE, CHARLES:** Principal residence, Jamaica. One of the most notorious pirates on Pearse's list. Veine was a member of Francis Fernando's crew from the *Bennet* who received a share of the plunder derived from the 1716 Spanish prize, *La Nuestra Señora de Belen*. After the pardon, Vane continued his predations throughout the summer of 1718 and famously orchestrated a daring escape when Woodes Rogers arrived that July. Vane continued his piracies for several more months before supposedly being shipwrecked on an uninhabited island off Panama. After being saved, a ship captain who recognized Vane brought him to Port Royal. After spending months in jail, Vane was tried and executed in March 1721.

WARD, RICHARD: Principal residence, Newport, Rhode Island. After the pardon he remained at Providence for several months. While conducting a trade mission to Cuba that summer, he was apprehended by Spanish *guardacostas*. He was married to a woman named Mary and had several children in the 1720s, presumably living out his days in Newport.

WATERS, JOHN: Principal residence, Jamaica. Probably born in St. Andrews Parish in 1691, Waters abandoned the sloop *Francis and Sarah* in September 1716 at Providence. His whereabouts after the pardon are unknown.

WELLS, EDWARD: Principal residence unknown. Possibly from Jamaica. After the pardon he bought a boat with several other pirates and surrendered again in Virginia in May 1718. There rumors indicated he intended to seize a sloop and resume piracy, but he never surfaced again in the historical record.

WHEELER, JAMES: Not identified conclusively in the historical record. Contemporaries from Portsmouth, England, Jamaica, and Barbados remain possibilities.

WHITE, DANIEL: Principal residence unknown. White receives mention as one of the individuals trading with pirates in the summer of 1717. In 1720 White was the captain of a privateer ship who delivered a message to Governor Rogers from Commodore Edward Vernon of the HMS *Mary*.

WHITEHEAD, CHARLES: Principal residence, Bahamas. Possibly descended from an early settler, Whitehead engaged in piracy first as a member of Francis Fernando's crew, receiving a share of the plunder derived from the *Nuestra Señora de Belen*. Ubiquitous in Bahamian records from the 1720s, Whitehead married in 1723, and he had at least three children and a slave. He served the government in minor capacities and mostly stayed out of trouble, except for rumors of his indebtedness and his role in instigating a strike of jurors in 1724. He appears in the 1731 census, after which he disappears from the historical record.

WILLIAMS, GRIFFITH: Principal residence, Jamaica. A carpenter, Williams served in the Royal Navy before and after the pardon. During Queen Anne's War he served for almost three years on the HMS *Foweys* and later did a peacetime stint aboard the *Shoreham*. His exact role in piracy is not known, but he reenlisted in the navy at Virginia in April 1718, joining Vincent Pearse on the *Phoenix*. He appears to have gravitated to Jamaica afterward. A sloop of his was destroyed in a 1722 hurricane, and he was buried in Kingston in 1727.

WILLIAMS, PALSGRAVE: Principal residence, Rhode Island. Supposedly born at Nantasket, Williams was the son of John Williams, former attorney general of Rhode Island. The Williams family owned property in Boston and at Block Island, Rhode Island, Williams's principal residence. Sailed in conjunction with the pirate Sam Bellamy on the *Marianne* and escaped the April 1717 storm that claimed the life of Bellamy and most of his crew. After the pardon he joined the pirates who ventured to West Africa. He presumably died there or in the Indian Ocean in the early 1720s.

WILLIAMS, WILLIAM: Principal residence, Bahamas and North Carolina. Most likely born in Jamaica before 1695 to a Kingston mariner by that name. Before the pardon, he had met and wed Frances, from Edenton, North Carolina. After the pardon he stayed at Providence, where he continued sailing trading vessels, engaged in privateering, and even did a short stint piloting the HMS *Flamborough* when it was stationed there. Fluent in Spanish, Williams was the colony's translator and served the government in minor capacities. He left the Bahamas around 1724, moving to Edenton, North Carolina, to run an inn with his wife. The couple had at least four children, and he died in 1732.

*WILLIAMSON, THOMAS:

WILLIS (WYLLYS), WILLIAM: Principal residence, Jamaica. Willis was a merchant whose principal involvement in piracy derived from his ownership of a quarter share of the *Bersheba*, which was involved in the 1716 piracies against Spanish shipping. He evidently joined the crew himself, perhaps to oversee the distribution of prizes. After the pardon, he returned to Kingston.

WILSON, TRISTRAM: Principal residence unknown. Probably English, Wilson served in the Royal Navy in the immediate aftermath of Queen Anne's War. He enlisted on the HMS *Speedwell* at Poole in January 1713 and transferred to the *Scarborough* that May, receiving a discharge at Jamaica in September 1715. He presumably joined one of the crews fitting out for the wrecks later that winter. After the pardon his whereabouts are unknown.

WISHART, ROBERT: Principal residence, South Carolina. Probably from Scotland, Wishart was married and living in South Carolina by 1714. At that time he commanded a Bermuda sloop and was the subject of a 1717 vice-admiralty case in which he was convicted of smuggling goods purchased from pirates at Providence. He returned to South Carolina after the pardon but left "clandestinely" to claim land at Providence. He died within a year of arriving there, although his wife Jane and their three children appear in the 1731 census.

WOODALE, NICHOLAS: Principal residence, Jamaica. As master of the *Wolfe* sloop, Woodale was among those who continued trading with Charles Vane before the institution of a royal government at the Bahamas. He died in Kingston in 1731.

WRIGHT, PEARSE: Principal residences, Jamaica and Bahamas. Wright engaged in piracy as a member of Benjamin Hornigold's crew on the sloop *Bennet*. He stayed in the Bahamas after the pardon and was accused of trading with pirates a few months later. He remained in the Bahamas until 1723, after which he disappears from the historical record.

NOTES

Introduction. Young, Resolute, and Wicked Fellows?

1. Vincent Pearse to Naval Secretary Josiah Burchett, August 15, 1717, Navy Department: Correspondence and Papers, Captain's Letters—P, ADM 1/2282, National Archives, Kew (hereafter TNA).
2. Admiralty: Captains' Logs, *Phoenix*, August 25–October 29, ADM 51/690 [unpaginated].
3. Pearse to Burchett, February 4, 1718, ADM 1/2282, TNA.
4. Pearse to Burchett, June 3, 1718, and the enclosed "A List of Names of Such Men as Surrendered to Capt. Vincent Pearse," ADM 1/2282.
5. Earle, *Pirate Wars*, 190, 269.
6. Stone, "Prosopography."
7. Karraker, *Piracy Was a Business*; Leeson, *Invisible Hook*; Leeson, "An-arrgh-chy"; Starkey, "Pirates and Markets."
8. Christopher Hill, "Radical Pirates?"; Rediker, *Villains of All Nations*; Rediker, "Under the Banner"; Mackie, "Welcome the Outlaw"; Burg, "Legitimacy and Authority"; Kuhn, *Life under the Jolly Roger*.
9. Earle, *Pirate Wars*; Ritchie, *Captain Kidd*; Cordingly, *Pirate Hunter of the Caribbean*.
10. Vickers, *Young Men and the Sea*; Kelleher, *Alliance of Pirates*.
11. Chet, *Ocean Is a Wilderness*, 9.
12. Burgess, *Politics of Piracy*.
13. Hanna, *Pirate Nests*; Hanna, "Pirates' Nest," quotation on 335.
14. Bialuschewski, *Raiders and Natives*; Bahar, *Storm of the Sea*.
15. David Wilson, *Suppressing Piracy*.
16. Bialuschewski, "Pirates, Markets and Imperial Authority," 65.
17. Hanna, *Pirate Nests*, 8, 423–25; Lipman, *Saltwater Frontier*; Pastore, *Between Land and Sea*; James L. Hill, "Bring Them What They Lack."
18. Hanna, "Pirates' Nest," 331–420.
19. Ginzburg et al., "Microhistory," 10–35; Szijarto, "Four Arguments for Micro-

history"; Richard D. Brown, "Microhistory and the Post-Modern Challenge"; Putnam, "To Study the Fragments/Whole"; Block, *Ordinary Lives*; Piker, *Four Deaths of Acorn Whistler*; Magnusson, "Singularization of History"; see also Magnusson, "Sites of Memory?"

20. Abraham Adams, born July 11, 1693, Boston, Births 1635–1744, Massachusetts, U.S. Town and Vital Records, 1620–1988, ancestry.com; Abraham Adams Sr., Will, April 6, 1700, Suffolk County Probate Records, 14:158–59, and Abraham Adams Estate Inventory, December 1717, Suffolk County Probate Records, 20:150–51, Massachusetts Wills and Records; Conveyance, Abraham Adams to John Clarke, May 19, 1715, Suffolk County Deeds, vol. 29, fol. 182; Conveyance, Abraham Adams to Gilbert Bant, June 25, 1723, Suffolk County Deeds, vol. 32, fol. 58; *Boston News Letter*, November 15, 1708, May 21, 1711, November 26, 1716.

21. Declaration of John Martin, May 13, 1713, in Sainsbury et al., *Calendar of State Papers, Colonial Series: America and the West Indies* (hereafter *CSP*), vol. 27, no. 510; Gov. Henry Pullein of Bermuda to the Board of Trade, January 9, 1714, *CSP*, vol. 27, no. 544; Henry Pullein to the Board of Trade, April 14, 1714, CO 37/10, fol. 13; Thomas Walker to the Board of Trade, March 14, 1715, CO 5/1265, fols. 16–17; *Articles Exhibited Against Governor Archibald Hamilton, Late Governor of Jamaica: With Depositions and Proofs Relating to the Same* (London: 1717); Jonathan Barnet, Deposition, Jamaica Council Minutes, August 10, 1716, CO 140/13, 77–79.

22. John and Lucy Brown v. Robert and Jane Wishart, 1715, box 5B, ITEM 395, Christian Cooper v. Robert Wishart, 1716, box 7A, ITEM 860, and William Hackett v. Robert Wishart, 1718, box 12A, ITEM 175A, South Carolina Court of Common Pleas—Judgment Rolls, SCDAH; Estate Inventory of John Crosskeys of Kingston, Inventories, vol. 10, 1B/11/3/10, fol. 202, Jamaica Archives; Benjamin Bennett to the Board of Trade, April 14, 1714, CO 37/10, fol. 13.

23. Mayor's Court Minute Book, June 21, 1720–August 13, 1723, 37–39, and New York Mayor's Court, August 20, 1723–April 30, 1728, 526, 536, 537, New York County Courts Division of Old Records.

24. Raymond, "Colonel William Stephens Smith."

25. Rediker, *Villains of All Nations*, chap. 1.

26. Schonhorn, *General History of the Pyrates*, 244.

Chapter 1. The Call of the Sea

1. Massachusetts, Town Clerk, Vital and Town Records, 1626–2001, familysearch.org.

2. Marmaduke Gee bapt. September 7, 1684, London, Church of England Records of Baptisms, Marriages, and Burials, 1538–1812, Southwark, St. Mary Magdalen Bermondsey, ancestry.com.

3. Jan Sipken bapt. June 10, 1688, New Amsterdam Reformed Dutch Church Baptisms, 1682–1689, Brooklyn Genealogical Society, https://brooklynancestry.com/new-amsterdam-reformed-dutch-church-baptisms-1682-1689/.

4. Edward Berry bapt. January 20, 1690, Jamaica, Church of England, St. Andrew's Parish Register Transcripts, Baptisms, Burials, Marriages, 1:32, familysearch.org.

5. Joseph Pearse, bapt. January 10, 1683, Jamaica, Church of England, St. Catherine's Parish Records, Baptisms, Burials, Marriages, 1:20, familysearch.org.

6. George Rouncifull, bapt. September 20, 1692, England, Dorset, Parish Registers, 1538–2001, familysearch.org.

7. Leigh Ashworth, bapt. April 4, 1693, Liverpool Parish Registers, Church of Our Lady and St. Nicholas [unpaginated], findmypast.uk.com.

8. Schonhorn, *General History of the Pyrates*, 71, 95, 585; Baylus C. Brooks, "Edward 'Blackbeard' Thache," http://baylusbrooks.com/index_files/Page613.htm (accessed October 5, 2020).

9. Faller, "Criminal Opportunities"; Mackie, *Rakes, Highwaymen, and Pirates*; Schonhorn, *General History of the Pyrates*, 153–55, 159–64, 318, 606.

10. Rediker, *Villains of All Nations*, 49.

11. Will of Thomas Mitchell, April 20, 1703, Middlesex (Mass.) Deeds, 13:540, familysearch.org.

12. John Stout (Sr.) to Thomas Wendham, Letter of Administration, April 20, 1699, in Keller and Pelletreau, *Abstracts of Wills on File* 25:305; Shipping Returns, Jamaica, March 7, 1699, CO 142/13.

13. Jamaica, Church of England, St. Catherine's Parish Registers, 1:38; William Williams Letter of Administration, February 5, 1711, Letters of Administration, 1B/11/17/1, fol. 18, Jamaica National Archives.

14. Moll, *Island of Barbadoes*; Francis Lesley, buried November 14, 1718, Church of England, Parish Burials, St. John Parish, Barbados, 25, familysearch.org; Deposition of John Bull, January 17, 1719, *CSP*, vol. 30, no. 797(vi).

15. Will of John Williams, April 18, 1687, proved October 25, 1687, inventoried May 1688, Suffolk Co. (Mass.) Probate Records, 10:329–33, ancestry.com.

16. Anonymous, *Report of the Committee*.

17. Shaw, *Calendar of Treasury Books*, 15:298–310.

18. Will of Abraham Adams, April 6, 1700, Suffolk County, Massachusetts Probate & Wills, 14:158–59; Depositions of Mary Grosse, Abraham Adams, and Francis Knox, ca. October 12, 1694, Massachusetts State Archives Collection, 8:25–28, familysearch.org (hereafter MAC).

19. Franklin, *Autobiography of Benjamin Franklin*, 8, 11, 13.

20. Deposition of James Moodie, December 22, 1719, South Carolina, Pre-federal Admiralty Court Records, vol. A-B, PART 2, National Archives and Record Administration, Washington, D.C.

21. Phillips, "Why Did Anyone Go?"

22. Vickers and Walsh, "Young Men and the Sea."

23. Pietsch, "Ships' Boys and Youth Culture."

24. Roger, *Wooden World*, 113–24.

25. Anonymous, *English Heroe*.

26. Lane, *Pillaging the Empire*, 96–129; Pestana, "Early English Jamaica without Pirates"; Pestana, *English Conquest of Jamaica*; Bialuschewski, *Raiders and Natives*, 13–27; Earle, *Sack of Panama*.

27. Johnson, *Enemy of All Mankind*; Margarette Lincoln, "Henry Every and the Creation of the Pirate Myth in Early Modern Britain," in Head, *Golden Age of Piracy*, 167–82.

28. Woodard, *Republic of Pirates*, 323.

29. Bulkley and Beckwith, *Chad Browne Memorial*, 6–12, 122–29.

30. *Boston News Letter*, June 19, 1704, June 1, 1713, April 19, 1714 (John); *Boston News Letter*, April 23, July 9, July 23, 1711, February 8, June 1, August 10, November 30, 1713, January 17, July 12, 1714 (Jeremiah); *Boston News Letter*, April 22, December 2, 1717, August 3, November 16, December 21, 1719, February 22, 1720 (William).

31. William Penn to the Board of Trade, April 28, 1700, CO 5/1288, fols. 136–43; Earl of Bellomont to the Board of Trade, May 25, 1700, with enclosures: Examination of James Brown, May 28, 1700, and Examination of William Markham, May 17, 1700, CO 5/1044, 1–7, 126, 161; Robert Snead to Gov. Nicholson, April 13, 1697, and Narrative of Capt. Robert Snead, n.d. [ca. 1697] in Browne, *Proceedings of the Council*, 561–63, 577; Richard Hogbin to James Brown, Conveyance, May 20, 1697, Kent County [Delaware] Deeds, roll 776, fol. 188, U.S. Land Records, 1677–1947, ancestry.com; John Graves to the Board of Trade, n.d. [ca. 1696], *CSP*, vol. 15, no. 744; Examination of John Dann, August 3, 1696, *CSP*, vol. 15, no. 517(iv).

32. Shipping Returns, Antigua, Leeward Islands: Miscellanea, CO 157/1, fol. 12; Shipping Returns, Barbados, CO 33/14, fol. 101.

33. Will of William Markham, December 13, 1703, Pennsylvania, U.S. Wills and Probate Records, 1683–1993, Philadelphia County, book B, 201, ancestry.com, 354; Will of Elizabeth Regnier, July 2, 1715, in *Collections of the New-York Historical Society for the Year 1893* (New York: New-York Historical Society, 1893), 153–54; *Boston News Letter*, October 10, 1723; Will of Joanna Markam, October 3, 1726, New York Wills, vol. 10, 354–55, familysearch.org; Indenture, Anne Brown to James Steel, January 18, 1728, Delaware, U.S. Land Records, New Castle County, roll 9, 616–17, ancestry.com; Board of Trade and Secretaries of State. America and West Indies, Original Correspondence, New York, Shipping Returns, CO 5/1222, fols. 173, 223, 233 and CO 5/1223, fols. 25, 28, 40, 58, 62.

34. Joseph Crispe to Governor Russell, July 16, 1695, *CSP*, vol. 14, no. 1,931.

35. Bourne, *Queen Anne's Navy*.

36. Rutledge, "Enemies Bound by Trade," 181–233; García del Pino, *Corsarios, Piratas, y Santiago*.

37. List of Vessels Registered in Boston, ca. 1687–1714, MAC, 7:209–18, 271, 369; Customs Officers to the Lords Commisioners of Their Majesties' Treasury, November 22, 1693, Act for the Regulation of Seamen, November 30, 1693, and John Ware and William Payne, Bill of Lading, February 1, 1694, MAC, 61:412, 418, 430.

38. Crew List of the Brig Adventure, Captain John Halsey, MAC, 62:412.

39. "An Account of Such Prizes as Were Condemned in Barbados," n.d. [ca. 1703], and Nicholas Rogers, "Abstract," February 4, 1704, CO 28/7, fols. 271–72; "Case of the *Charles the Second*," Barbados. Add Ch. 76087, British Library (BL).

40. Registration of the Brig *Sarah*, April 15, 1703, MAC, 7:220; Massachusetts, U.S. Town and Vital Records, Salem Registry of Marriages to 1800, 38, ancestry.com.

41. Satsuma, "Politicians," 317–36; Brunsman, *Evil Necessity*, chap. 2.

42. Deposition of John Lewis, September 17, 1709, Add Ms 61643, fol. 206, BL.

43. Shipping Returns, Jamaica, CO/142/14 [unpaginated], microfilm frames 389, 391,

393, 399, 402, 420, 421, 422, 423, 425, 428, 429, 431, 434, 448, 449, 451, 455; Thomas Handasyd to the Board of Trade, July 16, 1711, *CSP*, vol. 26, no. 18.

44. Will of Robert Brown, August 2, 1710, Jamaica Wills, vol. 13, fol. 2, Island Record Office.

45. David D. Moore, "Captain Edward Thatch"; Navy Board, Ships' Pay Books, *Speedwell*, ADM 33/304, TNA.

46. Ships' Pay Books, *Sorlings*, ADM 33/304.

47. Ships' Pay Books, *Anglesey*, ADM 33/229.

48. Ships' Pay Books, *Sweepstakes*, ADM 33/310.

49. Ships' Pay Books, *Windsor*, ADM 33/267.

50. Ships' Pay Books, *Foweys*, ADM 33/304; Ships' Pay Books, *Shoreham*, ADM 33/307.

51. Ships' Pay Books, *Sapphire*, ADM 33/304.

52. Ships' Pay Books, *Roebuck*, ADM 33/307.

53. Ships' Pay Books, *Shoreham*, ADM 33/302, fol. 474.

54. Ships' Pay Books, *Speedwell*, Scarborough, ADM 33/304.

55. Hancock, "Self-Organized Complexity."

56. Peterson, *City-State of Boston*; Jarvis, *In the Eye*; McCusker and Menard, *Economy of British America*, 144–68, 189–208, 175–88; Edelson, *Plantation Enterprise*.

57. Ubbehlode, *American Colonies*; Mattson, "Rethinking Mercantilism"; Andreas, *Smuggler Nation*.

58. Bradburn, "Visible Fist."

59. Peterson, *City-State of Boston*, 85–188.

60. Jarvis, *In the Eye*, 64–184, quotations on 5.

61. Massachusetts Treasury, 1693–1713, MAC, 122:231.

62. Registration for the sloop *Hannah & Mary*, November 16, 1711, MAC, 7:413; *Boston News Letter*, October 25, 1708, November 26, 1711, March 31, April 14, June 23, 1712, April 2 and 23, 1716; Board of Trade and Secretaries of State, America and West Indies, Original Correspondence, Massachusetts, Shipping Returns, CO 5/848, fols. 33, 43, 53, 56; John Montfort, Account, March 25, 1712, Colonial Court Records, North Carolina State Archives Digital Collections, 210–BIF4 Personal Accounts, 1709–1719, no. 58. https://digital.ncdcr.gov/Documents/Detail/personal-accounts-1709-1719/360239?item=360240.

63. Board of Trade and Secretaries of State, America and West Indies, Original Correspondence, Virginia, Shipping Returns, CO 5/1441, fols. 288, 290, 294, 296; Shipping Returns, Barbados, CO 33/13, fol. 71; Permits for Passing the Castle Granted to Ships and Other Vessels, ca. 1701–4 MAC, 7:77, 81; *Boston News Letter*, December 10, 1716, August 19, September 9, October 8, 1717.

64. Shipping Returns, Jamaica, CO 142/13, fol. 233; Shipping Returns, Jamaica, CO 142/14, frames 390, 399, 402, 431, 469; *Boston News Letter*, June 4, 1711, May 26, July 7, October 6, 1712.

65. *Boston News Letter*, March 17, 1711, January 26, June 9 and 30, July 7, 1712, January 16 and 30, 1716, March 12 and 26, September 4 and 10, 1716; Shipping Returns, Jamaica, CO 142/14, frames 463, 481; The West India and Guinea Company, The

Treasurer and the Merchant, St. Thomas and St. John: Books of Duties, kept at St. Thomas (1708–1755), vol. 446, entries for June 8–16, 1717, images 160–61, 182, 184, Danish National Archive.

66. Shipping Returns, Massachusetts, CO 5/848, fols. 32, 33, 42, 46, 48, 56, 64, 77, 97, 114; Shipping Returns, Jamaica, CO 142/13, frame 489.

67. Shipping Returns, Virginia, CO 5/1441, fols. 288, 290, 294, 296.

68. Jarvis, *In the Eye*, 137–41; Parsons and Murphy, "Ecosystems under Sail"; Murphy, "James Petiver's 'Kind Friends.'"

69. Hunnewell, *Records of the First Church*, 10; Wyman, *Genealogies and Estates of Charlestown*, 2:824.

70. Ships' Pay Books, Ship: *Rose*, Entry for February 3, 1689, ADM 33/123.

71. Pitt, "City upon the Atlantic Tides," 16–59.

72. Deposition of Robert Small, William Rouse, William Mims, John Sholls, and John Wister, April 29, 1689, MAC, 107:4.

73. Shipping Returns, Barbados, CO 33/13, p. 65.

74. Massachusetts, Town and Vital Records, 1620–1988, vol. 3, Charlestown, 33; Charlestown Archives Part J, 1662–1719, 125; Inventory of Thomas Peachee, June 19, 1683, Middlesex Deeds, 6:68.

75. Hunnewell, *Records of the First Church*, 83 (William), 90 (Mary 1), 97 (John), 111 (Mary 2), 113 (Peachie); Massachusetts, Town and Vital Records, 1620–1988, Charlestown Archives, Births, Marriages, and Deaths, 1638–1800, 102, 110, 120, 126, 146, 153, 156, 157, 176, ancestry.com.

76. Peter Landry, "Captain John Rous," Nova Scotian Biographies, last updated 2020, http://www.blupete.com/Hist/BiosNS/1700-63/Rous.htm#rfn2.

77. Hunnewell, *Records of the First Church*, 41.

78. Frothingham, *History of Charlestown*, 245.

79. Vol. 90: The Colonial Records of King's Chapel, 1686–1776, Vestry Minutes: vol. 1, The Colonial Society of Massachusetts, https://www.colonialsociety.org/publications/3640/vestry-minutes-1686-1776; Vol. 91: The Colonial Records of King's Chapel, 1686–1776, Register of Births, Weddings, and Burials, vol. 2, Colonial Society of Massachusetts, https://www.colonialsociety.org/node/3650#ch02.

80. Massachusetts, Middlesex County, Clerk of Courts, Court Papers—folio 118A-2, February 24, 1730, LDS REEL no. 008292123, familysearch.org.

81. Karraker, "Treasure Expedition"; Deposition of William Rouse, November 16, 1694, CO 5/858, fol. 244–45.

82. Deposition of Isaac Robinson and Robert Rogers, August 18, 1697, Massachusetts, Suffolk County, Court Files, case no. 3564, 40:36, familysearch.org.

83. Massachusetts Registry of Ships in the Port of Boston, ca. 1687–1714, MAC, 7:95.

84. Massachusetts Treasury, MAC, 122:139; Tapely, *Province Galley of Massachusetts Bay*, 5–6; Hitchings, "Guarding the New England Coast."

85. Receipt of John Champante to William Rouse, January 28, 1701, CO 5/862, 148.

86. Let pass to William Rouse, September 5, 1701, MAC, 7:73; Massachusetts Registry of Ships in the Port of Boston, 7:205; List of Merchant Ships at Jamaica bound for London, May 15, 1703, in Mahaffy, *Calendar of State Papers*, 17.

87. Conveyance of Watkins and Dowse to William Rouse, January 25, 1690, Middlesex Deeds, 12:436; Conveyance of John Phillips to William Rouse, June 10, 1704, Middlesex Deeds, 13:600.

88. Minutes of the Massachusetts Council, February 22, 1706, MAC, 81:574; Massachusetts Treasury, MAC, 122:277; Petition of William Rouse, John Phillips, and Ebenezer Coffin, n.d. [ca. January 1707], Privy Council, PC 1/46/9, TNA.

89. Gov. Paul Dudley to William Rouse, April 26, 1706, MAC, 63:11.

90. Waller, *Samuel Vetch*, 83–98.

91. Examination of a Mohogg [Mohawk] Indian Named Tayorhenseone, November 15, 1705, Clarendon Papers, vol. 102, fol. 99, Bodleian Library, Oxford University.

92. Waller, *Samuel Vetch*, 86.

93. Deposition of Abraham Miller, August 20, 1706, County Court Records, Suffolk County [Mass.], vol. 76, case no. 7603, item 2.

94. Deposition of Henry Darling, June 14, 1706 (sworn August 19), Suffolk County Court Records, vol. 76, case no. 7603, item 3.

95. Deposition of John Collins, July 1, 1706, Suffolk County Court Records, vol. 76, Case No. 7603, item 4; Deposition of Nicholas Merrit, June 14, 1706, Suffolk County Court Records, vol. 68, case no. 6893, fol. 58; Deposition of Robert Wing, July 6, 1706, MAC, vol. 63, fol. 25.

96. Bigelow and Goodell, *Acts and Resolves*, 65–66.

97. Petition of Rouse, Phillips, and Coffin.

98. Philopolites, *Memorial*, 7–9.

99. William Popple Jr. to Mr. Borret, February 27, 1707, *CSP*, vol. 23, no. 787; Edward Northey to the Board of Trade, March 28, 1707, *CSP*, vol. 23, no. 832; Privy Council Order of September 24, 1707, in Grant et al., *Acts of the Privy Council*, 2:516; William Popple to Paul Dudley, October 3, 1707, MAC, 51:175.

100. Minutes of the Massachusetts Council, November 29, 1707, MAC, 81:618.

101. Minutes of the Massachusetts Superior Court of Judicature, LDS FILM #007943508, fols. 223, 229–30, 233, familysearch.org. The two separate trials can be found in Suffolk County Massachusetts Court Files, vol. 75, case no. 7561, items 72–73, and vol. 76, case no. 7603, items 1–4.

102. Ship registers April 5, 1710, MAC, 7:366; July 7, 1710, Let pass for ship *King of Spain*, MAC, 7:83; *Boston News Letter*, February 11, November 19, 1711, January 26, February 16, May 19, 1712, April 6, 1713; Shipping Returns, Jamaica, CO 142/13, frame 449, also CO 142/14, frame 406.

103. Conveyance, Elizabeth Smith to William Rouse, March 17, 1709, Middlesex Deeds, 14:709; Conveyance, Steven Ford to Rouse, May 9, 1709, Middlesex Deeds, 15:8; Conveyance, Samuel Blunt to Rouse, April 3, 1710, Middlesex Deeds, 15:205–6; Conveyance, Joseph Lynde to Rouse, July 26, 1710, Middlesex Deeds, 15:289–90; Conveyance, Steven Ford to Rouse, August 29, 1710, Middlesex Deeds, 15:315–16.

104. Massachusetts Shipping Registers (sloop *Neptune*), August 3, 1713, and (sloop *Friends Adventure*) June 18, 1714, MAC, 7:477, 510.

105. Minutes of the Massachusetts Council, November 23, 1711, MAC, 81:789; Massachusetts, Middlesex County Court Paper Indexes, 1705–26, LDS FILM no. 008292104, fols. 237–Group 1, 238–42, 245–45, familysearch.org.

106. County Court (Suffolk County), case no. 10127, vol. 91, fols. 8–10; Minutes of the Massachusetts Superior Court of Judicature, Familysearch.org, LDS FILM no. 007943509, fol. 64.

107. The exact nature of the dispute is unknown. The case was postponed three times due to Rouse Jr.'s absence. William Rouse Jr. v. William Rouse Sr., agent for Lewis, March 2, June 8, and December 14, 1714, Middlesex County Inferior Court of Common Pleas, December 1699–January 1722, 191–92, 198, familysearch.org.

108. William Rouse v. John Paige, 1715, County Court (Suffolk County), case no. 8384, vol. 83, fol. 16; William Rouse v. Aeneas Salter, January 4, 1715, Suffolk Co. Inferior Court of Common Pleas, 1706–1725, 181.

109. John Oliver v. William Rouse, 1715, County Court (Suffolk County), case no. 10456, vol. 99, fol. 367.

110. Ebenezer Wentworth v. William Rouse, April 3, 1716, Suffolk County, Inferior Court of Common Pleas, 1716, fol. 29.

111. Mortgage, William Rouse to John Campbell, January 8, 1715, Middlesex Deeds, 17:185–87; Mortgage, Rouse to Charles Chambers et al., February 18, 1717, Middlesex Deeds, 19:79–80.

112. Massachusetts Treasury, MAC, 123:76.

Chapter 2. A New Madagascar

1. John Graves to the Board of Trade, ca. April 19, 1706, in *CSP*, vol. 23, no. 277.
2. Benjamin Bennett to the Board of Trade, May 31, 1718, *CSP*, vol. 30, no. 551.
3. Craton and Saunders, *Islanders in the Stream*, 1:4–7; Carew and Mylroie, "Geology of the Bahamas."
4. Schonhorn, *General History of the Pyrates*, 31.
5. Craton and Saunders, *Islanders in the Stream*, 1:63–80; Miller, "Colonization of the Bahamas."
6. Craton and Saunders, *Islanders in the Stream*, 1:92–103.
7. Thomas Lynch to William Blathwayt, June 2, 1684, William Blathwayt Papers, vol. 24, folder 5, familysearch.org.
8. Isaac Rush to Thomas Lynch, February 19, 1683, Blathwayt Papers, vol. 23, folder 4; Thomas Lynch to William Blathwayte, August 8, 1684, Blathwayt Papers, vol. 24, fol. 6.
9. Craton and Saunders, *Islanders in the Stream*, 1:103–8.
10. Craton and Saunders, 1:107.
11. Petition of the Inhabitants of New Providence to Ellis Lightwood, October 14, 1701, Board of Trade and Secretaries of State, America and West Indies, Original Correspondence, Bahamas, Secretary of State: Miscellaneous, CO 23/12—part 1, fol. 72; Thomas Walker to Gov. Francis Nicholson, October 11, 1701, Board of Trade and Secretaries of State, America and West Indies, Original Correspondence, Virginia, Board of Trade, 1700–1702, CO 5/1312, fol. 218; "Articles, Depositions, &c of the People of New Providence, in an Assembly Held at Nassau, October 5, 1701 against Elias Haskett" (London, 1702), Eighteenth Century Collections Online; New York (Col-

ony), Court of Vice Admiralty, Charges against Elias Haskett, n.d. [ca. 1701] (Washington, D.C.: National Archives and Records Administration, Central Plains Region, 1973, microfilm), 12.

12. Mr. Moore to the Board of Trade, September 17, 1703, CO 5/1, fol. 18; "Descripción de la isla de la Providencia, año de 1703," Archivo General des Indias, MP 115.

13. Graves to the Board of Trade, April 19, 1706, *CSP*, vol. 23, no. 277.

14. Eck, "Wampanoags, Wrecking, and Watlings Island."

15. John Graves to the Board of Trade, April 19, 1706, *CSP*, vol. 23, no. 277.

16. Petition of the Inhabitants of Providence to John Graves, November 30, 1704, *CSP*, vol. 23, no. 277(i).

17. Report of twenty-two sailors under the command of Thomas Walker, January 2, 1707, Records of the Secretary of the Province and Register of the Province of South Carolina, 1705–9, 249, familysearch.org.

18. Henry Wigington to the Lords Proprietors, March 31, 1708, *CSP*, vol. 23, no. 1422.

19. Capt. Samuel Chadwell to William Holden, October 3, 1707, *CSP* 5/1264, fol. 85.

20. Information of Mrs. Elizabeth Stroude [Strode], October 26, 1708, Blenheim Papers, vol. 545, British Library, Add Ms 61645, fol. 48 (hereafter Blenheim Papers).

21. Information of Samuel Harvey, October 26, 1708, Blenheim Papers, fols. 50–51.

22. The Information and Attestation of Capt. Edward Holmes, April 20, 1709, Blenheim Papers, fols. 74–75.

23. Petition of Mary Fox, January 10, 1726, CO 23/13, fol. 416.

24. Several passages taken from Coll Rhett's Letters, February–May 1709, CO 5/1264, fol. 150.

25. Capt. Samuel Chadwell to William Holden, October 3, 1707, CO 5/1264, fol. 85.

26. Copy of a Letter from Capt. Smith of the Enterprise, August 10, 1710, CO 5/1264, fols. 291–92.

27. Declaration of John Martin, May 30, 1713, *CSP*, vol. 27, no. 510; Lord Bolingbroke to the Board of Trade, December 3, 1713, and Petition of the Inhabitants of Massachusetts Bay to the Queen, n.d. [ca. 1713], *CSP*, vol. 27, nos. 513 and 513(ii); Gov. Henry Pullein to the Board of Trade, January 9, 1714, with enclosed depositions, *CSP*, vol. 27, nos. 544, 544(i), 544(i.a.), 544(i.b.).

28. Deposition of Samuel Sherlock, January 4, 1714, CO 37/9, fol. 213.

29. Gov. Henry Pullein to the Board of Trade, April 14, 1714, CO 37/10, fol. 13.

30. Thomas Walker to Francis Nicholson and enclosures, March 14, 1715, CO 5/1265, fol. 29.

31. Thomas Walker to Gov. Archibald Hamilton, January 21, 1715, Receipt of Capt. John Chace, January 2, 1715, the Marquis de Cassatores to Thomas Walker, February 15, 1715, Deposition of Richard Ward, August 6, 1716, CO 5/1264, fols. 30–32, 108.

32. Thomas Walker to the Board of Trade, August 6, 1716, CO 5/1265, fol. 105.

33. Anonymous, "Short Journal of my Voyages & Travels, 1714–1716," British Library Add Ms. 39946.

34. Deposition of John Vickers, n.d. [ca. June 1716], CO 5/1317, fol. 247.

35. Deposition of Thomas Walker Jr., August 6, 1716, CO 5/1265, fol. 107.

36. Deposition of John Vickers.

37. "The Case of the Marquis de Navarres," n.d. [ca. 1716] CO 23/13, fol. 18.

38. Deposition of John Vickers; Court of Chancery, Marquess of Navarres v. Charles Craven, C 11/227/34, C 11/1947/29, TNA.

39. Thomas Walker to the Board of Trade, n.d. [ca. August 1716], CO 5/1265, fols. 105–106.

40. Depositions of Robert Daniel, Nathaniel Partridge, George Rodd, Thomas Hepworth, Joseph Swaddell, and Thomas Walker, July 14–16, 1716, Board of Trade and Secretaries of State, America and West Indies, Original Correspondence, South Carolina, Correspondence, Original—Secretary of State, 1715–1729, CO 5/387, fols. 27–28, 37–42; James Fellowes to Josiah Burchett, July 19, 1716, CO 5/387, fols. 29–31.

41. Deposition of Michael Cole, September, 27, 1716, Treasury Board Papers and In-Letters, T 1/205, 142–45, TNA.

42. Depositions of Thomas Howard, Roger Butler, Henry Shrimpton, James Fellowes, Richard Wigg, John Hogg, Samuel Barlow, Edward Brooke, Cooper Wheeler, Bernhard Christian Cooper, and Neville Birdwell, July 20, 1716, Treasury Board Papers and In-Letters, T 1/201, 38–57.

43. Arrest Warrant for James Fellowes, July 19, 1716, Depositions of James Hepworth, Joseph Swaddell, and David Bourke, July 14, 1716, Deposition of Thomas Walker, July 10, 1716, and Depositions of William Gibbon and Andrew Allen, n.d. [ca. July 1716], CO 5/387, fols. 38–42; James Fellowes to Josiah Burchett, August 3, 1716, CO 5/387, fols. 32–33.

44. List of Vessels Commissioned by Archibald Hamilton, n.d. [ca. January 1716], CO 137/12, fol. 288; Deposition of Matthew Musson, Jamaica Council Minutes, October 19, 1716, CO 140/13, fol. 999.

45. Deposition of Benjamin Quelch, March 20, 1717, Treasury Board Papers and In-Letters, T 1/204, 111–13.

46. William Rhett to the Lords of Treasury, October 3, 1716, Treasury Board Papers and In-Letters, T 1/200, 177–80.

47. Hanna, *Pirate Nests*, 150–51, 189, 265; Burgess, *Politics of Piracy*, 103, 109, 218–22.

48. Ritchie, *Captain Kidd and the War*, 144; Hanna, *Pirate Nests*, 289–91.

49. Burgess, *Politics of Piracy*, 103, 109, 218–22, Ritchie, *Captain Kidd and the War*, 145–55; Hanna, *Pirate Nests*, 289–91.

50. Hanna, *Pirate Nests*, 245–50.

51. Lords of the Admiralty to Capt. Thomas Reynolds, n.d. [ca. May 8–9, 1716], and Same to Capt. Francis Hume, ADM 2/48, 585, 616; Lords of the Admiralty to Bennington Whitworth, August 23, 1716, ADM 2/49, 27.

52. Alexander Spotswood to the Lords of the Admiralty, July 3, 1716, in Brock, *Official Letters of Alexander Spotswood*, 168; Alexander Spotswood to the Board of Trade, July 3, 1716, and enclosed Deposition of John Vickers, ca. June 1716, CO 5/1317, fols. 245–48; Paul Methuen to the Board of Trade, November 30, 1716, CO 137/12, fol. 53.

53. Lords of the Admiralty to Bartholomew Candler, Francis Hume, and Thomas Rose, March 4, 1717, and Lords of the Admiralty to Ellis Brand, April 11, 1717, ADM 2/49, 184–85, 210.

Chapter 3. "All Mad to Go a Wrecking"

1. John Balchen to Josiah Burchett, May 13, 1716, Navy Department: Correspondence and Papers, ADM 1/1471, TNA.
2. Zahedieh, "Commerce and Conflict"; Rutledge, "Enemies Bound by Trade"; Finucane, *Temptations of Trade*, 21–52.
3. Zahedieh, "Commerce and Conflict," 74–76.
4. Anonymous, *Humble Address*.
5. [Rigsby], *Observations*.
6. Anonymous, *Groans of Jamaica*; Anonymous, *Case of the Poor Sailors*.
7. Governor Thomas Handasyd to the Board of Trade, July 22, 1710, and Proclamation for Pardoning Certain Pirates, November 19, 1709, Jamaica, Correspondence, CO 137/9, fols. 13, 35, TNA.
8. William Dummer to Alured Popple, January 31, 1710, *CSP*, vol. 25, no. 84.
9. Richard Lloyd to the Board of Trade, July 6, 1710, *CSP*, vol. 25, no. 289.
10. Finucane, *Temptations of Trade*, 21–52; Rutledge, "Enemies Bound by Trade," 32–38.
11. Anonymous, *Trade of the South-Sea Company*.
12. Archibald Hamilton to the Secretary of State, March 5, 1713, *CSP*, vol. 27, no. 291.
13. Hovenden Walker to Burchett, n.d. [ca. March 1713], ADM 1/230.
14. An Account of the Ships and Vessels taken by the Spaniards in the West Indies since the peace, n.d. [ca. October 1714], CO 137/10, fol. 352.
15. Extract of a letter from James Knight to Francis Melmoth, October 15, 1714, CO 137/10, fol. 66; J. Balchen to Burchett, July 20 and August 24, 1715, ADM 1/1471; Hamilton to the Board of Trade, November 14, 1715, CO 137/10, fols. 3–4; Lords of the Admiralty to Capt. Thomas Reynolds, n.d. [ca. May 8–9, 1716], ADM 2/48, fol. 585.
16. A List of the Many Ships, Sloops, and other Vessels taken from the Subjects of Great Britain in America by the Subjects of the King of Spain, n.d. [ca. 1718], Add Ms 61644A, British Library.
17. Walton, *Spanish Treasure Fleets*, 117–62; Newton, "Juan Esteban de Ubilla."
18. Walton, *Spanish Treasure Fleets*, 159–60; DeBry, "Concise History."
19. Link, "Spanish Camp Site"; Dubcovsky, "When Archaeology and History Meet."
20. Samuel Meade to Josiah Burchett, September 30, 1715, ADM 1/2095.
21. Josiah Soames to Josiah Burchett, December 18, 1715, ADM 1/2451.
22. Alexander Spotswood to Secretary James Stanhope, October 24, 1715, in Brock, *Official Letters of Alexander Spotswood*, 1:132–33.
23. *Evening Post*, November 12–15, 1715; *Evening Post*, November 26–29, 1715; *Daily Courant*, December 6, 1715; *Flying Post*, December 13–15, 1715; *British Weekly Mercury*, December 14–21, 1715.
24. *Boston News Letter*, December 19, 1715.
25. Hamilton to the Board of Trade, November 14, 1715, CO 137/11, fols. 3–4.
26. John Balchen to Josiah Burchett, May 12, 1716, ADM 1/1471; Jonathan Barnet Deposition, August 10, 1716, and John Wright Deposition, September 5, 1716, Jamaica Council Minutes, CO 140/13, 77–79, 344.
27. Jonathan Barnet Deposition, August 10, 1716, and Jamaica Council Minutes, Jan-

uary 27, 1716, CO 140/13, 77–79, 145–46; Commission and Instructions for Jonathan Barnet, November 24, 1715, CO 137/12, fols. 282–85.

28. Lewis Galdy and Jonathan Barnet Depositions, Jamaica Council Minutes, August 10, 1715, CO 140/13, 76–79.

29. Jamaica Council Minutes, January 27, 1716, CO 140/13, 145–46.

30. Thomas Bendysh Deposition, August 14, 1716, William Wyllis Deposition, August 16, 1716, John Beswick Deposition, August 19, 1716, Sarah Lopes Tores Deposition, August 21, 1716, Jamaica Council Minutes, CO 140/13, 93–95, 112–17, 153–54, 165–66; Edward James Deposition, August 16, 1716, John Beswick Deposition, August 19, 1716, and Archibald Hamilton's Interview, September 7, 1716, Jamaica Council Minutes, CO 140/13, 127–29, 351–57.

31. Deposition of Samuel Liddale, August 7, 1716, Jamaica Council Minutes, CO 140/13, 519–21.

32. Deposition of Sarah Fernando, August 27, 1716, Jamaica Council Minutes, CO 140/13, 689–98.

33. Deposition of William Willis, August 15, 1716, Jamaica Council Minutes, CO 140/13, 581–83.

34. Woodard, *Republic of Pirates*, 111–14; Depositions of Richard Ashley and David Middleton, August 22, 1716, Jamaica Council Minutes, CO 140/13, 635–36; Deposition of Joseph Lorrain, August 27, 1716, Jamaica Council Minutes, CO 140/13, 632–34; Deposition of Turner Stevenson, September 27, 1716, Jamaica Council Minutes, CO 140/13, 957–59; Memorials of Don Juan de Valle and Capt. Don Manuel de Arumburu, August 28, 1716, Jamaica Council Minutes, CO 140/13, 699–714, 715–20.

35. Marques de Cassatorres to Archibald Hamilton, January 8, 1716, CO 137/12, fols. 23–24; Depositions of Sebastian Fernando de Velasco, Nicholas Fernandes de Velasco, Capt. Balthasar de Herrera, Capt. Manuel de la Salde, James de la Quadra, Capt. Don Francisco de la Quadra y Achiaga, January 24, 1716, CO 137/12, fols. 457–67; Deposition of George Gosling, October 26, 1716, Jamaica Council Minutes, CO 140/13, 1000–1003.

36. Jamaica Council Minutes, January 26 and February 9, 1716, CO 140/13, 361, 373, 375–79.

37. Hamilton to the Marques de Cassatorres, February 27, 1716, CO 137/12, fols. 30–31; Jamaica Council Minutes, February 9, 1716, CO 140/13, 375–79.

38. Deposition of Samuel Page, with enclosed let pass for Henry Jennings dated February 28, 1716, Jamaica Council Minutes, September 19, 1716, CO 140/13, 897.

39. Memorial of Monsieur Moret and extract of a letter by Escoubet and the Comte de Blenac to Archibald Hamilton, June 18, 1716, Jamaica Council Minutes, August 1–2, 1716, CO 140/13, 483–91.

40. Depositions of James Forster, August 17, 1716, and Christopher Feake, August 19, 1716, Jamaica Council Minutes, CO 140/13, 605–8, 627–31.

41. Testimony of Pierre Leguardieu, September 4, 1716, Jamaica Council Minutes, CO 140/13, 807–9.

42. Jamaica Council Minutes, April 24–24, 1716, CO 140/13, 443–51.

43. Jamaica Council Minutes, May 15–16, 1716, CO 140/13, 453–60; Depositions of Alan Bernard, August 10, George Daws, August 17, Sarah Fernando, August 27, Thomas Johnson and Samuel Smith, August 31, and Joseph Eels, December 20, 1716,

Jamaica Council Minutes, CO 140/13, 444–51, 589–603, 689–98, 746–57, and CO 140/15, 25–30.

44. Hamilton to the Board of Trade, June 12, 1716, CO 137/11, fols. 178–81; Hamilton, Commission for the Investigation, July 9, 1716, CO 137/13—Part 1, fols. 3–7.

45. Board of Trade Instructions to Peter Heywood, May 28, 1716, CO 5/190, fol. 172.

46. Jamaica Council Minutes, July 31–August 3, 1716, CO 140/13, 467–601.

47. Jamaica Council Minutes, August 20, 1716, CO 140/13, 623; Francis Fernando to George Hall, Conveyance, June 29, 1716, Jamaica Deeds, vol. 54, fol. 82, Island Record Office.

48. Jamaica Council Minutes, August 19, 1716, CO 140/13, 612.

49. Hamilton to the Board of Trade, June 12, 1716, CO 137/11, fols. 178–81.

50. Peter Heywood to the Board of Trade, August 11, 1716, CO 137/12, fols. 65–68.

51. Bowes to Mr. Onslow, n.d. [ca. August 1716], CO 137/12, fols. 35–36.

52. Letter of William Rhett, August 3, 1716, Jamaica Council Minutes, October 17, 1716, CO 140/13, 977–78.

53. Jamaica Council Minutes, August 21 and August 30, 1716, CO 140/13, 625–26, 736–38.

54. Deposition of Samuel Liddale, August 7, 1716, Jamaica Council Minutes, CO 140/13, 519–22.

55. Deposition of Alan Bernard, August 10, 1716, Jamaica Council Minutes, CO 140/13, 544–51.

56. Deposition of Jonathan Barnet, August 10, 1716, Jamaica Council Minutes, CO 140/13, 542–44.

57. Depositions of John Cockram, Richard Ashley, Joseph Loraine, and David Middleton, August 10, 1716, Jamaica Council Minutes, CO 140/13, 551–59; Depositions of William Wyllis and John Cavalier, August 15–16, 1716, Jamaica Council Minutes, CO 140/13, 578–83, 585–86.

58. Extract of a Letter from Mr. [Thomas] Bernard to Hamilton, n.d. [ca. June 1717] and Hamilton's let pass for Page to depart the island, February 5, 1716, CO 137/12, fols. 319–20; Samuel Page to Gilbert Heathcoate, May 8, 1716, CO 137/11, fols. 107–8; Depositions of Samuel Page and Walter Adlington, May 15, 1716, CO 137/11, fols. 99–104; Jamaica Council Minutes, November 21, 1718, CO 140/14, 1–17 (inserted between 498 and 558).

59. "Nolle prosequi," Merriam-Webster Dictionary Online, https://www.merriam-webster.com/dictionary/nolle%20prosequi (accessed October 2020).

60. Jamaica Council Minutes, May 15 and August 8, 1716, CO 140/13, 455–56, 535–36; Peter Heywood to the Board of Trade, December 3, 1716, CO 137/12, fol. 120.

61. Jamaica Council Minutes, August 14, 16–17, 19, 21, 27, and September 10, 1716, CO 140/13, 574–75, 586, 597–621, 624–25, 688–89, 858–61; Jamaica Council Minutes, September 14, October 17, 1716, CO 140/13, 883–86, 996–97; Jamaica Council Minutes, December 19, 1716, CO 140/15, 25.

62. Depositions from Thomas Bendysh, August 14, 1716, George Daws, August 17, 1716, William Leaver and Edwyn Sandys, August 18, 1716, Jamaica Council Minutes, CO 140/13, 560–65, 598–603, 612–18.

63. Jamaica Council Minutes, October 13, 1716, CO 140/13, 989.

64. Nicholas Harris Deposition, August 15, 1716, Jamaica Council Minutes, CO 140/13, 573–75.

65. Depositions from William Wyllis, August 15, 1716, John Cavalier, August 16, 1716, John Reeves, August 19, 1716, Jamaica Council Minutes, CO 140/13, 578–83, 587–91, 620–21.

66. James Neilson Deposition, August 25, 1716, and Archibald Hamilton Interview, September 7, 1716, Jamaica Council Minutes, CO 140/13, 679–84, 822–24.

67. Justice, *General Treatise of the Dominion*, 113; Molloy, *De Jure Maritimo et Navali*, 267.

68. Archibald Hamilton Interview, September 7–8, Jamaica Council Minutes, CO 140/13, 819–37.

69. Jamaica Council Minutes, September 12–13, CO 140/13, 860–73.

70. William Bryan Deposition, September 25, 1716, Jamaica Council Minutes, CO 140/13, 959–63.

71. Jamaica Council Minutes, September 25–26, 1716, CO 140/13, 963–67; Jamaica Council Minutes, September 28, 1716, CO 140/13, 969; Messieur Niegre's Memorial, October 12, 1716, Jamaica Council Minutes, CO 140/13, 976–77.

72. Jamaica Council Minutes, October 12, 1716, CO 140/13, 973–81.

73. "Archibald Hamilton," History of Parliament Online, https://www.historyofparliamentonline.org/volume/1690-1715/member/hamilton-lord-archibald-1673-1754 (accessed July 19, 2023).

74. William Bryan Deposition, September 25, 1716, Jamaica Council Minutes, CO 140/13, 959–63.

75. William Quarrel Deposition, October 17, 1716, Jamaica Council Minutes, CO 140/13, 991–93.

76. Matthew Musson Deposition, October 19, 1716, Jamaica Council Minutes, CO 140/13, 999; Benjamin Quelch Jr. to Matthew Musson, Release, May 19, 1716, South Carolina, Records of the Secretary and Register of the Province, 1712–1713, 151, familysearch.org.

77. Joseph/George Gosling Deposition, October 26, 1716, Jamaica Council Minutes, CO 140/13, 1000–1006.

78. Jamaica Council Minutes, December 19, 1716, January 22, 1717, February 5, 1717, November 22, 1717, December 20, 1717, CO 140/15, 15–24, 62–66, 127–30, 134–37; Henry Timberlake Deposition, December 19, 1716, CO 140/15, 19–21.

79. Joseph Eels Deposition, December 20, 1716, CO 140/15, 24–30.

80. Jamaica Council Minutes, December 20, 1716, CO 140/15, 30–31.

81. Jamaica Council Minutes, January 15, January 22, February 19, and March 19, 1717, CO 140/15, 39, 64, 81, 84.

82. Jamaica Council Minutes, October 26, 1716, CO 140/13, 1005–6.

83. Robert Hawks Deposition, Bahamas Council Minutes, December 22, 1721, CO 23/13, fol. 320, TNA; DEPOsition of Nathaniel Hudson, June 6, 1718, New York Colony Council Papers, 61:34–40, New York State Archives; Robert Brown and Pearse Wright Depositions, December 22, 1721, Bahamas Council Minutes, CO 23/13, fols. 319–20.

84. *Cochran v. Jennings*, n.d. [ca. 1721], Jamaica Grand Court Records, vol. 10, 1A/5/10, fol. 64, JNA.

85. Inventory of William Turner, n.d. [ca. October 31, 1716], Jamaica Inventories, 1B/11/3/10, fol. 251, JNA; Nathaniel Hudson to John Dunk, Conveyance, October 29, 1718, recorded July 17, 1719, N.Y. Deeds, 28:522, familysearch.org.

86. Will of John Crossley, May 15, 1715, Jamaica Wills, vol. 14, fol. 166; Governor Robert Johnson, Pardon for Pirates, June 30, 1718, South Carolina, Secretary of the Province, Miscellaneous Documents, microfilm reel 50IA, 64, SCDAH; Letter of Administration for Othenias Davis and Richard Allen, March 1, 1716, Jamaica—Letters of Administration, 1B/11/17/1, fol. 177, JNA; Alan Bernard and John Cockram Depositions, August 10, 1716, Jamaica Council Minutes, CO 140/13, 545, 552–54; Turner Stevenson Deposition, September 27, 1716, Jamaica Council Minutes, CO 140/13, 957–59.

87. Jamaica Council Minutes, December 18–19, 1716, CO 140/15, 7–9, 12–19.

88. Jamaica Council Minutes, January 15, January 22, and December 20, 1717, CO 140/15, 36–59, 64, 136.

89. William Quarrel Deposition, October 17, 1716, Jamaica Council Minutes, CO 140/13, 991; Robert Johnson's Pardon of July 10, 1718, South Carolina, Secretary of the Province, Miscellaneous Documents, microfilm reel 50IA, 65.

Chapter 4. The Pardon and Its Discontents

1. Admiralty: Captains' Logs, *Phoenix*, entries for February 23–March 1, 1718, ADM 51/690, TNA.

2. Commons House of Assembly Journals, ca. 1708–18, John Green Transcripts, December 3, 1717, 5:389, SCDAH.

3. Rediker, *Villains of All Nations*, 29.

4. Woodard, *Republic of Pirates*, 169–93; Schonhorn, *General History of the Pyrates*, 585–92; Clifford et al., *Real Pirates*.

5. Woodard, *Republic of Pirates*, 194–225; Schonhorn, *General History of the Pyrates*, 71–94.

6. Nicholas Lawes to the Board of Trade, March 24, 1719, CO 137/13, fol. 132, TNA.

7. Wingate Gale to Col. Thomas Pitt Jr., November 4, 1718, Bahamas, Correspondence, Original—Board of Trade, A. 1717–1725, CO 23/1, fol. 48.

8. Bermuda, Miscellanea, Shipping Returns, 1715–1731, entry for October 19, 1715, CO 41/6, fol. 14.

9. Bermuda, Shipping Returns, CO 41/6, fols. 14–16.

10. Bermuda, Shipping Returns, CO 41/6, fol. 2.

11. Bermuda, Shipping Returns, CO 41/6, fol. 3.

12. Bermuda, Shipping Returns, CO 41/6, fols. 2–11.

13. Bermuda, Shipping Returns, CO 41/6. See especially entries for February 22, April 2, May 21, June 7, June 28–29, July 9, July 16–17, October 2–4, and October 13, 1716; Samuel Meade to Secretary Burchett, December 27, 1715, ADM 1/2095; Commons House of Assembly Journals, November 30 and December 1, 1716, Green Transcripts, 5:184–85, 188.

14. Board of Trade and Secretaries of State, America and West Indies, Original Correspondence, South Carolina, Shipping Returns, Cleared Outward October 19, 1716, to June 22, 1717, CO 5/508, fols. 2–3, 6–8, 13–16.

15. Board of Trade and Secretaries of State, America and West Indies, Original Cor-

respondence, Massachusetts, Shipping Returns, CO 5/848, fols. 33, 36, 50, 55, 61, 65, 67, 75, 79, 87, 92, and for the port of Salem, see fols. 128–29, 132–33, 144, 146; *Boston News Letter*, May 9 and October 31, 1715, January 23, March 12, April 30, May 7, and May 28, 1716, March 25, June 24, July 8, and July 29, 1717, and May 26, 1718.

16. Board of Trade and Secretaries of State, America and West Indies, Original Correspondence, New York, Shipping Returns, CO 5/1222, fols. 149–50, 163–64.

17. New York, Shipping Returns, fols. 56–57, 78, 84, 87, 112–15, 143–44, 157, 159–61.

18. New York, Shipping Returns, fols. 78, 87.

19. Bermuda, Shipping Returns, June 24, 1717, CO 41/6, fol. 7.

20. Massachusetts (Salem), Shipping Returns, July 25 and November 15, 1716, CO 5/848, fols. 75, 114; *Boston News Letter*, July 8, 1717.

21. New York, Shipping Returns, May 11, 1717 (Mutlow), October 5, 1717 (Pinfold), and March 24, 1718 (Stout), CO 5/1222, fols. 112, 143, 148.

22. Board of Trade and Secretaries of State, America and West Indies, Original Correspondence, South Carolina, Shipping Returns, 1716–1719 and 1721–1735, CO 5/508, fols. 5–6, 14, 23.

23. South Carolina, Shipping Returns, fol. 6; John Crosskeys, Inventory, February 7, 1716, 1B/11/3/10, fol. 202, JNA.

24. See from South Carolina Court of Common Pleas, Judgment Rolls, 1703–1790 (hereafter SCCP Judgment Rolls), SCDAH: Daniel Green, Robert Wishart and Jane, His Wife, Exors. of Joseph Merry v. James Burt, Exor. of William Sherman, 1714, box 4B, ITEM 232; Robert Wishart v. Mary Ellicott, Exix. of Joseph Ellicott, 1714, box 4B, ITEM 246; Henry Wigington, v. Robert Wishart and Jane, His Wife, Exix. and Daniel Green, Exor. of Joseph Merry, box 5A, ITEM 334; John Brown and Lucy, His Wife v. Robert Wishart and Jane, His Wife and Daniel Green, 1715, box 5B, ITEM 395; John Hale v. Robert Wishart and Jane, His Wife and Daniell Greene, Exors. of Joseph Merry, 1715, box 6A, ITEM 704; Catherine Robinson, Exix. of John Robinson vs Robert Wishart, 1716, box 7A, ITEM 858; Catherine Robinson, Exix. of John Robinson v. Robert Wishart, 1716, box 7A, ITEM 859; Robert Wishart and Jane, His Wife, and Daniell Green, Exors. of Joseph Merry v. Dr. Archibald Stobo, 1716, box 8A, ITEM 1092. See also Commons House of Assembly Minutes, February 17, 22, and 24, 1715, Green Transcripts, 5:355, 374, 385.

25. South Carolina, Shipping Returns, CO 5/508, fols. 6, 14.

26. South Carolina Court of Vice Admiralty Minute Books, September 23–October 15, 1717, v. A-B, PART 1, 107–39, in Pre-federal Admiralty Court Records, Province and State of South Carolina, 1716–1789, National Archives and Record Administration, Washington, D.C.

27. Richard Floyd v. Robert Wishart, December 1717 to May 1718, SCCP Judgment Rolls, box 12A, ITEM 177A.

28. Massachusetts, Shipping Returns, CO 5/848, fols. 50, 58, 61, 65, 67, 75, 79, 87, 128, 132, 144, 146.

29. New York, Shipping Returns, New York, CO 5/1222, fols. 26, 113.

30. Deposition of Samuel Vincent, June 4 and June 15, 1717, Deposition of Richard Caverly, June 15, 1717, Deposition of William Dobbs, June 22, 1717, Deposition of Henrick Van Dyke, July 4, 1717, Deposition of Jeremiah Higgins, July 12, 1717, Deposition of

Jonathan Brodrick, June 12, 1717, and Deposition of Catherine Dobbs, June 15, 1717, in Papers Relating to a Piracy Case, June 3–July 12, 1717, New York Vice Admiralty Court Records, no. 4545839, United States National Archives and Record Administration, New York City.

31. *Boston News Letter*, June 17 and June 24, 1717; New York, Shipping Returns, CO 5/1222, fol. 107; Deposition of John Cockram and Samuel Vincent, April 6, 1720, Colonial Office and Predecessors: Bahamas, Correspondence, Original—Board of Trade, A. 1717–1725, CO 23/1, fol. 134.

32. New York, Shipping Returns, CO 5/1222, fols. 127, 135, 143, 148, 150, 164.

33. Ship Captains Petition to Don Alonso Philippe de Andrada, n.d. [ca. November 29, 1715], Leeward Islands, Correspondence, CO 152/39, fol. 161, TNA.

34. Captain's Logs, *Rose*, entry for July 26, 1718, ADM 51/892/2, and Thomas Whitney, entry for August 7, 1718, ADM 51/801/4, TNA; Bahamas Vice-Admiralty Court Minutes, September 1–5, 1718, Admiralty, and Ministry of Defense, Navy Department: Correspondence and Papers—Original Series (1st Group): 1660–1839, ADM 1/1597.

35. New York, Shipping Returns, entry for October 6, 1718, CO 5/1222, fol. 187.

36. South Carolina, Shipping Returns, CO 5/508, fols. 5, 7, 13, 18.

37. New York, Shipping Returns, fols. 112, 149, 157, 163, 187.

38. Bermuda, Shipping Returns, CO 41/6, fols. 2–3.

39. Bermuda, Shipping Returns, fols. 3, 17–18.

40. Bermuda, Shipping Returns, fols. 8–11, 16–19, 21, 24.

41. Kelleher, *Alliance of Pirates*, 292–94.

42. Earle, *Pirate Wars*, 60–63, 96; Ritchie, *Captain Kidd and the War*, 137, 142, 212–13, 233–34; Hanna, *Pirate Nests*, 49, 54, 134, 180.

43. Information of Darby Donovan, October 11, 1709, and Thomas Handasyd to the [Earl of Sunderland], December 17, 1709, Add Ms 61643, fols. 203–4, 209, British Library.

44. Thomas Handasyd to the Board of Trade, November 9, 1709, *CSP*, vol. 25, nos. 313 and 313i; Jeremy Dummer to William Popple, January 31, 1710, *CSP*, vol. 25, no. 84.

45. Deposition of Sarah Fernando, Jamaica Council Minutes, August 27, 1716, Colonial Office: Jamaica, Sessional Papers, Journals of the Council, Assembly, and Council in Assembly, 1713–1724, CO 140/13, fols. 695–97.

46. Stephen Smith to Peter Heywood, September 23, 1716, Colonial Office and Predecessors: Jamaica, Correspondence, Original—Board of Trade, O. nos. 52–205, 1716–1718, CO 137/12, fol. 36.

47. Bartholomew Candler to Burchett, July 19, 1717, ADM 1/1597.

48. Nicholas Laws to the Board of Trade, August 29, 1717, CO 137/12, fol. 301.

49. 1717: 4 George I c.11: The Transportation Act, The Statutes Project, http://statutes.org.uk/site/the-statutes/eighteenth-century/1717-4-george-1-c-11-the-transportation-act/ (accessed November 14, 2020); "William III, 1698–9: An Act for the more effectuall Suppressions of Piracy. [Chapter VII. Rot. Parl. 11 Gul. III. p. 2. n. 5.]," in Raithby, *Statutes of the Realm*, 7:590–94.

50. Council of Trade and Plantations to Mr. Secretary Addison, May 31, 1717, *CSP*, vol. 29, no. 596.

51. Board of Trade Journals, August 7, 1717, in Ledward, *Journals of the Board of Trade*

(hereafter *JBT*), 3:253–63, British History Online. An original printed copy of the proclamation can be found in State Paper Office: Printed Proclamations, 1708–1722, SP 45/14, fol. 55.

52. Fox, "Jacobitism and the 'Golden Age'"; Bialuschewski, "Jacobite Pirates?"; Woodard, *Republic of Pirates*, 122–23, 142–43; Monod, *Jacobitism and the English People*, 111–19.

53. Guthrie, *Material Culture of the Jacobites*, 106; Rogers, "Riot and Popular Jacobitism"; Rogers, "Popular Jacobitism in Provincial Context"; Kathleen Wilson, *Sense of the People*, 101–17.

54. Papers Laid before the Committee, June 9, 1717, SP 35/9, fol. 27, TNA.

55. Black, *Politics and Foreign Policy*, 83.

56. *Original Weekly Journal*, September 28–October 5, 1718.

57. *London Evening Post*, September 12–14, 1717; *London Post Boy*, September 12–14, 1717; *London Gazette*, September 14–17, 1717.

58. Bennet to the Board of Trade, February 3, 1718, CO 37/10, fol. 19; *Boston News Letter*, December 9, 1717.

59. Jamaica Council Minutes, November 22, 1717, CO 140/15, 128.

60. Deposition of Henry Bostock, December 19, 1717, CO 157/1, fol. 219.

61. Bennet to the Board of Trade, February 3, 1718; Bermuda, Shipping Returns, CO 41/6, fol. 24.

62. Deposition of Thomas Nichols, June 3, 1718, New York Colony Council Papers, series A1894, 61:73–74, microfilm reel 20, NYSA. ALL further depositions cited in this chapter come from this source.

63. Deposition of Peter Miller, May 31, 1718, 61:32, microfilm reel 20; *Weekly Journal or British Gazeteer*, May 31, 1718.

64. Francis Lesley to Benjamin Bennet, January 7, 1718, and Thomas Nichols to Bennet, January 10, 1718, CO 37/10, fols. 23, 25.

65. Bermuda, Bonds, Bills, Deeds and Protests, book 6, 186–221, and book 7, 57, familysearch.org (accessed June 10, 2020).

66. *Weekly Journal or Saturday's Post*, April 12, 1718.

67. Lesley to Bennet, January 7, 1718, CO 37/10, fol. 25.

68. Nichols to Bennet, January 10, 1718, CO 37/10, fol. 23.

69. Bennet to the Board of Trade, March 29, 1718, CO 37/10, fol. 29.

70. Bennet to the Board of Trade, March 29, 1718.

71. Great Britain, Privy Council, January 30–February 9, 1718, in Grant et al., *Acts of the Privy Council*, 2:723–25.

72. Jamaica Council Minutes, January 3, 1718, CO 140/15, 138–40; Peter Heywood to the Board of Trade, February 7, 1718, CO 137/13, fol. 11.

73. William Smith Deposition, May 31, 1718, Nathaniel Hudson Deposition, June 6, 1718, and William Smith Deposition, June 9, 1718, 61:30, 55, 75.

74. William Smith Deposition, June 9, 1718, 61:75.

75. *Weekly Journal or British Gazeteer*, May 3, 1718; *Weekly Journal or Saturday's Post*, March 15, 1718.

76. "Declared Accounts, 1704–5: Navy," in Shaw, *Calendar of Treasury Books*, 20:cciii–ccxl, available at British History Online, http://www.british-history.ac.uk/cal-treasury

-books/vol20/ccii-ccxl; "Principal Officers and Commissioners," in Collinge, *Office-Holders in Modern Britain*, 18–25, available at British History Online, http://www.british-history.ac.uk/office-holders/vol7/pp18-25; Hasted, *History and Topographical Survey*, 463–70.

77. Vincent Pearse to Josiah Burchett, October 12, 1715, SP 42/14, fol. 276.
78. Admiralty Board to Vincent Pearse, November 12, 1715, SP 42/14, fol. 320; Mr. Hawes to Secretary Townsend, January 26, 1716, SP 54/11, fol. 128.
79. Lords of the Admiralty to Vincent Pearse, November 20, 1716, ADM 2/49, 84.
80. Captain's Logs, *Phoenix*, ADM 51/690; Ships Pay Books, *Phoenix*, ADM 33/298.
81. Lords of the Admiralty to Vincent Pearse, and Same to Thomas Jacobs, June 19, 1717, ADM 2/49, 263–65, 267–69; Pearse to Burchett, February 4, 1718, ADM 1/2282; New York Council Minutes, January 27, 1718, CO 5/1186, fol. 150.
82. Captain's Logs, *Phoenix*, ADM 51/690; Ships Pay Books, *Phoenix*.
83. Captain's Logs, *Phoenix*, entries for February 23–26, ADM 1/2282; Nathaniel Hudson Deposition, June 6, 1718, 61:55.
84. Pearse to Burchett, March 4, 1718, ADM 1/2282.
85. Captain's Logs, *Phoenix*, entries for March 1–23, ADM 1/2282.
86. Captain's Logs, *Phoenix*, entries for March 24–May 19, 1718, ADM 1/2282.
87. Pearse to Burchett, June 3, 1718, ADM 1/2282.
88. New York Council Minutes, May 27, 1718, CO 5/1222, fol. 156.
89. Earle, *Pirate Wars*, 188; Rutledge, "Enemies Bound by Trade," 88–89.
90. Deposition of Benjamin Bill, May 27, 1718, 61:22.
91. Depositions of Benjamin Bill and Alexander Gilmore, May 30, 1718, John Parsons, May 28, 1718, and Richard Liscum, Thomas Leach, Edward Bigeley, and David Clerk, May 30, 1718, 61:22–24, 26, 27.
92. Deposition of Benjamin Bill, May 27, 1718, New York Council Papers, series A, 61:21, New York State Archive.
93. New York, Shipping Returns, CO 5/1222, fols. 8, 48, 61, 80, 90, 117, 131.
94. Deposition of William Smith, June 9, 1718, 61:75–85.
95. Deposition of Nathaniel Hudson, June 6, 1718, Deposition of Samuel Tynes, June 3, 1718, Deposition of William Smith, June 9, 1718, 61:31–36.
96. Depositions of William Connor and Thomas Nicolls, June 3, 1718, 61:39–41.
97. Depositions of William Connor, June 3, 1718, and William Smith, June 9, 1718, 61:39, 75–85.
98. Vincent Pearse to the Navy Board, August 28, 1718, ADM 106/721/178.
99. Deposition of Nathaniel Hudson, May 31, 1718, 61:31.
100. Deposition of Nathaniel Hudson, June 6, 1718, 61:33–35.
101. Deposition of Peter Miller, May 31, 1718, and Nathaniel Hudson, June 6, 1718, 61:32, 33–35.
102. Depositions of Nathaniel Hudson, June 6, 1718, and William Smith, June 9, 1718, 61:35, 85.
103. Deposition of William Smith, June 9, 1718, 61:75–85.
104. Deposition of Nathaniel Hudson, June 6, 1718, 61:33–35.
105. Deposition of Benjamin Bill, May 27, 1718, 61:22.
106. Depositions of Alexander Gilmore and John Parsons, May 28, 1718; Alexander

Gilmore, May 30, 1718; Richard Liscum, Thomas Leach, Edward Bigeley, and David Clerk, May 30, 1718; Benjamin Bill, May 27, 1718, 61:22–24, 26.

107. Deposition of Benjamin Bill, May 27, 1718, 61:22.
108. Deposition of Richard Symonds, May 30, 1718, 61:25.
109. Depositions of Benjamin Bill, May 27, 1718, and William Smith, June 9, 1718, 61:22, 75–85.
110. Depositions of Thomas Odell and William Smith, June 3, 1718, 61:38, 41.
111. Deposition of Thomas Nicolls, June 3, 1718, 61:40.
112. Ships Pay Books, *Phoenix*, ADM 33/298.
113. Depositions of William Smith, Nathaniel Hudson, Peter Miller, May 31, 1718, and William Smith, June 9, 1718, 61:30–32, 75–85.
114. Depositions of Benjamin Bill, May 30, 1718, and William Smith, Nathaniel Hudson, and Samuel Tynes, May 31, 1718, 61:29–31, 33.
115. Deposition of Benjamin Bill, May 27, 1718, 61:22.
116. Vincent Pearse to Burchett, September 5, 1718, and February 13, 1721/2, ADM 1/2282.
117. Vincent Pearse to the Navy Board, February 4, 1718, Navy Board In-Letters, ADM 106/721/135; Pearse to the Navy Board, August 28, 1718, ADM 106/721/178.
118. Lewis Morris to Cadwaller Colden, July 23, 1720, in Sheridan, *Papers of Lewis Morris*, 1:203–4; also Lewis Morris to Robert Hunter Morris, December 14, 1737, in Sheridan, *Papers of Lewis Morris*, 1:299.
119. Deposition of John Sipkins, 61:42.

Chapter 5. "Pirates Expelled—Commerce Restored"

1. Pearse to Burchett, June 3, 1718, with enclosure "A List of Names of Such Pirates as Surrendered Themselves at Providence to Capt. Vincent Pearse," ADM 1/2282, TNA.
2. London, Freedom of the City Admission Papers, 1681–1930, 1689–90, April 25, 1690, 2383, ancestry.com (accessed April 5, 2021); Shaw, *Calendar of Treasury Books*, 9:824–35, 1940–48; England Marriages 1538–1973, findmypast.co.uk; Hardy, *Calendar of State Papers Domestic*, 178–222; *London Flying Post*, April 28, 1698; Minutes of the House of Commons, 12:313–17; Anonymous, *Report of the Committee*; Roberts, "Law of Impeachment"; London, Church of England Records of Baptisms, Marriages, and Burials, 1538–1812, City of London, St. Swithins London Stone, February 24, 1699, 52, ancestry.com; Apprentice agreement between John Goudet and Daniel Motet, 1695, London Apprenticeship Abstracts, 1442–1850, findmypast.co.uk; Tax List for the Inhabitants of London, St. Mary Bothaw Precinct, 1703, findmypast.co.uk.
3. Bahamas Council Minutes, December 22, 1721, Bahamas, Correspondence, CO 23/1, part 3, fol. 63, TNA.
4. Bahamas Council Minutes, December 23, 1723, CO 23/1, part 3, fol. 63 (informal appointment keeping government accounts); G. Phenney to the Board of Trade, April 16, 1725, CO 23/1, part 3, fol. 103 (Crown clerk); G. Phenney to the Board of Trade, April 20, 1727, CO 23/2, part 1, fol. 115 (Crown clerk); G. Phenney to the Board

of Trade, January 1, 1729, CO 23/2, part 2, fol. 46 (Crown clerk); G. Phenney to the Board of Trade, March 16, 1728, CO 23/2, part 2, fol. 116 (Crown clerk); "An Account of What Ordnance, Powder, Shott, and Other Stores of War," January 1, 1725, CO 23/1, fol. 109 (store keeper); Bahamas Council Minutes, January 20, 1724, CO 23/13, fol. 390 (treasurer); Bond, G. Phenney, Samuel Lawford, and William Pindar to Peter Goudet, November 26, 1729, CO 23/2, part 2, fol. 234 (treasurer); Bahamas Council Minutes, January 20, 1724, CO 23/13, fol. 390 (customs receiver); Bahamas Council Minutes, November 18, 1728, CO 23/14, fols. 55–56 (Dispute with Fairfax).

5. Minutes of the Bahamas Assembly, September 29, October 8, October 9, 1729, Colonial Office and Predecessors: Bahamas, Sessional Papers, Council, Assembly, Council in Assembly, 1729–1738, CO 26/2A, fols. 115–18.

6. Shipping Returns, Bahamas, CO 23/13, fols. 251, 257, 260, 262; Colonial Office and Predecessors: Bahamas, Miscellaneous, Shipping and Other Returns, 1721–1751, CO 27/12, fol. 62.

7. Church of England, St. Michael Parish, Bahamas Births, Marriages, and Burials, CO 23/2, part 2, fol. 51, familysearch.org; Johnston and Hallet, *Early Colonists of the Bahamas*, 25, 33.

8. Commission to Peter Goudet, July 5, 1731, South Carolina, Charleston County Wills, 64:285, familysearch.org; *South Carolina Gazette*, June 24, 1732.

9. Joseph Fox to the Board of Trade, May 20, 1734, Shipping Returns, South Carolina, CO 5/509, fol. 127.

10. *South Carolina Gazette*, December 23, 1732; Estate Inventory of John Gardner, March 16, 1733, South Carolina Probate Records, Loose Files, 1732–1736, 97, 99; Estate Inventory of Benjamin Hall, October 16, 1750, South Carolina Probate Records, Loose Files, 1748–1751, 385, familysearch.org.

11. Minutes of the Bahamas Assembly, February 7, February 22, 1734, and November 26, 1735, CO 26/2A, fols. 44–46, 61–62; Will of Peter Goudet, February 14, 1729, proved September 18, 1735, in Johnston and Hallet, *Early Colonists of the Bahamas*, 65. Goudet lived at least through the first six months of 1735. See Account of Taxes per Polls and Lots of Land from Christmas 1734 to the following Midsummer, Colonial Office and Predecessors: Bahamas, Correspondence, Original—Board of Trade, B. Nos. 90–158, 1731–1737, CO 23/3, fol. 180.

12. Cordingly, *Pirate Hunter of the Caribbean*, chaps. 3–6.

13. Craton and Saunders, *Islanders in the Stream*, 1:115–17.

14. Ships' Paybook, *Rose*, 1717–20, Navy Board, Navy Pay Office, Ships Pay Books (Series I), ADM 33/294, TNA.

15. Captains' Logs, *Rose*, ADM 51/801; Woodes Rogers to the Board of Trade, October 31, 1718, CO 23/1, fols. 16–17.

16. George Pomeroy to Josiah Burchett, September 3, 1718, ADM 1/2282.

17. Rogers to the Board of Trade, October 31, 1718, CO 23/1, fol. 16.

18. Minutes of the Bahamas Council, August 2–5, 1718, CO 23/1, fols. 32–33.

19. "A General List of Soldiers, Saylours & Passengers Deceased Since We Arrived at Providence," ca. October 31, 1718, CO 23/1, fol. 29.

20. Whitney to Burchett, September 7, 1718, ADM 1/2684; Log of HMS *Mil-*

ford, January 16, 1718, to December 31, 1719, entry for August 8, 1718, Captains' Logs, ADM 51/606; Rogers to the Board of Trade, October 31, 1718, CO 23/1, fol. 20.

21. Rogers to the Board of Trade, October 31, 1718, CO 23/1, fol. 22.

22. Log of HMS *Rose*, entry for August 7, 1718, Captains' Logs, ADM 51/801; Peter Chamberlain to Burchett, January 29, 1719, with the enclosures "An Account of the Wine, Flower, and Beef Belonging to the Brigantine call'd the St. Martin of Bordeaux," January 24, 1719, and Vice-Admiralty Proceedings, August 7, 1718, Great Britain, Admiralty, Captain's Letters, ADM 1/1597, TNA.

23. Rogers to the Board of Trade, October 31, 1718, CO 23/1, fol. 27.

24. Bennet to the Board of Trade, March 29, 1718, CO 37/10, fol. 29.

25. Woodard, *Republic of Pirates*, 264.

26. Rogers to the Board of Trade, October 31, 1718, CO 23/1, fol. 23; Thomas Whitney to Burchett, September 8, 1718, ADM 1/2684.

27. Log of the HMS *Milford*, January 16, 17188, to December 31, 1719, entry for August 15, 1718, Captains' Logs, ADM 51/606; Log of HMS *Rose*, September 15, 1718, to December 31, 1719, entries for September 15, 1718, Captains' Logs, ADM 51/801; Log of the *Shark*, entry for August 15, 1718, Captains' Logs, ADM 51/892; Thomas Whitney to Burchett, September 8, 1718, ADM 1/2684.

28. W. Rogers to the Board of Trade, October 31, 1718, CO 23/1, fol. 23; Thomas Whitney to Burchett, September 8, 1718, ADM 1/2684; George Pomeroy to Burchett, September 3, 1718, ADM 1/2282.

29. Rogers to the Board of Trade, October 31, 1718, CO 23/1, fol. 23.

30. Deposition of John King, n.d. [ca. 1719], High Court of Admiralty, Instance and Prize Courts: Examinations and Answers, HCA 13/136.

31. Deposition of John King, fol. 24–25.

32. Bahamas Council Minutes, September 20 and 28, 1718, CO 23/1, fol. 35.

33. Rogers to the Board of Trade, January 24, 1719, CO 23/13, fol. 25.

34. Depositions of Thomas Bowlin, September 8, 1718, William Dewick, September 15, 1718, and Richard Taylor, August 4, 1718, CO 23/1, fols. 36–38, 42.

35. Rogers to Secretary James Craggs, December 24, 1718, CO 23/13, fol. 21.

36. Woodes Rogers's November 4 postscript to his letter to the Board of Trade, October 31, 1718, CO 23/1, fol. 26; Schonhorn, *General History of the Pyrates*, 626–60.

37. Schonhorn, *General History of the Pyrates*, 646.

38. Schonhorn, 652, 655.

39. Schonhorn, 660.

40. Schonhorn, 657–60.

41. Anthony Cacherode to the Lords of the Treasury, n.d. [ca. 1721] in Treasury Board Papers and In-Letters, T 1/220, fols. 27–30, TNA.

42. Rogers to Secretary Craggs, December 24, 1718, CO 23/13, fols. 20, 22; Bahamas Council Minutes, January 12, 1719, CO 23/13, fol. 47; Rogers to Craggs, January 24, 1719, CO 23/13, fol. 25.

43. Rogers to Craggs, January 30, 1719, CO 23/13, fols. 28–29.

44. Rogers to Craggs, December 24, 1718, and January 30, 1719, CO 23/13, fols. 21, 29; Anthony Cacherode to the Lords of the Treasury.

45. Rogers to Craggs, December 24, 1718, fol. 23.

46. Bahamas Council Minutes, January 12, 1719, CO 23/13, fol. 47; Rogers to Craggs, February 10, 1719, CO 23/13, fol. 38.
47. Rogers to the Governors of Jamaica, Barbados, New York, Virginia, etc., March 3, 1719, CO 23/13, fol. 36.
48. Bahamas Council Minutes, March 31, 1719, CO 23/13, fol. 48.
49. Oates, *Last Spanish Armada*.
50. Bahamas Council Minutes, March 31, 1719, CO 23/13, fol. 48.
51. Bahamas Council Minutes, May 7, 1719, CO 23/13, fol. 49; Minutes of William Martindale, ca. December 4, 1719, CO 37/10, fol. 80.
52. Bahamas Council Minutes, April 9, 1723, CO 23/1, part 3, fol. 66.
53. Schonhorn, *General History of the Pyrates*, 42.
54. Whitney to Burchett, July 3, 1719, ADM 1/2649.
55. Will of Richard Barret and Thomas Samson, December 9, 1719, in Johnston and Hallet, *Early Colonists of the Bahamas*, 56.
56. Schonhorn, *General History of the Pyrates*, 640–41.
57. Josiah Burgess to Lydia Tarkenton, Power of Attorney, December 8, 1719, Josiah Burgess, Will, December 9, 1719, Deposition of Nicholas Seley and Thomas Terrill, September 10, 1720, Josiah Burgess, Estate Inventory, September 30, 1720, Thomas Walker Affidavit, June 12, 1720, in Josiah Burgess Estate File, no. 31, Pennsylvania, Philadelphia County Register of Wills, 1718–22.
58. Bahamas Council Minutes, CO 23/13: May 11, 1719, fol. 49; May 19, 1719, fol. 50; May 26, 1719, fol. 52.
59. Bahamas Council Minutes, February 9, March 15, March 19, and May 15, 1720, fols. 55, 60, 62, 68.
60. Depositions of John Cockram, Samuel Vincent, Fathers Antonio Escobar and Antonio Toledo, and William Williams, n.d. [ca. April 19, 1720], CO 23/1, fol. 134.
61. Deposition of William South, May 10, 1719, CO 23/1, fol. 59.
62. Bahamas Council Minutes, June 21, 1720, CO 23/13, fol. 69; Rogers to the Board of Trade, July 28, 1720, CO 23/1, part 2, fol. 20; Edward Vernon to Bennington Whitworth, August 3, 1720, Vernon to Burchett, August 24, 1720, Vernon to the Marquis de Sorrell, August 20, 1720, Vernon to Nicholas Lawes, September 8, 1720, Vernon to Burchett, September 12, 1720, and Joseph Lawes to Vernon, October 20, 1720, Vernon Papers, vol. 43, fols. 44, 51, 53, 60–61, 64, 125, Add Ms 40812, British Library.
63. Woodard, *Republic of Pirates*, 315–16.
64. *Boston News Letter*, October 17, 1720; *The Trials of John Rackham and Other Pyrates* (Kingston, Jamaica: Robert Baldwin, 1721), 8–10, in CO 137/14, fols. 12–14.
65. Bahamas Council Minutes, September 2, 1720, CO 23/13, fols. 70–71.
66. Bahamas Shipping Returns, CO 23/13, fol. 253.
67. Gov. Phenney's Answers to Queries from the Board of Trade, n.d. [ca. December 1721], CO 23/13, fols. 235–36; Craton and Saunders, *Islanders in the Stream*, 1:119.
68. Michael Johnson v. William Williams, July 17, 1716, Court of Common Pleas, Judgment Rolls, 1703–1790, box 7A, NO. 909, SCDAH.
69. Colonial Office: Jamaica, Miscellanea, Shipping Returns, 1680–1705, dates unknown [ca. 1705–1728, 1729–1753], CO 142/14, fols. 79, 84, 90, 95; Bahamas Shipping Returns, CO 23/13, fol. 256.

70. *American Weekly Mercury*, October 27, 1720, and February 12, 1723; Bahamas Shipping Returns, CO 23/13, fols. 245–46, 249–62; Shipping Returns, South Carolina, CO 5/509, fols. 1, 3–4, 37, 39.

71. Shipping Returns, Bahamas, CO 23/13, fols. 251, 257, 260, 262, 425, 435, 437.

72. Shipping Returns, South Carolina, CO 5/509, fols. 62, 64, 67, 246, 255, 261; Shipping Returns, Bahamas, CO 23/14, fols. 62–63, 65.

73. Shipping Returns, Bermuda, CO 41/6, fol. 12; *Boston Gazette*, December 21, 1719; Shipping Returns, Bahamas, CO 23/13, fols. 255, 258.

74. Shipping Returns, Jamaica, CO 142/14, fol. 85; Shipping Returns, South Carolina, CO 5/509, fols. 39, 46, 53, 57; Shipping Returns, Bahamas, CO 23/13, fols. 251–52, 260–62, 441.

75. Colebrooke and Rogers Account Book, 1725–1731, NYHS.

76. Shipping Returns, Bahamas, CO 23/13, fol. 435; Shipping Returns, Jamaica, CO 142/15, fol. 34; Shipping Returns, Bahamas, CO 23/12, fols. 41–43, 46, 48.

77. Shipping Returns, Bahamas, CO 23/13, fols. 246, 255–56, 261, 487.

78. Bahamas Council Minutes, December 4, 1720, and the bond of Terrill and Petty, April 21, 1721, CO 23/1, fols. 88–89.

79. Bahamas Council Minutes, April 13, 1722, CO 23/13, fol. 344.

80. Bahamas Council Minutes, January 7, 1729, CO 23/14, fol. 91.

81. Pennsylvania Council Minutes, July 22, 1718, in Hazard, *Minutes of the Provincial Council*, 50–52.

82. Deposition of Thomas Bowlin, Phillip Cockram, William Rutherford, Nathaniel Baran, and Joseph Mickelburrow, September 8, 1718, CO 23/1, fols. 36–37.

83. Bahamas Council Minutes, November 21, 1721, CO 26/1, 4–5.

84. G. Phenney to the Board of Trade, September 14, 1722, CO 23/1, part 2, fol. 110; Phenney to the Board of Trade, April 16, 1725, CO 23/13, fol. 189; Bahamas Council Minutes, January 10, 1726, CO 23/13, fol. 416.

85. Deposition of John Cullimore, April 16, 1725, Depositions of Ridley Pindar, William Adams, and Richard Thompson, April 22, 1725, and Deposition of Thomas Petty, April 15, 1725, CO 23/13, fols. 195–99.

86. Deposition of Lane Whitehall, September 12, 1729, SP 94/101, fols. 34–36.

87. Trial of Richard Hancock and other pirates, including Campbell's testimony of October 12, 1722, CO 23/1, part 3, fols. 32–35.

88. Bahamas Council Minutes, March 2, 1722, CO 23/13, fol. 333; James Mynde after an unknown artist, ca. 1740–70, *King George I Portrayed on the Great Seal*, National Portrait Gallery, London, https://www.npg.org.uk/collections/search/portrait/mw139236/King-George-I-portrayed-on-the-Great-Seal.

89. Rogers to the Board of Trade, May 29, 1719, CO 23/1, fol. 68.

90. Craton and Saunders, *Islanders in the Stream*, 1:110–27.

91. Johnston and Hallet, *Early Colonists of the Bahamas*, 2–3; [Woodes Rogers], "An Account of the families I have given land or lotts in Providence since my arrival and are there now," n.d. [ca. 1721], CO 23/1, part 3, fol. 58.

92. Craton and Saunders, *Islanders in the Stream*, 1:119–27.

93. John Arturreal m. Mary Low, July 12, 1721 (CO 23/13, fol. 269); John Bley, wife

Rose (1731 Census); John Carey (1731 Census); David Champion (1731 census); John Cullimore, wife Lavinia Gibbons, (1731, 1734, 1740 censuses); John Edwards m. Ann Knowles, February 20, 1727 (CO 23/2, part 2, fol. 18); William Grahame (1731 census); Robert Hunter, wife Elizabeth (Johnston and Hallet, *Early Colonists of the Bahamas*, 7); Anthony Kemp (1731 and 1734 censuses); John Kemp, wife Mary (CO 23/2, part 2, fol. 143); Edward Kerr, m. Ann Carter May 1723 (CO 23/2, part 2, fol. 28); Richard Legatt (1731 census); David Meredith, will of Ruth Meredith, 1740 (Johnston and Hallet, *Early Colonists of the Bahamas*, 70); Joseph Pearse, wife Martha, CO 23/2, part 2, fol. 124; George Raddon, wife Elizabeth (CO 23/2, part 2, fol. 28); Thomas Reynolds, wife Ruth (CO 23/2, part 2, fol. 28); Samuel Richardson, wife Dorothy (CO 23/1, fol. 80); Jacob Roberts, wife Martha (CO 23/2, part 2, fol. 30); Michael Rogers, wife Mary (CO 23/2, part 1, fol. 124); Henry Shipton, wife Ann (CO 23/2, part 2, fol. 28); Daniel Stillwell, wife Rebecca d. 1728 (CO 23/2, part 2, fol. 51); Thomas Terrill, wife in Jamaica, (CO 23/14, fol. 91); Joseph Thompson, m. Anna Bradwell, January 17, 1723/4 (CO 23/2, part 2, fol. 28); Charles Whitehead, m. Katherine Saunders April 3, 1723 (CO 23/2, part 2, fol. 29). For Cockram, see Henry Pullein to the Board of Trade, April 14, 1714, CO 37/10, fol. 13. For Wishart see chapter 4, note 24. For Robert Brown, see note 99 below.

94. Johnston and Hallet, *Early Colonists of the Bahamas*, 29.
95. Craton and Saunders, *Islanders in the Stream*, 1:122.
96. Deposition of Robert Brown, December 22, 1721, CO 23/1, fol. 55 (from Cork, Ireland); Bahamas Births, Marriages, and Burials, CO 23/2, part 2, fols. 28–29, 124.
97. Deposition of Dorothy Richardson, February 21, 1721, CO 23/2, part 1, fol. 99; Johnston and Hallet, *Early Colonists of the Bahamas*, 3.
98. Deposition of Dorothy Richardson, Bahamas Council Minutes, December 15, 1721, CO 23/13, fol. 313.
99. Kathleen Brown, *Good Wives*, 99–103, 285–86, 306–13.
100. Craton and Saunders, *Islanders in the Stream*, 1:119–26.
101. Jarvis, *In the Eye*, 102–6, 147–50.
102. Johnston and Hallet, *Early Colonists of the Bahamas*, 25, 29, 33, 65, 58.
103. Bialuschewski, "Black People"; Bialuschewski, "Pirates, Black Sailors."
104. Bahamas Council Minutes, May 2, 1723, CO 23/13, fols. 374–75.
105. Johnston and Hallet, *Early Colonists of the Bahamas*, 67; Bahamas Council Minutes, July 9, 1725, CO 23/13, fol. 412.
106. Bahamas Council Minutes, February 19, 1723, CO 23/13, fol. 365.
107. Bahamas Council Minutes, November 3, 1723, August 15 and September 8, 1724, CO 23/13, fols. 386–87, 402–3.
108. The Publick Treasurer's Account of Cash for the Years 1724, 1725, 1726, CO 23/13, fols. 223–24, 241–42, 482–83; Publick Treasurer's Account of Cash for the Years 1727, 1728, CO 23/2, part 2, fols. 2, 48.
109. Minutes of the Bahamas Assembly, September 29, October 8, October 9, 1729, CO 26/2A, fols. 115–18; Minutes of the Bahamas Assembly, November 28, 1734, CO 23/14, fol. 259.
110. Minutes of the Bahamas Assembly, December 24, 1729, CO 26/2A, fol. 8.

111. Bond of Governor Phenney, Samuel Lawford and William Pinder to Peter Goudet, November 29, 1729, CO 23/2, part 2, fols. 231–34; Journals of the Board of Trade, June 3, 1731, in "Journal, June 1731: Journal Book H.H," in Ledward, Journals of the Board of Trade and Plantations, vol. 6, January 1729–December 1734, 204–16; Board of Trade to the Privy Council, June 9, 1731, CSP, vol. 38, no. 222; Great Britain, Privy Council, July 7, 1731, in Grant et al., *Acts of the Privy Council*, 3:317–18.

112. Commission to Peter Goudet, July 5, 1731.

113. Muster List of Captain Palmer's Company, in Great Britain Public Record Office et al., *Records in the British Public Record Office*, 13:196.

114. Bahamas Grand Jury addresses to Gov. Phenney, August 29, 1722, May 24 and August 24, 1724, February 26, 1726, and February 28, 1727, CO 23/13, fols. 83, 501, 503, 505, 507; Bahamas Council Minutes, November 26, 1735, CO 26/2A, fol. 61; Governor, Council, and Grand Jury address to the King, n.d. [ca. March 1723], CO 23/13, fol. 90; Grand Jury Address to Gov. Fitzwilliam, n.d. [ca. 1736], CO 23/3, fol. 205.

115. Court of Oyer and Terminer, Bahamas, March 11, 1719, CO 23/13, fols. 42–45.

116. Court of Common Pleas, Bahamas, February 13, 1722, CO 23/2, part 1, fol. 63.

117. Bahamas Council Minutes, May 29, 1721, and also Thomas Petty and Thomas Terrill to John Bessard, Bond, April 25, 1721, CO 23/1, part 2, fols. 67, 89; Bahamas Court of Admiralty, testimony of Valentine Rodrigo, August 2, 1722, CO 23/13, fol. 120.

118. "List of All Men That Can Bear Arms," December 1727, CO 23/2, part 2, fols. 18–19.

119. Bahamas Council Minutes, December 31, 1721, January 3, 1722, September 5, September 24, and November 26, 1722, CO 23/13, fols. 324–26, 350, 353, 356.

120. Bahamas Council Minutes, December 24, 1721, February 11, 1722, and March 6, 1722, CO 23/13, fols. 323, 332–34.

121. G. Phenney to the Duke of Newcastle, June 20, 1726, Petition of Governor Phenney, the Council, and the regiment to the King, July 26, 1726, and Bahamas Council Minutes, July 13–September 2, 1726, CO 23/13, fols. 428, 431–66; Bahamas Council Minutes, April 26, May 11, May 18, CO 23/14, fols. 80–85.

122. Charles Townshend to the Board of Trade, including his notes on the charges against Phenney, August 13, 1728, Thomas Curphey to Charles Wager, July 24, 1728, Curphey to [Charles Townsend?], June 28, 1728, Edward Hughes to the Duke of Newcastle, July 22, 1728, Memorial of Martha Vere, n.d. [ca. June 1728], Richard Harris to the Board of Trade, August 24, 1728, Cuthbert Jackson to the Board of Trade, September 10, 1728, CO 23/2, part 2, fols. 6–16, 26–30.

123. Bahamas Births, Marriages, and Burials, CO 23/2, part 1, fols. 28–29; Johnston and Hallet, *Early Colonists of the Bahamas*, 22–29.

124. Will of Benjamin Clouge, January 29, 1725, Jamaica Wills, vol. 16, fols. 146–47, Island Record Office, Jamaica; Bahamas Council Minutes, January 2, 1729, CO 23/14, fols. 90–91 (Williams and Terrill); A List of Such Persons Proper to Supply Vacancies in Council, 1721, CO 23/13, fol. 277 (Cockram); John Mouncey's Interview before the Board of Trade, September 3, 1728, in "Journal, September 1728: Journal Book E.E," in Ledward, *Journals of the Board of Trade and Plantations*, vol. 5, January 1723–December 1728 (London: His Majesty's Stationery Office, 1928), 426–28.

125. London, Bethlem Hospital Patient Admission Registers and Casebooks 1683–1932, 229, findmypast.co.uk (accessed April 15, 2023).

126. Bahamas Censuses of 1731 and 1734, in Johnston and Hallet, *Early Colonists of the Bahamas*, 22–41.

127. "Account of taxes per polls and town lots, from Christmas 1736 to the following midsummer," CO 23/4, fol. 39; Deposition of George Raddon, September 10, 1736, CO 23/3, fol. 222; Johnston and Hallet, *Early Colonists of the Bahamas*, 41–49; "An Account of the Taxes per Polls and Lots of Land, from December 1741 to the next Midsummer," CO 23/5, fols. 11–12.

128. Johnston and Hallet, *Early Colonists of the Bahamas*, 51.

129. Ledward, *JBT*, 9:354–69, British History Online.

130. "Account of Taxes per Poll and Lands from Christmas 1744 to Midsummer 1745," CO 23/5, fol. 111; Will of John Thompson, February 18, 1746, and Will of John Blay, June 1, 1758, in Johnston and Hallet, *Early Colonists of the Bahamas*, 58, 79.

131. Storr, "Enterprising Slaves and Master Pirates."

132. Anonymous, *Apology or Vindication*.

133. Bahamas Council Minutes, December 10, 1721, CO 23/13, fols. 294–99.

134. Bahamas Council Minutes, December 14–18, 1721, CO 23/13, fols. 299–317.

135. Bahamas Council Minutes, December 19, 1721, CO 23/13, fols. 318–22.

136. Bahamas Council Minutes, October 7, 1722, and April 14, 1726, CO 23/13, fols. 354, 420.

137. Bahamas Vice Admiralty Court Proceedings against Wyat, Jarvis, Tomkins, and Rodrigo, August 2–4, 1722, CO 23/13, fols. 115–22.

138. Kevin J. Hayes, "Richard Fitzwilliam (d. 1744)," *Dictionary of Virginia Biography*, Library of Virginia, 2018, http://www.lva.virginia.gov/public/dvb/bio.asp?b=Fitzwilliam_Richard.

139. Richard Fitzwilliam to the Board of Trade, September 6, 1734, CO 23/3, fols. 98–99.

140. Fitzwilliam to the Board of Trade, February 10, 1734, and July 2, 1734, CO 23/3, fols. 113–14, 116–17.

141. Richard Fitzwilliam to the Board of Trade, September 6, 1734, CO 23/3, fols. 98–99.

142. Bahamas Council Minutes, February 22, 1734, CO 26/2A, fol. 45.

143. Bahamas Council Minutes, November 8, 1734, CO 26/2A, fol. 52.

144. Shipping Returns, Bahamas, CO 27/12, fols. 62–63; Fitzwilliam to William Yonge, March 25, 1726, CO 23/3, fols. 170–72.

145. Fitzwilliam to the Board of Trade, November 12, 1736, CO 23/3, fols. 218–20; Alured Popple to Francis Fane, February 16, 1737, and Popple to John Scrope, March 9, 1737, CO 24/1, fols. 160–61.

146. Craton and Saunders, *Islanders in the Stream*, 1:114.

147. This description derives from the author's visit to Nassau in February 2019. See the websites for Pirates of Nassau (http://www.piratesofnassau.com) and Pirate Republic Brewing Company (https://www.piraterepublicbahamas.com) for online presentations of these two sites.

Chapter 6. A Pirate's Life No More

1. Board of Trade and Secretaries of State, America and West Indies, Original Correspondence, South Carolina, Shipping Returns, 1716–1719 and 1721–1735, CO 5/508, fols. 62, 68; James Fasset to James Whippo, Power of Attorney, August 19, 1718, recorded November 7, 1718, New York, Wills and Deeds, 28:452, familysearch.org.

2. Crews of the *Sea Nymph, Mediterranean Galley, King William,* and *Revenge* to Fayrer Hall, Letter of Administration, December 17, 1718, South Carolina, Records of the Secretary and Register of the Province, 1714–19, 276–280, microfilm reel 0756, familysearch.org.

3. *Boston Gazette,* June 20, 1720; *New England Courant,* January 1, 1722; *Boston News Letter,* April 11, 1723.

4. Will of James Fasset, August 1, 1720, Massachusetts, Wills and Probate, 1635–1991, Suffolk County Probate Records, 12:400, ancestry.com.

5. James Fasset v. Thomas Glen, January 17, 1723, Massachusetts, Suffolk County, Court Files, vol. 151, case no. 17054, familysearch.org.

6. Letter of Administration to George Skinner, April 26, 1723, Letter of Attachment to Thomas Glen, April 29, 1723, Deposition of William Mayle, May 6, 1723, Deposition of George Berwick, May 27, 1723, Depositions of Stephen Pearkes and Benjamin Gallop, June 10, 1723, Letter of Administration to Mark Potts, June 17, 1723, Suffolk County, Mass. Inventories, 12:401–3; Deposition of George Skinner, April 25, 1723, James Fasset, Estate Inventory, February 26, 1724, and George Skinner, Administrator's Account for James Fasset, June 6, 1724, Massachusetts, Wills and Probate, 1635–1991, Suffolk County Probate Records, 23:117, 261–62, box 27, case no. 4729, ancestry.com.

7. Pearse to Burchett, March 4, 1718, ADM 1/2282, TNA; Admiralty: Captains' Logs, *Phoenix,* entries for February 24 and March 4, 1718, ADM 51/690, TNA.

8. Governor Robert Johnson, Pardon to James Harding, Edward Chaviler, Oliver Vapier, John Rogers, John Alberson, John Lewis, Philip Dawharty, Andrew Foster, James Whitlock, Joseph Binks, and Anthony Faz, February 6, 1718, South Carolina Miscellaneous Records, Charleston County, 1716–1721, 29, familysearch.org.

9. Robert Johnson, Pardon of Daniel Arowsmith and Francis Charnock, April 7, 1718, South Carolina Miscellaneous Records, Charleston County, 1716–1721, 33.

10. Robert Johnson, Pardon to Othenias Davis, Thomas Reynolds, Marmaduke Ge[e], Samuel Richardson, James Gartrick, Robert Hawks, and Benjamin Turner, June 30, 1718, South Carolina Miscellaneous Records, Charleston County, 1716–1721, 38.

11. Robert Johnson, Pardon to Thomas Emly, Richard Legat, John Eling, Edmond Berry, and John Osborn, July 10, 1718, South Carolina Miscellaneous Records, Charleston County, 1716–1721, 39.

12. Shipping Returns, South Carolina, CO 5/508, fols. 43, 48, 52; Colonial Office: Jamaica, Miscellanea, Shipping Returns, 1680–1705, CO 142/14, fol. 69.

13. Shipping Returns, South Carolina, CO 5/508, fol. 67.

14. Colonial Office and Predecessors: Barbados, Miscellaneous, Shipping and Other Returns, 1708–1726, CO 33/15, fol. 105.

15. *Boston News Letter,* June 2 and July 28, 1718.

16. Shipping Returns, South Carolina, CO 5/508, fols. 51, 62, 66.

17. Robert Johnson, Pardon to Thomas Emly, Richard Legat, John Eling, Edmond

Berry, and John Osborn, July 10, 1718, South Carolina Miscellaneous Records, Charleston County, 1716–1721, 39; Crews of the Sea Nymph, Mediterranean Galley, King William, and Revenge to Fayrer Hall, Letter of Administration, December 17, 1718, South Carolina, Records of the Secretary and Register of the Province, 1714–19, 276–80.

18. Virginia Council Journal, April 30 and May 12, 1718, in McIlwaine, *Executive Journals*, 466–67, 469.

19. Ship Pay Books, *Phoenix*, ADM 51/298, fols. 11–12.

20. *Boston News Letter*, April 7, April 21, April 28, and May 19, 1718.

21. Church of England, Kingston Parish Burials, 1:10, 91 (Dunkin and Williamson); London, Church of England Records of Baptisms, Marriages, and Burials, 1538–1812, Kingston Parish Baptisms, 1:1, 11 (Austin); Church of England, Kingston Parish Marriages, 1:1 (Crew), ancestry.com.

22. Church of England, St. Michael Parish, Barbados, Births, Marriages, Burials, 1702–1739, 216, 308; John Smith v. Jeffrey Grey, December 19, 1720, Bermuda Court of Assizes, Book of Actions, AZ101–3, 44, familysearch.org.

23. Shipping Returns, South Carolina, CO 5/509, fols. 42, 47; Shipping Returns, Bahamas, CO 23/13, fols. 250, 260; Salley, *Register of St. Phillips Parish*, 235.

24. Thames Watermen and Lightmen, 1688–2010, Binding Records, 1692–1949, January 3, 1706 (Trouton) and May 21, 1708 (Adams), findmypast.co.uk (accessed April 16, 2021).

25. Ships' Pay Books, *Blandford*, ADM 33/293/6.

26. Lords Proprietors of South Carolina, Order to Charles Craven, February 23, 1716, CO 5/290, fol. 44.

27. Breage, Cornwall Parish Registers, in England Births and Christenings, 1538–1975, familysearch.org (accessed April 16, 2021).

28. New York Court of General Sessions, August 1695, 2:7, familysearch.org; Oliver, *Caribbeana*, 172; Memorial of Peter Melotte, https://www.findagrave.com/memorial/166095115/peter-mellotte (accessed April 16, 2021).

29. Estate Inventory of William Rouse, February 11, 1721, Middlesex County, Mass. Deeds, 16:217–19.

30. Elizabeth Mitchell, William Montfort, and Joseph York, Power of Attorney to James Nichols, June 3, 1718, Document 1, Colonial Court Records, North Carolina State Archives Digital Collections.

31. Joseph Lampson v. Elizabeth Mitchell, July 1719, in Massachusetts, Middlesex County, Clerk of Courts, Court Papers, fols. 111X–120X, FOL. 113X, familysearch.org.

32. Mitchell et al. vs. Edward Mayo, 1722–1724, Documents 2–16, Colonial Court Records, North Carolina State Archives Digital Collections.

33. Attachment of Elizabeth Mitchell, October 5, 1727, and Mitchell's response of December 12, 1727, in Middlesex County, Clerk of Courts, Court Papers, fols. 75X–110X, FOL. 108X.

34. *Boston News Letter*, September 23, 1717.

35. Bahamas Court of Vice Admiralty, case of the *St. Martin* of Bordeaux, September 1–5, 1718, included in the letters of Capt. Peter Chamberlain, ADM 1/1597, TNA.

36. Shipping Returns, Massachusetts, CO 5/848, fol. 61; *Boston News Letter*, January 7 and August 27, 1717.

37. Captain's Log Book of the *Shark*, entry for July 26, 1718, Captain's Logs, ADM 51/892; Bahamas Court of Vice Admiralty, case of the *St. Martin* of Bordeaux.

38. Great Britain, Privy Council, May 26 and November 25, 1719, in Grant et al., *Acts of the Privy Council*, 2:760–61.

39. Robert Johnson, Pardon of Charles Yates, William Tinsley, Thomas Winbourn, John South, John Mounsey, Francis Carter, Peter Legront, David Stephens, and Henry Hambliton, September 10, 1718, in South Carolina Miscellaneous Records, Charleston County, 1716–1721, 41–42.

40. Schonhorn, *General History of the Pyrates*, 135–47; Jamaica, Court of Vice-Admiralty, *The Trials of John Rackham and Other Pyrates* (Jamaica: Robert Baldwin, 1721), Colonial Office and Predecessors: Jamaica, Correspondence, Original—Board of Trade, Q. nos. 1–103, 1721–1724, CO 137/14, 36–40, fols. 27–30; Petition of William Margarritte, n.d. [ca. 1721], T 1/233, 25, TNA.

41. Robert Johnson, Pardon of Charles Yates, William Tinsley, Thomas Winbourn, John South, John Mounsey, Francis Carter, Peter Legront, David Stephens, and Henry Hambliton; Board of Trade Journals, September 3, 1728, in Ledward, *JBT*, 5:426–28.

42. Depositions of John King, July 22, 1719, and Thomas Stone, September 19, 1719, High Court of Admiralty, Instance and Prize Courts: Examinations and Answers, HCA 13/136, TNA.

43. Schonhorn, *General History of the Pyrates*, 145–46; Jamaica, Church of England, Kingston Parish Burials, 1722–74, 1:86.

44. Virginia Council Journals, December 9, 1718, and March 11, 1719, in McIlwaine, *Executive Journals*, 495, 497.

45. David Wilson, "From the Caribbean to Craignish"; Graham, *Seawolves*, 47–60.

46. *London Journal*, January 21, 1721; David Wilson, "From the Caribbean to Craignish," 459n100.

47. Deposition of Walter Canaday, April 21, 1721, HCA 1/54, fols. 121–22.

48. Shipping returns, Barbados, CO 33/15, fols. 48–49; Deposition of Richard Taylor, August 4, 1718, CO 23/1, fol. 42; Pennsylvania Council Minutes, February 22, 1718, in Hazard, *Minutes*, 3:28; *Boston News Letter*, September 10 and December 31, 1716, March 11, May 13, and July 8, 1717, and March 17, 1718. However, two Richard Taylors circulated in the Bahamas at that time, the other being a man who signed articles aboard a wrecking vessel in New York. See New York Council Minutes, September 3, 1718, Board of Trade and Secretaries of State. America and West Indies, Original Correspondence. New York, Sessional Papers, 1713–1720, CO 5/1186, fols. 102–4.

49. Ships' Pay Books, *Shark Sloop*, ADM 33/318.

50. Bialuschewski, "Blackbeard off Philadelphia," 177; William Hamilton to the Board of Trade, December 19, 1718, and enclosed depositions, *CSP*, vol. 30, nos. 797–797(vi), British History Online.

51. Deposition of John Matthews, October 12, 1722, HCA 1/55, fol. 20.

52. Depositions of Clement Downing and Gyles Neal, October 28, 1724, HCA 1/55, fols. 92–93.

53. Depositions by Richard Lazinby, n.d. [ca. October 1723], India Office Records, BL IOR-E-1-13, fols. 163–77.

54. Schonhorn, *General History of the Pyrates*, 114–34; *London Post Boy*, April 22 and 25, 1721; Downing, *Compendious History*, 44–47.

55. Deposition of Richard Moore, October 31, 1724, HCA 1/55, fols. 94–97.

56. Unknown to Humphrey Morrice, May 23, 1723, IOR-E-1–13, fol. 298.

57. Snelgrave, *New Account*, 271–72.

58. Brooks, *Jacob de Bucquoy*, 11–25.

59. Earle, *Pirate Wars*, 166. Earle misidentifies him as "John Taylor."

60. Deposition of Richard Moore, October 31, 1724, HCA 1/55, fols. 94–97.

61. "Petition of the Pirates on Board the Cassandra" to Capt. John Laws, April 10, 1723, CO 137/14, fol. 314.

62. Captain Laws's Letter to the Pirates, n.d. [ca. April 10, 1723], CO 137/14, fol. 315.

63. John Laws to the Duke of Portland, May 5, 1723, with enclosed Petition of the Pirates, April 26, 1723, and the Duke of Portland to Laws, May 29, 1723, CO 137/14, fols. 315–17.

64. Barrow Harris to Josiah Burchett, July 16, 1723, SP 42/17/281; Geronimo Badillo to the Duke of Portland, October 5, 1723, CO 137/14, fol. 321.

65. Extracts of two letters by Capt. Jeremy Pearce and Capt. James Pearce to Humphrey Morrice, July 4 and 19, 1723, IOR-E-1–13, fol. 299.

66. Laws to the Pirates, May 6, 1723, Laws to the Duke of Portland, June 4, 1723, Richard Taylor to Laws, May 14, 1723, Laws to the Governor of Panama, May 31, 1723, Laws to the Governor of Portobello, May 5, 1723, Laws to the Governor of Panama, June 3, 1723, Duke of Portland to the Governor of Panama, n.d. [ca. June 1723], and the Governor of Panama to the Duke of Portland, October 5, 1723, CO 137/14, fols. 317–21; Barrow Harris to Secretary Burchett, June 16–17, 1723, SP 42/17, fol. 601, TNA; Earle, *Pirate Wars*, 125–26; Schonhorn, *General History of the Pyrates*, 134; Brooks, *Jacob de Bucquoy*, 22–23.

67. Snelgrave, *New Account*, 257–59.

68. New York Council Minutes, October 28, 1718, CO 5/1186, fols. 190–91.

69. John Lewis to Love West, Promissory Note, December 10, 1719, Bermuda, Bonds, Bills, Deeds, Protests, Grants, etc., book 6, 1713–21, 313.

70. Ships' Pay Books, *Flamborough*, ADM 33/299.

71. *Boston News Letter*, September 5, 1720; *Boston Gazette*, October 17, 1720.

72. Will of William Joell, August 13, 1719, Bermuda, Book of Wills, vol. 6, part 1, 52.

73. John Lewis v. William Martindale, March 2–3, 1721, Bermuda Court of Assizes, Book of Actions, AZ101/3, 50; Lewis v. Martindale, May 19, 1721, Bermuda Court of Assizes, Proceedings, AZ102/5, 67–68; Samuel Smith, John and Mary Lewis against William Dunscombe, July 28, 1721, Bermuda Court of Assizes, Book of Actions, AZ101/3, 56; Named as Juror, December 5, 1721, Bermuda Court of Assizes, Proceedings, AZ102/5, 79.

74. Lewis v. Thomas Joell, February 19, 1722 (two cases), Bermuda Court of Assizes, Book of Actions, AZ101/3, 74.

75. Florentius Cox et al., Coroner's Report, March 20, 1722, Bermuda Bonds, Bills, Deeds, Grants, etc., book 7, 56; Lieutenant Governor John Hope to the Board of Trade, March 26, 1722, CO 37/10, fols. 183–84.

76. Trial of John Lewis, June 4–7, 1722, Bermuda Court of Assizes, Proceedings, AZ102/5, 104–13.

77. Petition of Mary Lewis to the King, January 28, 1723, CO 37/26, fol. 130; Will of Samuel Smith, March 25, 1729, Bermuda Book of Wills, vol. 6, part 2, 231–37.

78. South Carolina Court of Vice-Admiralty, *Tryals of Major Stede Bonnet*; Records of the Vice-Admiralty Court of South Carolina, October 28–November 12, 1718, books A–B, part I, fols. 234–98; Woodard, *Republic of Pirates*, 298–300; Earle, *Pirate Wars*, 192–93; Hanna, *Pirate Nests*, 389–90; Rediker, *Villains of All Nations*, 100–101, 129–30.

79. Hall, *Importance of the British Plantations*.

80. (Richard Rawlins) Crew of the *Henry*, Conveyance to John Masters, December 17, 1718, and (Edward Berry) Crew of the *Sea Nymph*, Conveyance to Fayrer Hall, December 17, 1718, and South Carolina Records of the Secretary and Register of the Province 1714–1719, 252–55, 263–65. Accessible at familysearch.org, DGS #8688781.

81. South Carolina Court of Vice-Admiralty, *Trials of Major Stede Bonnet*, iv–v.

82. Schonhorn, *General History of the Pyrates*, 301.

83. Jamaica Council Minutes, October 26, 1716, CO 140/13, 1005; New York Council Minutes, September 3, 1718, CO 5/1186, fols. 102–4.

84. South Carolina, Court of Vice-Admiralty, November 19–24, 1718, book A-B, PART 1, 291–98.

85. (Richard Rawlins) Crew of the *Henry*, Conveyance to John Masters, December 17, 1718, and (Edward Berry) Crew of the *Sea Nymph*, Conveyance to Fayrer Hall, December 17, 1718, and South Carolina Records of the Secretary and Register of the Province 1714–1719, 252–55, 263–65.

86. Crews of the *Sea Nymph*, *Mediterranean Galley*, and *King William*, Conveyance to John Masters and to Fayrer Hall, December 17, 1718, South Carolina, Records of the Secretary and Register of the Province, 1714–1719, 259–62, 276–81.

87. William Rhett to the Lords of Treasury, n.d. [ca. 1719], T 1/200, fols. 177–79; Anthony Cacherode to the Lords of Treasury, June 20, 1719, T 1/220, fols. 27–30; A. Cacherode to the Lords of Treasury, March 18, 1720, T 1/227, fols. 134–36; A. Cacherode to the Lords of Treasury, August 27, 1723, T 1/244, fols. 73–74, all from Treasury Board Papers and In-Letters, TNA; Privy Council Order, August 24, 1721, in Grant et al., *Acts of the Privy Council*, 3:23–24.

88. South Carolina, Court of Vice-Admiralty, November 19 to December 26, 1718, book A-B, PART 2, 304–444; from Court of Common Pleas, Judgment Rolls, 1703–1790, SCDAH, SEE John Mason, Lionel Wood, John Smith, and John Howard v. Thomas Bee, 1719, box 11B, NO. 10A; Mason et al. v. George Duckat, February 12, 1719, box 11B, N. 55A; Smith et al. v. James Jones, March 11, 1719, box 11B, NO. 98A; Smith et al. v. James Mazyck, February–March, 1719, box 12A, N. 110A.

89. Deposition of William South, May 10, 1719, CO 23/1, fol. 59.

90. South Carolina Vice-Admiralty Proceedings, August 11–19, 1719, South Carolina Court of Vice Admiralty, book A-B, PART 2, 446–55.

91. Othenias Davis and Thomas Porter to William Gibbon and Andrew Allen, Power of Attorney, n.d. [ca. September 1719], South Carolina Miscellaneous Records, microfilm reel 501A, FOLS. 113–14, SCDAH.

92. Othenias Davis v. Robert Hawkins, June 21, 1720, Davis (attorney for Robert In-

gersoll) v. Richard Richards, July 29, 1720, Davis v. Peter Johnson, July 29, 1720, and Davis v. John Shackleford, in North Carolina Wills and Probate Records, 1665–1998, Chowan County, Suits Dismissed and Court Papers, 1712–1724, images 359–60, 462, Ancestry.com (accessed December 7, 2020).

93. *Boston Gazette*, October 17, 1720.

94. Ships' Pay Books, *Milford*, ADM 33/310; *Shark Sloop*, ADM 33/318; *Flamborough*, ADM 33/299; *Pearl*, ADM 33/311.

95. Bahamas Council Minutes, February 28–29, 1724, CO 23/13, fol. 393.

96. Writ of Attachment for William Cooper (or Cope), October 27, 1724, North Carolina Wills and Probate Records, 1665–1998, Chowan County, Suits Dismissed and Court Papers, Suits Dismissed 1695–1725, image 359.

97. Records of the Proceedings of the Vestry of St. Paul's Church Edenton, N.C., 1701–1841, 54, 61–62, 67. NCDAH, familysearch.org (accessed June 2, 2021).

98. Complaint of Bartholomew and Margaret Scott, July 1726, and Attachment of William Williams, June 8, 1726, in North Carolina Wills and Probate Records, 1665–1998, Chowan County, Suits Dismissed and Court Papers, Suits Dismissed 1714–1728, reel 18565, image 52.

99. Attachment of William Williams and William Rowden to answer John Bole, December 7, and William Williams and William Rowden, Bond to Robert Hicks, Provost Marshal, December 8, 1726, North Carolina Wills and Probate Records, 1665–1998, Chowan County, Suits Dismissed and Court Papers, Suits Dismissed 1721–30, images 52–54.

100. Minutes of the General Court of North Carolina, March 28, 1727–April 5, 1727, in Saunders, *Colonial Records of North Carolina*, 2:695–96.

101. Attachment of William Mullers, July 24, 1732, and Williams's Complaint of October 1732, in North Carolina Wills and Probate Records, 1665–1998, Chowan County, Suits Dismissed and Court Papers, 1721–34, image 36.

102. Williams's minor offices can be chronicled in (as Grand Juror) Minutes of the General Court of North Carolina, March 30, 1725–April 7, 1725, (as head of the Powder Office) Minutes of the Lower House of North Carolina, April 5, 1726–April 13, 1726, in Saunders, *Colonial Records of North Carolina*, 585–90, 608–24; (as constable) Writ of Attachment for William Cooper (or Cope), October 27, 1724, in North Carolina Wills and Probate Records, 1665–1998, Chowan County, Suits Dismissed and Court Papers, 1695–1725, image 359.

103. Will of William Williams, May 7, 1730, proved December 20, 1732, North Carolina Secretary of State, Wills vol. 3, 1722–1735, 264.

104. Attachment of Frances Williams, to answer the charges of Samuel Lawford, June 19, 1736, in North Carolina Digital Collections, Colonial Court Records; Attachment of Frances Williams, to answer the charges of Susannah Everard, November 3, 1736, in North Carolina Wills and Probate Records, 1665–1998, Chowan County, Suits Dismissed and Court Papers, 1731–1738 (no. 007639583), image 4, ancestry.com (accessed December 9, 2020).

105. Nugent, *Cavaliers and Pioneers*, 132; Tyler, "Old Tombstones in Gloucester County," 253–55.

106. A report from Boston indicated the arrival of one "John Verin" from Virginia.

As there were no ship captains from Virginia with that name, it was likely a misspelling of "Perrin." See *Boston News Letter*, June 7, 1708.

107. Shipping Returns, Virginia, CO 5/1442, fol. 6.

108. Virginia, York County, Wills and Orders, vol. 15, 1716–1720, 627; Virginia, York County Wills, Orders, 19:258, 304, 432, 446, 454, 472.

109. *Virginia Gazette*, January 14 and 21, 1736, January 13 and 20, October 21 and 28, November 11, December 9, 16, 23, and 30, 1737, November 23, 1738, June 22 and 29, 1739, April 18, October 31, and November 7, 1745; *Pennsylvania Gazette*, May 9, 1745; *New York Gazette*, September 19, 1748; *New York Weekly Herald*, October 24, 1748.

110. Board of Trade and Secretaries of State, America and West Indies, Original Correspondence, Virginia, Shipping Returns, 1726–1735, CO 5/1443, fols. 52, 80–81, 103–4, 110–14, 135–37; Board of Trade and Secretaries of State, America and West Indies, Original Correspondence, Virginia, Shipping Returns, 1715–1727, CO 5/1442, fols. 3–5, 7–10, 15, 26, 29, 38, 49.

111. Historic American Buildings Survey, Little England, State Route 672 vicinity, Bena, Gloucester County, Virginia, Documentation compiled after 1933, photograph, https://www.loc.gov/item/va0462/.

112. *Records of Colonial Gloucester County, Virginia*, 2:121.

113. "Virginia SP Little England," National Register of Historic Places, RG 79, Records of the National Park Service, reference no. 70000795, National Archives Catalog, https://catalog.archives.gov/id/41680912.

114. *Boston News Letter*, July 9, 1719, May 30, 1720, March 13, April 3, June 26, and November 3, 1729, September 24 and December 31, 1730, June 3 and 28, 1731, February 3, 1732, June 21, 1733; *Boston Gazette*, March 13 and May 15, 1727; *New England Weekly Journal*, April 7 and September 30, 1729, July 9, 1733, January 21, 1734; *Boston Weekly Rehearsal*, May 29, 1732.

115. *Boston News Letter*, December 21, 1719, December 12, 1720, September 17 and October 15, 1722, May 27, 1723, September 10, 1724, July 19, 1725; *New England Courant*, December 4, 1721, September 17 and October 15, 1722; Shipping Returns, Leeward Islands—Antigua, CO 157/1, fols. 63, 88–89.

116. *Boston News Letter*, May 12, 1718; Will of William Rouse, June 26, 1718, in Middlesex County (Mass.) Probate Papers, 19436–19539, no. 19533.

117. Shipping Returns, Massachusetts, CO 5/848, fols. 97, 113; *Boston News Letter*, June 9, October 6, December 8, 1718, July 4, 1720, May 14, 1722, April 11, 1723, April 9, 1724; *American Weekly Mercury*, May 12 and June 16, 1720, August 30, 1722, October 4 and December 10, 1723, May 7, 1724; *Boston Gazette*, August 22, October 3 and 17, 1720, September 10, 1722, April 7, May 9 and 25, 1724; *New England Courant*, May 14 and June 4, 1722, April 8, 1723.

118. Massachusetts Court of Vice Admiralty, Cox, Adams, and Wood v. Joshua Norman, December 22, 1720, Suffolk County, Vice Admiralty Records, vol. 2, fol. 66.

119. *Boston News Letter*, July 21, 1718, September 12 and November 21, 1720, March 20 and April 10, 1721, August 6 and September 10, 1722, February 14, May 2, and June 13, 1723.

120. Fiske, *Gleanings from Newport Court Files*, case no. 104.

121. Patrick Gould to Isaac Hobhouse, January 4, 1723, in Minchinton, *Trade of Bristol*, 83–84.

122. St. Michael Parish, Barbados, Baptisms, Marriages, Burials, vol. 3, 1702–1739, 39, 55, 216, 308; 1715 Barbados Census, St. Michael Parish, CO 28/16, fol. 213.

123. Kingston Parish, Jamaica, Marriages, 1721–1825, 1:1–2; Kingston Parish, Jamaica, Baptisms, 1722–1779, 1:5; Kingston Parish, Jamaica, Burials, 1722–1774, 1:10, 25, 29, 32, 39–40.

124. Will of William Rouse, June 26, 1718; William Rouse to John Foy, Conveyance, June 30, 1718, Middlesex County, Mass. Deeds, 20:57; William Keen to William Rouse, Conveyance, April 29, 1719, Middlesex County, Mass. Deeds, 20:287–288.

125. Estate Inventory of William Rouse, February 11, 1721, in Middlesex County (Mass.) Probate Papers, 19436–19539, no. 19533.

126. Thomas Newton et al., Executors of William Rouse to William Wyer and Samuel Carey, Conveyance, April 29, 1721, in Middlesex County (Mass.) Deeds, 21:320–21.

127. Mary Rouse to Charles Foxcroft, Middlesex County Probate Judge, November 22, 1722, with attached inventory, in Middlesex County (Mass.) Probate Papers, 19436–19539, no. 19533.

128. Mary Rouse to John Rouse, Conveyance, November 2, 1737, in Middlesex County (Mass.) Deeds, 39:536–37; Solomon and Catherine Phipps, Stephen and Mary Ford, and William Rouse Jr. to John Rouse, Conveyance, January 17, 1738, in Middlesex County (Mass.) Deeds, 39:537; Jonathan Remington, Commission to Thomas Jenners, Stephen Hall, Isaac Parker, Joseph Phillips, and Thomas Syms, November 2, 1737, and the Commission's Assessment of the Rouse Estate, November 24, 1737, in Middlesex County (Mass.) Probate Papers, 19436–19539, no. 19533.

129. Charlestown, Mass., Archives Births Marriages Deaths, 1629–1800, in Massachusetts, U.S., Town and Vital Records, 1620–1988, 599, ancestry.com; Coss, *Fever of 1721*.

130. Charlestown, Mass., Archives Births Marriages Deaths, 1629–1800, 193, 200, 204, 207, 213, 215, 220, 228, 265, 419, 433, 458, images 156, 160, 162–63, 166–67, 170, 174, 191, 269, 276, 289; Joseph Collier and Mary Ford, Bans of November 20, 1742, Charlestown, Marriage Intentions, vol. 1, 1725–1826, image 26, in Massachusetts, U.S., Town and Vital Records, 1620–1988; Hunnewell, *Records of the First Church*, 163.

131. William Harris et al. v. Capt. Price, April 11, 1729, Mass. Court of Admiralty (Suffolk County), Court Records and Account Books, 1718–72, fol. 62, familysearch.org.

132. Deposition of Samuel Boyce, August 21, 1727, in Suffolk County (Mass.) Probate Records, 16:19.

133. (As petit juror) July 6, 1725, Suffolk Co. Inferior Court of Common Plea Records, 1725–1728, 1; Copp v. Boies, October 1727, Suffolk County (Mass.) Court Files, case no. 20732, vol. 180, fol. 108; Leahy v. Ledbetter, n.d. [ca. 1729], Suffolk County (Mass.) Court Files, case no. 27978, vol. 214, fol. 127.

134. Letter of Administration, Samuel and Abigail Boyce, April 9, 1729, Suffolk County (Mass.) Court Files, case no. 22670, vol. 195, fol. 51.

304 NOTES TO CHAPTERS SIX AND SEVEN

135. Samuel and Abigail Boyce to Edward Tillet, Conveyance, April 9, 1729, Suffolk County (Mass.) Deeds, vol. 43, fols. 146–47.
136. Nicholas Bowes, attorney for Samuel and Abigail Boyce to Joseph Prout, Treasurer of the Town of Boston, November. 1, 1736, Suffolk County (Mass.) Deeds, vol. 53, fol. 156.
137. Richards v. Samuel Holland, n.d. [ca. 1726], Suffolk County (Mass.), Court of Common Pleas Records, 1725–1728, 166–67; Richards v. Nathaniel Fadre, April 24, 1730, Suffolk County (Mass.) Court of Common Pleas Records, 1728–1730, 511.
138. John and Mary Richards to Joseph Grafton, Conveyance, November 30, 1727, Essex County (Mass.) Deeds, vol. 50, fol. 5.
139. John Richards et al. to Thomas Hutchinson, Conveyance, September 21, 1731, Suffolk County (Mass.) Deeds, vol. 46, fols. 80–81.
140. Benjamin Alford to John Richards, Conveyance, September 5, 1732, Essex County (Mass.) Deeds, vol. 49, fol. 55.
141. Lynn: Vital Record Transcripts, 580, Massachusetts, U.S. Town and Vital Records, 1620–1988; Tuller, "American Family History."
142. Mary Richards to Ebenezer Newhouse, Conveyance, March 16, 1734, Essex County (Mass.) Deeds, 64:149; Tuller, "American Family History."

Chapter 7. The Respectable Pirates of New York

1. Deposition of William Smith, May 31, 1718, New York Colony Council Papers, 61:30, NYSA.
2. Deposition of William Smith, June 3, 1718, New York Council Papers, 61:77.
3. Deposition of William Smith, June 9, 1718, New York Council Papers, 61:79; Board of Trade and Secretaries of State, America and West Indies, Original Correspondence, New York, Shipping Returns, 1713–1722, CO 5/1222, fols. 48, 61, 80, 90, 117, 131.
4. Goodfriend, *Before the Melting Pot*, 31–37, 82.
5. Goodfriend, 91, 142–43.
6. Goodfriend, 66.
7. Archdeacon, *New York City*, 61–64.
8. New York Court of General Sessions for August 1695 and February 2, 1697, 2:7, 19; Will of John Peter Melotte, January 30, 1703, in William Nelson, *Documents*, 314–15; "John Peter Melotte," https://www.findagrave.com/memorial/54941879/john_peter-malott; "Mary Melotte New," https://www.findagrave.com/memorial/166109094/mary_new.
9. Scott, "Jacob Leisler's Fifty Militiamen," 67, 69; New Amsterdam Reformed Dutch Church Baptisms, 1682–1689, Brooklyn Genealogical Society, https://brooklynancestry.com/new-amsterdam-reformed-dutch-church-baptisms-1682-1689/.
10. Otto and Aeltyans Grim to Jan Sipken, Lease and Release, June 2, 1679, New York, Wills and Deeds, 5:181–182, familysearch.org.
11. Selyns, *Records of Domine Henricus Selyns*, 12, 17.
12. Scott, "Jacob Leisler's Fifty Militiamen," 67, 69.
13. New-York Historical Society, *Tax Lists*, 19, 54, 72, 149, 199.

14. Sypher, *Liber A*, 21, 171, 175, 287.

15. N.Y. Court of General Sessions, Minute Books, 1683–1731, 3:17, familysearch.org.

16. Minutes of the Supreme Court of Judicature, *Collections of the New York Historical Society for the Year 1912* (New York: Printed for the Society, 1913), 123; New York Council Minutes for November 27, 1700, in *New York Calendar of Council Minutes, 1683–1786*, New York State Library Bulletin no. 58 (Albany: State University of New York, 1902), 151.

17. P. D. Smith, 1703 Census of New York City, August 23, 1998. http://files.usgwarchives.net/ny/newyork/census/1703/1703-nyc.txt.

18. *Boston News Letter*, March 17, 1711, January 12 and 26, May 30, June 9 and 30, July 7, 1712; Colonial Office: Jamaica, Miscellanea, Shipping Returns, 1680–1705, dates unknown [ca. 1705–1728, 1729–1753], December 1713, CO 142/14, frames 463, 481.

19. *Boston News Letter*, January 16 and 30, March 12 and 26, September 4 and 10, 1716.

20. C. E. Long, Jamaica Wills and Marriages, fol. 7, Add Ms 21921, British Library; Petition of Amerens Stout, June 19, 1700, in *Calendar of New York Colonial Manuscripts: Endorsed Land Papers, 1643–1803* (Albany: Weed, Parsons, 1864), 53.

21. Lilliard, *Stout Family*.

22. Letter of Administration to Thomas Wenham, April 20, 1699, with accompanying letter from John Stout, in Keller and Pelletreau, *Abstracts of Wills*, 25:305; Shipping Returns, Jamaica, September 1698–December 1699, CO 142/13, frames 259–60.

23. New-York Historical Society, *Collections . . . 1885*, 616.

24. Stout was admitted as a freeman as a barber on February 12, 1717. New-York Historical Society, *Collections . . . 1885*, 96.

25. Shipping Returns, New York, CO 5/1222, 44, 126.

26. Lilliard, *Stout Family*.

27. Shipping Returns, New York, CO 5/1222, 141, 148.

28. Richie, *Captain Kidd and the War*, 33–55, 112–26; McDonald, *Pirates, Merchants, Settlers, and Slaves*, 37–55.

29. Shipping Returns, Jamaica, ca. 1713, CO 142/14, frame 463.

30. Foote, *Black and White Manhattan*, 130–40; Huth, "Slave Revolt of 1712."

31. *New York Genealogical and Biographical* Society, "Register Book," 53.

32. James Riker Jr., *Annals of Newtown*, 334–38.

33. *New York Genealogical and Biographical* Society, "New York Marriage Licenses," 7.

34. *New York Genealogical and Biographical* Society, "Records of the Reformed Dutch Church of New York—Marriages," 188, and "Records of the Reformed Dutch Church of New York—Baptisms," 171.

35. Thomas Palmer, "Vessels Cleared Out from the Customs Office of New York for Curacao, 25 March 1698 to 17 August, 1698," William Blathwayt Papers, vol. 8, folder 8, familysearch.org.

36. *Boston News Letter*, March 12, June 11, November 19, 1705, May 13, June 3, 1706, and July 21, 1707.

37. Slave Voyages Database, Voyage ID 21334.

38. *Boston News Letter*, November 19, 1705, May 13, 1706, July 21, 1707.

39. *Boston News Letter*, March 5, 1710, March 10, September 10, November 26, December 3, 1711, October 5, 1713.

40. John Stout to Benjamin Bill, Conveyance, September 8, 1716, Richmond County, New York, Wills and Deeds, C:155–57, familysearch.org; Historical Records Survey, *Earliest Volume of Staten Island Records*, 131; Clute, *Annals of Staten Island*, 167; Davis et al., *Church of St. Andrew*, 70; New-York Historical Society, "Colonial Commissions," 32; List of Jurors, September 3, 1717, New York, Richmond County Court of General Sessions Records, 23.

41. Gov. Ellis Lightwood, Order to Benjamin Bill, William Lince, and Daniel Cock, December 28, 1702, Massachusetts State Archives Collection, 62:424, familysearch.org.

42. Shipping Returns, New York, CO 5/1222, fol. 57.

43. Shipping Returns, New York, fol. 141.

44. Will of Edmund Pinfold, January 4, 1657, Prerogative Court of Canterbury, Wills, PROB 11/289/356, fols. 381–82, TNA; City of London, Haberdashers, Apprentices, and Freemen, 1526–1923, fols. 97, 103, 156, 159, 235, findmypast.co.uk (accessed March 22, 2021); Church of England, St. Sepulchre (London) Church Registers, April 29, 1683, findmypast.co.uk (accessed March 22, 2021).

45. Shipping Returns, New York, CO 5/1222, fol. 44.

46. Shipping Returns, New York, fols. 48, 61, 80, 90, 117, 131, 208.

47. David M. Riker, "Genealogy"; Charles A. Nelson, *Minutes*, 181, 210.

48. John Frost Deposition, July 15, 1717, NYHS.

49. William Smith to William Stroud, Bond, September 17, 1709, Bermuda Colonial Records, vol. 9, 1677–1713 (deeds, bonds, receipts, letters of attorney, acts, orders from London), 13–14; Bermuda Court Records, Book of Actions, Cox v. Smith, November 11, 1712, AZ101/2, 319; Shipping Returns, New York, CO 5/1222, fol. 46; Shipping Returns, Barbados, CO 33/15, fols. 43, 50, 59–60; Peter Courant to William Smith and Joseph Young, Sailing Orders for the sloop *Love*, June 12, 1717, Bermuda Deeds, book 6, 164.

50. Shipping Returns, New York, CO 5/1222, fols. 197–98, 228, 234.

51. Depositions of William Connor and Thomas Nichols, June 3, 1718, New York Colony Council Papers, 61:71–73, NYSA.

52. *Boston News Letter*, October 17, 1717 (Nichols), and November 4, 1717 (Sipkins).

53. Shipping Returns, New York, CO 5/1222, fols. 127, 135, 144, 148.

54. Indenture, Peter Vallet, John Moore, Henry Cuyler, and Joseph Murray (executors of the estate of Nicholas Mathyson), October 28, 1734, New York City Deeds, 1712–1739, box 4, NYHS; New York Genealogical and Biographical Society, "New York City Assessment Rolls," 29.

55. Will of Richard Alsop, October 11, 1718, proved November 4, 1718, in Smith and Kelby, *Abstracts of Wills on File*, 181–82.

56. Charles Moore, "Early History of Hempstead," 11; James Riker Jr., *Annals of Newtown*, 110, 131; O'Callaghan, *Documentary History*, 1:313–14, 2:354, 351, 363.

57. Will of John Bayley, May 26, 1719, proved December 24, 1720, Westchester N.Y. Deeds, J0038–92: Probated Wills, 1662–1827, no. 219, ancestry.com; Finch v. Connor, New York Mayor's Court Minutes, 1720–23, 159–62, New York County Courts Division of Old Records.

58. *Collections of the New-York Historical Society*, 43:210, 246, 285.
59. In Richmond County, New York, Wills and Deeds: Benjamin Bill to Garret Keteltas, June 29, 1716, B:76; Bill to the Church of St. Andrews and to Aeneas Mackinsie, B:630–32; Bill to Jacob Billow, March 4, 1723, C:113; Bill to Jacob Billow, June 8, 1727, B:250.
60. Records of the Reformed Dutch Church in New York, Brooklyn Genealogical Society, https://brooklynancestry.com/new-amsterdam-reformed-dutch-church-baptisms-1690-1696/; New York Genealogical and Biographical Society, "Records of the Reformed Dutch Church of New York—Marriages," 191.
61. Gronning, "Early New York Turned Chairs"; Will of Teunis Blom, proved November 24, 1714, New York Wills, 8:268–69.
62. Selyns, *Records of Domine Henricus Selyns*, 6.
63. *Collections of the New-York Historical Society*, 43:22, 52.
64. Will of Aaron Bloom, October 19, 1702, proved 1709, New York Wills, 7:552; Conveyance, Hester Bloom to Joost Lynsen, April 2, 1714, New York Deeds, 28:66–70.
65. Archdeacon, *New York City*, 64.
66. Hoadly, *Public Records*, 526, 542.
67. Will of Justus Bosch, June 4, 1737, New York Wills, 13:292–94; Conveyance, Richard Ogden to Justus Bosch, January 26, 1725, Westchester County New York Deeds, F:26; New York Genealogical and Biographical Society, "New York City Assessment Rolls," 28.
68. Smith, 1703 Census of New York City.
69. Gardener, "Census of Newtown"; Will of Richard Alsop, October 11, 1718, *AWNY*, 26:181–82.
70. Shipping Returns, New York, CO 5/1222, fols. 148, 150, 163, 164, 185.
71. Shipping Returns, Bermuda, CO 41/6, fol. 42; Shipping Returns, New York, CO 5/1222, fol. 197.
72. Shipping Returns, New York, CO 5/1222, fol. 208.
73. Governor Robert Hunter's Accounts, May 18, 1719, Robert Hunter Papers, box 1, folder 3, NYHS; Shipping Returns, New York, CO 5/1222, fol. 211.
74. *Boston Gazette*, August 22, 1720; *American Weekly Mercury*, January 17, 1721.
75. Letter of Administration to Deborah Sipkins, February 2, 1721, in Eardeley, *Records*, 74; New York Genealogical and Biographical Society, "Records of the Presbyterian Church, Newtown," *New York Genealogical and Biographical Record* 56, no. 1 (January 1925): 80.
76. Thomas Nichols to Joseph Halstead, March 6, 1724, Nichols to Andrew Hunter, March 12, 1724, Nichols to Ithmar Pelton, 1726, and Nichols to John Ferris, Westchester County, New York Deeds, F:12, 15, 105, 106, 145; Fourneur v. Nichols, December 7, 1721, Hayward v. Nichols, and Nichols v. Fourneur, June 7, 1722, Westchester Land Records, D:117, 131; Will of Thomas Nichols, May 2, 1733, New York Wills, 11:135–37; Peter Vallet v. T. Nichols, November 24, 1724, and the King v. Isaac Mense, December 6, 1724, New York Supreme Court Minute Book, 1723–1728, 115, 120, New York County Courts Division of Old Records.
77. Navy Board, Navy Pay Office, Ships' Pay Books (Series I), HMS *Phoenix*, ADM 33/298, TNA.

78. Shipping Returns, New York, CO 5/1222, fol. 256.
79. Shipping Returns, New York, fols. 197–98, 228, 234, 250.
80. Shipping Returns, New York, fol. 266; Shipping Returns, New York, CO 5/1223, fols. 4, 6.
81. Shipping Returns, New York, CO 5/1223, fols. 36, 41, 44, 47–48, 52, 54, 59, 63, 67, 71, 73, 77, 81, 84, 89, 95, 98, 103; Shipping Returns, New York, CO 5/1224, fols. 2, 8, 18, 24, 29.
82. Gelfand, "Gomez Family."
83. Shipping Returns, New York, CO 5/1224, fols. 35, 39, 42, 45, 51, 53, 63, 70, 73, 101.
84. Christopher Bancker Account Book, 1726–1731, NYHS; PETEr Jay Ledger, 1724–1768, fols. 8, 13–14, NYHS.
85. Shipping Returns, New York, CO 5/1224, fols. 135, 139, 145, 165, 176, 190, 192; Shipping Returns, Jamaica, entries for October 21, 1729, and March 10, 1730, CO 142/14.
86. *American Weekly Mercury*, July 20, 1727.
87. *Maryland Gazette*, March 25, 1729.
88. Shipping Returns, New York, CO 5/1224, fols. 178, 195–96, 205, 209.
89. Shipping Returns, New York, CO 5/1225—Part 1, fols. 27, 63, 68, 72, 78, 90, 192; Shipping Returns, New York, CO 5/1225—Part 2, fols. 137, 189, 193, 204, 218.
90. Shipping Returns, New York, CO 5/1224, fol. 180; Shipping Returns, New York, CO 5/1225—Part 1, fols. 2, 4, 5, 11, 15, 27, 31, 35, 51, 52, 62, 67, 71, 75, 84, 91, 93, 104, 112, 114; *New York Weekly Journal*, December 3, 1733, March 25 and November 4, 1734.
91. *New York Weekly Journal*, December 25, 1738, May 7 and December 24, 1739, November 30, 1741, November 8, 1742, March 28, 1743; *Pennsylvania Journal or Weekly Advertiser*, March 10, 1743; Shipping Returns, New York, CO 5/1227, fols. 56, 68, 82, 152; Shipping Returns, Jamaica, entries for December 7, 1742, May 30, 1743, January 25, 1744, January 12, May 21, December 18, 1745, January 9, 1746, March 21, 1746, April 5, June 16 and 27, 1746, January 9, 1747, April 11, 1747, CO 142/15; Shipping Returns, Jamaica, entries for December 30, 1743, January 24, 1744, May 7 and 8, December 7, 1744, July 15, November 27, December 16, 1745, January 11, 1746, March 15, 1746, April 5, July 1, December 9, 1746, January 7 and 10, 1747, April 26, May 27, July 6, July 22, December 18, 1747, May 14, 1749, CO 142/15.
92. Shipping Returns, Jamaica, entries for May 8, 1744, January 10, 1747, April 11, 1747, CO 142/15.
93. Shipping Returns, New York, CO 5/1222, fol. 240; Shipping Returns, New York, CO 5/1223, fols. 15, 18, 28; Phillip Van Cortlandt to Cornelius De Ruyter, to Peter Gravaer and Peter Toomen, and to Jean Jacques Japin, September 24, 1720, Letterbook of Philip Van Cortlandt, fols. 243–45, NYHS.
94. Shipping Returns, New York, CO 5/1223, fols. 54, 61, 68–69, 76, 84, 87, 94; Shipping Returns, New York, CO 5/1224, fols. 1, 7, 11, 16, 22, 34, 39, 46, 57, 61, 66, 76, 91, 107, 124.
95. Shipping Returns, New York, CO 5/1224, fols. 195, 222; *Boston Gazette*, December 14, 1730, May 31, 1731; *American Weekly Mercury*, March 31, 1731.
96. Shipping Returns, New York, CO 5/1222, fols. 149, 161, 197, 200; The West India and Guinea Company, The Treasurer and the Merchant, St. Thomas and St. John: Books of Duties, kept at St. Thomas (1708–1755), vol. 446, entries for September 25–26, October 22 and 30, images 253–55, 270–71, Danish National Archive.

97. Shipping Returns, New York, CO 5/1222, fols. 256, 276; Shipping Returns, New York, CO 5/1223, fols. 33, 40; Shipping Returns, Perth Amboy, New Jersey, CO 5/1035, fols. 2, 5.

98. Foote, *Black and White Manhattan*, 63–70. Calculations for the 1720s are my own, encompassing Voyage ID#S 102469 to 107712. For the single largest importation of enslaved people, see Voyage ID# 107448. Slave Voyages, Inter-American Database, slavevoyages.com (accessed March 25, 2021).

99. Shipping Returns, New York, CO 5/1223, fols. 36, 67, 89; Shipping Returns, New York, CO 5/1224, fols. 18, 80, 125, 139, 165, 221; Shipping Returns, New York, CO 5/1225, fols. 2, 4–5, 11, 31, 75, 114; Shipping Returns, New York, CO 5/1227, fol. 2. Calculations for New York's intra-American slave imports (1723–39) are my own, encompassing Voyage ID#S 102481 to 111358. Slave Voyages, Inter-American Database, slavevoyages.com (accessed February 17, 2022).

100. Shipping Returns, New York, CO 5/1222, fol. 208; Shipping Returns, New York, CO 5/1223, fol. 87; Shipping Returns, New York, CO 5/1224, fols. 57, 222.

101. James Riker Jr., *Annals of Newtown*, 351; Will of Richard Pinfold, December 15, 1763, proved February 25, 1764, New York Wills, 24:339–341.

102. New York Genealogical and Biographical Society, "Records of the First Presbyterian Church at Newtown Queens," *New York Genealogical and Biographical Record* 55, no. 2 (April 1924): 164, 175, 55, no. 3 (July 1924): 285, 287; Onderdonk, *Documents and Letters*, 40–41, 87, 93, 126.

103. New Amsterdam Reformed Dutch Church Baptisms, Brooklyn Genealogical Society, https://brooklynancestry.com/new-amsterdam-reformed-dutch-church-baptisms-1720-1724/.

104. U.S. Selected States Dutch Reformed Church Records, 1639–1994, Collegiate Church, New York, Burials, 1726–1802, 11–13, ancestry.com; Goodfriend, *Before the Melting Pot*, 154.

105. New York Genealogical and Biographical Society, "Records of Trinity Church Parish," *New York Genealogical and Biographical Record* 69, no. 3 (July 1938): 280; Will of Aaron Mutlow, November 28, 1745, proved February 8, 1748, New York Deeds, 33:210–11.

106. New Amsterdam Reformed Dutch Church Baptisms; *New York Weekly Journal*, July 21, December 15, 1740, and June 22, 1741; Harlow, *Old Bowery Days*, 103–5; McParland, "Colonial Taverns and Tavernkeepers," 161; "65 Attend Stout Family Reunion," *Courier-News* (Bridgewater, N.J.), August 16, 1937, 12; "97 Stout Family Descendants Turn Out for Reunion," *New York Times*, August 16, 1976.

107. New Amsterdam Reformed Dutch Church Baptisms; Anne Marten "Jauncey" to Abigail Johnson, n.d. [ca. 1819], Johnson Family Papers, box 2, folder 8, 110–13, Cornell University Library; New York Genealogical and Biographical Society, "Notes and Queries," *New York Genealogical and Biographical Record* 11, no. 3 (July 1880): 145–46.

108. U.S., Selected States Dutch Reformed Church Membership Records, 1701–1995, New York, Manhattan, Collegiate Church, Ecclesiastical Records, Baptisms, Members, Marriages, 1639–1774, February 19, 1725, 505, ancestry.com.

109. First Presbyterian Church in the City of New York Records at Presbyterian Historical Society, Philadelphia, series I: First Presbyterian Church in the City

of New York, 1717–1954, Trustee Records, 1717–1775, box 10, folder 1, 7–25, 35, and Register of Baptisms, 1728–1790, box 3, folder 11, 5, 11; Anne Marten "Jauncey" to Abigail Johnson.

110. "New Amsterdam Reformed Dutch Church Baptisms, 1731–1734," Brooklyn Genealogical Society, https://brooklynancestry.com/new-amsterdam-reformed-dutch-church-baptisms-1731-1734.

111. James Gibson Account Book, 25–27, 33–38, 66, 75–76, 82–83, NYHS.

112. New-York Historical Society, *Collections . . . 1885*, 96, 98.

113. *Connor v. Villant*, December 13, 1718, New York Mayor's Court Minute Book 1718–20, 91; *Todd v. Conner*, July 12, 1720, New York Mayor's Court Minute Book 1720–23, 16.

114. *Daniel Fournier v. Nichols*, December 7, 1721, *Haywood v. Nichols* and *Nichols v. Fournier*, June 7, 1722, Westchester (N.Y.) Court of Common Pleas, vol. D, fols. 117, 129, 131; Rex v. Isaac Mense, 1725, New York Supreme Court Minute Book 1723–28, 124.

115. New York Mayor's Court Minutes, 1715–18, 45, 57–60, 185; New York Mayor's Court Minutes, 1720–23, 223, 227, 229, 239, 246, 249, 265, 267, 269, 275.

116. New York Supreme Court of Judicature Minute Book, June 4, 1723–June 13, 1724, 24, 104.

117. New York Mayor's Court Minute Book 1723–28, 526, 536, 537; New York Mayor's Court Minute Book, 1728–31, 320; New York Mayor's Court Minute Book 1731–36, 120–24.

118. New York Supreme Court Minute Book 1723–28, 124.

119. New York Mayor's Court Minute Book 1720–23, 37–39; New York Mayor's Court Minute Book 1723–28, 297.

120. "New Amsterdam Reformed Dutch Church Baptisms, 1731–1734."

121. Will of Thomas Nichols, May 2, 1733, proved February 14, 1734, Westchester (N.Y.) Wills, 12:132–33.

122. Will of Arent (Aaron) Mutlow, November 28, 1745, New York Deeds, 33:200–201.

123. New York Genealogical and Biographical Society, "Records of the Presbyterian Church," 355.

124. Will of William Smith, February 12, 1752, New York, U.S., Wills and Probate Records, 1659–1999, 18:109–12, ancestry.com (accessed March 16, 2021).

125. *New York Genealogical and Biographical Society*, "New York City Assessment Rolls," 28; *New York Evening Post*, July 29, 1749, May 21, 1750.

126. *New York Gazette or Weekly Post Boy*, November 12, 1750, April 29, October 28, 1751.

127. Dawes, "Titles as Symbols of Prestige."

128. Anne Marten "Jauncey" to Abigail Johnson.

129. Will of William Smith, February 12, 1752.

130. Anne Marten "Jauncey" to Abigail Johnson.

131. *New York Gazette or Weekly Post Boy*, May 25 and June 22, 1752.

132. Joseph O. Brown, *Jaunceys of New York*, 3, 14–21.

133. Will of René Het, April 1, 1754, *Abstracts of Wills on File in the Surrogate's Office*,

City of New York, vol. 7 (New York: Collections of the New-York Historical Society, 1899), 211; Chapman, *Chapman Family*, 107–9.

134. New York Genealogical and Biographical Society, "Notes and Queries"; Raymond, "Colonel William Stephens Smith," 153–61; New York Genealogical and Biographical Society, "King's College (now Columbia) and Some of Its Earliest Alumni," *New York Genealogical and Biographical Record* 26, no. 4 (October 1895): 187.

135. Abigail Adams to John Quincy Adams, February 29, 1796, Adams Family Correspondence, Adams Papers Digital Collection, vol. 2, Massachusetts Historical Society; McCullough, *John Adams*, 457–58, 529, 548, 555, 573, 601.

Conclusion. Noncanonical Pirates

1. *Weekly Journal or Saturday's Post*, May 9, 1724.

2. *Parker's London News or the Impartial Intelligencer*, September 9, 1724. See also September 11–October 9, 1724.

3. Schonhorn, *General History of the Pyrates*, xxxiii–xlii; *Dublin Gazette*, February 3, 1725.

4. *Weekly Journal or Saturday's Post*, June 1 and 22, November 23, 1717; *Weekly Journal or British Gazetteer*, August 10, 1717.

5. *Weekly Journal or British Gazeteer* (London), January 18, 1718 ("noted") and April 11, 1719 ("famous"); *Applebee's Weekly Journal* (London), July 30, 1720 ("noted").

6. *Whitehall Evening Post* (London), December 27–30, 1718; *Weekly Journal or Saturday's Post* (London), January 3 and 17, February 28, 1719.

7. Boyer, *Political State of Great Britain*, 447–48, 550–54, 443–45.

8. South Carolina Court of Vice-Admiralty, *Trials of Major Stede Bonnet*; *The Trials of Captain John Rackham and Other Pyrates* (Jamaica: R. Baldwin, 1721), CO 134/14, fols. 9–31.

9. *Full and Exact Account*; *Daily Post* (London), February 6, 1723.

10. Bialuschewski, "Daniel Defoe"; Brooks, "Capt. Charles Johnson."

11. Schonhorn, *General History of the Pyrates*, 76, 82, 84–85, 153–54, 159–64, 326, 606–14.

12. Rediker, *Villains of All Nations*, 60–102, 148–69 (quotations on 157–59); Schonhorn, *General History of the Pyrates*, 244.

13. Schonhorn, *General History of the Pyrates*, 135–48 (Vane), 41–42, 71, 146, 615–16, 639, 643 (Hornigold), 42, 627, 651, 658–59, 695 (Augur), 41, 615, 616, 623, 640, 644 (Burgess), 121–22, 127, 131, 134 (Taylor), 142 (Brown), 145 (Woodale), 146, 643 (Cockram), 616 (Clark), 43, 617, 653, 659 (Macarty), 585, 591 (Williams).

14. *American Weekly Mercury*, December 29, 1724, January 12, 1725.

15. Wall, "William Bradford, Colonial Printer."

BIBLIOGRAPHY

Archival Records—Manuscript and Digitized

ANCESTRY.COM

Delaware, U.S. Land Records, 1677–1947.
London, Church of England Records of Baptisms, Marriages, and Burials, 1538–1812. St. Mary Magdalen Bermondsey.
London, Freedom of the City Admission Papers.
Massachusetts, U.S., Town and Vital Records, 1620–1988.
Massachusetts, U.S., Wills and Probate Records, 1635–1991.
North Carolina Wills and Probate Records, 1665–1998, Chowan County, Suits Dismissed and Court Papers, 1712–24.
North Carolina Wills and Probate Records, 1665–1998, Chowan County, Suits Dismissed and Court Papers, Suits Dismissed, 1695–1725.
North Carolina Wills and Probate Records, 1665–1998, Chowan County, Suits Dismissed and Court Papers, 1721–34.
North Carolina Wills and Probate Records, 1665–1998, Chowan County, Suits Dismissed and Court Papers, 1731–38.
Pennsylvania, U.S. Wills and Probate Records, 1683–1993.
Rhode Island Town Council and Probate Records. Newport, R.I., vols. 1–3, 1702–19.
U.S. Selected States Dutch Reformed Church Membership Records, 1701–1995, New York, Manhattan, Collegiate Church, Ecclesiastical Records, Baptisms, Members, Marriages, 1639–1774.
U.S. Selected States Dutch Reformed Church Records, 1639–1994. Collegiate Church, New York. Burials, 1726–1802.

BRITISH HISTORY ONLINE
(https://www.british-history.ac.uk/)

House of Commons, Journal of the House of Commons, vol. 12, 1697–99. London: His Majesty's Stationery Office, 1803.
Ledward, K. H., ed. *Journals of the Board of Trade and Plantations*. Vols. 1–9. London: His Majesty's Stationery Office, 1920–32.

Sainsbury, Noel J., James Fortescue, Cecil Headlam, and A. P. Newton, eds. *Great Britain Public Record Office, Calendar of State Papers, Colonial Series: America and the West Indies*. 38 vols. London: H. M. Stationery Office, 1860–1919. [Cited as *CSP*.]

Shaw, William A., ed. *Calendar of Treasury Books*, vol. 15. London: His Majesty's Stationery Office, 1933.

BRITISH LIBRARY, LONDON (BL)

Add Ms 61643.
Add Ms 19038.
Anonymous. "Short Journal of My Voyages & Travels, 1714–1716," Add Ms. 39946.
Blenheim Papers, vol. 545. Add Ms 61645.
"Case of the *Charles the Second*," Barbados. Add Ch. 76087.
India Office Records, IOR E-1-13-15.
C. E. Long, Jamaica Wills and Marriages. BL ADD Ms 21921.
Sir Edward Vernon Papers, vol. 43. Add Ms 40812.

CORNELL UNIVERSITY LIBRARY, DIVISION OF RARE AND MANUSCRIPT COLLECTIONS, ITHACA, NEW YORK

Johnson Family Papers, box 2. https://ecommons.cornell.edu/handle/1813/56427.

DANISH NATIONAL ARCHIVE (ARKIVERONLINE)

The West India and Guinea Company (Denmark). The Treasurer and the Merchant, St. Thomas and St. John: Books of Duties, Kept at St. Thomas (1708–1755), vol. 446. https://www.sa.dk/ao-soegesider/en/billedviser?epid=20202851#293408,59291428.

EIGHTEENTH CENTURY COLLECTIONS ONLINE, GALE PUBLISHING.

"Articles, Depositions, &c of the People of New Providence, in an Assembly Held at Nassau, October 5, 1701 against Elias Haskett." London, 1702.

FAMILYSEARCH.ORG

Bermuda, Bonds, Bills, Deeds and Protests, Books 6, 7, 9, Bermuda Public Records, 1612–1937.
Bermuda, Book of Wills, vol. 6.
Bermuda Court of Assizes, Book of Actions, AZ101/2.
Bermuda Court of Assizes, Book of Actions, AZ101/3.
Bermuda Court of Assizes, Proceedings, AZ102/5.
William Blathwayt Papers at Colonial Williamsburg, 1661–1722. 41 vols.

Church of England, Dorset, Parish Registers, 1538–2001.
Church of England, St. Michael Parish, Barbados, Births, Marriages, Burials, 1702–1739.
Jamaica, Church of England, Port Royal Parish Register Transcripts, Baptisms, Burials, Marriages, 1725–1835.
Jamaica, Church of England, St. Andrew's Parish Register Transcripts, Baptisms, Burials, Marriages, vol. 1, 1664–1807.
Jamaica, Church of England, St. Catherine's Parish Register Transcripts, Baptisms, Burials, Marriages, vol. 1, 1669–1764.
Massachusetts Court of Admiralty (Suffolk County), Court Records and Account Books, 1718–1772.
Massachusetts Land Records, 1620–1986.
Massachusetts, Middlesex County, Clerk of Courts, Court Papers—folios 104A–133A 1652–1735.
Massachusetts, Middlesex County Inferior Court of Common Pleas.
Massachusetts, Middlesex County, Record Books of the Registry of Deeds, 1649–1900.
Massachusetts State Archives Collection, 1629–1799. 328 vols.
Massachusetts, Suffolk County, Court Files, vols. 10–240, ca. 1689–1732.
Massachusetts, Suffolk County, Court of Common Pleas Records, 1724–28.
Massachusetts, Suffolk County, Court of Common Pleas Records, 1728–30.
Massachusetts, Suffolk County Deeds, 1639–1886.
Massachusetts, Town Clerk, Vital and Town Records, 1626–2001.
New Shoreham (R.I.) Town Records, vol. 1, part 2, 1675–1744.
New York Court of General Sessions, Minute Book from August 1694 to February 2, 1697.
New York, Land Records, 1630–1975.
New York, Wills and Deeds, ca. 1700s–2017.
North Carolina Secretary of State, Wills, vol. 3, 1722–35.
Pennsylvania, Philadelphia County Register of Wills, 1718–22.
Records of Colonial Gloucester County, Virginia, vol. 1. Compiled by Polly Cary Mason. 1948.
Records of the Proceedings of the Vestry of St. Paul's Church, Edenton, N.C., 1701–1841.
South Carolina, Charleston County Wills, vol. 64.
South Carolina Miscellaneous Records, Charleston County, 1716–21.
South Carolina Probate Records, Bound Volumes, 1677–1971.
South Carolina Probate Records, Loose Files, 1732–36.
South Carolina Probate Records, Loose Files, 1748–51.
South Carolina, Records of the Secretary of the Province and Register of the Province, 1705–9.
South Carolina, Records of the Secretary of the Province and Register of the Province, 1712–13.
South Carolina, Records of the Secretary of the Province and Register of the Province, 1714–19.
York County, Virginia, Orders and Wills, vol. 15, 1716–20.

FINDMYPAST.CO.UK

City of London, Haberdashers, Apprentices, and Freemen, 1526–1923.
Church of England, St. Sepulchre (London) Church Registers, April 29, 1683.
England Marriages 1538–1973, St. Peter le Poer, Register of Births, Marriages, Deaths.
Liverpool Parish Registers, Church of Our Lady and St. Nicholas.
London Apprenticeship Abstracts, 1442–1850.
Tax List for the Inhabitants of London, St. Mary Bothaw Precinct, 1703.
Thames Watermen and Lightmen, 1688–2010. Binding Records, 1692–1949.

HARVARD BUSINESS SCHOOL, BAKER LIBRARY HISTORICAL COLLECTIONS, CAMBRIDGE, MASSACHUSETTS

Peter Faneuil papers, 1716–39, Invoice book, 1725–29, MSS 766, 1712–1854, H234, vol. F-3. Online at https://iiif.lib.harvard.edu/manifests/view/drs:422465421$17i.
Daniel Henchman Papers, 1718–1763, MSS 766, 1712–1854, H234, vol. DH-1. Online at https://hollisarchives.lib.harvard.edu/repositories/11/archival_objects/2445232.

ISLAND RECORD OFFICE, TWICKENHAM PARK, JAMAICA

Deeds, vol. 54.
Wills, vols. 12–17.

JAMAICA NATIONAL ARCHIVES, SPANISH TOWN, JAMAICA (JNA)

Grand Court Records, 1A/5/10.
Inventories, 6 vols., 1B/11/3/9–15.
Letters of Administration, 4 vols., 1B/11/17/1–4.

MASSACHUSETTS HISTORICAL SOCIETY

Adams Papers Digital Collection, vol. 2. https://www.masshist.org/publications/adams-papers/index.php/view/ADMS-04-11-02-0100.

OXFORD UNIVERSITY, BODLEIAN LIBRARY

Clarendon Papers, 1661–1713.

NATIONAL ARCHIVES, KEW, GREAT BRITAIN (TNA)

Admiralty, and Ministry of Defense, Navy Department: Correspondence and Papers—ADM 1—ORiginal Series (1st Group): 1660–1839.

BIBLIOGRAPHY

Admiralty: Captains' Logs, ADM 51.
Admiralty: Navy Board, Navy Pay Office, Ship's Pay Books (Series 1), 1669–1778, ADM 33.
Admiralty: Navy Board Records, ADM 106.
Admiralty: Out Letters, Lords Letters: Orders and Instructions, ADM 2.
Board of Trade and Secretaries of State, America and West Indies, Original Correspondence, Bahamas, Correspondence, Original—Secretary of State: Miscellaneous, CO 23/12.
Board of Trade and Secretaries of State, America and West Indies, Original Correspondence, Carolina (Proprietary), Entry Book of Letters, Instructions, Commissions, Warrants, etc., 1710–1726, CO 5/290.
Board of Trade and Secretaries of State, America and West Indies, Original Correspondence, Entry Book of Letters, Instructions, Commissions, Warrants, Licenses, etc., 1714–1716, CO 5/190.
Board of Trade and Secretaries of State, America and West Indies, Original Correspondence, Expedition against Canada, 1710–1713, CO 5/9.
Board of Trade and Secretaries of State, America and West Indies, Original Correspondence, Massachusetts, Shipping Returns, 1686–1719, CO 5/848.
Board of Trade and Secretaries of State, America and West Indies, Original Correspondence, New Jersey, Shipping Returns, 1722–1751, CO 5/1035.
Board of Trade and Secretaries of State, America and West Indies, Original Correspondence, New York, 1700–1701, Correspondence, Original—Secretary of State, CO 5/1044.
Board of Trade and Secretaries of State, America and West Indies, Original Correspondence, New York, 1702–1711, Correspondence, Original—Secretary of State, CO 5/1084.
Board of Trade and Secretaries of State, America and West Indies, Original Correspondence, New York, Sessional Papers, 1702–1711, CO 5/1185.
Board of Trade and Secretaries of State, America and West Indies, Original Correspondence, New York, Sessional Papers, 1713–1720, CO 5/1186.
Board of Trade and Secretaries of State, America and West Indies, Original Correspondence, New York, Shipping Returns, 1713–1722, CO 5/1222.
Board of Trade and Secretaries of State, America and West Indies, Original Correspondence, New York, Shipping Returns, 1722–1725, CO 5/1223.
Board of Trade and Secretaries of State, America and West Indies, Original Correspondence, New York, Shipping Returns, 1725–1730, CO 5/1224.
Board of Trade and Secretaries of State, America and West Indies, Original Correspondence, New York, Shipping Returns, 1731–1738, CO 5/1225, parts 1–2.
Board of Trade and Secretaries of State, America and West Indies, Original Correspondence, New York, Shipping Returns, 1735–1752, CO 5/1226.
Board of Trade and Secretaries of State, America and West Indies, Original Correspondence, New York, Shipping Returns, 1739–1753, CO 5/1227.
Board of Trade and Secretaries of State, America and West Indies, Original Correspondence, Pennsylvania, 1690–1767, CO 5/1233.
Board of Trade and Secretaries of State, America and West Indies, Original Correspondence, Proprietaries, Board of Trade Correspondence B, 1699–1701, CO 5/1288.

Board of Trade and Secretaries of State, America and West Indies, Original Correspondence, Proprietaries, Correspondence, Original—Board of Trade, P and Q, 1707–1720, CO 5/1264–65.

Board of Trade and Secretaries of State, America and West Indies, Original Correspondence, South Carolina, Correspondence, Original—Secretary of State, 1715–1729, CO 5/387.

Board of Trade and Secretaries of State, America and West Indies, Original Correspondence, South Carolina, Shipping Returns, 1716–1719 and 1721–1735, CO 5/508–9.

Board of Trade and Secretaries of State, America and West Indies, Original Correspondence, Virginia, Correspondence, Original—Board of Trade, 1700–1702, CO 5/1312.

Board of Trade and Secretaries of State, America and West Indies, Original Correspondence, Virginia, Correspondence, Original—Board of Trade, 1705–1707, CO 5/1315.

Board of Trade and Secretaries of State, America and West Indies, Original Correspondence, Virginia, Correspondence, Original—Board of Trade, 1715–1717, CO 5/1317.

Board of Trade and Secretaries of State, America and West Indies, Original Correspondence, Virginia, Correspondence, Original—Secretary of State, 1706–1714, CO 5/1341.

Board of Trade and Secretaries of State, America and West Indies, Original Correspondence, Virginia, Shipping Returns, 1699–1706, CO 5/1441.

Board of Trade and Secretaries of State, America and West Indies, Original Correspondence, Virginia, Shipping Returns, 1715–1727, CO 5/1442.

Board of Trade and Secretaries of State, America and West Indies, Original Correspondence, Virginia, Shipping Returns, 1726–1735, CO 5/1443.

Board of Trade and Secretaries of State, America and West Indies, Original Correspondence, Virginia, Shipping Returns, 1735–1752, CO 5/1444.

Colonial Office and Predecessors: Bahamas, Correspondence, Original—Board of Trade, A. 1717–1725, CO 23/1.

Colonial Office and Predecessors: Bahamas, Correspondence, Original—Board of Trade, B. Nos. 1–89, 1726–1731, CO 23/2.

Colonial Office and Predecessors: Bahamas, Correspondence, Original—Board of Trade, B. Nos. 90–158, 1731–1737, CO 23/3.

Colonial Office and Predecessors: Bahamas, Correspondence, Original—Board of Trade, C. 1736–1743, CO 23/4.

Colonial Office and Predecessors: Bahamas, Correspondence, Original—Board of Trade, D. Nos. 1–59, 1743–1753, CO 23/5.

Colonial Office and Predecessors: Bahamas, Correspondence, Original—Secretary of State: Despatches, Letters from Phenney, Fitzwilliam, and Tinker, 1728–1746, CO 23/14.

Colonial Office and Predecessors: Bahamas, Correspondence, Original—Secretary of State: Letters from Woodes Rogers and Phenney, 1718–1727, CO 23/13.

Colonial Office and Predecessors: Bahamas, Miscellaneous, Shipping and Other Returns, 1721–1751, CO 27/12.
Colonial Office and Predecessors: Bahamas, Sessional Papers, Council, 1721–1729, CO 26/1.
Colonial Office and Predecessors: Bahamas, Sessional Papers, Council, Assembly, Council in Assembly, 1729–1738, CO 26/2A.
Colonial Office and Predecessors: Barbados, Miscellaneous, Shipping and Other Returns, 1679–1709, CO 33/14.
Colonial Office and Predecessors: Barbados, Miscellaneous, Shipping and Other Returns, 1708–1726, CO 33/15.
Colonial Office and Predecessors: Barbados, Miscellaneous, Shipping and Other Returns, 1728–1753, CO 33/16.
Colonial Office and Predecessors: Barbados, Original Correspondence—Board of Trade, 1715, T. nos. 64, 136, 203, CO 28/16.
Colonial Office and Predecessors: Bermuda, Correspondence, Original—Board of Trade, 1709–1716 and 1716–1723, CO 37/9–10.
Colonial Office and Predecessors: Bermuda, Miscellanea, Shipping Returns, 1715–1731, CO 41/6.
Colonial Office and Predecessors: Jamaica, Correspondence, Original—Board of Trade, 1710–1713, N. CO 137/9.
Colonial Office and Predecessors: Jamaica, Correspondence, Original—Board of Trade, 1713–1715, N. CO 137/10.
Colonial Office and Predecessors: Jamaica, Correspondence, Original—Board of Trade, 1715–1716, O. nos. 1–51, CO 137/11.
Colonial Office and Predecessors: Jamaica, Correspondence, Original—Board of Trade, 1716–1718, O. nos. 52–205, CO 137/12.
Colonial Office and Predecessors: Jamaica, Correspondence, Original—Board of Trade, 1721–1724, Q. nos. 1–103, CO 137/14.
Colonial Office: Jamaica, Miscellanea, Shipping Returns, 1680–1705, dates unknown [ca. 1705–1728, 1729–1753], CO 142/13–15.
Colonial Office: Jamaica, Sessional Papers, Journals of the Council, Assembly, and Council in Assembly, 1713–1724, CO 140/13–18.
Colonial Office and Predecessors: Leeward Islands, Correspondence, Original—Board of Trade and Secretaries of State, 1693–1720, CO 152/39.
Colonial Office: Leeward Islands, Miscellanea, Naval Office Returns (Shipping Returns), CO 157/1.
Court of Chancery, Six Clerks Division, Pleadings, 1714–1758, Marquis de Navarres v. Craven, 1716, C 11/227/34.
Court of Chancery, Zincke Division, Pleadings, 1714–1758, Marquis de Navarres v. Craven, 1716, C 11/1947/29.
High Court of Admiralty, Instance and Prize Courts: Examinations and Answers, HCA 13.
High Court of Admiralty, Oyer and Terminer Records: Examinations of Pirates and Other Criminals, HCA 1/54–55.

High Court of Admiralty, Proceedings of Vice-Admiralty Courts in North America, the West Indies, and Africa, HCA 1/99.
Navy Board, In-Letters, ADM 106.
Navy Board, Navy Pay Office, Ships Pay Books (Series I), ADM 33.
Prerogative Court of Canterbury, Wills, PROB 11/289/356.
Privy Council and Privy Council Office, Miscellaneous Unbound Papers, Colonial Papers, 1707, PC 1/46/9.
Secretaries of State, State Papers Domestic, George I, 1714–1727, SP 35/9.
Secretaries of State, State Papers Foreign, Spain, SP 94/101.
Secretaries of State, State Papers Naval, Lords of the Admiralty, SP 42/14.
Secretaries of State, State Papers Naval, Lords of the Admiralty, SP 42/17.
Secretaries of State, State Papers Scotland Series II, SP 54/11.
State Paper Office: Printed Proclamations, 1709–1722, SP 45/14.
Treasury: Miscellaneous Records, Colonies, Barbados: Ships Entered and Cleared with Cargoes, T 64/47.
Treasury: Treasury Board Papers and In-Letters, August–October 1716, T 1/200.
Treasury: Treasury Board Papers and In-Letters, November 1–December 31, 1716, T 1/201.
Treasury: Treasury Board Papers and In-Letters, January 1–April 30, 1719, T 1/220.
Treasury: Treasury Board Papers and In-Letters, January 1–April 30, 1720, T 1/227.
Treasury: Treasury Board Papers and In-Letters, July 1–December 31, 1723, T 1/244.

NEW YORK COUNTY COURTS DIVISION OF OLD RECORDS, NEW YORK CITY

New York Mayor's Court Minute Books, ca. 1700–1730.
New York Supreme Court Minute Book, 1723–1728.

NEW-YORK HISTORICAL SOCIETY, NEW YORK CITY (NYHS)

Christopher Bancker Account Book, 1726–1731.
Colebrooke and Rogers Account Book, 1725–1731.
John Frost, Deposition, July 15, 1717.
James Gibson Account Book, 1726–1731.
Robert Hunter Papers, 1699–1744.
Peter Jay Ledger, 1724–1768.
New York City Indentures, 1718–1727.
New York City Deeds, box 4, 1723–1739.
Philip Van Cortlandt Letterbook, 1713–1722.
Stephen Van Cortlandt Day Book, 1716.

NEW YORK STATE ARCHIVES, ALBANY (NYSA)

New York Colony Council Papers, vols. 60–61, series A1894.

NORTH CAROLINA STATE ARCHIVES DIGITAL COLLECTIONS

Colonial Court Records, https://digital.ncdcr.gov/collections/colonial-court-records.

PRESBYTERIAN HISTORICAL SOCIETY, PHILADELPHIA

First Presbyterian Church in the City of New York Records, series I.

SOUTH CAROLINA DEPARTMENT OF ARCHIVES AND HISTORY, COLUMBIA (SCDAH)

Commons House of Assembly Journals, ca. 1708–18, John Green Transcripts, vols. 4–5, microfilm reel AD40.
Court of Common Pleas, Judgment Rolls, 1703–1790.
Secretary of the Province, Miscellaneous Documents, microfilm reel 501A.

UNITED STATES NATIONAL ARCHIVES AND RECORD ADMINISTRATION, NEW YORK CITY

New York Vice-Admiralty Court, record group 21: Records of District Courts of the United States, 1685–2009, Piracy Case of 6/2/1717 to 7/12/1717, NARA NO. 4545839.

UNITED STATES NATIONAL ARCHIVES AND RECORD ADMINISTRATION, WASHINGTON, D.C.

Pre-federal Admiralty Court Records, Province and State of South Carolina, 1716–1789, vol. A-B, PARTs 1–2.

Newspapers

American Weekly Mercury (Philadelphia)
Applebee's Weekly Journal (London)
Boston Gazette
Boston News Letter
Boston Weekly Rehearsal
British Weekly Mercury (London)
The Courier-News (Bridgewater, N.J.)
Daily Courant (London)
Dublin Gazette (Ireland)
Evening Post (London)
Flying Post (London)
London Gazette
Maryland Gazette (Annapolis)

New England Courant (Boston)
New England Weekly Journal (Boston)
New York Evening Post
New York Gazette or Weekly Post Boy
New York Weekly Journal
Original Weekly Journal (London)
Parker's London News or the Impartial Intelligencer (London)
Pennsylvania Journal or Weekly Advertiser (Philadelphia)
Post Boy (London)
Weekly Journal or British Gazeteer (London)
Weekly Journal or Saturday's Post (London)
Whitehall Evening Post (London)

Published Primary Sources

Anonymous. *An Apology or Vindication of Governor Nicholson, Esq.; His Majesty's Governor of South Carolina, from the Unjust Aspersions Cast upon Him by Some of the Members of the Bahama-Company*. London, 1724.

Anonymous. *The Case of the Poor Sailors (Captors of Several Prizes) Brought into Jamaica, and Several Other Inhabitants of the Island Concern'd Therein*. London, 1713.

Anonymous. *The English Heroe, or, Sir Francis Drake Revived Being a Full Account of the Dangerous Voyages, Admirable Adventures, Notable Discoveries, and Magnanimous Atchievements of That Valiant and Renowned Commander*. London: Nathaniel Crouch, 1687.

Anonymous. *The Groans of Jamaica, Expressed in a Letter by a Gentleman Residing There to a Friend in London*. London, 1714.

Anonymous. *The Humble Address of the Governor, Council, and Assembly of Jamaica to the Queen; and Some Instances of Duties Demanded on Prize Goods Brought into That Island*. London, 1711.

Anonymous. *Sir Francis Drake Revived . . . Being a Summary and True Relation of Foure Severall VOYAGES Made by the Said Sir FRANCIS DRAKE to the WEST-INDIES*. London: Nicholas Bourne, 1626.

Anonymous. *The Trade of the South-Sea Company: Considered with Relation to Jamaica. In a Letter to One of the Directors of the South-Sea Company, from a Gentleman Who Has Resided Several Years in Jamaica*. London: Samuel Crouch, 1714.

Anonymous [Adrien Van Brock]. *The Life and Adventures of Capt. John Avery; the Famous English Pirate, Now in Possession of Madagascar*. London: J. Baker, 1707.

Bigelow, Melville M., and Abner C. Goodell. *The Acts and Resolves, Public and Private, of the Province of the Massachusetts Bay: to Which Are Prefixed the Charters of the Province: with Historical and Explanatory Notes, and an Appendix*. Boston: Wright & Potter, 1869.

Bigges, Thomas. *A Summary and True Account of Sir Francis Drake's West India Voyage*. London: Richard Field, 1589.

Boyer, Abel. *The Political State of Great Britain*. Vol. 15. London: J. Baker & T. Warner, April 1718.

———. *The Political State of Great Britain.* Vol. 16. London: J. Baker & T. Warner, December 1718.
———. *The Political State of Great Britain.* Vol. 17. London: J. Baker & T. Warner, April 1719.
Brock, R. A., ed. *The Official Letters of Alexander Spotswood, Lieutenant Governor of Virginia, 1710–1722.* Vols. 1–2. Richmond: Virginia Historical Society, 1932.
Brooklyn Genealogical Society. New Amsterdam Dutch Reformed Church Records—Baptisms and Marriages. Brooklyn Genealogy, https://brooklynancestry.com/new-york-church-records/.
Brooks, Baylus, ed. *Jacob de Bucquoy: Pirates of Madagascar at Rio Delagoa.* Lulu.com, 2018.
Browne, William H., ed. *Proceedings of the Council of Maryland, 1698–1731.* Baltimore: Maryland Historical Society, 1905.
Clarke, Samuel. *The Life & Death of the Valiant and Renowned Sir Francis Drake His Voyages and Discoveries in the West-Indies, and about the World, with His Noble and Heroick Acts.* London: Samuel Miller, 1671.
Collinge, J. M. *Office-Holders in Modern Britain.* Vol. 7: *Navy Board Officials, 1660–1832.* London: University of London Press, 1978.
Davis, William T., Charles W. Leng, and Royden Woodward Vosburgh, eds. *The Church of St. Andrew, Richmond, Staten Island: Its History, Vital Records, and Gravestone Inscriptions.* Staten Island, N.Y.: W. C. Davis for the Staten Island Historical Society, 1925.
Downing, Clement. *A Compendious History of the Indian Wars, with an Account of the Rise, Progress, Strength, and Forces of Angria the Pyrate. Also the Transactions of a Squadron under Commodore Matthews, Sent to the East Indies to Suppress Pyrates.* London: T. Cooper, 1737.
Eardeley, William Applebie. *Records in the Office of the County Clerk at Jamaica, Long Island, New York: 1680–1781.* Brooklyn, N.Y., 1918.
Every, Henry. *A Copy of Verses, Composed by Captain Henry Every, Lately Gone to Sea to Seek His Fortune.* London: Theophilus Lewis, 1696.
Fernow, Berthold, and Arnold J. F. Van Laer, eds. *New York Calendar of Council Minutes, 1683–1786.* New York State Library Bulletin no. 58. Albany: State University of New York, 1902.
Fiske, Jane F., ed. *Gleanings from Newport Court Files, 1653–1783.* Boxford, Mass.: J. F. Fiske, 1998.
Franklin, Benjamin. *The Autobiography of Benjamin Franklin.* In Larzer Ziff, ed., *The Portable Benjamin Franklin.* New York, Penguin, 2005.
Frothingham, Richard, Jr. *History of Charlestown, Massachusetts.* Boston: Charles C. Little and James Brown, 1845.
A Full and Exact Account, of the Tryal of All the Pyrates, Lately Taken by Captain Ogle, on Board the Swallow Man of War, on the Coast of Guinea. London: J. Roberts, 1723.
Gardener, Charles Carroll. "Census of Newtown, Long Island, August, 1698." *American Genealogist* 24, no. 3 (July 1948).
Grant, W. L., James Munro, and Almeric Fitzroy, eds. *Acts of the Privy Council of England: Colonial Series.* Vol. 2: 1680–1720. Hereford, U.K.: H. M. Stationery Office, 1910.

———. *Acts of the Privy Council of England: Colonial Series.* Vol. 3: 1720–1745. Hereford, U.K.: H. M. Stationery Office, 1910.

Great Britain, House of Commons. *The Report of the Committee of the House of Commons, to Whom the Petition of the Royal Lustring-Company of England, Was Referred Together with the . . . Relating to the Smuggling-trade.* London: E. Whitlock, 1698.

Great Britain Public Record Office, W. Noel Sainsbury, and Alexander S. Salley, eds. *Records in the British Public Record Office Relating to South Carolina.* Vol. 13: 1728–1729. Atlanta: Foote & Davies, Printed for the Historical Commission of South Carolina, 1947.

Greepe, Thomas. *The true and perfecte newes of the woorthy and valiaunt exploytes, performed and doone by that valiant knight Syr Frauncis Drake not onely at Sancto Domingo, and Carthagena, but also nowe at Cales, and vppon the coast of Spayne.* London: I. Charlewood, 1587.

Hall, Fayrer. *The Importance of the British Plantations in America to This Kingdom: with the State of Their Trade, and Methods for Improving It; as Also a Description of the Several Colonies There.* London: J. Peele, 1731.

Hardy, William J., ed. *Calendar of State Papers Domestic: William III, 1697.* London: His Majesty's Stationery Office, 1927.

Hazard, Samuel, ed. *Minutes of the Provincial Council of Pennsylvania.* Vol. 3. Philadelphia: Jo. Stevens, 1852.

Historical Records Survey (New York, N.Y.). *The Earliest Volume of Staten Island Records, 1678–1813.* New York: Works Projects Administration, 1942.

Hoadly, Charles J., ed. *Public Records of the Colony of Connecticut.* Vol. 4. Hartford, Conn.: Case, Lockwood & Brainard, 1868.

Hunnewell, James Frothingham, ed. *Records of the First Church in Charlestown, Massachusetts, 1632–1789.* Boston: David Clapp & Son, 1880.

Johnston, F. Claiborne, Jr., and C. F. E. Hollis Hallet, eds. *Early Colonists of the Bahamas: A Selection of Records.* Bermuda: Juniperhill, 1996.

Justice, Alexander. *A General Treatise of the Dominion of the Sea: and a Compleat Body of the Sea-laws: Containing What Is Most Valuable on That Subject in Antient and Modern Authors; and Particularly the Antient Laws of the Rhodians and Romans; Those of Oleron, Wisbuy, and Other Countries; with Curious Notes and Observations.* London: Thomas Page & William Fisher, 1724.

Keller, John, and William S. Pelletreau, eds. *Abstracts of Wills on File in the Surrogate's Office: City of New York.* Vol. 26. New York: New-York Historical Society, 1893.

Landry, Peter. *Nova Scotia Biographies.* http://www.blupete.com/Hist/BiosNS/1700-63/Rous.htm#rfn2.

Lilliard, Jacques Ephraim Stout. *The Stout Family of New York City and Kentucky: Pedigree.* Washington, D.C., 1939. Allen County, Ky. Public Library Genealogy Center. https://archive.org/details/stoutfamilyofnewoolill/page/n15/mode/2up.

Mahaffy, Robert Pentland, ed. *Calendar of State Papers, Domestic Series, of the Reign of Anne, I. 1702–1706, Preserved in the State Paper Department of Her Majesty's Public Record Office.* Vol. 1: March 1702–May 1703. London: His Majesty's Stationery Office, 1916.

McIlwaine, H. R., ed. *Executive Journals of the Council of Colonial Virginia*. Vol. 3: May 1, 1705–October 23, 1721. Richmond: Virginia State Library, 1928.

Minchinton, W. E., ed. *The Trade of Bristol in the Eighteenth Century*. Bristol Record Society Publications, vol. 20. Bristol: Bristol Record Society, 1957.

Moll, Herman. *The Island of Barbadoes. Divided into Its Parishes, with the Roads, Paths, &c. According to an Actual and Accurate Survey*. London: Thomas & Isaac Bowles, ca. 1736.

Molloy, Charles. *De Jure Maritimo et Navali, or A Treatise of Affairs Maritime and of Commerce*. London: John Walthoe & John Wotton, 1722.

Nelson, Charles A., ed. *Minutes of the Common Council of the City of New York, 1675–1776*. Vol. 3: 1712–1729. New York: Dodd, Meade, 1905.

Nelson, William, ed. *Documents Relating to the Colonial History of the State of New Jersey*. Vol. 23: Calendar of *New Jersey Wills*, vol. 1: *1670–1730*. Paterson, N.J.: Press Printing and Publishing, 1901.

New York Council. *New York Calendar of Council Minutes, 1683–1786*. New York State Library Bulletin no. 58. Albany: State University of New York, 1902.

New York Genealogical and Biographical Society. "New York City Assessment Rolls, 1730." *New York Genealogical and Biographical Record* 95, no. 1 (January 1964): 27–32.

———. "New York Marriage Licenses, 1694–95." *New York Genealogical and Biographical Record* 98, no. 1 (January 1967): 1–10.

———. "Records of the Presbyterian Church, Newtown (now Elmhurst) Queens County, Long Island." *New York Genealogical and Biographical Record* 56, no. 4 (October 1925): 353–68.

———. "Records of the Reformed Dutch Church of New York—Marriages." *New York Genealogical and Biographical Record* 12, no. 4 (October 1881): 187–95.

———. "Records of the Reformed Dutch Church of New York—Baptisms." *New York Genealogical and Biographical Record* 13, no. 4 (October 1882): 165–73.

———. "The Register Book for the Parish of Jamaica [Queens], 1710–1732." *New York Genealogical and Biographical Record* 19, no. 2 (April 1888): 53–59.

New-York Historical Society. "Colonial Commissions, 1680–1772." *New York Historical Society Quarterly Bulletin* 9, no. 1 (April 1925): 32–35.

———. Collections of the New York Historical Society for the Year 1885, vol. 18. New York: Printed for the Society, 1885.

———. *Collections of the New-York Historical Society for the Year 1893*. New York: New-York Historical Society, 1893.

———. *Tax Lists of the City of New York, December, 1695–July 15th, 1699: Assessment of the Real and Personal Property of the East Ward, City of New York, June 24, 1791*. Collections of the New-York Historical Society, vol. 43. New York: Printed for the Society, 1910.

Nugent, Nell Marion. *Cavaliers and Pioneers: Abstracts of Virginia Land Patents and Grants, 1623–1800*. Richmond: Dietz, 1934.

O'Callaghan, E. B., ed. *Documentary History of the State of New York*. Vols. 1–2. Albany: Weed, Parsons, 1849.

Oliver, Vere Langford, ed. *Caribbeana: Being Miscellaneous Papers Relating to the His-

tory, Genealogy, Topography, and Antiquities of the British West Indies. Vol. 2. London: Mitchell, Hughes, & Clark, 1912.

Onderdonk, Henry, Jr. *Documents and Letters Intended to Illustrate the Revolutionary Incidents of Queens County.* New York: Leavitt, Trow, 1848.

Philopolites [Cotton Mather]. *A Memorial of the Present Deplorable State of New England.* Boston: S. Phillips, N. Buttolph, B. Elliot, 1707.

Raithby, John. *Statutes of the Realm.* Vol. 7: 1695–1701. London: Great Britain Record Commission, 1820.

[Rigsby, Richard]. *Observations on, and Reasons Against Vacating the Bonds Taken by Her Majesty's Customs Collector at Jamaica.* London, 1712.

Riker, James, Jr. *The Annals of Newtown in Queens County, New York.* New York: D. Fanshaw, 1852.

Salley, Alexander S, ed. *Register of St. Phillips Parish, Charlestown, South Carolina, 1720–1758.* Charleston: Walker, Evans, Coggswell, 1904.

———. *Journal of the Commons House of Assembly of South Carolina, March 6, 1705/6– April 9, 1706.* Columbia: Printed for the Historical Commission of South Carolina by the State Company, 1937.

Saunders, William, ed. *The Colonial Records of North Carolina.* Vol. 2. Raleigh: PM HALE, 1886.

Schonhorn, Manuel, ed. *A General History of the Pyrates.* By Daniel Defoe. Mineola, N.Y.: Dover, 1999.

Selyns, Domine Henricus. *Records of Domine Henricus Selyns of New York, 1686–7: With Notes and Remarks by Garret Abeel Written a Century Later, 1791–2.* Collections of the Holland Society of New York, vol. 5. New York: Holland Society of New York, 1916.

Shaw, William, ed. *Calendar of Treasury Books.* Vol. 9: 1689–1692. London: His Majesty's Stationery Office, 1931.

———. *Calendar of Treasury Books.* Vol. 15: 1699–1700. London: His Majesty's Stationery Office, 1933.

———. *Calendar of Treasury Books.* Vol. 20: 1705–1706. London: Her Majesty's Stationery Office, 1952.

Sheridan, Eugene R., ed. *The Papers of Lewis Morris.* Vol. 1: 1698–1730. Newark: New Jersey Historical Society, 1991.

———. *The Papers of Lewis Morris.* Vol. 2: 1731–1737. Newark: New Jersey Historical Society, 1993.

Smith, William P., and Robert Kelby, eds. *Abstracts of Wills on File in the Surrogate's Office, City of New York.* Vol. 26. New York: New-York Historical Society, 1893.

Snelgrave, William. *A New Account of Some Parts of Guinea, and the Slave-trade: Containing I. The History of the Late Conquest of the Kingdom of Whidaw by the King of Dahomè . . . II. The Manner How the Negroes Become Slaves . . . III. A Relation of the Author's Being Taken by Pirates, and the Many Dangers He Underwent.* London: James, John & Paul Knapton, 1734.

South Carolina Court of Vice-Admiralty. *The Tryals of Major Stede Bonnet, and Other Pirates.* London: Benjamin Cowse, 1719.

Sypher, Francis J., Jr., ed. and trans. *Liber A 1628–1700: Of the Collegiate Churches of*

New York. The Historical Series of the Reformed Churches of America, vol. 61. Grand Rapids, Mich.: William B. Eerdmans, 2009.

Wyman, Thomas B. *The Genealogies and Estates of Charlestown, in the County of Middlesex and Commonwealth of Massachusetts, 1629–1818.* Boston: Joseph Clapp, 1879.

Secondary Sources

Andreas, Peter. *Smuggler Nation: How Illicit Trade Made America.* Oxford: Oxford University Press, 2014.

Archdeacon, Thomas J. *New York City, 1664–1710: Conquest and Change.* Ithaca, N.Y.: Cornell University Press, 1976.

Bahar, Matthew R. *Storm of the Sea: Indians and Empires in the Atlantic's Age of Sail.* Oxford: Oxford University Press, 2019.

Bailyn, Bernard, and Lotte Bailyn. *Massachusetts Shipping, 1697–1714: A Statistical Study.* Cambridge, Mass.: Harvard University Press, 1959.

Bassi, Ernesto. *An Aqueous Territory: Sailor Geographies and New Granada's Transimperial Greater Caribbean World.* Durham, N.C.: Duke University Press, 2016.

Baugh, Daniel A. "Great Britain's 'Blue Water' Policy, 1689–1815." *International History Review* 10, no. 1 (February 1988): 33–58.

Bialuschewski, Arne. "Blackbeard off Philadelphia: Documents Pertaining to the Campaign against Pirates in 1717 and 1718." *Pennsylvania Magazine of History and Biography* 134, no. 2 (April 2010): 165–78.

———. "Black People under the Black Flag: Piracy and the Slave Trade on the West Coast of Africa, 1718–1723." *Slavery and Abolition* 29, no. 4 (December 2008): 461–75.

———. "Daniel Defoe, Nathaniel Mist, and the General History of the Pyrates." *Papers of the Bibliographical Society of America* 98, no. 1 (2004).

———. "Jacobite Pirates?" *Histoire sociale / Social history* 44, no. 87 (May 2011): 147–64.

———. "Pirates, Black Sailors and Seafaring Slaves in the Anglo-American Maritime World, 1716–1726." *Journal of Caribbean History* 45, no. 2 (2011): 143–58.

———. "Pirates, Markets and Imperial Authority: Economic Aspects of Maritime Depredations in the Atlantic World, 1716–1726." *Global Crime* 9, nos. 1–2 (2008): 52–65.

———. *Raiders and Natives: Cross-Cultural Relations in the Age of Buccaneers.* Athens: University of Georgia Press, 2022.

Black, Jeremy. *Politics and Foreign Policy in the Age of George I, 1714–1727.* New York: Routledge, 2014.

Block, Kristen. *Ordinary Lives in the Early Caribbean.* Athens: University of Georgia Press, 2012.

Bourne, Ruth. *Queen Anne's Navy in the West Indies.* New Haven, Conn.: Yale University Press, 1939.

Bradburn, Douglas. "The Visible Fist: The Chesapeake Tobacco Trade in War and the Purpose of Empire, 1690–1715." *William and Mary Quarterly,* 3rd ser., 68, no. 3 (July 2011): 361–86.

Brooks, Baylus C. "'Capt. Charles Johnson' Was Indeed Nathaniel Mist." *B. C. Brooks' Writer's Hiding Place* (blog), April 27, 2021, http://bcbrooks.blogspot.com/2021/04/capt-charljohnson-is-indeed-nathaniel.html.

Brown, Joseph O. *The Jaunceys of New York*. New York: Thitchener & Glastaeter, 1876.

Brown, Kathleen. *Good Wives, Nasty Wenches, and Anxious Patriarchs: Gender, Race, and Power in Colonial Virginia*. Chapel Hill: University of North Carolina Press, 1996.

Brown, Richard D. "Microhistory and the Post-Modern Challenge." *Journal of the Early Republic* 23, no. 1 (Spring 2003): 1–20.

Brunsman, Denver. *The Evil Necessity: British Naval Impressment in the Eighteenth-Century Atlantic World*. Charlottesville: University of Virginia Press, 2013.

Bulkley, Abby Isabel, and Henry Truman Beckwith. *The Chad Browne Memorial, Consisting of Genealogical Memoirs of a Portion of the Descendants of Chad and Elizabeth Browne; with an Appendix, Containing Sketches of Other Early Rhode Island Settlers, 1638–1888*. Brooklyn, N.Y.: Brooklyn Daily Eagle Book Printing Dept., 1888.

Burg, R. R. "Legitimacy and Authority: A Case Study of Pirate Commanders in the Seventeenth and Eighteenth Centuries," *American Neptune* 37, no. 1 (January 1977): 40–49.

Burgess, Douglas R. *The Politics of Piracy: Crime and Civil Disobedience in Colonial America*. Lebanon, N.H.: University Press of New England, 2014.

Carew, James, and John E. Mylroie. "Geology of the Bahamas." In H. L. Vacher and T. Quinn, eds., *Geology and Hydrogeology of Carbonate Islands*. Developments in Sedimentology 54. Amsterdam: Elsevier Science, 1997.

Chapman, Rev. F. W. *The Chapman Family: Or, the Descendants of Robert Chapman, One of the First Settlers of Saybrook, Connecticut*. Hartford, Conn.: Case, Tiffany, 1854.

Chet, Guy. *The Ocean Is a Wilderness: Atlantic Piracy and the Limits of State Authority, 1688–1856*. Amherst: University of Massachusetts Press, 2014.

Clifford, Barry, Kenneth Kinkor, and Sharon Simpson. *Real Pirates: The Untold Story of the Whydah from Slave Ship to Pirate Ship*. New York: National Geographic, 2007.

Clute, John J. *Annals of Staten Island, from Its Discovery to the Present Time*. New York: C. Vogt, 1877.

Coclanis, Peter A., ed. *The Atlantic Economy during the Seventeenth and Eighteenth Centuries: Organization, Operation, Practice, and Personnel*. Columbia: University of South Carolina Press, 2005.

Cordingly, David. *Pirate Hunter of the Caribbean: The Adventurous Life of Captain Woodes Rogers*. New York: Random House, 2011.

———. *Under the Black Flag: The Romance and Reality of Life among the Pirates*. New York: Random House, 1996.

Coss, Stephen. *The Fever of 1721: The Epidemic That Revolutionized Medicine and American Politics*. New York: Simon & Schuster, 2016.

Craton, Michael, and Gail Saunders. *Islanders in the Stream: A History of the Baha-*

mian People. Vol. 1: *From Aboriginal Times to the End of Slavery*. Athens: University of Georgia Press, 1992.

Craven, Wesley Frank. *The Colonies in Transition: 1660–1713*. New York: Harper & Row, 1968.

Cromwell, Jesse. "Life on the Margins: (Ex) Buccaneers and Spanish Subjects on the Campeche Logwood Periphery, 1660–1716." *Itinerario* 33, no. 3 (2009): 42–71.

Davis, Ralph. *The Rise of the English Shipping Industry in the 17th and 18th Centuries*. London: Macmillan, 1962.

Dawes, Norman. "Titles as Symbols of Prestige in Seventeenth-Century New England." *William and Mary Quarterly* 6, no. 1 (January 1949): 69–83.

Dawson, Kevin. "Enslaved Swimmers and Divers in the Atlantic World." *Journal of American History* 92, no. 4 (March 2006): 1327–55.

———. *Undercurrents of Power: Aquatic Culture in the African Diaspora*. Philadelphia: University of Pennsylvania Press, 2018.

DeBry, John. "A Concise History of the 1715 Spanish Plate Fleet." The 1715 Fleet Society: An Educational Forum, August 2018, https://1715fleetsociety.com/history/.

Dubcovsky, Alejandra. "When Archaeology and History Meet: Shipwrecks, Indians, and the Contours of the Early-Eighteenth-Century South." *Journal of Southern History* 84, no. 1 (February 2018): 39–68.

Earle, Peter. *The Pirate Wars*. New York: St. Martin's Griffin, 2013.

———. *The Sack of Panama: Captain Morgan and the Battle for the Caribbean*. New York: St. Martin's Press, 2007.

Eck, Christopher R. "Wampanoags, Wrecking, and Watlings Island: A Group of Documents Relating to the Voyage of the Ship Portsmouth Galley from Boston to the Bahamas 1703–04." *Journal of the Bahamas Historical Society* (October 1999): 13–20.

Edelson, S. Max. *Plantation Enterprise in Colonial South Carolina*. Cambridge, Mass.: Harvard University Press, 2006.

Enthoven, Victor. "'That Abominable Nest of Pirates': St. Eustatius and the North Americans, 1680–1780." *Early American Studies* 10, no. 2 (Spring 2012): 239–301.

Faller, Lincoln. "Criminal Opportunities in the Eighteenth Century: The 'Ready-Made' Contexts of the Popular Literature of Crime." *Comparative Literature Studies* 24, no. 2 (1987): 120–45.

Finucane, Adrian. *The Temptations of Trade: Britain, Spain, and the Struggle for Empire*. Philadelphia: University of Pennsylvania Press, 2016.

Foote, Thelma Willis. *Black and White Manhattan: The History of Racial Formation in Colonial New York City*. Oxford: Oxford University Press, 2004.

Fox, E. T. "Jacobitism and the 'Golden Age' of Piracy, 1715–1726." *International Journal of Maritime History* 22, no. 2 (December 2010): 277–303.

García del Pino, César. *Corsarios, Piratas, y Santiago de Cuba*. Havana: Editorial de Ciencias Sociales, 2009.

Geanacopoulos, Daphne Palmer. *The Pirate Next Door: The Untold Story of Eighteenth Century Pirates' Wives, Families and Communities*. Durham, N.C.: Carolina University Press, 2016.

Gelfand, Noah L. "The Gomez Family and Atlantic Patterns in the Development of New York's Jewish Community." The Gotham Center for New York City History, July 21, 2020, https://www.gothamcenter.org/blog/the-gomez-family-and-atlantic-patterns-in-the-development-of-new-yorks-jewish-community.

Ginzburg, Carlo, John Tedeschi, and Anne C. Tedeschi. "Microhistory: Two or Three Things That I Know about It." *Critical Inquiry* 20, no. 1 (Autumn 1993): 10–35.

Goodall, Jamie L. H. *Pirates of the Chesapeake Bay: From the Colonial Era to the Oyster Wars*. Charleston, S.C.: History Press, 2020.

Goodfriend, Joyce D. *Before the Melting Pot: Society and Culture in Colonial New York City, 1664–1730*. Princeton, N.J.: Princeton University Press, 1992.

Graham, Eric J. *Seawolves: Pirates and the Scots*. Edinburgh: Birlinn, 2007.

Gronning, Erik. "Early New York Turned Chairs: A Stoelendraaier's Conceit." In Luke Beckerdite, *American Furniture 2001* (American Furniture Annual), Chipstone Foundation, December 2001, https://www.chipstone.org/html/publications/2001AF/gronning/gronningtext.html.

Guthrie, Neil. *The Material Culture of the Jacobites*. Cambridge: Cambridge University Press, 2013.

Hahn, Steven C. "The Atlantic Odyssey of Richard Tookerman: Gentleman of South Carolina, Pirate of Jamaica, and Litigant before the King's Bench." *Early American Studies* 15, no. 3 (Summer 2017): 539–90.

Hancock, David. "Self-Organized Complexity and the Emergence of an Atlantic Market Economy, 1651–1815: The Case of Madeira." In Coclanis, *Atlantic Economy*, 30–71.

Hanna, Mark. *Pirate Nests and the Rise of the British Empire, 1570–1740*. Chapel Hill: University of North Carolina Press, 2015.

———. "The Pirates' Nest: The Impact of Piracy on Newport, Rhode Island and Charles Town, South Carolina." PhD diss., Harvard University, 2006.

———. "Well-Behaved Pirates Seldom Make History: A Reevaluation of the Golden Age of English Piracy." In Peter C. Mancall and Carole Shammas, eds., *Governing the Sea in the Early Modern Era: Essays in Honor of Robert C. Ritchie*. San Marino, Calif.: Huntington Press, 2015, 129–68.

Harlow, Alvin. *Old Bowery Days: The Chronicles of a Famous Street*. New York: D. Appleton, 1931.

Hasted, Edward. *The History and Topographical Survey of the County of Kent*. Vol. 4. Canterbury: W. Bristow, 1798.

Head, David, ed. *The Golden Age of Piracy: The Rise, Fall, and Enduring Popularity of Pirates*. Athens: University of Georgia Press, 2018.

Hill, Christopher. "Radical Pirates?" In *The Collected Essays of Sir Christopher Hill: Writing and Revolution in Seventeenth-Century England*, vol. 2. Brighton, UK: Harvester, 1986, 161–87.

Hill, James L. "'Bring Them What They Lack': Spanish-Creek Exchange and Alliance Making in a Maritime Borderland, 1763–1783." *Early American Studies* 12, no. 1 (Winter 2014): 36–67.

Hitchings, Sinclair. "Guarding the New England Coast: The Naval Career of Cyprian Southack." *Seafaring in Colonial Massachusetts: Publications of the Colonial Society of Massachusetts*, v. 52. Boston: University Press of Virginia, 1980, 43–65.

Holmes, Geoffrey. *British Politics in the Age of Anne*. London: Bloomsbury, 2003.

Huth, Geof. "The Slave Revolt of 1712: The Provision and Omission of Justice in Early New York." *Metropolitan Archivist*, December 18, 2019, https://medium.com/metropolitan-archivist/the-slave-revolt-of-1712-the-provision-and-omission-of-justice-in-early-new-york-8f6aae2adbd3.
Jarvis, Michael J. *In the Eye of All Trade: Bermuda, Bermudians, and the Maritime Atlantic World, 1680–1783*. Chapel Hill: University of North Carolina Press, 2010.
Johnson, Steven. *Enemy of All Mankind: A True Story of Piracy, Power, and History's First Global Manhunt*. New York: Riverhead, 2020.
Joseph, Gilbert M. "British Loggers and Spanish Governors: The Logwood Trade and Its Settlements in the Yucatan Peninsula: Part II." *Caribbean Studies* 15, no. 4 (January 1976): 43–52.
Kane, David. "Nostos and Kleos in the Iliad and Odyssey, Respectively." *Pyrrhic Victories* (blog), April 18, 2014, https://davidakane.wordpress.com/2014/04/18/nostos-and-kleos-in-the-iliad-and-odyssey-respectively/.
Karraker, Cyrus. *Piracy Was a Business*. Rindge, N.H.: Richard R. Smith, 1953.
———. "The Treasure Expedition of Captain William Phips to the Bahama Banks." *New England Quarterly* 5, no. 4 (October 1932): 731–52.
Kelleher, Connie. *The Alliance of Pirates: Ireland and Atlantic Piracy in the Early Seventeenth Century*. Cork: Cork University Press, 2020.
Kuhn, Gabriel. *Life under the Jolly Roger: Reflections on Golden Age Piracy*. Oakland, Calif.: PM PRESS, 2009.
Lane, Kris. *Pillaging the Empire: Piracy in the Americas, 1500–1750*. New York: Routledge, 1998.
Leeson, Peter. "An-arrgh-chy: The Law and Economics of Pirate Organization." *Journal of Political Economy* 115, no. 6 (2007): 1049–94.
———. *The Invisible Hook: The Hidden Economics of Piracy*. Princeton, N.J.: Princeton University Press, 2009.
Link, Marion Clayton. "The Spanish Camp Site and the 1715 Plate Fleet Wreck." *Tequesta* 26 (1966): 21–30.
Lipman, Andrew. *The Saltwater Frontier: Indians and the Contest for the American Coast*. New Haven, Conn.: Yale University Press, 2015.
Lovejoy, David S. *The Glorious Revolution in America*. Hanover, N.H.: Wesleyan University Press, 1972.
Mackie, Erin. *Rakes, Highwaymen, and Pirates: The Making of the Modern Gentleman in the Eighteenth Century*. Baltimore, Md.: Johns Hopkins University Press, 2009.
———. "Welcome the Outlaw: Pirates, Maroons, and Caribbean Countercultures." *Cultural Critique* 59 (Winter 2005): 24–62.
Magnusson, Sigurdur Gylfi. "The Singularization of History: Social History and Microhistory within the Postmodern State of Knowledge." *Journal of Social History* 36, no. 3 (Spring 2003): 701–36.
———. "Sites of Memory? Institutionalization of History: Microhistory and the Grand Narrative." *Journal of Social History* 39, no. 3 (Spring 2006): 891–913.
Mattson, Cathy. "Rethinking Mercantilism: Political Economy, the British Empire, and the Atlantic World in the Seventeenth and Eighteenth Centuries." *William and Mary Quarterly*, 3rd ser., 69, no. 1 (January 2012): 3–34.

McCullough, David. *John Adams*. New York: Simon & Schuster, 2001.
McCusker, John J., and Russell R. Menard. *The Economy of British America, 1607–1789*. Chapel Hill: University of North Carolina Press, 1985.
McDonald, Kevin. *Pirates, Merchants, Settlers, and Slaves: Colonial America and the Indo-Atlantic World*. Sacramento: University of California Press, 2015.
McKendrick, Neil, John Brewer, and J. H. Plumb. *The Birth of a Consumer Society: The Commercialization of Eighteenth-Century England*. Bloomington: Indiana University Press, 1982.
McParland, Eugene. "Colonial Taverns and Tavernkeepers of British New York City." *New York Genealogical and Biographical Record* 106, no. 3 (July 1975).
Meyer, W. R. "English Privateering in the War of the Spanish Succession, 1702–1713." *Mariner's Mirror* 69 (1983): 435–46.
Miller, W. Hubert. "The Colonization of the Bahamas, 1647–1670." *William and Mary Quarterly* 2, no. 1 (January 1945): 33–46.
Monod, Paul. *Jacobitism and the English People, 1688–1788*. Cambridge: Cambridge University Press, 1993.
Moore, Charles. "Early History of Hempstead, Long Island." *New York Genealogical and Biographical Record* 10, no. 1 (January 1879).
Moore, David D. "Captain Edward Thatch: A Brief Analysis of the Primary Source Documents Concerning the Notorious Blackbeard." *North Carolina Historical Review* 95, no. 2 (April 2018): 147–85.
Morley, Nicholas. "British-Colonial Privateering in the War of the Spanish Succession, 1702–1713." M.Phil. thesis, University of Glasgow, 2000.
Morsink, Joost. "Spanish-Lucayan Interaction: Continuity of Native Economies in Early Historic Times." *Journal of Caribbean Archaeology* 15 (2015): 103–19.
Muldrew, Craig. *The Economy of Obligation: The Culture of Credit and Social Relations in Early Modern England*. New York: Macmillan, 1998.
Murphy, Kathleen. "James Petiver's 'Kind Friends' and the 'Curious Persons' in the Atlantic World: Commerce, Colonialism, and Collecting." *Notes and Records of the Royal Society* 74, no. 2 (October 2020): 259–74.
Newton, Lowell. "Juan Esteban de Ubilla and the *Flota* of 1715." *Americas* 33, no. 2 (October 1976): 267–81.
Oates, Jonathan D. *The Last Spanish Armada: Britain and the War of the Quadruple Alliance, 1718–1720*. Warwick, UK: Helion, 2019.
Parsons, Christopher, and Kathleen Murphy. "Ecosystems under Sail: Specimen Transport in the Eighteenth Century British and French Atlantic." *Early American Studies* 10, no. 3 (Fall 2012): 503–29.
Pastore, Christopher. *Between Land and Sea: The Atlantic Coast and the Transformation of New England*. Cambridge, Mass.: Harvard University Press, 2014.
Pestana, Carla. "Early English Jamaica without Pirates." *William and Mary Quarterly*, 3d ser., 71 (2014): 321–60.
———. *The English Conquest of Jamaica: Oliver Cromwell's Bid for Empire*. Cambridge, Mass.: Belknap Press of Harvard University Press, 2017.
Peterson, Mark. *The City-State of Boston: The Rise and Fall of an Atlantic Power, 1630–1865*. Princeton, N.J.: Princeton University Press, 2019.

Phillips, Carla Rahn. "Why Did Anyone Go to Sea? Structures of Maritime Enlistment from Family Traditions to Violent Coercion." In Lauren Benton and Nathan Perl-Rosenthal, eds., *A World at Sea: Maritime Practices and Global History*. Philadelphia: University of Pennsylvania Press, 2020, 17–36.

Pietsch, Roland. "Ships' Boys and Youth Culture in Eighteenth-Century Britain: The Navy Recruits of the London Marine Society." *Northern Mariner / Le marin du nord* 14, no. 4 (October 2004): 11–24.

Piker, Joshua. *The Four Deaths of Acorn Whistler: Telling Stories in Colonial America*. Cambridge, Mass.: Harvard University Press, 2013.

Pitt, Steven John James. "City upon the Atlantic Tides: Merchants, Pirates, and the Seafaring Community of Boston, 1689–1748." PhD diss., University of Pittsburgh, 2015.

Putnam, Lara. "To Study the Fragments/Whole: Microhistory as Atlantic History." *Journal of Social History* 39, no. 3 (Spring 2006): 615–30.

Raymond, Marcus. "Colonel William Stephens Smith." *New York Genealogical and Biographical Record* 25, no. 4 (October 1894): 153–54.

Rediker, Marcus. "'Under the Banner of King Death': The Social World of Anglo-American Pirates." *William and Mary Quarterly* 38, no. 2 (April 1981): 203–27.

———. *Villains of All Nations: Atlantic Pirates in the Golden Age*. Boston: Beacon, 2011.

Riker, David M. "Genealogy of a Colonial Dutch Bush Family." *De Halve Maen: Magazine of the Dutch Colonial Period in America* 64, no. 2 (Summer 1991): 29–33.

Ritchie, Robert J. *Captain Kidd and the War against the Pirates*. Cambridge, Mass.: Harvard University Press, 1989.

Roberts, Clayton. "The Law of Impeachment in Stuart England: A Reply to Raoul Berger." *Yale Law Minutes* 84, no. 7 (June 1975): 1419–39.

Roger, N. A. M. *The Wooden World: An Anatomy of the Georgian Navy*. New York: Norton, 1986.

Rogers, Nicholas. "Popular Jacobitism in Provincial Context: Eighteenth-Century Bristol and Norwich." In Eveline Cruickshanks and Jeremy Black, eds., *The Jacobite Challenge*. Edinburgh: John Donald, 1988, 123–41.

———. "Riot and Popular Jacobitism in Early Hanoverian England." In Eveline Cruickshanks, ed., *Ideology and Conspiracy: Aspects of Jacobitism, 1689–1759*. Edinburgh: John Donald, 1982, 70–88.

Rupert, Linda. *Creolization and Contraband: Curaçao in the Early Modern Atlantic*. Athens: University of Georgia Press, 2012.

Rutledge, Andrew. "Enemies Bound by Trade: Jamaica, Cuba, and the Shared World of Contraband in Atlantic Empires, 1710–1760." PhD diss., University of Michigan, 2018.

Satsuma, Shinsuke. "Politicians, Merchants, and Colonial Maritime War: The Political and Economic Background of the American Act of 1708." *Parliamentary History* 32, part 2 (2013): 317–36.

Schneider, Elena A. *The Occupation of Havana: War, Trade, and Slavery in the Atlantic World*. Chapel Hill: University of North Carolina Press, 2018.

Scott, Kenneth. "Jacob Leisler's Fifty Militiamen." *New York Genealogical and Biographical Record* 94, no. 2 (April 1963): 65–72.

Starkey, David. "Pirates and Markets." In C. R. Pennell, ed., *Bandits at Sea: A Pirates Reader*. New York: New York University Press, 2001, 107–23.

Stone, Lawrence. "Prosopography." *Daedalus* 100, no. 1 (Winter 1971): 46–71.

Storr, Virgil Henry. "Enterprising Slaves and Master Pirates: Understanding Economic Life in the Bahamas." PhD diss., George Mason University, 2000.

Szijarto, Istvan. "Four Arguments for Microhistory." *Rethinking History* 6, no. 2 (2002): 209–15.

Tapely, Harriet Silvester. *The Province Galley of Massachusetts Bay, 1694–1716: A Chapter of Early American Naval History*. Salem, Mass.: Essex Institute, 1922.

Tuller, Roberta. "Captain John Richards." An American Family History, 2023, https://www.anamericanfamilyhistory.com/Richards%20Family/RichardsJohn1677.html.

Tyler, Lyon G. "Old Tombstones in Gloucester County." *William and Mary Quarterly* 3, no. 4 (April 1895).

Ubbehlode, Carl. *The American Colonies and the British Empire: 1607–1763*. New York: Wiley & Sons, 1975.

Vickers, Daniel. "Beyond Jack Tar." *William and Mary Quarterly* 50, no. 2 (April 1993): 418–24.

———. *Young Men and the Sea: Yankee Seafarers in the Age of Sail*. New Haven, Conn.: Yale University Press, 2005.

Vickers, Daniel, and Vince Walsh. "Young Men and the Sea: The Sociology of Seafaring in Eighteenth-Century Salem, Massachusetts." *Social History* 24, no. 1 (January 1999): 17–38.

Wall, Alexander J. "William Bradford, Colonial Printer: A Tercentenary Review." *American Antiquarian* 73, no. 2 (October 1963): 361–84.

Waller, George M. *Samuel Vetch: Colonial Enterpriser*. Chapel Hill: University of North Carolina Press, 1960.

Walton, Timothy R. *The Spanish Treasure Fleets*. Sarasota, Fla.: Pineapple Press, 1994.

Wilson, David. "From the Caribbean to Craignish: Imperial Authority and Piratical Voyages in the Early Eighteenth-Century Atlantic Commons." *Itinerario* 42, no. 3 (2018): 430–60.

———. *Suppressing Piracy in the Early Eighteenth Century : Pirates, Merchants and British Imperial Authority in the Atlantic and Indian Oceans*. Woodbridge, UK: Boydell, 2021.

Wilson, Kathleen. *The Sense of the People: Politics, Culture and Imperialism in England, 1717–1785*. Cambridge: Cambridge University Press, 1995.

Woodard, Colin. *The Republic of Pirates: Being the True and Surprising Story of the Caribbean Pirates and the Man Who Brought Them Down*. New York: Harcourt, 2007.

Zahedieh, Nuala. "Commerce and Conflict: Jamaica in the War of the Spanish Succession." In A. B. Leonard and David Pretel, eds., *The Caribbean and the Atlantic World Economy: Circuits of Trade, Credit, and Knowledge, 1650–1914*. London: Palgrave Macmillan, 2015, 68–86.

INDEX

Locators in *italics* indicate a figure. Locators in **bold** indicate the appearance of individual pardoned pirates in the appendix.

Act of Grace: bounties and, 188–91; *General History* and, 240; New York pirate ring and, 217, 236; Pearse arrival with, 94–95; Pearse's list and, 2, *3–5*, 7, 14, 244; pirate surrenders and, 1–2, 111–15, 117–20, 243–44, 247; requirements of, 171. *See also* pardoning mission to the Bahamas; Pearse, Vincent
Adams, Abraham, 12, 20, *31*, 174, 199, 244, **249**
Adams, Packer, 27, 174, **249**
Addey, Samuel, 93, **249**
Allen, Arthur, **249**
Allen, John, **250**
Alsop, Deborah, 212, 218, 220
America Act, 26, 46, 71
Anne (ship), 108
anti-piracy acts, 66, 81–82, 110
anti-piracy commissions investigation (Jamaica Council): acts of piracy and, 89–91; class and, 93; Hamilton testimony and, 87–89; merchant testimonies and, 85–88; Pearse's pardoned pirates and, 91–93; pirate flight and, 82–83; recovery of stolen goods and, 88–89; wrecking and, 84–85
Antsis play, 240
apprehension of pirates: bounties for, 111; colonial governance and, 65–66; Craignish and, 181; executions/convictions and, 65–66, 137–39, 168, 179–81, 189–90, 239; Hamilton inquest and, 82–83, 88; Jamaica Council and, 82–85; Lewis and, 61, 187–88; Pearse tactics and, 126; Perrin sloop conflict and, 61–64; Phenney efforts and, 164–65; Rogers efforts and, 137–38, 178; Walker and, 59–60
Archdeacon, Thomas, 207
Arterile/Arturreal, John, 152, 160, **250**
articles of agreement, 240
Ashworth, Leigh: background of, 17–20; *Lovely Mary* and, 80–84, 90–91; on Pearse's list, 144, **250**; postpardon employment of, 171–72; privateering and, 192
asiento, 70, 73
Atlantic commercial networks, 29–30, 36, 99. *See also* imperial trade system
Augur, John, 93, 115–18, 136–37, 139, 240, **250**
Austin, William, 93, 174, **250**
Axtell, Daniel, 81, 86

INDEX

Bahama Merchant (ship), 53
Bahamas: bounty system in, 188–89, 190–91; censuses in, 154, 161; corruption in, 160–61; court of admiralty and, 132–33; evidence of pardoned pirates in, 6; flourishing of piracy in, 7–8, 15, 49–50; governance in, 52–54, 132–33, 150–51, 157–58, 160–63; Jamaica inquest and, 83; map of, *51*; modern pirate tourism and, 167; pirate concerns in, 57–60; as pirate nest, 49–50, 60–62, 66–67; pirate trade in, 99–102, 145–46, 243; Queen Anne's War and, 54–57; race and slavery in, 154–55; relations with Spain, 140–44, 148–50; Revolution of 1701 in, 53–54; settlement of, 52; shadow of piracy in, 162–63, 166; Spanish attacks on, 136; suppression of piracy in, 62, 132–40, 164–66; trajectories of pardoned pirates in, 130; wrecking expeditions and, 52–53. *See also* New Providence; Rogers, Woodes
Bahamas Assembly, 150–51, 157–58, 162, 165
Bahamas Company, 52, 131, 151
Bahamas Society, 159
Bahar, Matthew, 10
Balchen, John, 68–69
Barker, John, *31*, 250
Barnet, Jonathan, 76–77, 85
Barrow, Thomas, 61
Bass, Robert, 194, 250
Bead, Edward, 190–91, 251
Belcher, Andrew, 45
Bellamy, Samuel, 98, 241
Bendysh, Thomas, 78, 81, 86
Benjamin (ship), 108
Bennet (ship), 77, 78–79, 86–88
Bennet, Benjamin, 107–8, 112–14
Bennet, John, 108, 112
Bermuda, 29, 58, 100–102, 107–8, 112–15, 154
Bernard, Alan, 84
Berry, Edward, 17, 19, 171–72, 189–90, 199, 251
Berry, Henry, 27, 174, 199, 251
Berry, James, 191

Bersheba (ship), 77, 78, 80, 87–88
Bialuschewski, Arne, 10
Bill, Benjamin, 120–21, 123, 125, 212–18, 219. *See also* New York pirate ring
Bishop, Richard, 251
Blackbeard. *See* Thache, Edward
Blanco, Augustine, 149–50
Blankenshire, Ralph, 58
Bley, John, 152, 154–55, 161–62, 173–74, 251
Bonnet, Stede, 8, 138, 172, 189–90
Bonny, Anne, 167
Bosch, Justus, 121–22, 215, 220, 222–23
Boston, Mass., 25, 29, 42, 102, 170
bounty system, 188–91
Bourne, James, 58
Bowlin, Thomas, 149
Boyce, Samuel, 29–30, *31*, 37, 171, 198, 202, 251
Bradford, William, 247–48
Bradley, Thomas, 139–40, 251
Bradshaw, James, 181
Bridges, William, 159, 251
Brown, James, 22–23, 27, *31*, 199, 251
Brown, Robert (Jamaica/Bahamas), 26–27, 91, 152–53, 159, 164, 252
Brown, Robert (R.I.), 133, 177–78, 241, 252
Brown, William, 22
Bryan, James, 252
Buck (ship), 180–81
Bucquoy, Jacob de, 183–94
Bunce, Phineas, 136–37, 167
Burchett, Josiah, 1, 68, 120
Burgess, Douglas, 9, 65
Burgess, Josiah, 2, 92, 112, 117–18, 133, 138, 142–43, 161, 243–45, 252
buried treasure, 166

Cale, Edward, 158
Calverley, Phillip, 252
Campbell, Alexander, 150, 152, 154, 252
Campbell, James, 46
canonization of pirates, 239–41. *See also* noncanonical pirates
Carey, John, 58, 152
Carman, Daniel, 172, 252
Carnegie, James, 80, 81–82

INDEX

Carr/Kerr, Edward, 152, 164, 258
carrying trade, 19–20, 28–30, 221. *See also* trade
Carye, John, 252
Cat Island attack, 149–50
Champion, David, 27, 155, 252
Chandler, Thomas, *31*, 172, 252
Charles Town, S.C., 171–72
Charnock, Francis, 91, *96*, 171, 181, 199, 253
Chet, Guy, 9
Chick, Henry, 27, 253
Chissem, George, 93, 253
Clapp, Joseph, 253
Clark, Richard, 164
Clark/Clarke, John, 181, 241, 253
Clies, Thomas, 174–75, 253
Coates, James, 253
Cocklyn, Thomas, 182–83
Cockram, John, 253; anti-piracy cause and, 137–38, 140, 240; *Bersheba* and, 91; civic participation and, 245; debts issues of, 161; estate of, 152, 156; map of, 132; as merchant, 147; Spanish encounters of, 58, 143–44, 149
Colebrook, John, 166
colonization, piratical, 24
Company of Eleutherian Adventurers, 52
Congdon, Edward, 122, 139–40
Connelly, Darby, 253
Connor, William, 122–23, 215–16, 219, 221–22, 231, 233, 253–54
conviction and execution of pirates, 65–66, 137–39, 168, 179–81, 189–90, 239
Courant, Peter, 160, 163
Cracraft, John, 186
Craton, Michael, 53, 153
Craven, Charles, 61
Creigh/Creagh, John, *31*, 254
Crew/Crow, John, 174, 194, 254
crucifix case, 163–64
Cuba, 72–73
Cullemore/Cullimore, John, 148–56 passim, 159, 161–62, 245, 254

Dalrimple/Dalrymple, John, 161, 194, 254
Daniel, Robert, 62–65, 83
Darling, Henry, 43
Darville, Zaccheus, 58–59
Davis, Howell, 170, 180, 183
Davis, Othenias, 91, 133, 171, 186, 192–93, 245, 254
debt cases, 11, 46–47, 175–76, 195, 231–32
Delicia (ship), 137, 141–42
demise of piracy, 244–45
De Peyster, Abraham, 121–22, 126, 205, 215
Derickson, Clois (Cornelius), 217, 254
diaspora of pardoned pirates. *See* pirate diaspora
Dively, Richard, 104, 254
Dolphin (ship), 81, 90, 149
Drake, Francis, 21
Dudley, Paul, 41–44
Dudley proclamation, 42
Dunkin, John, 174, 190–91, 199, 254
Dutch West India Company (WIC), 206

Eagle (ship), 77–78, 87, 177, 181, 191
Ealing, John, 92, 171, 254–55
Earle, Peter, 184
Earle, Richard, 91, 255
Edmundsen, William, 255
Edwards, John, 152, 255
Eels, Joseph, 90–91
Elding, Read, 53
Eleuthera, Bahamas, 51–52, 57–59
Emly, Thomas, 171, 255
England, Edward, 22, 26, 177, 182–83, 241
enslaved people, 52, 154–55
Escheverz y Zubiza, Antonio, 75
estates and wills. *See* wills and estates
Every, Henry, 21–23, 53
execution and conviction of pirates, 65–66, 137–39, 168, 179–81, 189–90, 239

Fairfax, William, 158, 162–64
Fancy (ship), 22–23, 53
Fasset, James, 168–69, 172, 190–91, 255
Fellowes, James, 63–64
Fernando, Francis, 76, 78–79, 81–83, 86, 88
Ferrall, Simon, 160
Feversham, George, 255
Fitzwilliam, Richard, 165–66

Fletcher, Robert, 179–80
flota (New Spain fleet), 69, 74–76, 81–82, 99, 242–43. *See also* wrecking expeditions
forced men. *See* impressment
Francis and Sarah (ship), 89, 92, 146
Franklin, Benjamin, 20
Fred, John, 106, 133, 216–17
free people of color, 154–56

Gee, Marmaduke, 17, 171, 192–93, 255
General History of the Pyrates (Johnson), 18–19, 50, 238–41, 247–48
George (ship), 108
George I, King of England, 111–12
Glinn, Henry, 32, 93, 255–56
Gohier, James, 162–64
golden age of piracy, 8–9, 12, 82–83, 93, 98–99, 177, 243
Goodsir, James, 256
Goudet, Peter, 16, 20, 128–30, 147, 152, 155–59, 161, 165, 245, 256
Graham/Grahame, Thomas, 123, 125, 173, 256
Gratricks, James, 96, 171, 256
Graves, John, 49–50, 53–55
Great Seal of the Realm defacement, 150–51
Greenway, William, 136–37, 148–49
Groans of Jamaica, The (anonymous), 72–73
guardacostas, 24, 57–58, 66, 73–74, 79, 130, 148–49
Guerrero, Domingo, 92
Gunsway (ship), 22

Halsey, John, 25
Hamilton, Archibald, 15, 64, 68–69, 73–74, 76–77, 79, 81–83. *See also* anti-piracy commissions investigation
Hancock, David, 28
Hancock, Richard, 149–50
Hanna, Mark, 9, 65–66
Harbin, Rowland, 256
Harbon, Rowland, 92
Harris, William, 32, 104, 133, 177–78, 197–98, 202, 243, 256

Haselton, William, 174, 199, 256
Haskett, Elias, 53–54
Hawkins, Henry, 27, 256
Hawks, Richard, 256
Heywood, Peter, 69–70, 82–83
Hildesey, John, 194
Hipperson, John, 93, 199, 257
Hipps, John, 138
Holmes, Edward, 56
Holmes, Mark, 257
Hornigold, Benjamin, 257; anti-piracy assistance and, 134–35, 137–38, 140; death of, 142, 161, 245; *General History* and, 239–40; investigations into, 89, 98; on Pearse's list, 3; as pirate commander, 243; pirate voyages of, 58–62, 74, 80, 84, 91–92, 163–64; surrender of, 1, 98, 114–15, 118
Howard, Thomas, 62–64, 66
Howell, John, 160, 161, 162, 163, 257
Hudson, Nathaniel, 32, 91, 103, 115, 122, 123, 257
Hunt, John, 257
Hunt, William, 257
Hunter, Robert, 148, 257

illicit trade. *See* trade
imperial trade system (Britain), 29, 58, 69, 127, 207, 242, 244, 247
impressment, 25–26, 46, 137
Isaacs, Henry, 80–81

Jackson, John, 32, 173, 258
Jacobs, Anthony, 27, 93, 258
Jamaica: contributions to piracy, 15, 68–70, 93; duties in, 71–72; *guardacosta* attacks and, 73–74; Hamilton and, 81–83; monopoly companies and, 72–73; pardoned pirates and, 6, 114–15; privateering and wartime customs in, 71–72; role of geography of, 30; slave trade and, 70–71; wrecking expeditions and, 76–79. *See also* anti-piracy commissions investigation
Jamaica Act, 66
Jarvis, Michael, 29

INDEX

339

Jauncey, James, 225, 235
Jennings, Henry, 78, 79–81, 87–89, 98, 113
John and Elizabeth (ship), 120–26, 179, 204–5, 214–18
Johnson, Charles, 239; *General History of the Pyrates*, 18–19, 50, 238–41, 247–48
Johnson, Jacob, 258
Johnson, John, 174, 258
Johnson, Peter, 161, 192–93, 258
Johnson, Robert, 171, 189–90
Jones, Daniel, 216, 258

Kaine, Richard, 174, 258
Karraker, Cyrus, 8
Keith, William, 191
Kemp, Anthony, 92, 161–62, 258
Kemp, John, 58, 148, 161–62, 258
Kennedy, Walter, 22, 180–81
Kensington (ship), 78–79
Kerr, James, 173, 259
Kerr/Carr, Edward, 152, 164, 258
Kidd, William, 40
King of Spain (ship), 45, 201
King William's War, 24

La Bouche, Olivier Levasseur, 182–83, 185
Lane, Henry, 126
Lark (ship), 61, 94–95, 118–19, 122
Laws, John, 184
Leeson, Peter, 8
Legatt, Richard, 154, 171, 259
Lesley, Francis, 2, 19, 91, 113, 118, 175, 245, 259
Lester, Territ, 210
Lewis, Herman, 46
Lewis, John, 26, 30, 32–33, 61, 118, 125, 145, 185–88, 259
Lewis, Mary, 187–88
Lewis, William, 139
Liddale, Samuel, 77, 80, 84
Lightwood, Ellis, 53–54
Linn, Benjamin, 58, 163
Lovely Mary of Rochelle (ship), 80–82, 84, 88–90
Lowe, Matthew, 58

Madagascar, 22, 182–83
Magness, John, 259
Mahon, Cornelius, 174, 199, 259
Mallet, Peter, 33, 175, 208, 245, 259
manumission, 155–56
Marianne (ship), 80, 88, 90
maritime historical research, 241–42
Martel, Louis, 55–56, 57–58
Martin, Bartholomew, 56
Martin, John, 33, 91, 216, 233, 259
Mayflower (ship), 41, 42
McCarty, Denis/Dennis, 27, 136, 138, 139, 240, 260
Mense, Isaac, 232
mercantilism, 28–29
merchant voyages of pardoned pirates, 31–36. *See also* carrying trade
Meredith, David, 161, 260
Mickelbro, Joseph, 148–49, 260
Mist, Nathaniel, 239–41. See also *General History of the Pyrates*
Mitchell, Elizabeth, 175
Mitchell, John, 19, 27–29, 33, 37, 173, 175–76, 244, 245, 260
Moodey/Moodie, James, 20, 260
Moody, William, 185, 190
Morgan, Henry, 21
Morris, Lewis, 14, 126
Mounsey, John, 161, 179, 190–91, 260
Movil Trader (ship), 180, 192–93
Mowat, James, 93, 260
Murray, Archibald, 18, 19, 181, 260
Musson, Matthew, 62, 64–65, 112, 117–18
mutinies, 136–37, 180–81
Mutlow, John, 33–34, 104, 214, 219–21, 225–30, 233, 243, 261

Nassau, Bahamas, 167. *See also* Bahamas; New Providence
Navarres, Marquis de, 61, 185–86
Navigation Acts, 28–29
Neville, James, 27, 261
New Amsterdam. *See* New York
Newland, Edward, 261
Newland, Richard, 91, 122–23, 147–48, 161–64, 261

New Providence: anti-piracy policies and, 66–67; demographics in, 154; development as pirate lair, 59, 60–61; disease and, 161; Jamaican pirates and, 70; Pearse logbook and, 94–95, 97; rebuilding fortifications in, 135–36; reception of pirates, 59–62, 88, 243–44; Spain and, 55, 143–44; use of term, 16. *See also* Bahamas; pardoning mission to the Bahamas; Rogers, Woodes

New York: origins and English influence in, 206–7; pardoned pirates and, 16, 208–12; slave rebellion in, 211–12; Smith case in, 204–5; trade networks and, 30, 207; wealth in, 207–8. *See also* New York pirate ring

New York pirate ring: Bill circle, 213–18; children of, 227–28, 230, 235–37; church membership and, 228–29; estate planning and death in, 230, 233–35; family backgrounds of, 208–12, 218; legal entanglements of, 231–32; maritime status and, 217, 221, 223–24; marriages of, 218–20; pardoned pirates in, 205; post-pardon careers of, 218, 221–26; reputation in, 234–38; slave trade and, 227; wealth and, 207–8, 233–35

Nichols, Edward, 261

Nichols, Thomas, 2, 112, 118, 122–23, 215–16, 218, 221–22, 231–33, 243, 261

Noland, Edward, 104

noncanonical pirates, 16, 241–42, 246–48; canonization, 239–41

Nuestra Señora de Belen (ship), 79, 81, 86

Odell, Thomas, 121, 123–24

Old Bunce, 167

origins of pirates: carrying trade and, 28–30, 36; maritime backgrounds and, 19–22; merchant voyages and, *31–36*; privateering and, 24–26, 27–28; romantic appeal and, 21–24; Royal Navy and, 26–28; warfare and, 18, 24–28, 242. *See also* Royal Navy service

Pajoean, 56

pardoned pirates: class and, 13, 14–15; Every link to, 22–23; in *General History*, 240; governance and, 150–51; historical evidence of, 6–7, 127; integration into colonial life, 10–14, 15, 16; intelligence gathering and, 143–44; Jamaican piracies and, 91–92; Johnson pardon certificate and, *96*; land holding and, 152; memorization and, 124; merchant voyages of, *31–36*; rank and, 13; reconceptualization of, 245–46; reputation of, 170–71, 236; rootlessness of, 37; Royal Navy service and, 27; as victims of piracy, 148–49; War of the Quadruple Alliance and, 142; work ethic of, 133. *See also* Act of Grace; New York pirate ring; origins of pirates; pardoning mission to the Bahamas; pirate diaspora; pirate rehabilitation; privateers/privateering; *and individual pardoned pirates*

pardoning mission to the Bahamas: background and precedents for, 108–14; Pearse and, 97, 117, 120; Pearse's list and, 2, *3–5*, 14, 244; Piracy Act and, 110; rouge pirates and limitations of, 119–20; success of, 126–27; surrender and, 97–98, 112–16, 118–19. *See also* Act of Grace; Bahamas; *John and Elizabeth*; Pearse, Vincent

Parmyter, Edward, 261

Partridge, Nathaniel, 62

Pearse, John, 261

Pearse, Joseph, 17, 19, 92, 147–48, 156, 261

Pearse, Thomas, 92, 261

Pearse, Vincent: arrival at Providence, 117–18; background as captain, 116–17; captain's log, 94–95, 97; contrasting depictions of, 125–26; efforts to suppress and pardon pirates, 15; illicit activity and, 14–15, 97, 120–25, 204–5; pardon list of, 1–2, *3–5*, 14, 217, 244. *See also*

Act of Grace; pardoning mission to the Bahamas
Perrin, John, *34*, 62, 64–65, 196–97, 261–62
Peters, William, 262
Peterson, Mark, 29
Phenney, George, 145, 158, 160–61
Phillips, John, 42–43
Phoenix (ship), 94, 116–17, 119–20, 123–24, 173, 214, 222
Phoenix, Jacob, 106, 216
Pinfold, William, 104, 106, 214–18 passim, 221, 227–28, 233, 243–44, 262
piracy: anti-piracy acts/commissions and, 66, 81–82, 110; class and, 93; context and, 242–43; definitions of, 110; demise of, 8–10, 12, 244–45; "enemies of all mankind" and, 10; golden age of, 8–9, 12, 82–83, 93, 98–99, 177, 243; historical sources and, 2, 6–7, 11, 18–19; indigenous maritime history and, 10; "marooners" and, 13; motivations to pursue, 8–9, 15, 18–19; murder and, 114; political weaponization of, 162–64; reconceptualization of, 245–46; settler colonialism, 246; shadow of, 162–63; suppression of, 9, 127, 132–40; war on, 9, 189. *See also* origins of pirates; pardoned pirates; pirate trade
piracy, acts of: anti-piracy acts and, 66, 81–82; Bahamas and, 57–59; Bellamy, 98; crucifix case and, 163–64; Cuba trade voyage and, 136–37; Fernando, 78–79, 81; Hamilton commissions inquest and, 82–83; Hornigold, 60–61; Jamaican seamen and, 69–70; Jennings and, 80; *John and Elizabeth* and, 120–26, 179, 204–5, 214–18; John Lewis and, 61, 185–86; Musson and, 64–65; noncanonical pirates and, 246–47; against pardoned pirates, 148–50; Perrin sloop conflict and, 61–65; proprietary governors and, 65; against Spanish shipping, 74; Thache, 98–99; wreckage commissions and, 79–81. *See also* anti-piracy commissions investigation; golden age of piracy; piracy; wrecking expeditions
Piracy Act of 1698, 66
Piracy Act of 1717, 110
piracy investigation of 1716 (Governor and Council), 6, 15
pirate diaspora, 16, 170–75, 197, 202–3
pirate hunting, 189–92
pirate literature, 238–41. *See also General History of the Pyrates*
pirate rehabilitation: civic participation and, 156–60; death and, 161, 175, 203, 245; domestic life and, 10–13, 152–54, 194–97, 199–201; merchant trade and, 195–99; postpardon careers and, 16, 130, 170–71, 245; property holding and, 151–52, 199–202; return to piracy and, 176–85; wealth and, 156, 197, 205, 207, 234–35; wills/estates and, 168–70, 188, 195, 197–202, 219, 230, 233–34. *See also* pirate diaspora; Royal Navy service
pirate republics, 12
pirate trade: Bermudians and, 100–102, 107–8; merchants and, 99–100, 107; pardoned pirates and, 103–4; unprosecuted activity and, 105–7; Wishart and, 104–5. *See also* trade
pirate utopias, 22
piratical colonization, 24
Porter, Thomas, 192–93
Potts, Mark, 168–69
prisoner exchanges, 41–42, 141
privateers/privateering: financial incentives and, 192–93; Jamaica and, 71–72, 74; John Lewis and, 186; as occupation interruption, 242; Queen Anne's War and, 24–28; turn to piracy and, 144; wrecking expeditions and, 64–65
proprietary governors and piracy, 65, 69–70
Providence. *See* New Providence
proximity principle, 7
Pullein, Henry, 58, 107

Quarrel, William, 92
Queen Anne's Revenge (ship), 99
Queen Anne's War, 7–8, 24–28, 54–57, 70–71

Rackham, John "Calico Jack," 8, 144–45, 164, 167
Raddon, George, 148, 154, 159, 161–62, 262
Rawlings, Richard, *34*, 172, 189–90, 191, 262
Read, Mary, 167
Real Factorías de Tobacos, 72–73
reconceptualization of piracy/pirates, 245–46
Rediker, Marcus, 8, 19, 240
reputation of pardoned pirates, 170–71, 236
retirement from piracy. *See* pirate rehabilitation
Reveare, Matthew, 91, 262
Revenge (ship), 168, 189–90
Revolution of 1701, 53–54
Reynolds, Thomas, 171, 262
Rhett, William, 57, 62–65, 83, 189
Richards, John, 17, 25, *34*, 37, 173, 202, 262
Richards, Richard, *34*, 92, 174, 192–93, 262
Richardson, Dorothy, 153
Richardson, Samuel, 171, 262–63
Roberts, Bartholomew, 170, 180–81, 240
Roberts, Jacob, 161, 263
Roberts, William, 263
Rogers, Michael, 27, 263
Rogers, Woodes: accommodation of pirates and, 133–34, 139–40, 151; background of, 131–32; Bahamian government and, 13, 130, 132; contraband cases and, 177–78; Cuba supply trade incident and, 136–37; executions and, 137–39; pardoned pirates and, 134–35, 143–44; suppression of piracy and, 140; war with Spain and, 140–41, 143
Roper, Francis, 263
Ross, David, 92, 263
Rouncifull, George, 17, 19, 136, 138, 142, 161, 240, 245, 263
Rouse, Mary, 200–201

Rouse, William, 263; background of, 38–40; carrying trade and, 40–41; death of, 175, 245; estate planning of, 198–202; illicit activity of, 42–44, 47–48; legal entanglements of, 44–47; merchant voyages of, *34–35*; pirate diaspora and, 174; property holdings of, 41, 47; Queen Anne's War and, 41–42; sunken merchant ships and, 47
Royal Navy service, 18, 21, 25–27, 180, 188, 194; impressment, 25–26, 46, 137
royal proclamation of 1717, 13

sailor geographies, 6
Satsuma, Shinsuke, 26
Saunders, Gail, 53, 153
Sayle, William, 52
sea robbery. *See* piracy
settler colonialism and piracy, 246
shadow of piracy, 162–63
Shipton, Henry, 156, 161, 172, 263
Shoar, Robert, 161–62, 263
Sims, Benjamin, 166
Sinclair, George, 27, 174, 263
Sipkins, John, 263; background of, 17, 19, 208–10, 218; death of, 233; estate of, 244; *John and Elizabeth* and, 120–26, 204, 214–17; merchant voyages of, 30, 35; New York and, 211–12; postpardon trajectory of, 221
Skinner, George, 169
slaveholding, 122, 129, 154–56, 200, 220, 234
slave trade: *asiento* and, 70, 72; demographics of Bahamas and, 145; New York and, 206, 211–12, 227; privateering and, 192
Smith, Charity (Bosch), 215, 220, 222–23, 228–29, 232, 245
Smith, John, *35*, 174, 263–64
Smith, John (son of William), 234–36
Smith, Nicholas, 57
Smith, Samuel, 188
Smith, William, 264; background of, 218; domestic life of, 228–32; evidence against Pearse, 124; *General History* and, 247–48; *John and Elizabeth* and,

204–6; *Lark* and, 121–22; legacy of, 13–14; marriage of, 220; merchant voyages of, *35–36*; New York pirate ring and, 215–18; postpardon trajectory of, 221–25, 245; royal proclamation voyage and, 115; slave trade and, 227; will of, 233–36
Smith, William Stephens, 236
Snelgrave, William, 183, 185
South, William, 93, 144, 173, **264**
South Carolina, 64–66, *98*, 102–4, 129, 168, 171–72, 188–92
South Sea Company, 73
Spain. See *flota*; *guardacostas*; Queen Anne's War
Spanish-Bahamian relations, 140–44, 148–50
Spanish fleet system, 74–76; *Tierra Firme*, 74–75. See also *flota*; *guardacostas*
Spencer, William, *36*, **264**
Spotswood, Alexander, 66, 76, 173
Stanberry/Stanbury, Adonijah, 159, **264**
Stevenson, John, 191
Stillwell, Daniel, 58–59, 147–49, 156, 159, 161, 163, **264**
St. Martin (ship), 132–33, 177
Stoneham, Thomas, 174, 194, **264**
Stout, John, 19, 104, 210–11, 214, 218–21, 226, 228–33, 243–44, **264**
suppression of piracy in Bahamas, 132–40
Susannah (ship), 23, 30
Sutton, John, *36*, 91, **265**
Swaddell, Joseph, 64
Sword, David, 92, 136, **265**
Symonds, Richard, 1, 117

Taylor, Richard, *36*, 181–85, 241, **265**
Terrill, Thomas, 58, 138, 146–48, 152, 156, 159–61, 163, **265**
Thache, Edward (Blackbeard), 8, 26, 27, 90, 98, 112
Thompson, Joseph, **265**
Tickell, John, 106, 216, 221
Tierra Firme (fleet), 74–75. See also *flota*
Tisso, William, **265**
Tores, Sarah Lopes, 77
trade: British imperial, 29, 58, 69, 127, 207, 242, 244, 247; carrying, 19–20, 28–30, 221; illicit, 29, 42–44, 62, 121, 178, 204; merchant voyages and, *31–36*; pardoned pirates and, 146–49, 196–97; pirate, 99–108; Royal Navy and, 121
Treaty of Utrecht, 57, 73, 141
Trott, Nicholas, 22, 53
Trouton, Thomas, 174, **265**
Turner, David, **265**
Turn Joe, 137
Turnor, Benjamin, 93, **265**
Tynes, Samuel, 121–22

Ubilla, Juan Esteban de, 75

Valle, Juan del, 79
Vane, Charles, **266**; Bahamas court of admiralty and, 132–33; Bill and, 123; defiance of Rogers, 130–31, 134–35, 177; Fred and, 106; *General History* and, 240; Jamaican piracies and, 91; Pearse pursuit of, 120; trial of, 178–79
Van Hoven, Hendrjik, 53
Van Pelt, Arthur, 179–80, 194, **266**
Vetch, Samuel, 42
Vickers, Daniel, 221–22
Vincent, Samuel, 105–6, 143–44

Wake, Thomas, 22
Walker, Charles, 144, 166
Walker, John, 166
Walker, Thomas, 55, 57, 59–62, 141, 160, 163–64
Walton, William, 214
Ward, Richard, 148–49, **266**
warfare and origin of pirates, 18, 24–28, 242. See also privateers/privateering; Royal Navy service
War of the Quadruple Alliance, 140–41, 143–44
war on piracy, 9, 126, 189
Waters, John, 92, **266**
Webb, Nicholas, 53
Wells, Edward, **266**
Wells, John, 78, 79, 82
Wentworth, John, 52

Wheeler, James, 266
White, Daniel, 266
White, Henry, 136–37
Whitehead, Charles, 91, 142, 145, 152, 155, 159–60, 194, 266
widows, 152, 175–76, 188, 199–200
Williams, Griffith, 27, 173, 199, 267
Williams, John, 10
Williams, Palsgrave, 19–20, 98, 105–6, 185, 240–41, 243, 267
Williams, William, 19, 93, 142, 144, 146, 152, 156, 160–61, 194–95, 267
Williamson, Thomas, 174
Willis, William, 78, 267
wills and estates, 168–70, 188, 195, 197–202, 219, 230, 233–34
Wilson, David, 10
Wilson, Tristram, 27, 267
Wishart, Robert, 36, 104–5, 152, 154, 161, 172, 243, 245, 267
women, 19, 55, 145, 153, 155, 239; Bonny, 167; Read, 167. *See also* widows
Woodale, Nicholas, 174, 179, 241, 268
Woodward, Colin, 22
Worley, Richard, 173, 190
wrecking expeditions: Bahamian government and, 52, 108; Bermudians and, 100; *flota* and, 68, 76–81; Jamaicans and, 242–43; privateering commissions for, 83. *See also* anti-piracy commissions investigation
Wright, Pearse, 91, 139–40, 164, 268

Yates, Charles, 178–79

EARLY AMERICAN PLACES

*On Slavery's Border: Missouri's Small
Slaveholding Households, 1815–1865*
BY DIANE MUTTI BURKE

*Sounds American: National Identity and the Music Cultures
of the Lower Mississippi River Valley, 1800–1860*
BY ANN OSTENDORF

*The Year of the Lash: Free People of Color in Cuba
and the Nineteenth-Century Atlantic World*
BY MICHELE REID-VAZQUEZ

*Ordinary Lives in the Early Caribbean: Religion,
Colonial Competition, and the Politics of Profit*
BY KRISTEN BLOCK

*Creolization and Contraband: Curaçao in
the Early Modern Atlantic World*
BY LINDA M. RUPERT

*An Empire of Small Places: Mapping the
Southeastern Anglo-Indian Trade, 1732–1795*
BY ROBERT PAULETT

*Everyday Life in the Early English Caribbean: Irish,
Africas, and the Construction of Difference*
BY JENNY SHAW

*Natchez Country: Indians, Colonists, and the
Landscapes of Race in French Louisiana*
BY GEORGE EDWARD MILNE

Slavery, Childhood, and Abolition in Jamaica, 1788–1838
BY COLLEEN A. VASCONCELLOS

*Privateers of the Americas: Spanish American Privateering
from the United States in the Early Republic*
BY DAVID HEAD

*Charleston and the Emergence of Middle-
Class Culture in the Revolutionary Era*
BY JENNIFER L. GOLOBOY

*Anglo-Native Virginia: Trade, Conversion, and
Indian Slavery in the Old Dominion, 1646–1722*
BY KRISTALYN MARIE SHEFVELAND

*Slavery on the Periphery: The Kansas-Missouri
Border in the Antebellum and Civil War Eras*
BY KRISTEN EPPS

*In the Shadow of Dred Scott: St. Louis Freedom Suits and
the Legal Culture of Slavery in Antebellum America*
BY KELLY M. KENNINGTON

Brothers and Friends: Kinship in Early America
BY NATALIE R. INMAN

*George Washington's Washington: Visions for the
National Capital in the Early American Republic*
BY ADAM COSTANZO

*Patrolling the Border: Theft and Violence on
the Creek-Georgia Frontier, 1770–1796*
BY JOSHUA S. HAYNES

*Borderless Empire: Dutch Guiana in
the Atlantic World, 1750–1800*
BY BRAM HOONHOUT

*Complexion of Empire in Natchez: Race and
Slavery in the Mississippi Borderlands*
BY CHRISTIAN PINNEN

*Toward Cherokee Removal: Land, Violence,
and the White Man's Chance*
BY ADAM J. PRATT

Generations of Freedom: Gender, Movement, and Violence in Natchez, 1779–1865
BY NIK RIBIANSZKY

A Weary Land: Slavery on the Ground in Arkansas
BY KELLY HOUSTON JONES

Rebels in Arms: Black Resistance and the Fight for Freedom in the Anglo-Atlantic
BY JUSTIN IVERSON

The Good Forest: The Salzburgers and the Trustees' Plan for Georgia
BY KAREN AUMAN

From Empire to Revolution: Sir James Wright and the Price of Loyalty in Georgia
BY GREG BROOKING

A Southern Underground Railroad: Black Georgians and the Promise of Spanish Florida and Indian Country
BY PAUL M. PRESSLY

The Mosquito Confederation: A Borderlands History of Colonial Central America
BY DANIEL MENDIOLA

A Pirate's Life No More: The Pardoned Pirates of the Bahamas
BY STEVEN C. HAHN

www.ingramcontent.com/pod-product-compliance
Lightning Source LLC
Chambersburg PA
CBHW020240240426
43672CB00006B/588